Why Look at Plants?

Why Look at Plants?

The Botanical Emergence in Contemporary Art

Written and Edited by

Giovanni Aloi

BRILL

RODOPI

LEIDEN | BOSTON

This paperback was originally published in hardback as Volume 05 in the series *CPST*.

Cover illustration: Giovanni Aloi, *The Window: Plant Ontology*, 2014 © Aloi.

Library of Congress Cataloging-in-Publication Data

Names: Aloi, Giovanni. | Picard, Caroline. | Davis, Lucy, 1970-
Title: Why look at plants? : the botanical emergence in contemporary art /
  written and edited by Giovanni Aloi.
Description: Leiden ; Boston : Brill, 2018. | Series: Critical plant studies
  : philosophy, literature, culture, ISSN 2213-0659 ; Volume 5 | Includes
  bibliographical references and index.
Identifiers: LCCN 2018041943 (print) | LCCN 2018042948 (ebook) | ISBN
  9789004375253 (E-book) | ISBN 9789004375246 (hardback : alk. paper)
Subjects: LCSH: Plants in art. | Arts, Modern--20th century--Themes, motives.
  | Arts, Modern--21st century--Themes, motives. | Plants and civilization.
Classification: LCC NX650.P53 (ebook) | LCC NX650.P53 W49 2018 (print) | DDC
  700/.464--dc23
LC record available at https://lccn.loc.gov/2018041943

Typeface for the Latin, Greek, and Cyrillic scripts: "Brill". See and download: brill.com/brill-typeface.

ISSN 2213-0659
ISBN 978-90-04-40958-3 (paperback)
ISBN 978-90-04-37524-6 (hardback)
ISBN 978-90-04-37525-3 (e-book)

Copyright 2019 by Koninklijke Brill NV, Leiden, The Netherlands.
Koninklijke Brill NV incorporates the imprints Brill, Brill Hes & De Graaf, Brill Nijhoff, Brill Rodopi, Brill Sense,
Hotei Publishing, mentis Verlag, Verlag Ferdinand Schöningh and Wilhelm Fink Verlag.

This book is printed on acid-free paper and produced in a sustainable manner.

Contents

Acknowledgements

Because of its coauthored nature, this has been one of the most exciting and rewarding books I have worked on. First and foremost, I am particularly grateful to all the coauthors listed in the table of contents for bringing such wealth of original perspectives and information to this book. Everyone's enthusiasm, dedication, knowledge, and professionalism have made working on this book a truly amazing and enriching experience. More especially, I would like to thank Michael Marder for including this book in his *Critical Plant Studies* and for his inspirational contribution to the field of critical plant studies.

The research and writing in this book are the result of important discussions with colleagues, students, artists, curators, and friends. Needless to say, I will not be able to mention everyone here, but the following do deserve a special mention if only because they have carefully listened to my plant-ruminations with genuine interest and because they have shared valuable insights on plant-being with me: Chris Hunter, Susan McHugh, Jenny Kendler, Marlena Novak, Joela Jacobs, Joshi Radin, Linda Tegg, Michael Marder, Sara Black, Amber Ginsburg, and Darius Jones have all helped to think about and around plants in new ways.

Also, important to the development of this book was the exhibition *Imperceptibly and Slowly Opening*, curated by Caroline Picard at Sector 2337 in 2015, as well as the reading materials and the contribution of those who attended the 2014 and 2015 incarnations of *Following Nonhuman Kinds*, a Chicago based reading group organized by Caroline Picard, Andrew Yang, and Rebecca Beachy.

Lastly, I am particularly grateful to all the artists featured in this book for their kind collaboration and patience in answering my questions and for helping with clearing permission rights. Most especially I would like to thank image researchers at The National Gallery of Art in Washington DC; Chris Jacob at Wilkinson Gallery; Mark Geary at Marshmallow Laser Feast; Kiko Aebi at Matthew Marks Gallery; Hollis McGregor and Stef Tanki at Lisson Gallery; Chiara Costa at Fondazione Prada; Elizabeth Wayne at Studio Marc Quinn; Saskia Coombs at Thomas Dane Gallery; Sanne van Ettinger at KesselsKramer; Myungwon Kim at Tanya Bonakdar Gallery; Jari-Juhani Lager at Thomas Erben Gallery; Mai Pham at Bridgeman Images; Mattias Vendelmans at Carsten Höller Stuido; and Julia Lenz at Hauser and Wirth.

Lastly, many thanks to Jennifer Pavelko and Meghan Connolly at Brill, and to Trevor Perri for his assistance with copy editing.

List of Figures

Notes on Contributors

Giovanni Aloi

is a thinker, maker, and writer who studied History of Art and Art Practice in Milan and then moved to London in 1997 to further his studies at Goldsmiths University where he obtained a Postgraduate Diploma in Art History, a Master in Visual Cultures, and a PhD on the subject of natural history in contemporary art. Aloi currently teaches at the School of the Art Institute of Chicago, Sotheby's Institute of Art New York and London, and Tate Galleries. He has curated art projects involving photography and the moving image, contributes to BBC radio programs, and is involved in museum education programs at the Art Institute of Chicago. His work has been translated in Italian, Chinese, French, Russian, Polish, and Spanish. His first book titled *Art & Animals* was published in 2011 (IB Tauris) and *Antennae 10: A Decade of Art and the Non-Human 07-17* in 2017 (AntennaeProject and Forlaget 284). Since 2006, Aloi has been the Editor in Chief of *Antennae, the Journal of Nature in Visual Culture* (www.antennae.org.uk). *Speculative Taxidermy: Natural History, Animal Surfaces, and Art in the Anthropocene* was published in 2018 by Columbia University Press. With Caroline Picard, he is the coeditor of the University of Minnesota Press series *Art after Nature*.

Monika Bakke

PhD (1967) works at the Philosophy Department at the Adam Mickiewicz University, Poznan, Poland. She writes on contemporary art and aesthetics with a particular interest in posthumanist, gender, and cross-species perspectives. She curated a group show Seeing the Forest Through the Trees, AND Festval, UK 2015.

Katherine Behar

is a new media and performance artist based in Brooklyn, New York. Her work focuses on exploring contemporary digital culture through interactive installation, performance art, public art, photography, and video art.

Sara Black

is an artist who uses conscious processes of carpentry, woodworking, and repair as a time-based method; inherited building materials or other exhausted objects as material; and creates works that exposes the complex ways in which things and people are suspended in worlds together. Sara is currently an assistant professor of sculpture at the School of the Art Institute of Chicago. She has given talks and presented workshops at the MassArt, Harvard University, and more. Her work has been exhibited in a variety of spaces including Chicago's Museum of Contemporary Art, The Smart Museum of Art, Gallery 400, Threewalls; Portland's Museum of Contemporary Craft; New York's Park Avenue Armory and Eyebeam; Boston's Tufts University Gallery; Minneapolis's Soap Factory, and more.

Shannon Castleman

has been an assistant professor in the School of Art, Design and Media since 2006. Before joining NTU she taught at Dar Al Hekma College in Jeddah, Saudi Arabia. She graduated from San Francisco Art Institute with an MFA in Photography in May of 2004. She received a BFA from Tisch School of the Arts at New York University in 1993. She was the recipient of Murphy Fine Arts Fellowship from the San Francisco Foundation in 2003. Castleman has worked as a freelance photographer for clients and publications including Ray Gun, Rolling Stone, Alternative Press, and Workman Publishing. Her work has been included in a number of exhibitions, both in her native United States and internationally. Most recently her series entitled "Hanoi Ve Dem" was included in the Viet Nam! From Myth to Modernity exhibition at Singapore's Asian Civilizations Museum. In June 2008 she was commissioned by Substation to produce a video installation in conjunction with SeptFest 2008. Her project "Jurong West Street 81" was featured in a solo exhibition at the Substation Gallery.

Fatma Çolakoğlu

earned her undergraduate degree in Film Directing and History of Cinema at Emerson Collage and received her MA in Arts Administration & Cultural Policy from Goldsmiths College. She founded the first museum cinema programme in Turkey at İstanbul Museum of Modern Art in 2005.

Mat Collishaw

(b. 1966) is a key figure in the important generation of British artists who emerged from Goldsmiths' College in the late 1980s. He participated in *Freeze* (1988) and since his first solo exhibition in 1990 has exhibited widely internationally. Recent solo exhibitions include The Centrifugal Soul (2017); *Mat Collishaw*, The New Art Gallery Walsall (2015); *In Camera*, Library of Birmingham (2015); *Black Mirror*, Galleria Borghese, Rome (2014); *This Is Not An Exit*, Blain|Southern, London (2013); Bass Museum of Art, Florida (2013); Pino Pascali Museum Foundation, Bari (2013); *Mat Collishaw: Afterimage*, Arter, Istanbul (2013); and *Magic Lantern* at the Victoria and Albert Museum, London (2010).

Lucy Davis

Artist and writer's interdisciplinary practice examines notions of nature in art and visual culture, science and indigenous knowledge, natural histories, materiality and urban memory primarily but not exclusively in Southeast Asia. Most notably, Davis is the founder of The Migrant Ecologies Project—the product of her longstanding interest in the mid-twentieth century Singapore Modern Woodcut movement which later informed a six-year long, material-led cumulative series of investigations under the auspices of The Migrant Ecologies Project. Davis was also the founding editor of the Singapore critical publication series *focas: Forum on Contemporary Art & Society* from 2000 to 2007. She was previously an assistant professor at School of Art, Design and Media (ADM) at Nanyang Technological University.

Mark Dion

is an internationally renowned artist whose practice engages with natural history methodologies, anthropology, and museology. Dion was born in 1961 in New Bedford, Massachusetts. He initially studied in 1981–82 at the Hartford School of Art in Connecticut, which awarded him an honorary doctorate in 2002, and from 1982–84 at the School of Visual Arts in New York. He also attended the prestigious Whitney Museum of American Art's Independent Study Program (1984–85). He is an Honorary Fellow of Falmouth University in the UK (2014) and received an Honorary Doctorate of Humane Letters (PhD) from The Wagner Free Institute of Science in Philadelphia (2015).

Lindsey French

is an artist and educator whose work engages in gestures of communication with landscapes and the nonhuman. Embracing a number of mediation strategies, her projects materialize as texts written in collaboration with trees, video performances of attempted dialogues with the landscape, and sound installations of distant and displaced forests. She currently teaches courses that explore new media practices and site specific research at the School of the Art Institute of Chicago in the Art and Technology Studies, Sculpture, and Contemporary Practices Departments.

Joela Jacobs

is an assistant professor of German Studies, and is affiliated with the Institute of the Environment, the Department of Gender and Women's Studies, and the Arizona Center for Judaic Studies. She earned her PhD in Germanic Studies at the University of Chicago, where she subsequently held a postdoctoral position as Humanities Teaching Scholar. Prior to coming to the US from Germany, she studied at the Universities of Bonn, St. Andrews, and the Freie Universität Berlin to receive her MA in German and English Philology. Dr. Jacobs's research focuses on nineteenth to twenty-first century German literature and film, animal studies, environmental humanities, Jewish studies, the history of sexuality, and the history of science. She has published articles on monstrosity, multilingualism, literary censorship, biopolitics, animal epistemology, zoopoetics, critical plant studies, cultural environmentalism, and contemporary German Jewish identity.

Brian M. John

is interested in the ways that our relationship to the world is mediated by technology and technical media. Believing that technology must be understood not only as a tool, but as a material, he investigates mediation through photography, video, sound, music, and software. Engaging critically with contemporary apparatuses, both technical and systemic, the artist demonstrates their malleability as mediums of aesthetic expression. As an artist and a technologist, John manipulates sound, light, color, and space in order to subvert the intended uses of mediating technologies. Selected group exhibitions include: Mercury, The LeRoy Neiman Center Gallery, SAIC, Chicago, Illinois, 2015; Surface Area, Studio 109, Brooklyn, New York, 2014, and New Constructions, Pump Project's Flex Space, Austin, Texas, 2014.

Jenny Kendler

is an interdisciplinary artist, environmental activist, forager & naturalist based in Chicago and elsewhere. Her intimate sculptures and interactive projects have been exhibited nationally & internationally at museums and biennials including the Albright-Knox, Pulitzer Arts Foundation, MCA Chicago, iMOCA, DePaul Art Museum, Yeosu International Art Festival and the Kochi-Muziris Biennale. She has been commissioned to create public projects for locations as diverse as downtown Louisville and a Costa Rican tropical forest. She is vice-president of the artist residency ACRE, and cofounder of OtherPeoplesPixels and The Endangered Species Print Project. Kendler is the first ever Artist-in-Residence with environmental nonprofit NRDC.

Luftwerk

creates immersive art installations using light, color, and sculpture to augment experiences of space and site, blending history and contemporary media to open new aesthetic conversations. Luftwerk is the artistic vision of Petra Bachmaier and Sean Gallero. Petra Bachmaier, originally from Munich, holds an MA from the University of Fine Arts of Hamburg, Germany, and BFA from The School of the Art Institute of Chicago (SAIC). Sean Gallero, originally from the Bronx, NYC, studied art and humanities at Lehman College with a focus on applied arts and continued his studies at The School of the Art Institute of Chicago. The artist duo have collaborated since 2000 and formed Luftwerk in 2007.

Michael Marder

is Ikerbasque Research Professorof Philosophy at the University of the Basque Country, Vitoria-Gasteiz and Professor-at-Large in The Humanities Institute at Diego Portales University, Santiago, Chile. His work spans the fields of phenomenology, environmental philosophy, and political thought. His books includeThe Philosopher's Plant: An Intellectual Herbarium (2014, Columbia University Press); Dust (Object Lessons) (2016, Bloomsbury Academic); Grafts: Writings on Plants (2016 Univocal Publishing).

Susan McHugh

teaches courses in writing, literary theory, and animal studies. She is the author of Animal Stories: Narrating across Species Lines (2011), a volume in the University of Minnesota Press's Posthumanities series, as well as Dog (2004), a volume in Reaktion Books' groundbreaking Animal series. She coedited Indigenous Creatures, Native Knowledges and the Arts: Human-Animal Studies in Modern Worlds (2017), The Routledge Handbook of Human-Animal Studies, and Literary (2014) and Literary Animals Look (2013), a special issue of Antennae: The Journal of Nature in Visual Culture. Additionally, she has published dozens of essays in edited collections and peer-reviewed journals such as Critical Inquiry, Literature and Medicine, and PMLA: Publications of the Modern Language Association of America. She has delivered keynote lectures and invited talks in Canada, Germany, New Zealand, Norway, South Africa, Sweden, the UK, and the US. Her ongoing research focuses on the intersections of biological and cultural extinction.

Natasha Myers

is the director of the Institute for Science and Technology Studies and an associate professor in the Department of Anthropology at York University. Her ethnographic research examines forms of life in the contemporary arts and sciences. Her forthcoming book, Rendering Life Molecular (Duke University Press, 2015) is an ethnography of an interdisciplinary group of scientists who make living substance come to matter at the molecular scale.

Heidi Norton

is an artist whose 1970s upbringing as a child of New Age homesteaders in West Virginia resulted in a strong connection to the land, plant life, and nature. She received her BFA from University of Maryland, Baltimore, her MFA from The School of the Art Institute of Chicago. She was a recent recipient of a residency at Elmhurst Art Museum where her solo exhibition, Prismatic Nature, a major site responsive exhibition was on view. Additionally, Norton has had solo exhibitions at the Museum of Contemporary Art Chicago, Northeastern Illinois University, Monique Meloche Gallery Chicago, among others. Selective group exhibitions include Contemporary Museum Baltimore, Knitting Factory NY, Chicago Cultural Center, Ohio State University, Gallery 400 University of Illinois Chicago, La Box Gallery National School of Art France. Recent publications include Art21, BOMB magazine, Journal for Artistic Research, *My Green City* by Gestalten, and *Grafts* by Michael Marder. Her work has been reviewed in *Art 21, Frieze, Art Slant*, among others. She is an adjunct professor at the International Center of Photography.

Laurie Palmer

is an artist, writer, and teacher. Her work is concerned, most immediately, with resistance to privatization, and more generally, with theoretical and material explorations of matter's active nature as it asserts itself on different scales and in different speeds. Her work takes various forms as sculpture, installation, public projects, and writing. In 2014, Palmer published In the Aura of a Hole an extended exploration of mineral extraction sites in the US (Black Dog Publishing, UK). Palmer collaborated with the four-person art collective Haha for twenty years. In 2008, WhiteWalls Press published With Love from Haha documenting Haha's site-based work (distributed by the University of Chicago Press). Palmer teaches in the Art Department at the University of California, Santa Cruz.

Caroline Picard

is a writer, curator, and cartoonist who explores the figure in relation to systems of power through ongoing investigations of interspecies borders, how the human relates to its environment, and what possibilities might emerge from upturning an anthropocentric world view. Her writing has appeared in publications like ArtForum (critics picks), Flash Art International, Hyperallergic, Paper Monument, The Seen, and others. In 2014 she was the Curatorial Fellow at La Box, ENSA in France, and became a member of the SYNAPSE International Curators' Network of the Haus der Kulturen der Welt in Berlin in 2015. She is the executive director of The Green Lantern Press—a nonprofit publishing house and art producer in operation since 2005—and codirector of Sector 2337, a hybrid artspace/bar/bookstore in Chicago.

Joshi Radin

works independently and collaboratively on performance, video, installation, and writing projects dealing with themes of power, empathy and ritual. She is currently an SAIC New Artist Society Scholar and MFA candidate in the Photo department.

Greg Ruffing

is an artist, writer, and organizer working on topics around the production of space at different scales—from the macro level of sociopolitical structures and architecture in the built environment, down to an emphasis on community, collaboration, and exchange on the interpersonal level. Often looking critically or conceptually at the specifics of site and place, he has facilitated exhibitions and programming at venues such as Public Access (Chicago), Sector 2337 (Chicago), The Perch (Chicago), SPACES (Cleveland, OH), and the Terrain Biennial (various locations). Additionally, his own work in photography, sculpture, installation, and performance has been exhibited at The Cleveland Museum of Art, Johalla Projects (Chicago), Sullivan Galleries (Chicago), Schneider Gallery (Chicago), Triumph Gallery (Chicago), Laura (Chicago), Forum Artspace (Cleveland, OH), and elsewhere.

Dawn L. Sanders

is an associate professor at the Institute for Didaktik och Pedagogiska Profession, University of Goteborg, Sweden.

Ulya Soley

is a Turkish art historian, born in Istanbul, who studied within the booming art scenes of Montreal and Glasgow. Upon returning to Istanbul, she started working at Pera Museum as one of their collection supervisors, as well as taking part in the museum's contemporary projects.

Linda Tegg

explores the contingent viewing conditions through which we orient ourselves in the world. Driven by curiosity, her work oscillates from the romantic to the forensic, in efforts to decipher abstract concepts through concrete models. The artist was the Samstag Scholar of 2014, The Georges Mora Foundation Fellow of 2012 and has been the recipient of numerous Australia Council for the Arts and Arts Victoria Grants. She has degrees from the University of Melbourne and RMIT University. Recent solo exhibitions include; Grasslands, the State Library of Victoria, Melbourne, 2014; Choir, Westspace, Melbourne 2014; Coexistence, MARSO Galleria, Mexico City, 2012. Selected group exhibitions include: Don't Talk to Strangers, Random

Institute, Brooklyn, 2014 and NEW13, Australian Centre for Contemporary Art, Melbourne, 2013. Linda has collaborated with Architects Baracco + Wright as the Creative Directors of the Australian Pavilion at the 16th International Architecture Biennale, Venice, 2018.

Lois Weinberger

works on a poetic-political network that draws our attention to marginal zones and questions hierarchies of various types. Weinberger, who sees himself as a field worker, embarked in the 1970s on ethno-poetic works that form the basis for his ongoing artistic investigations of natural and manmade spaces. Ruderal plants—weeds—involved in all areas of life, are initial and orientation points for notes, drawings, photographs, objects, texts, films as well as projects in public space. In 1991 he designed the WILD CUBE, a rib steel enclosure for spontaneous vegetation to grow without human intervention—a RUDERAL SOCIETY that creates a gap in the urban environment. With his work he has contributed significantly to the recent discussion on art and nature since the early 1990s.

Wendy Wheeler

is professor emeritus of English Literature and Cultural Inquiry at London Metropolitan University. She is also a visiting professor at Goldsmiths, University of London and RMIT in Melbourne, Australia. She has taught at the universities of Oregon and of Kansas. In 2014, she gave the first annual University of Tartu Jakob von Uexküll Lecture to the European Association for the Study of Literature, Culture and the Environment in Estonia, and she has been involved in many environmental projects. Author of many books and essays on biosemiotics, her most recent book—Expecting the Earth: Life|Culture|Biosemiotics—was published in 2016.

Amanda White

is a Toronto-based artist and PhD candidate in Cultural Studies at Queen's University, Canada. Her current work combines research and collaborative, participatory and interdisciplinary arts practices looking at cultural imaginings of nature with a particular interest in human-plant encounters, interspecies exchange, and permaculture.

Andrew S. Yang

works across the visual arts, the sciences, and natural history to explore the cosmological flux. Exhibiting from Oklahoma to Yokohama, his writing and research can be found in journals including Biological Theory, International Studies in the Philosophy of Science, Current Biology, and Leonardo. He currently is an associate professor at the School of the Art Institute of Chicago and a research associate at the Field Museum of Natural History. He earned his PhD in Biology at Duke University.

About this Book

Why look at plants? The question posed by the title of this book might seem redundant to some. Haven't we been looking at plants for millennia already? What's there to see that we haven't already? Aren't plants carefully identified, recorded, represented, and classified in many prestigious botanical works? Don't we look at plants every time we take a walk in the park, stroll in a forest, eat our greens, or tend to our flowers in the garden? Well yes and no is the answer to all these questions.

The title of this book adopts and reworks that of John Berger's seminal essay "Why Look at Animals?" and it does so provocatively, as well as politically. Berger's essay identified and criticized fundamental aspects of our limited ability to look at animals through different media, spaces, theoretical contexts, and historical milieus. A key to his main argument is the notion that photography and film have contributed to a counterproductive assimilation of animals within an objectifying bourgeois culture of consumption. In short, stripped of their mystical powers, animals have been reduced to economic tokens in reckless, capitalist economies. Through this desacralizing process, their representational function has been that of normativizing and moralizing humans, serving as identity-building blocks. For this reason, the visual centrality occupied by animals in specific photographic and filmic genres is in truth fictitious—yes, we do look at animals in our everyday lives, but we only do so in the implicit hope of discovering a "natural truth" about our ourselves. When that process fails, we rapidly lose interest, as in the case of animals confined in zoos, which are dependent on keepers and are alienated from their natural environments—they languish as evidential tokens of their relatives in the wild, but nothing more.[1] What is at play in our looking at animals, according to Berger is, therefore, a form

of *animal-blindness*—the impossibility to see animals beyond the reflections of ourselves; beyond the cultural norms that have been constructed for us by centuries of philosophical thinking and scientific practices that, more or less directly, have enabled the objectification and marginalization of animals in today's world.

It is in this context that this book addresses the equivalent cultural phenomenon to animal-blindness concerning the ultimate otherness of the vegetal world. *Plant-blindness* essentially is our cultural inability to conceive plants beyond the prefixed cultural schemata. It is that which simultaneously reduces them to resources or aesthetic objects. From an aesthetic perspective, more specifically, paying attention to plants entails the possibility of considering new modes of attention and crafting new modalities of perception. Both opportunities can bear substantial productivities in our relationship with the current challenges impacting our planet. At stake is the opportunity to understand plants as integral, coexisting *actants* that play defining roles in the functioning of ecosystems on this planet. What we look at, and how we look, constitute essential parameters in the recuperation of "alternative gazes" and the crafting of new ones—modalities of engagement that entail more than the ocular—modalities that can lead to a reontologization of the living.

Although this notion is neither new nor necessarily hard to assimilate in scientific discourses, the humanities have been severely lagging behind in their move towards a posthumanist conception of plants. However, the reluctance to disavow an inherent anthropocentric framework that still pervades many disciplines is now being challenged by a new level of global urgency, the environmental threat we all face might just shift our focus at las.

On August 29, 2016, the Working Group on the Anthropocene, chaired by Jan Zalasiewicz,

---

1   Berger, J. (1980) 'Why Look at Animals?' in *About Looking* (New York: Vintage), p. 25.

presented the recommendation to the International Geological Congress in Cape Town that the term "Anthropocene" should be used to define the current geological epoch.[2] Far from being uncontroversial,[3] the concept inscribes humanity's detrimental impact on earth as the most defining upon climate and environments. Thereafter, on October 24 it was announced that the world entered a new era of "climate change reality" defined by the crossing of 400 CO2 parts per million in the atmosphere—a level which will not dip for many generations.[4] This news was followed by the startling revelation that Arctic and Antarctic sea-ice reached record lows, melting much faster than scientists had anticipated.[5] And in July 2017 an iceberg twice the size of Luxembourg (5,800 square km) broke off the Antarctic peninsula.[6] Despite the denial that seems to pervade the current US administration, signs that something is changing are undeniable. So, while the label "sixth extinction" is widely being used to help us envision the gravity

of the current changes in climatic balance, not much is actually known about how plants, upon which all biodiversity on the planet depends, will be affected. A 2015 study claims that:

> The effects of climate change on plant growth will likely vary by region, with northern areas in places like Russia, China and Canada gaining growing days. However, already hot tropical regions could lose as many as 200 growing days per year. In total, 3.4 billion people would live in countries that lose nearly a third of their growing days. More than 2 billion of those people live in low-income countries, according to the study.[7]

As I write this introduction, president Donald Trump has officially announced that he will pull the United States of America from the Paris Climate Agreement which in 2015 brought together 195 countries with the goal of preventing global temperatures from rising by 2 degrees Celsius by the end of the century. This move casts a dark shadow over the already critically fragile ecological balance of our planet. However, while it is easy to claim that individuals can do little in the face of catastrophic climate change, it is important to remember that the environmental alterations caused by multinationals, intensive agriculture and farming, deforestation, and transportation are all dependent on individual's choices that can be positively altered.

Since the beginning of this millennium, the field of human-animal studies has achieved the heroic task of awakening the conscience of western philosophy to the objectification of animals which has led to their unethical cultural marginalization and abhorrent treatment.[8]

---

2   Carrington, D. (2016) 'The Anthropocene epoch: scientists declare dawn of human-influenced age' in *The Guardian*, Monday, August 29, online: [<https://www.theguardian.com/environment/2016/aug/29/declare-anthropocene-epoch-experts-urge-geological-congress-human-impact-earth>] accessed on November 10, 2016.

3   For a compressive and accessible overview of the current critiques of the Anthropocene label see Colebrook, C. (2016) 'Twilight of the Anthropocene Idols' in *After Us* (Open Humanities Press).

4   Press Association (2016) 'New era of climate change reality as emissions hit symbolic threshold' in *The Guardian*, Monday, October 24, online [<https://www.theguardian.com/environment/2016/oct/24/new-era-of-climate-change-reality-as-emissions-hit-symbolic-threshold>] accessed on November 10, 2016.

5   Fountain, H., and Schwartz, J. (2016) 'Spiking Temperatures in the Arctic Startle Scientists' in *The New York Times*, Wednesday, December 21, online [<http://www.nytimes.com/2016/12/21/science/arctic-global-warming.html>] accessed on December 21, 2016.

6   *Viñas, M-J.* (2017) 'Massive Iceberg Breaks Off From Antarctica' in *NASA* website, published on July 12, online [<https://www.nasa.gov/feature/goddard/2017/massive-iceberg-breaks-off-from-antarctica>] accessed on July 30, 2017.

7   Worland, J. (2015) 'The Weird Effect Climate Change Will Have On Plant Growth' in *Time*, Thursday, June 11, online [<http://time.com/3916200/climate-change-plant-growth/>] accessed November 2016.

8   For an overview of the emergence of animal studies see Weil, K. (2012) *Thinking Animals: Why Animal*

While human-animal studies might not singlehandedly prevent the sixth extinction or reverse climate change, thus far it has certainly outlined a productive arena for the discussion of human/animal relations in universities around the world. Its influence has already spilled into popular culture. It is therefore common today to encounter human-animal studies student groups in many campuses and a greater visibility of related classes in the curriculum. For the first time, discussing animals outside the scientific and veterinarian remit is no longer a matter of curiosity. The hope is that, with time, human-animal studies arguments will substantially impact on human perception of animals, making more and more of us aware of the challenges involved in overcoming the limitations imposed by cultural blinkers, and thus enabling the emergence of new, more ethically considerate, and sustainable human/animal relations. Similar to these positive strides in animal studies, this book offers the opportunity to further the dialogue about plants that has been recently beginning to emerge.[9]

The increased presence of plants in contemporary art is a relatively recent phenomenon that can be read in conjunction with the emergence of animals in the gallery space witnessed over the past thirty years.[10] Plants in the gallery space can be interpreted as a symptom of the wrongness characterizing human/plant relationships but also as a wake-up-call to reappraise this relationship at a time of crisis. The hope is that like human-animal studies, the field of plant studies will enrich our perspectives on plants, thus leading to different modalities in what right now constitutes a mostly unacknowledged critical node in the survival of life on the planet.

This book focuses on representation and contemporary art to counterbalance the predominantly scientific attention that has been given to plants in the traditional disciplinary structure. It does so in the belief that representation, as implicitly argued by Berger, constitutes the most agentially-charged, world-forming tool at our disposal. The last century, more than any previous, has been characterized by a heightened, critical approach to representation. Just consider the essential contributions of race and gender studies, feminist theories, and the more recent emphasis on cultural decolonization. We therefore now stand at a unique point in the production of knowledge itself—a point in which we can identify the shortcomings of past representational strategies in order to devise new, speculative approaches capable of decentering fictitious anthropocentric

Studies Now? (New York: Columbia University Press) and, specifically in relation to contemporary art, Aloi, G. (2011) Art & Animals (London: IB Tauris).

9   Amongst the most visible recent contributions on the field of plant studies see Antennae: The Journal of Nature in Visual Culture, Issues 17 and 18, 2011, online: [<http://www.antennae.org.uk/back-issues/4583697895>]. Books: Hall, M. (2011) Plants as Persons (Albany: SUNY Press); Gessert, G. (2012) Green Light: Toward An Art Of Evolution (Cambridge: MIT Press); Marder, M. (2013) Plant-Thinking: A Philosophy of Vegetal Life (New York: Columbia University Press); Marder, M. (2014) The Philosopher's Plant (New York: Columbia University Press); Marder, M. (2016) Grafts (Minneapolis: University of Minnesota Press); Marder, M. and Irigaray, L. (2016) Through Vegetal Being (New York: Columbia University Press); Mabey, R. (2012) Weeds (New York: Ecco); Mabey, R. (2016) The Cabaret of Plants (New York: W. W. Norton & Company); Veira, P., Gagliano, M. and Ryan, J. (Eds.) (2015) The Green Thread: Dialogues in the Vegetal World (Ecocritical Theory and Practice); Wohlleben, P. and Flanery, T. (2016) The Hidden Life of Trees: What They Feel, How They Communicate—Discoveries from a Secret World (Vancouver:

Greystone Books); Essays: Myers, N. (2016) 'Photosynthesis' in 'Lexicon for an Anthropocene Yet Unseen' (Eds.) Howe, C. and Pandian, A. Theorizing the Contemporary, Cultural Anthropology Website, January 21, 2016; Myers, N. (2015) 'Conversations on Plant Sensing: Notes from the Field,' NatureCulture 03, pp. 35–66; Bakke, M. (2012) 'Art for Plants' Sake? Questioning Human Imperialism in the Age of Biotech,' Parallax, pp. 18, 4.

10   Aloi, G. (2011) Art & Animals (London: IBTauris); Baker, S. (2000) The Postmodern Animal (London: Reaktion); Broglio, R. (2011) Surface Encounters: Thinking with Animals and Art (Minneapolis: Minnesota University Press).

exceptionalisms that have led us where we are today. The mapping of new, intra-active, agential interconnectedness of human-nonhuman biosystems is already central to many artistic and philosophical discourses and is only bound to acquire more traction over the next few years.

Central to the reconfiguration of the anthropocentric paradigm in this book are posthumanist approaches based on the work of Donna Haraway and Cary Wolfe, notions of Dark Ecology conceived by Timothy Morton, Mark Fisher's paradigm of Capitalist Realism, Jason W. Moore's conception of the Capitalocene, and most importantly Foucault's theorizations of power and biopolitics.[11] Essentially this is a multi-authored/collaborative book—not quite an edited collection—but a gathering of multidisciplinary perspectives, voices, experiences, perceptions, and reflections on plant-being. When I set off to write a book about plants in contemporary art and culture, I realized that the subject called for abandoning the monographic format. I focused on my personal and cultural relationships with plants and considered the

wealth of my colleagues' and friends' experiences to constitute a large part of my own interest in plants. Plants' fixity, perceived passivity, and resilient silent presence have, for over two thousand years relegated plants to cultural backgrounds. These reductionisms have been used to assess plants' ontological inferiority towards animals and even more so, humans. I therefore became interested in the opportunity of upturning this very contingency in a productive way or at least taking it as a productive starting point around which to conceive plant-being from new perspectives. From this consideration, it followed that because of "plant fixity" and perceived "plant passivity," our experiences are predominantly mediated by the *spaces* in which we interact *with them* as well as by our cultural lenses that these spaces inscribe. Inspired by Berger's essay and its implicit reference to the act of looking as a fundamental tool of power, I thus returned to Foucault's notions of the *panopticon* and *biopower*. But, more specifically, I decided to focus on his interest in epistemic spatializations: the ability space, materials, architectural, and representational dimensions have to define power/knowledge relations. In other words, this book's structure is devised upon the notion that the interaction between plants, humans, and animals are deeply defined on material grounds; that meaning is constructed through spatial relations shared by actants, and by the cultural laws and power dynamics inscribed in such spatializations.

The first two chapters titled "Lost in the Post-Sublime Forest" and "Trees: Upside-Down, Inside-Out, and Moving" are an exception. They directly address sublimity and anthropomorphism as two of the primary epistemic modalities that limit our relationships with plants through outdated, culturally encoded epistemic dimensions.[12] Neither wholly negative nor

11   Haraway, D. (1991, 2013) *Simians, Cyborgs, and Women: The Reinvention of Nature* (London: Routledge); Haraway, D. (2008) *When Species Meet* (Minneapolis: University of Minnesota Press); Wolfe, C. (2010) *What Is Posthumanism?* (Minneapolis: Minnesota University Press); Morton, T. (2016) *Dark Ecology* (New York: Columbia University Press); Fisher, M. (2009) *Capitalist Realism: Is There No Alternative?* (Portland: Zero Books); Moore, J. (2015) *Capitalism In The Web Of Life* (New York: Verso); Foucault, M. (1966) *The Order of Things: An Archaeology Of The Human Science* (London and New York: Routledge), 1970, 2003; Foucault, M. (1964) *Madness and Civilization: A History of Insanity in the Age of Reason* (New York: Vintage Books), 1967, 1988; Foucault, M. (1963) *The Birth of the Clinic: An Archaeology of Medical Perception* (London and New York: Routledge) 1973, 2003; Foucault, M. (1972) 'The eye of power' in *Power/Knowledge: Selected Interviews and Other Writings, 1972–1977* (Brighton: The Harvester Press) p. 146–165; Foucault, M. (1976a) *The History of Sexuality 1—The Will to Knowledge* (London and New York, Penguin), 1998; Foucault, M. (1975b) *Discipline and Punish: The Birth of the Prison*, translation Sheridan, A. 1977 (London: Penguin), 1991.

12   Histories of representation in Western art and science have, over the past three hundred years, trained the popular gaze to look at plants (and animals) through two primary lenses: the sublime

inherently positive, both sublimity and anthropomorphism most regularly still define objectifying and superficial modes of engagement that prevent us from moving in new epistemic directions. Following this ground-priming pair, each chapter moves beyond classical epistemic limitations by focusing on a, more or less, delineated space in which plants/human interactions take place. The garden, the greenhouse, the store, the house, and the laboratory have been identified as spaces/situations that have recurred more frequently and productively in contemporary art.[13] Therefore, all coauthors were asked to identify a particular plant-being relationality defined by the space in which the plant lives and to use that as a starting point to articulate new perspectives, approaches, symbolisms, and considerations. The last chapter, titled "Of Other Spaces" is concerned with the alternative and fluid spatializations of *transitional spaces*—places like lobbies, offices, laundromats, restaurants, or gallery spaces.[14]

I also very much cared that this book should be as accessible as possible while retaining academic integrity. *Antennae: The Journal of Nature in Visual Culture* of which I have been the Editor in Chief since 2006 has consistently promoted multidisciplinarity and knowledge-transfer amongst students, artists, scholars, curators, and general readers. Widening participation

and reaching beyond the boundaries of the academic community has also played a vital role in everything I have published so far, including my first book *Art & Animals* (2011).[15] Therefore, the contributions in this book have tried to avoid, at all costs, a "purely-philosophical" treatment of plants in which living beings are reduced to tokens performing intellectual acrobatics designed to impress a scholarly elite. The field of human-animal studies knows a thing or two about this counterproductive approach marked by an utter disconnect between the living and the ethical urgency that the living imposes upon those working/making/writing/thinking with it. Contemporary art has the ability to complement, unhinge, problematize, and challenge philosophical concepts—the synergy between the two can constitute a powerful tool just as long as it is put to work to achieve actual change.

Following these parameters has produced a thoroughly heterogeneous gathering of insights, stories, experiences, perspectives, and arguments encompassing multiple disciplines and methodologies. As much as it was possible, I wanted all coauthors to own and interpret their "thinking space" in format and content for the purpose of enabling as many plant-human becomings and coevolutions to emerge. In every chapter, my own contribution outlines the emergence of a specific modality of plant-being through a selection of contemporary art examples that challenges preestablished norms, approaches, and methodologies. The contributions of my colleagues aptly problematize, expand, or upturn my own perspectives in creative and original ways. Ultimately, I wanted this book to be kaleidoscopic in essence, and to provide as many different thinking-models dedicated to the structuring of new innovative and challenging ways to conceive plants. By no means did I hope for it to be comprehensive and to chart a history of plants in contemporary art. That is a book I am not interested in writing, at

---

and the anthropomorphic. As it is explained in the chapter titled "Lost in the Post-Sublime Forest," the sublime reassessed the separation between man and nature dramatizing the forest into a fictional space enmeshed in symbolism and mythology. While in "Trees: Upside-Down, Inside-Out, and Moving" anthropomorphism is identified as a limiting epistemic tool which continuously reduces trees to a metaphorical mirror of human existence.

13   See Nemitz, B. (2000) *Trans Plant: Living Vegetation In Contemporary Art* (Berlin: Edition Kantz); Tweed Museum of Art (1999) *Botanica: Contemporary Art And The World Of Plants* (Duluth: Tweed Museum of Art); Fisher, P., and Burgi, B. (2015) *About Trees* (Koln: Snoeck Verlag).

14   Foucault, M. (1984) 'Of other spaces' in *Diacritics*, Spring 1986, pp. 22–27.

15   G. Aloi (2011).

least not yet. In this instance, I instead focused on specific examples, which helped me to develop my knowledge and thinking and which I hope will instigate, or further, the interest of many readers. These are examples that test the boundaries of representation, epistemology, ontology, and ethics against the ultimate otherness of plant-being.

INTRODUCTION

Why Look at Plants?

Giovanni Aloi

Amarcord[1]

Plants on the table, plants on the floor, plants on chairs, plants hanging on the walls, plants perched on windowsills, plants spilling over either side of the balcony railings—my grandmother's terrace was a miniature forest in its own right, or at least, so it seemed to me. I was five years old. From my lower than average viewpoint, her balcony was a true wilderness: one with its mythologies, enchanted inhabitants, unrepentant villains, and secret passages. A climbing jasmine, a honeysuckle, different varieties of pansies, variegated petunias, the sculptural dish-like foliage of leopard plants, red geraniums, deep red gloxinias, tall ferns, fuzzy fern-asparagus, a giant rubber plant, slender orange and yellow zinnias, African daisies, sharp mother-in-law tongues, dark-leaved Irish roses, two small palms, nasturtium, nasturtium, nasturtium, and a bonsai-like money-tree were only some of the many plants she grew there. These varieties did not come from fancy gardening centers.

Her botanical collection was assembled between the 1960s and 1970s, and was at its peak in the early 1980s. Each plant had a story: almost all came from local friends or family members. My grandmother's passion for plants was well-known in the small Calabrian village, Italy's deep south, where she lived. It was therefore not unusual for a friend to come around for coffee—always unannounced—with a cutting wrapped up in wet cotton wool, or sticking out of a small container of some sort. Small size terracotta pots were not readily available, and plastic ones were rare too, so anything from an empty coffee tin, to a jam jar, or a well-rinsed tuna tin could do. My grandmother would duly transplant the cuttings into bigger containers, but tins and jars would always stay around. She needed them to reciprocate vegetal gifts at the earliest opportunity. So, some small plants would spend prolonged periods of time growing out of a beans tin, waiting for the next family friend to stop by.

Cuttings were part of an open-ended botanical-dialogue between plants, people, balconies, and gardens. Giving cuttings was a deep sign of affection—a heartfelt gift—a sharing of something personally treasured to whose growth and well-being a person had directly contributed over time. Care was inscribed in this gift on two registers: in the act of giving and in the gift itself. In time, the plants would become place-markers for memories, special occasions, alternative family genealogies, births, and deaths. They were much more precious than any plant bought at the market on the streets behind the church. Biologically speaking, these plants were most regularly "old" varieties, some of which could not be found, or were never available, in the commercial realm at the time.

---

1   The first section of this introduction is titled after Federico Fellini's film *Amarcord* from 1973. The film proposes a fragmented narrative in which the idiomatic of film is made to function as a repository of childhood memories. Vignettes dotted by colorful characters alternate each other in the piecing of a bygone time that was not necessarily better than the present but that surely seemed magical as seen through the dimension of memory. The film thus acknowledges that memory is a temporally defined space in which places, people, nonhumans, and narratives are constructed in specific ways that vastly differ from other perceptual instances. To highlight this specificity, Fellini created the neologism *amarcord*, which echoes the word *ricordare*, to remember, and *amar* which could equally allude to *amaro* which translates in bitter, and *amare*, to love. Fellini, F. (1973) *Amarcord* (dist. PIC Distribuzione / Warner Brothers).

There was a sense of magic to those gifts—some plants would acquire mythical status. You'd regularly hear that such and such had a blue variety of this usually white flowering plant; or that an elusive giant strand of this or that had been sighted, somewhere, in someone's garden many moons ago.

My grandmother and other relatives had a few plants that, they claimed, came from cuttings gifted to them by the richest woman in town. She was only ever referred to as "the Baroness" and lived in a beautiful villa a couple of miles inland. My grandmother helped with the housekeeping. The building was surrounded by acres of land planted with bergamot, figs, and olive trees—that was partly where her wealth came from. A giant palm grew next to the building, granting a stately demeanor. She lived in Milan for most of the year and only stayed at the villa during the summer months. She loved plants and regularly shipped rare and expensive varieties down south from the most prestigious gardening business in Italy: The Fratelli Ingegnoli. The business opened its doors in 1789 and pioneered crossbreeding as well as genetic manipulation techniques in Italy.[2] Their catalog was simply jaw-dropping: amongst others, it featured utterly beautiful exotic varieties, and rare European strands of sought after roses. My great-aunt owned a mesmerizing wholly white tropical hibiscus, claimed to be from the Baroness's own collection—she was very proud of it and would not make cuttings from it very often. I remember looking at those pure-white flowers against the dark green foliage—it was somewhat unreal—the unicorn of flowering shrubs—I have never encountered it ever again, anywhere.

But my grandmother didn't seem to be preoccupied with notions of rarity just as much as she was not concerned at all with a systematic approach to her collection—and that is what made her gathering of plants so interesting and unique. She deeply loved them and regularly anthropomorphized them. Her plants could be "sad," or they would "smile at her," or could be "annoyed with her." To a certain degree, it was all knowingly humorous. Despite the popular culture stereotype that casts those who love plants as lonely lunatics, my grandmother was the center of the family—she was deeply loved. Yet, there was something fascinating about her enjoyment of plants that surpassed the simple notion of "hobby" or "pastime." They made her world so rich. She cared for them on the grounds of this joy they brought to her life. She loved them just as much as she loved animals. She never liked captivity—most of her pets came and went as they pleased. Like plants, they were usually brought to her by friends and family—a nestling found under a tree and unable to fly, or a bird with a broken leg, or wing, due to a window collision. She would take care of them and release them thereafter—some of them would stick around for a while. I remember that, for years, a magpie would come back to visit after being cared for by her as a chick. My mom remembers an owl that, well before my time, used to come back to visit almost every evening. It is safe to say that when it came to plants and animals, my grandmother instinctively operated a flat ontology of some sort—an ontological orientation of compassion for the nonhuman that much anticipated contemporary philosophical concerns in the posthuman sphere.[3] Today, at the tender age of forty-one, as I continue to cultivate my own interest for plants and animals,

---

2 Gandini, G. (2004) *I Locali Storici di Milano* (Milano: Touring Editore), pp. 68–69.

---

3 The term "flat ontology" is used here in reference to Object Oriented Ontology theorist Graham Harman and his intent to avoid overmining as well as undermining objects in philosophical discourses. Flat ontology is a challenge to the intrinsic anthropocentrism of correlationsim, and it involves an invitation to forget what we already know about objects to attempt to see beyond the cultural connotations that generally make them present-at-hand. Bryant, L., Srnicek, N., and Harman, G. (2011) *The Speculative Turn: Continental Materialism and Realism* (Melbourne: re.press).

I consider myself lucky to have been exposed to her influence.

But back then, things were different. Towards the end of the 1980s, her nonscientific approach to the nonhuman became the point of divergence between us. My early interest in animals and plants, for which she was largely responsible, began to be influenced by the disciplinary optics of natural history and its patriarchal ways. Around the age of ten, David Attenborough became my undisputed hero—I watched every single one of his wildlife documentaries with religious devotion. A couple of years later, my science teacher set Gerald Durrell's *My Family and Other Animals* as summer reading—I was ready. Jars, meshes, boxes, tweezers … anything I could use to catch an animal or put an animal into, to look at, for a while, was fit for purpose. My grandmother did not approve—the question: "and when are you going to release that?" would be inevitably directed at me with impeccable timing. I could no longer see the magic in her terrace. To my eyes, the adventurous wilderness had turned into a jumble of intricate and unguided vegetal growth. Mind you, not much had changed with it, but I had. I was more and more interested in taxonomy, collecting, archiving, drawing what I found, taking notes, and reading "young naturalist" manuals.

My grandmother passed away in 2003 after a long battle with cancer. Much of her exuberant plant collection had already been dispersed when she moved from her old home by the creek to a modern apartment with a narrow and smaller south east facing balcony which, she lamented, was "always too sunny and baked the plants." Some of the original plants still exist today. They are in family members' homes and gardens. The plants that outlived her have become invaluable material markers of absence in a complex and lengthy process of mourning: an extension of our dead ones in the silence of the living.

The Silence of the Plants

In the years that followed my grandmother's death, my interest in nature remained constant. However, growing up, I struggled to find ways to incorporate this interest in my professional life. Nature was the subject of my photographic work while studying at the London College of Printing. It was at Goldsmiths University that I had the opportunity to shape my own views on animal presence in art for my MA thesis whilst attending the meetings of the British Animal Studies Network.[4] Animal Studies was still much of an underground movement—for better or worse, it has since been institutionalized and incorporated in the fierce capitalist system that now rules academia worldwide. Publishers have quickly taken note of the field's commercial potential and conferences on the subject are now a regular occurrence around the globe. Twenty years ago, the so-called "animal-turn" was still "philosophically fresh" and conceptually exciting—its promise was to recover animals from the anthropocentric erasure operated by the sciences and the humanities to rethink our entanglements and coevolution beyond the traditional ontology of species. It was this genuinely bold proposal that brought me to launch *Antennae: The Journal of Nature in Visual Culture* in March 2007. The journal pioneered a hybrid magazine/academic approach, mixing scholarly texts with interviews, fiction, artists' portfolios, and poetry to widen participation in cultural/artistic discourses. Since its inception, *Antennae* has encouraged multidisciplinary dialogue and knowledge crossover among artists, scientists, environmental activists, museum curators, scholars, and most importantly students around the world.

What's in its name? The word *antennae* was lifted from Ezra Pound's (famously requoted by Marshall McLuhan) essay titled "Henry James" in

---

4 *The British Animal Studies Network—London Meetings: 2007–2009*, organized by Erica Fudge, Middlesex University, <http://www.britishanimalstudiesnetwork.org.uk/>.

which he wrote: "Artists are the *antennae* of the race, but the bullet-headed many will never learn to trust their great artists."[5] Still today, this quote underlines *Antennae*'s ethos and cultural mission. I had no other alternative names in mind for it. The animal/technology connotation the word *antennae* encapsulates seemed to perfectly nod to the posthuman sensitivities emerging at the time. Yet, I knew that the masthead needed a line to more clearly fasten the content—that is when I decided that "animals in art" would have been far too restrictive. I wanted the journal to be as open as possible to reflect my understanding of an ontological turn, not simply an animal one. So, I decided to settle with the utterly complex, old-fashion, and stereotypically open term *nature*. At that time, I had come to conclusion that nature is nothing more than a representational construct—the multiple overlapping configurations through which we reduce, rationalize, and moralize the nonhuman as Other. From the word go, it was evident to me that discussing human/animal relations in an arena where human and animals ontologically occupy privileged agential roles, came with unsustainable critical limitations.

The epistemic limits of animal studies became very clear to me pretty early on, in 2008, when I was invited to speak at the first *The Animal Gaze* symposium. There I presented a paper titled "The Death of the Animal" on the controversial artists whose works included animal killings.[6] The argument was plain and simple: some contemporary art involving animals, despite its aesthetic appeal, is very classical in essence: animals are reduced to metaphors and the message being sent is deeply anthropocentric. In the impossibility of materializing human death, some artists used animals as proxy.

I thought this subject would be well received at a conference of this kind at which artists and humanities scholars constituted the vast majority in the audience. But I was about to find out otherwise. When time for the Q&A came, I was attacked on two fronts. On one side were those who just did not want to see those works. Instead of facing animal death in art for the purpose of critically understanding the phenomenon, some blamed me for "promoting" such works. On the other, were those who simply could not come to terms with my criticism of Peter Singer's conceptions of "journey model" and "interest".

According to Peter Singer's now mostly outdated and highly anthropocentric views, what outlines the possibility of granting equal consideration to a nonhuman being is an individual's capacity for "suffering and enjoying" which defines the trajectory of a "journey model of life" driven by agency and intentionality.[7] In other words, only animals that appear to share a similar understanding of a human conception of "being alive" deserve ethical consideration. I have always found this view, one of the foundations of animal rights, to be extremely problematic. On what account should I consider myself the arbiter, or the normative measure of other nonhuman beings' sentience or will to live? I provocatively addressed my critics, saying that both a cow and a carrot pursue equally valid "journey models" involving different forms of "personal interests" and displaying various forms of agency and intentionality. The attack intensified, my point of view was duly trivialized via wholly personal and nonacademic "ethical" and moral schemes—there was no mediation, no compromise, or remediation. I was laughed off—the horrid idea that animal and vegetal life could be, even momentarily, compared on any grounds was safely put in the back of everyone's mind—order was restored, coffee was served, everyone filled their mouths with pastries throughout the break.

5   Pound, E. (1918) 'Henry James' in *Literary Essays of Ezra Pound* (New York: New Directions Publishing) p. 297.

6   Aloi, G. (2008) 'The Death of the Animal' in *Antennae: The Journal of Nature in Visual Culture*, 5, Spring, pp. 43–53.

7   Singer, P. (1993) *Practical Ethics* (Cambridge: Cambridge University Press).

This experience marked the next few years of my involvement in Animal Studies. I kept thinking about plants and how they seem to short-circuit animal studies discourses in such a profound way. As a result, I became more and more fascinated by this phytophobia, so much that in 2011 I published two issues of *Antennae* entirely dedicated to plants in contemporary art. The autumn issue featured the results of an online experiment called "The Silence of the Plants." An article on the subject of plants and ethics published by *The New York Times* was offered for public commentary on a blog platform. It led to a challenging and interesting discussion amongst some of *Antennae*'s readers, contributors, and board members. The article titled "Sorry Vegans, Brussels Sprouts Like to Live Too" was an intentionally provocative piece that triggered interesting responses.[8] The exchange encompassed many important points including the Derridian notion of "eating well"; pressing questions about the possibility/impossibility of having compassion for the vegetal world; the vegan reluctance to acknowledge plant sentience as mitigator of animal killing; the questioning of the validity of sentience as a tool of measure in these discourses;[9] the possibility of envisioning new notions of "being sentient" that might exceed human phenomenology;[10] the primacy science still retains in shaping Western knowledge and ethical approaches in opposition to the holistic views of Eastern philosophies;[11] the anthropocentric privileging of mammals in animal studies discourses as a speciesist trait that prevents any serious consideration of plants; the challenges and limitations posed by anthropomorphism; the possibility or impossibility

to productively engage with biocontinuity; the productivities involved in the elusive search for an objective outlook;[12] and Peter Singer's rejection of the notion of "plant intelligence."[13]

The exchange was not meant to draw specific conclusions about the troubling ontological instability plants ignite when ousted from their objectified/silenced cultural dimension. However, it nonetheless proved extremely useful in mapping key concerns and anxieties as seen from an animal studies perspective. The following year, the animal/plant ethical debate gained momentum as Michael Marder and animal rights/vegan ambassador Gary Francione exchanged their views on ethics, plants, animals, and veganism on the Columbia University Press website.[14] Marder wisely opened the exchange acknowledging that "plant ethics" should not constitute a threat to, or invalidation of, veganism. He explained that it should rather constitute an invitation to surpass the obsolete conceptions of pain and sentience to consider the violence perpetrated on other living-beings, such as plants, which, in Marder's words, have been "thoroughly instrumentalized by the same logic that underpins human domination over other animal species."[15] Francione's line of defense, however, was defined by deeply misconstrued and obsolete notions about plants. He obstinately claimed that "they are not sentient," or that they "have no subjectivity," or that they "have no interest." Francione claimed: "They cannot desire, or want, or prefer anything."[16] He thus deliberately refused to acknowledge new evidence of scientific research to support the exceptionalism of animal life. Francione is in denial. His simplistic argument wrongly claims that we have no evidence of plant suffering or plant agency: the anthropocentric conception

8 Angier, N. (2009) 'Sorry Vegans, Brussels Sprouts Like to Live Too' in *The New York Times*, December 22, p. 2.

9 Various Authors (2011) 'The Silence of the Plants' in *Antennae: The Journal of Nature in Visual Culture*, 18, Autumn, pp. 11–23.

10 Ibid., p. 14.

11 Ibid., p. 15.

12 Ibid., p. 21.

13 Ibid., p. 22.

14 Marder, M. (2016) *Grafts: Writing on Plants* (Minneapolis: Univocal) pp. 175–82.

15 Ibid., p. 175.

16 Ibid., p. 176.

of pain therefore becomes the normative tool with which the worth of other beings' life is assessed and established. However, his personal views on plants are firmly contradicted by scientific evidence he would rather ignore.[17] This seems at odds with the demarcated interest vegan quarters have for recent scientific research demonstrating that lobsters suffer and that fish have longer memory spans than we previously thought.[18] So why is Francione insistently resistant to the notion that plants could also, in very different ways from our own, experience something akin to pain, and that they might also have, in their own ways, "desires"? Why should the idea that a plant could have "subjectivity" be so troubling? Even more uncanny is that Francione's position, and that of some vegan scholars I have encountered at animal studies conferences, is intrinsically based on the same hubristic logic perpetrated by those who, in the eighteenth and nineteenth centuries, proclaimed that animals had no souls, no intent; in brief: that animals are automata. The Cartesian paradigm is the same; only this time the target has changed.

In *Writing On An Ethical Life*, Peter Singer also discounted any conception of plant agency, their "will to live," or desire to seek nourishment as mechanical responses. He insisted, again based on no scientific research, that plants are not conscious and that they cannot engage in intentional behavior.[19] But what's most disconcerting is that Singer's deliberate reduction of plants to mechanized beings, in the context of his book, unfolds at the expense of holistic philosophical approaches. Singer's real targets were the theories of Albert Schweitzer and Paul Taylor whose principle of morality entailed revering the "will-to-live" in all beings, "whether it can express itself to my comprehension or whether it remains unvoiced." Paul Taylor's argument that every living being is "pursuing its own good in its own unique way" was equally dismissed.[20] Why would Singer undermine these productive holistic approaches and prioritize animal suffering against views that can benefit entire ecosystems? Likewise, on what ethical grounds can Francione state: "I reject completely the notion that we can have direct obligations to plants. I reject completely that plants have any interests whatsoever."[21] According to his philosophy then, razing a forest to the ground poses no ethical problem, as we do not have any moral obligations to any plants. Alternatively, do obligations arise only when we consider that animals and plants are closely interconnected in ecosystems? Does any ethical obligation simply rest on animals? I am afraid that matters are much more complex than this.

Francione's and Singer's arguments have been reverberating through the recent tilting of the animal studies axis towards vegan and animal rights agendas and away from truly

---

17   This is the content of a Facebook post by Francione, dated 08/09/2016. It was titled 'Thought of the day'. It clearly shows how Francione is indebted to Singer's legacy and how his thinking does not advance from Singer's *Animal Liberation* (1975). "There may be uncertainty as to whether some mollusks, such as clams or oysters, are sentient. With regards to any unclear cases, we believe it prudent to err on the side of caution and regard close cases as being sentient. There is, however, absolutely no doubt that the animals we routinely exploit—cows, pigs, sheep, goats, chickens, turkeys, fish, lobsters, etc.—are sentient. All sentient beings have at least two interests: the interest in not suffering and the interest in not dying. That is, although not all sentient beings may think about their lives in the same way, all of them desire or want to remain alive. And the use of animals as property for food, clothing, and other purposes implicates at least two related, but different, interests that animals have. That is, using animals in the ways that we use them involves doing things to animals that they want, desire, or prefer us not to do: we cause them suffering, and we kill them."

18   Gee, P., Stephenson, D., and Wright, D.E. (1994) 'Temporal Discrimination Learning of Operant Feeding in Goldfish (*Carassius auratus*)' in *Journal of the Experimental Analyses of Behaviour*, 1, pp. 1–13.

19   Singer, P. (2000) *Writings On An Ethical Life* (New York: Open Road Media).

20   Ibid.

21   Marder, M. (2016), p. 180.

innovative thinking on human-nonhuman relations. While this is not a problem, some issues are nonetheless caused by the inherent anthropocentric parameters of these frameworks. The initial premise of animal studies was to sidestep anthropocentrism to develop a more complex understanding of what animals might be and do. In this context, anthropocentrism requires a certain fine-tuning, and Singer's and Francione's ethical approaches are far from that.

Most importantly, underneath the unwillingness to acknowledge that plants are active agents, that they want and desire, that they are aware of their surroundings, and that they might even feel pain in very different ways from ours lies a form of deep anxiety that is entirely human and exclusively about us. I would hate to be misunderstood here: animal rights and vegan ideologies have positively contributed to the well-being of animals and, in some respect, of the planet more generally—at no stage do I deny this. Yet, the obsoleteness of their core foundational beliefs is now clearly undermining their credibility. The very idea of assessing a being's "sentience" to define ethical paradigms smacks of an anthropocentric arrogance that belongs to the nineteenth century.

Relying on anthropocentric notions like *sentience* and *intention,* or *pain*, and *desire*, implicitly forces specifically human parameters upon animals. In this way we build an empathic bridge of some sort. But ethically speaking, this is a highly problematic move, for it implies that the more an animal is human-like, the more likely it is that we can strike an empathic bond with it, and the more appropriate it seems that such animals should be granted rights. The problem lies in the measuring tools that words like pain, sentience, desire, interest, and will impose on discourse—how they limit it. Therefore, and paradoxically so, much in animal rights discourses is inherently speciesist. Whilst ethical consideration is reserved for primates and farm animals, or endangered charismatic megafauna, where is the objection to insecticides on sale in all supermarkets around the world? Animal rights activists have been quick at protesting the use of butterflies in Damien Hirst's work, but what about the millions of insects, arachnids, and rodents systematically exterminated every day by an agricultural industry worth millions of dollars?

What assures Singer and Francione that our senses might suffice to assess the sentience levels of beings with which we cannot communicate using language or establish meaningful eye contact? What about those animals that cannot make a sound, or at least a sound that we can hear, or those anchored at the bottom of sea beds? Do we owe them any ethical obligations? Are they too plant-like to be considered? At what point are we prepared to seriously acknowledge that our sensorial is just as partial as, and in many cases more limited than, those of other nonhuman beings? At what point can we acknowledge that we only access a very superficial notion of nonhuman perceptiveness and that ultimately animals and plants see, hear, smell, sense, and feel the world in ways we cannot yet even conceive? Most importantly, at what point can we incorporate these different modalities of awareness, something scientific research has been piecing together over the past century, within philosophical discourses without drowning into a naïve new age sensitivity based on personal mythologies alone? Feminist Science Studies, Multispecies Ethnography, and New Materialism have all capitalized on the latest scientific research for the purpose of speculating on human/nonhuman sympoiesis. However, the field of animal studies is, generally speaking, far from engaging with these approaches.

Ultimately, what do philosophers really know about animals or plants that is not derived from scientific knowledge and personal experiences? From Agamben's spider to Heidegger's lizard, or Deleuze's wolves, the continental tradition in Western philosophy has failed animals on two accounts: the constant use of the singular/plural 'animal' and the lack of actual engagement with specific species or individual animals. Derrida famously objected to the totalization operated by the word *animal* as it designates an undifferentiated multiplicity of nonhuman life-forms. His proposed neologism, *animot,* acknowledged the essential representative nature inscribed in the word while reminding the reader of the undermined human/animal complications the word animal has produced through history.[22] Indeed this largely is a matter of language—language inserts itself between human and animal, it wraps both, defining and problematizing beyond the register of materiality.

In addition to their anthropocentric reliance on a terminology that cannot account for the sensorial complexity of the variety of species on this planet, philosophers are guilty of not spending enough time with animals (and dogs and cats do not count here, sorry!), or with plants. This is the other way in which western philosophy has failed animals, and this essentially is the epistemic modality we need to avoid at all costs in our botanical speculations. Agamben, for instance, drew very generic and arbitrary conclusions on a spider's presumed lack of knowledge of what it feeds on and the coincidental affinity between the web it builds and the fly it catches. His notion of attunement between fly and web is purely poetic. At no stage did Agamben tell us which species of spider he is referring to—that's of course not relevant in the scope of the Western philosophical tradition. Spiders have very varied diets, they don't simply eat flies and have not evolved to exclusively aim to catch flies. In consequence, their webs are designed to catch a multitude of differently sized insects, that's what's marvelous about them. And beyond this, spiders exhibit an astute sense of awareness in deciding where to build their webs. They choose locations in which insect traffic is high, nearby stagnant water, light sources, in the undergrowth, dark

cavities—they make choices and take decisions that are directly linked to their survival. How they know about their preys is incomprehensible to us, so incomprehensible that the verb "know" loses all meaning.

Let's not mistake, Agamben's "spider" only exists as a word on the page of his book *The Open*—there the spider is written as a chimerical conglomerate of multiple species that paradoxically add up to a "dumb-spider": one which, in a Heideggerian sense, is not capable of grasping its own being nor that of the food it catches.[23] Similarly, Heidegger's (generic) lizard is caught up in a series of captivations with other objects or animals, but it lacks the ability to know the rock it sits on as a rock, never mind grasping an essential-notion of the sun. According to most Western philosophers, animals are akin to automata that hopelessly wander around the world with no reference points, priorities, knowledge, or ability to truly experience anything. The truth is that a lizard has no use for any essential construction of what a rock or the sun might be, at least not in the sense a Western philosopher might. We might never know what the stone or the sun "means" to the lizard that returns to the stone over and over. However, could the lizard know something we will never know about the stone? Who's the short-sighted, the limited, the one that lacks, here?

These reductionist approaches have brought me to wonder how many lizards Heidegger must have studied before coming to his conclusions. Likewise, how many spiders must have Agamben gazed at, days on end, before formulating his theory? Very likely, the answer, in both cases is very few, if any at all. These philosophers have written about animals as transcendental entities—place-markers of human finitude—their animals are specifically constructed and reduced to assess human's presumed exceptional position in the world, and so they implicitly contribute to the structure of an ethical scale of

---

22   Derrida, J. (1997) 'The animal that therefore I am (More to follow),' *Critical Inquiry,* 28, 2 (2002), pp. 369–418.

23   Agamben, G. (2002) *The Open: Man and Animal* (Redwood City: Stanford University Press).

compassion or lack of thereof. Why should one care for a dumb spider or a lizard that has no clue about the rock it sits on? Maybe spending some time with these animals prior to entrapping them in philosophical discourses could have produced different results. But perhaps spending time with animals might have been time badly spent. It might have undermined the hubris that suggests we can know everything about other beings and that our perception of them is wholly exhaustive.

Scientific advancements have, over time, substantially changed our perception of nonhuman life. From Anton van Leeuwenhoek's founding of microbiology and Lynn Margulis's work on eukaryotic cells to James Westwood's discovery that some parasitic plants meddle with their hosts on a genetic level, two hundred and fifty years of science have drastically reconfigured what we thought we knew. We have become aware of the importance of pheromones, or the ability certain insects have to see the infrared range, or the use of ultrasounds in bats and dolphins—and this sensorial range, which by far exceeds human abilities, only constitutes the tip of the iceberg. What else are we bound to discover about the many ways in which animals communicate with each other, and how they navigate or intermingle with the biosystems they inhabit? New technologies have enabled us to understand that individuals of some plant-species communicate to each other using their root systems; that plants under attack by parasites can release biochemical signals capable of attracting "companion insects" that will take care of the threat. More recently, a hormone which releases pain in stressed plant tissue has also been identified—this opens up the serious possibility for a notion of awareness and pseudo-sentience in plants to gain traction.[24] At this moment in time we are at an important junction. Philosophy has had the best part of twenty years to brush up with the animal and come to terms with its alterity. The time has come to reconsider the role of philosophical poetics in the face of ethical urgency. If one is to write about an animal or a plant, let's make it specific and learn from the perspectives of other disciplines first.

This picture might explain why plants still constitute the last frontier in ethical discourses involving animals and the nonhuman more generally. Which returns us to animal rights and vegan theories once more. In brief, vegan and animal rights philosophies rely on an intrinsic notion of shame, which implicitly articulates itself over a stark disassociation with human-on-human violence. As argued by Agamben in *The Open: Man and Animal*, during the Second World War, Jews (along with other minority groups) came to represent "the non-man produced within the man."[25] As it is known, direct comparisons between the structural overlaps in the mass slaughter of animals and the atrocities committed in concentration camps recur in animal rights arguments. Likewise, the invitation to think about animals as children also regularly plays a vital role in animal right's cry for empathy. From here, and understandably so, stems the desire not to inflict pain on sentient beings.

Whilst I could not agree more with this notion, it is also impossible to ignore that this very desire, because its roots are grounded in the shame which permeates the traumatic memories of the Holocaust, or more generally any type of genocide, leads to the forming of prioritized animal categories: those whose suffering is more similar to our own get attention. It is at this point that one thing becomes clear: to some radical animal rights and vegan discourses, acknowledging plants' agency or alternative modes of sentience entails risking the human once again, and this time, with that, risking the animal too. Not causing suffering is the essential aspiration of animal rights and vegan

24   Worrall, S. (2016) 'There is Such a Thing as Plant Intelligence' in *National Geographic*, online, February 21st, online [<http://news.nationalgeographic.com/2016/02/160221-plant-science-botany-evolution-mabey-ngbooktalk/> accessed on 23 February 2016.

25   Agamben, G. (2002), p. 22.

beliefs. Digging too deep into vegetal-being to detect forms of suffering, distress, or sentience poses a fundamental threat to the foundations of these philosophies. Yet is it ethically defensible to continually and deliberately deny the complexity of plants in order to retain the validity of one's beliefs? Acknowledging that plants are much more complex beings than previously thought should not involve a rethinking of what we eat and what we do not—like all other living beings on this planet we need to consume other living organisms to keep ourselves alive. In the context of the environmental global challenges we currently face, I seriously advocate that our responsibility as humans must encompass entire ecosystems rather than soley focus on outdated. Acknowledging that plant-being means much more than mechanistic responses to stimuli upturns the Cartesian perspectives that have culturally impoverished the world we live in. Now more than ever before, as digital technologies distract us from the natural world, we need to use the new types of knowledge we have at our disposal to generate curiosity for the living, not for the purpose of reassessing a hierarchy of animal life structured around anthropocentric values. Ultimately, I respect everyone's freedom to ignore new scientific research, but I object to the notion that someone's will to ignore should limit my own thinking about the living world.

Plants and Animals: Issues of Representation

Plants and animals share analogous histories of objectification that have been substantially defined by representation. This is why it is important to look at the presence of plants in art before engaging with contemporary practices that attempt to upturn plant objectification. For this purpose, a productive starting point is constituted by the European medieval period and the epistemic source that introduced a modern

conception of animal and plant objectification in Western culture.

During the Middle Ages, the *Physiologus*, a book likely to have originated from Egypt and written in Greek, became much more influential than any painting or other work of art.[26] It was translated in different languages including Syriac, Ethiopic, Coptic, Armenian, and Latin, and it traveled far and wide across the continent.[27] Essentially a religious text, the *Physiologus* gathered pagan tales of animal stories infused with Christian morals and became the most adopted reference of iconographical sourcing in art.[28] Its impact upon the epistemology of the natural world was defining and long-lasting. The book provided the visual and literary arts with many allegorical scenarios populated by phoenixes, unicorns, and an array of fantastical plants that generally served as backdrops, or as scenic dividers, in rare number of illuminated versions. In principle, the *Physiologus'* plants occupied a secondary/ornamental role in the narration of religious events.

As a didactic text, the *Physiologus* constituted a new epistemic spatialization in which humans, animals, plants, and fantastic beings were essentially represented through the enmeshing of *nature semantics.* Nature semantics are the words interwoven in the very fabric of "represented nonhumans.' Every representation of a human or nonhuman-being effectively is, to different degrees, inscribed with language, with an intrinsic signifying, symbolic register. A horse in a painting is never just a horse; dogs represent fidelity, butterflies the soul, cats witchcraft, and so on. In medieval and classical art, symbolism functioned as a representational crux between human and nonhuman. The representation of

---

26   Curley, M.J. (2009) *Physiologus: A Medieval Book of Nature Lore* (Chicago: University of Chicago Press) p. ix.

27   James, M.R. (1931) 'The Bestiary' in *History: The Quarterly Journal of the Historical Association*, XVI, 61, April, pp. 1–11, and p. 3.

28   Ibid.

certain nonhuman-beings and the exclusion of others in art is motivated by the cultural coordinates that make them worthy of representation in the first place. Nature semantics were, therefore, the linguistic elements that structured iconography beyond the formalist concerns of mimesis. Over time, nature semantics directly formed the essential representational sedimentations of an archive of symbolic modalities, practices, and discourses. Nature semantics are narratives—a chain-link of attributes, myths, and anecdotes all of which share a deep anthropocentric matrix.[29]

Thereafter, the formula of the *Physiologus* became the blueprint of the *Bestiarium*—a zoological-epistemological site that profoundly marked Medieval and Renaissance culture in Europe. The Latin text of the surviving early bestiaries effectively is a translation of the *Physiologus*.[30] However, most importantly, moving beyond the *Physiologus*' unorganized assemblage of information, the *Bestiarium* provided more visual representations, first unclassified (before the twelfth century) and thereafter classified in loose orders.[31]

In the *Bestiarium* nature semantics materialized animals and plants as morally charged, symbolic-objects of religious value: the "medieval naturalist" was a theologian.[32] With time, as collections of stories dispersed across different geographical and cultural areas, bestiaries established new iconographies that subsequently informed the discipline of natural history. In bestiaries, the newly formed relationship between animals, plants, text, and

FIGURE 0.1   The Tree Peridexion in *Oxford Bestiary*, c. 1220.

illustration was initially a substantially fluid one. Since the text was essentially religious, animals and plants appeared as actors on the stage of a morality play. Realism did not matter in this context, and in fact, many of the artists who illustrated multiple copies of bestiaries had never seen firsthand the animals and plants they represented.

Since the fall of the Roman Empire (5th century CE), realism had lost prominence in artistic production throughout Central and Eastern Europe.[33] Christianity appropriated artistic production for funerary and educational purposes. Thus, the role of representation was that of educating, and to do so in a clear way. The many details involved in a too realistic representation would distract the viewer from the essential moral teaching.[34] Therefore, naturalistic realism simply became inadequate to the rendition of a

29   As it will be seen later on, the work of nature semantics is also active in everyday life where living or preserved plants are clearly inscribed with shared symbolisms. A wrapped dozen of roses purchased from a florist shop never is just roses—it's a sign of love (as long as the roses are red).

30   Klingender, F. (1971) *Animals in Art and Thought to the End of the Middle Ages*, p. 341.

31   Ibid., p. 4.

32   Allen, R.J. (1887) *Lecture VI: The Medieval Bestiaries—The Rhind Lectures in Archaeology for 1885* (London: Whiting & Co.).

33   Richards, J. (2000) 'Early Christian Art' in Kemp, M. (ed.) *The Oxford History of Western Art* (Oxford: Oxford University Press) pp. 70–75, ref. p. 71.

34   Ibid.

world constructed through the "already coded eye" of God.

From an art historical perspective, the departure from naturalistic realism that characterized the postclassical Greek phase has generally been acknowledged to be the result of the influence of the art of Celtics, Germanics, Hiberno-Saxons, and Vikings.[35] In many ways, medieval painting was the result of discourses and practices that prioritized representation as an ordering agent in a highly dystopian world. Furthermore, nonnaturalistic approaches enhanced the urgency of appeal in the viewer—form became substantially subjugated to content, and it ostensibly veered towards flatness. Painting became the site of God's materialization on earth: a limited, filtered, flattened, and a miniaturized world better lent itself to metaphorical control and could be better assimilated into discourses. It is thus that medieval painting and manuscript illuminations reciprocally validated one another—God's word was the truth, and the representation of God was the word.

Within the flatness of medieval painting two major accomplishments took place. First of all, the flattening of animals and plants operated as the "marker of the spiritual." Flatness suggested the lifting of the object from the metaphysical—figures were deliberately extrapolated from the spatial as well as temporal flux of the world.[36] As such they exclusively existed in spiritual, symbolic registers. Second, extrapolating figures from the three-dimensionality of the world, medieval art enhanced the possibilities of organizing it according to the omnipotence of the word of God. Bypassing realism enabled artists to construct clear hierarchical structures in which human figures were arranged in size according to their theological importance, not their positioning in relation to the viewer's gaze. Thus, images and words ontologically coincided in the material condition they shared: the flatness of

the manuscript pages or the wooden boards of paintings. Repeated and disseminated through the manual reproduction of bestiaries around Europe, the newly acquired visibility of animals and plants defined a new representational space in which nature could be constructed.

The Flattening of Nature

By the second half of the thirteenth century, the flattened representations of animals and plants in bestiaries had become the aesthetic norm. One of the most widely circulated early natural history books to include illustrations was *Historia Animalium* by Conrad Gesner, published between 1551 and 1558.[37] One of the main innovations introduced by this book was the emergence of a new epistemological optic based on Aristotelian notions of empiricism. In the attempt of prioritizing order, that which will eventually become taxonomy, Gesner organized his collection alphabetically. Yet nature semantics still populated nature representations. The result still featured many symbols, emblems, and metaphors, but Gesner's work also demonstrated new awareness of the importance images played in the study of nature.[38] In the preface to the first volume, he states:

> princes of the Roman Empire used to exhibit exotic animals in order to overwhelm and conquer the minds of the populace, but those animals could be seen or inspected only for a short time while the shows lasted; in contrast, the pictures in the Historia animalium could be seen whenever and forever, without effort or danger.[39]

35   Klingender, F. (1971) p. 117.

36   Worringer, W. (1953) *Abstraction and Empathy: A Contribution to the Psychology of Style* (Chicago: Ivan R. Dee), 1997, p. 44.

37   Ashworth, W., B. (1996) 'Emblematic Natural History in the Renaissance' in Jardine, J., Secord, A., and Spary, E.C. (Eds.) *Cultures of Natural History* (Cambridge: Cambridge University Press) pp. 17–37, ref. p. 17.

38   Ibid.

39   Gesner, C. (1551) *Historia Animalium*, I, g1 v, as quoted in Kusukawa, S. (2010) 'The sources of Gesner's pictures for the *Historia animalium*' in *Annals of Science*, 76,3, pp. 303–28, quote, p. 307.

During the Renaissance, princes, kings, and aristocrats routinely used exotic animals and plants as markers of power—the possession of exotic species, live or preserved, immediately spoke of substantial wealth and intellectual ability. However, metaphorically, the taming and pacifying of these animals also implied a high moral strength of the owner—he, who could tame the wild beast, would also possess impressive ruling qualities. Gesner's passage demonstrates the importance of this power/knowledge relation and how representations of the natural world also mattered in this context. Books like those by Gesner's and other naturalists were extremely sought after as they encapsulated a more defined taste for erudition and art besides the spectacle of the menagerie. It is also in this context that the cabinets of curiosities became extremely popular in Europe around the same time. Developing knowledge of the natural world became a valuable way to demonstrate one's mastery over the world. The new importance images played in animal and plant representation contributed to the shift from the theological symbolism to a more empirical realm of early scientific concern where animals and plants could be inspected. This way, natural history contributed to a transhistorical process of objectification in which animals and plants essentially functioned as emblems of power.

A significant innovation in Gesner's work was the inclusion of exotic animals arriving to Europe from the far North, the New World, and the East Indies.[40] These new animals appeared somewhat suspended between the empirical and the fantastical as the novelty of their colors and shapes made them implicitly otherworldly. However, their newness challenged authors with a blank space in the place of narratives. These new animals were wholly or mostly unknown and did not carry with them any natural

semantics: they were symbolically bare. It is likely that the impossibility to interpret these animals through an anthropocentric, sociosymbolic schemata brought Gesner to focus on their surfaces and morphology in order to register with accuracy the only meaningful features at his disposal. As a result, his illustrations capitalized on a representational naturalism that had already resurfaced in the sculptural and pictorial arts through the revival of Classical art and Greek philosophy during the Renaissance.[41]

As these animals travelled to Europe accompanied by little or no information about what their environments looked like, Gesner left most of the backgrounds plain. In many cases, plants had disappeared entirely from their assigned backdrop role. In the absence of specific cultural knowledge of exotic animals, the new iconographical modality at play positioned animal bodies in a contextual vacuum.[42] This

---

40 Ashworth, W.B. (1996) p. 27. For a detailed analysis of Gesner's use of images in *Historia Animalium* including interesting information on the sources of his images, see Kusukawa, S. (2010).

41 It is important to mention that on many occasions, the images Gesner published were not made from life, but that they were instead purchased or incorporated from previous publications in his own. As argued by scientific historian Sachiko Kurosawa: "the sources of Gesner's images were thus varied— they included live, dried or partial specimens; images from other printed books, manuscripts, maps and prints; drawings made by artists at his request; drawings sent in by his friends and chosen by Gesner." Ibid., p. 327.

42 Gesner's approach to natural history has been center of much scrutiny from different historians. Whilst Foucault may be considered to be the most influential, it is important to take into consideration Kusukawa's research on Gesner's sources of the images he used in *Historia Animalium* for the purpose of better understanding how Gesner constructed his natural history optics. However, it is also interesting to see that all critiques of Gesner's work fail to consider the importance of his illustrations in relation to the broader contemporary context of painting and representation. Thus, Ashworth identifies a number of factors that may have been influential to Gesner's approach, like the renewed interest for hieroglyphs, antique coins and renaissance medals, Aesopic fables, classical mythology, epigrams, and emblems, but does not pause to consider the relevance which painting may bear on Gesner's representations.

aesthetic shift was also characterized by a different positioning of animal bodies within the space of the page, as they more regularly began to appear longitudinally. Unlike the animals in the illustrations of bestiaries, which usually participated in some narrative act surrounded by a contextualizing backdrop, Gesner's animals were still.

Transcribed into the discourses of natural history, starkly rendered, and longitudinally positioned in the pictorial plane so to display formal attributes with heightened clarity, animal bodies appeared aligned as closely as possible to the words that described them on the surface of the page. Simultaneously silenced, immobilized, posed, isolated, and flattened, they were fully exposed to the objectifying gaze of the natural historian.

Botany: Setting the Iconographies of Objectification

Having outlined the role played by representation in the process of animal objectification, it is now important to take a step back to evaluate the synergy involved in the illustration of plants and animals since this informs their shared ontologization as subjugated others. I will argue that the herbarium effectively was an iconographical precursor of natural history objectification; one in which the aesthetic "flattening of animals" of early natural history in the Renaissance was laid.

The work of Aristotle, Theophrastus, and that of Crateva di Mitridate from the 4th century BCE is considered the beginning of botanical studies. Crateva di Mitridate's body of work

has been entirely lost, but it is claimed that his drawings were incorporated in medieval texts.[43] Pliny (23–79 CE) and Pedanios Dioscorides (54–68 CE) also notably advanced the study of plants, although not much remains of their work.[44] However, one of the most interesting examples of the iconographical approach originally employed by botanical illustration can be identified in the *Vienna Dioscurides,* an early 6th century illuminated, medical manuscript from Greece that cataloged roughly five hundred plants.[45] In this collection of illustrations and medical texts, plants already appeared morphologically flattened—their parts were clearly manipulated to best fit the flatness and borders of the page upon which they were drawn. The background was neutral, like in the later images by Gesner, while the vast majority or totality of the leaves and flowers appeared parallel to the page.

These examples show that the iconographical modalities of zoological representations are discursively linked to the study of botany. A contemporary work, *Herbarium Apuleii Platonici* incorporated similar representational strategies, and it became one of the most popular herbaria of the middle ages.[46] Similarly, *The Old English Herbarium* (late 10th century) proposed flattened and largely synthetic representations of plants.[47] However, it was the *Codex Vindobonensis,* with its four hundred illustrations of Mediterranean plants, that introduced a new level of naturalism in the representation of plants—one that transcended

---

Likewise, Ashworth acknowledges that Gesner's iconographical choices may have been informed by the botanical revolution of the 1530s during which the prominence gained by herbaria vastly contributed to the circulation of illustrated books—yet he does not linger too long over the potentialities may have been at stake here and he is also perhaps far too quick at dismissing the influence that the Physiologus or that the Bestiary may have played too.

---

43   Savi, G., and Andres, G. (1840) *Istituzioni Botaniche* (Loreto: Tipografia Rossi), pp. x–xii.

44   Ibid., pp. xiv–xxiv.

45   Dioscorides, P. (50–70AD) *De Materia Medica* (Lugdunum: Apud Balthazarem Arnolletum) and Rix, M. (1981) *The Art of Botanical Illustration* (New York: Arch Cape Press) p. 10.

46   Pseudo-Apuleius (4th century CE) *Herbarium of Pseudo Apuleius*, Oxford, Bodleian Library, Ashmole, 1431 (7523).

47   De Vriend, H.J. (ed) (1984) *The Old English Herbarium and Medicina de Quadrupedibus* (London, Oxford, and Toronto: Oxford University Press).

FIGURE 0.2 *Diptannum (Dittany) and Solago maior (Heliotropium europaeum). Solago minor (African Marigold) and Peonia (Peony). Herbal* England, Ps. Apuleius, M.S. Ashmole, fols. 17v-18r, St. Augustine's Abbey, Canterbury; 11th century, c. 1070–1100.

the stylistic synthetic approaches of Byzantine art. The epistemic shifts that enabled the emergence of the new iconography of natural history simultaneously produced more realistic images in Brunfels's *Herbarum Vivae Eicones* (1532–36) and Fuchs's *De Historia Stirpium* (1542).[48]

But it was also around this time that, alongside the epistemic importance gained by illustration in the study of plants, the emergence of herbaria in which plants are not graphically illustrated but preserved as pressed specimens

started to rise. The practice of collecting live plant specimens for the purpose of studying them was introduced by Luca Ghini: founder of the academic study of nature in Bologna and Pisa.[49] In the 1530s, Ghini introduced field trips and specimen collections as essential parts of his courses in which he produced the first "modern" herbarium including dried specimens.

Flattened and dried, plants were affixed to sheets of paper in ways that aesthetically overlapped with the preceding tradition of botanical illustration. Leaves and flowers were made

48   Brunfels, O. (1532–36) *Herbarum Vivae Eicones* (Strasburg: Argentorati, Apud Joannem Schottum); Fuchs, L. (1547) *De Historia Stirpium Commentarii Insignes* (Leipzig: Kurt Wolff Verlag).

49   Findlen, P. (1994) *Possessing Nature: Museums, Collecting, and Scientific Culture in Early Modern Italy* (Berkeley: University of California Press), p. 166.

FIGURE 0.3 Leonhart Fuchs, *Papaver*. From *De Historia Stirpium*, 1542.

The introduction of dried specimens in botanical studies should not be understood as a replacement of the illustration methods that preceded it. In fact, Gherardo Cibo, one of Ghini's students, collected, pressed, and set specimens just as much as he illustrated them.[50] Alongside the complex changes and different alternatives that shaped the discursive field of botanical research, zoology and the illustration of animals defined their epistemic spatializations, organized their practices, and set their iconographical standards. This is moreover confirmed by the fact that the prominent Italian zoologist Ulisse Aldrovandi cited Cibo's influence on his own work on animal illustration in *Catalogus Virorum qui mea studia adjuvarunt*.[51] Aldrovandi built upon Cibo's contribution by developing a keen interest in the epistemic value of illustration and consistently advocating the importance of color in painting specimens *ad vivum* (from life). Aldrovandi claimed that:

> There is nothing on earth that seems to me to give more pleasure and utility to man than painting, and above all painting of natural things: because it is through these things, painted by an excellent painter, that we acquire knowledge of foreign species, although they are born in distant lands.[52]

to adhere to the surface of the page, while stems were organized to impose a sense of clarity and definition to the plant-body; the overlap of leaves and stems was avoided wherever possible. The drying process substantially distanced the specimen from the morphology of its living referent. Beyond the required flattening, which aesthetically aligned the specimen to the ontology of illustration, the color and texture of leaves and flowers would also be conspicuously altered. However, what the dried specimen provided was the much-needed evidential truth necessary to begin a secular, taxonomical project based on empirical scientific methodologies.

50   Ibid., pp. 166–67. However, interestingly, in some of his depictions, Cibo followed the tradition of botanical illustration in which the background appears plain, and the plant morphology is flattened, while in others, he constructed an entirely new iconography in which the specimen was situated against an accurately painted local landscape. In these instances, the representation of the plant in question was rendered in a more distinct three-dimensional style as Cibo carefully negotiated the aesthetic-epistemic demands of the study of plants with pictorial parameters relevant to the time and place in which he painted.

51   Tomasi, T. (2013) 'Gherardo Cibo: un percorso tra arte e scienza' in *Gherardo Cibo: Dilettante di Botanica e Pittore di Paesi* (Ancona: Il Lavoro Editorial).

52   Aldrovandi as quoted in Swan, C. (2005) *Art, Science and Witchcraft* (Cambridge University Press) p. 41.

It is at this point that the practices of illustration and specimen collection overlapped through the scientific desire to possess the animal or plant body. Aldrovandi's impression of painting's ability to replace the natural object was also expressed by Gesner's own collection. It is reported that Gesner sometimes settled for drawings and paintings of specimens because of the prohibitive costs of some exotic animals.[53]

Objectification and Painting

Renaissance herbaria were not only the domain of natural historians but, for practical reasons, they also quickly became a reference source for European painters, designers, and tailors. During the second half of the fifteenth century, the popularization of the printing press enabled a standardization of representational modes, which largely contributed to the reinstatement of a new realism in natural history illustrations. Up to this point, bestiaries and herbaria had been reproduced by copyists who, one version after version, approximated the content of texts and the accuracy of images. At the same time, a resurgence of naturalism in painting, and a keen desire to reproduce nature driven by the revival of classical art and philosophy, also impacted on the representational-modalities of plants. A revival of Aristotelian empiricism, and the emergence of competitive markets brought artists to strive for the most realistic representations of flowers and plants. At this point, plants began to occupy a more complex role within the semantic structure of classical representation. While in the Middle Ages they were relegated to the role of ornamental backdrops, during the Renaissance, plants' presence in paintings became charged with new symbolic meaning.

The presence of flowers, leaves, and fruits on the canvas was never coincidental. It was the result of careful negotiations with patrons. Flowers are seasonal and ephemeral, so herbaria, both illustrated and with dried specimens,

could be used as source-books from which artists would draw information at any time of the year. Accuracy in the representation of flowers gained importance mainly because intersections between art and science were at the core of the new classical spirit of the time. During the Renaissance, patrons indulged in "more sophisticated" forms of knowledge as power tool through which they validated themselves. Only the most skilled artists could capture optical accuracy in representation—the market began to demand realism. Representing natural objects accurately was so important that art historians and botanists have recently been able to use plants as evidence to dispute the attribution of a famous painting by Leonardo da Vinci.

The authenticity of da Vinci's *Virgin of the Rocks* at The National Gallery in London has been challenged on the grounds that the vegetation painted at the base of the painting does not match the artist's usual level of accuracy for detail. As it is known, another version of the work is at the Louvre, in Paris. For years, both museums have been interested in ascertaining the level of authenticity and age difference of their respective masterpieces, and plants have provided the necessary clue to answer some of their questions. Renaissance art historian Ann Pizzorusso has argued that the flowers in the London version have the wrong number of petals, while John Grimshaw, a leading horticulturist, has claimed that the London painting features chimeric plants in which flowers do not match foliage. To Renaissance scholar Charles Hope, the lack of accuracy with which the plants have been rendered in the London painting is enough to suggest that the work might be entirely by the hand of a copyist, rather than da Vinci's own. Another theory is that the painting was made by da Vinci's workshop assistants behind his back so that they might benefit from an unauthorized sale.[54]

---

53   Kusukawa, S. (2010), p. 312.

54   Alberge, D. (2014) 'The daffodil code: Doubts revived over Leonardo's *Virgin of the Rocks* in London,' *The*

FIGURE 0.4 Leonardo da Vinci, *Virgin of the Rocks* (detail), National Gallery, London. About 1491/2–9 and 1506–8.
PUBLIC DOMAIN.

FIGURE 0.5 Leonardo da Vinci, *Virgin of the Rocks* (detail), The Louvre, Paris. 1483–85.
PUBLIC DOMAIN.

In Renaissance painting, realism found a new spiritual dimension. In da Vinci's painting, a palm symbolized victory and referred directly to the Virgin Mary. Irises stood as symbols for the Immaculate Conception, while the daffodils might have been included as a funerary symbol of love after death.[55] Within the semantic structure of the painting, plants and flowers anchored meaning—they fixed the identities of the main figures and simultaneously extended the narrative alluding to future or related events. It was therefore crucial that species should not be mistaken for another due to inaccurate rendering.

Cast as vessels for entirely human affairs, plants and their flowers shared a very similar representational destiny with animals. Renaissance animal presence in art was characterized by the same symbolic trajectories defined by Medieval manuscripts and bestiaries—animals were always symbolically tamed and domesticated by representation. An emblematic example of this condition is provided by the whimsical use of plants in the late sixteenth century paintings of the Italian artist Giuseppe Arcimboldo. In some works based on the superficial notion of the "scherzo" or "capriccio," the artist produced vegetal compositions inscribing a human portrait.[56] It has been claimed that his "composite heads" aimed to criticize rich people's conduct, and their frivolous and superficial approach to culture. The flowers and fruits represented in these paintings essentially are an

FIGURE 0.6   Giuseppe Arcimboldo, *Four Seasons in One Head*, c. 1590, oil on panel. Paul Mellon Fund COURTESY OF THE NATIONAL GALLERY OF ART, WASHINGTON DC.

attention seeking device through which purely anthropocentric concerns are expressed.[57]

At this point in the history of Western representation, we witness a peculiar bifurcation in the processes of objectification of animals and plants. On the one hand, the scientific herbaria of natural history objectified plants (and animals) by representationally isolating them against a plain background for observation purposes. Through this process, a plant became a specimen, the generalized and ideal body representing a whole species in the taxonomic order. On the other hand, classical painting immersed plants (and animals) in complex anthropocen-

---

Guardian, 9 December; accessed online 08/08/2016 [<https://www.theguardian.com/artanddesign/2014/dec/09/leonardo-da-vinci-virgin-rocks-louvre-national-gallery>].

55   Impelluso, L. (2004) S. Sartarelli, trans. *Nature and Its Symbols* (Los Angeles: Getty Publications). Originally published 2003, as *La Natura e i suoi simboli* (Milano: Mondadori Electa).

56   DaCosta Kaufmann, T. (2009) *Arcimboldo: Visual Jokes, Natural History, and Still-Life Painting* (Chicago: University of Chicago Press).

57   Elhard, K.C. (2005) 'Reopening the book on Arcimboldo's librarian' in *Libraries & Culture*, 40, 2 Spring 2005, pp. 115–27.

tric tableaus in which they featured as silent and yet eloquent normative tools.

The Rise of Botanical Illustration

Another important factor that led to the prevalence of optical realism in the representation of plants was related to their medicinal importance. As previously seen, stylized representations dominated the pages of late medieval and early Renaissance herbaria—but thereafter, as the study of plants became central to medicine, mistaking one species for another could be fatal. For this very reason, the work of German physician and botanist Leonhart Fuchs helped to shift the representational register of plants towards a greater realism. His *De Historia Stirpium Commentarii Insignes* (*Notable Commentaries on the History of Plants*), published in 1542, featured 497 alphabetically ordered species, many of which were originally identified by Dioscorides, Hippocrates, and Galen. Its innovative aspect lied in the inclusion of more than five hundred woodcuts proposing the classical iconography of natural history representation, featuring a singled out plant, usually uprooted, (so that the root system could be seen) and flattened against a plain background.[58] This new iconographic standard was the result of the previous representational strategies of Italian natural history, the cataloging work of Ghini and Cibo, and an integration of the artistic dexterity of three artists who produced the plates for Fuchs: Albrecht Meyer, Heinrich Fullmaurer, and Veit Rudolf Speckle.

Thereafter, new standards in botanical illustration were set by Maria Sibylla Merian, the famous Swiss naturalist who researched, wrote about, and painted plants and insects in a male-dominated scientific field. Between 1701 and 1705 she produced sixty copperplate engravings

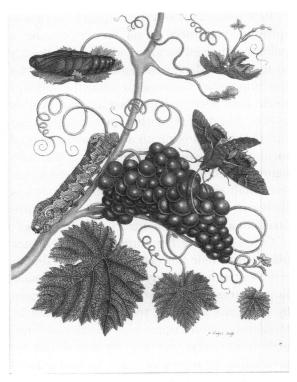

FIGURE 0.7 Maria Sibylla Merian, from *Metamorphosis Insectorum Surinamensium*, 1705.

documenting the lives of insects as connected to host-plants. Forming the core of *Metamorphosis Insectorum Surinamensium*, these were the first illustrations to closely consider biointerconnectedness between plants and animals and between different stages of a plant's and an insect's life. Her animal and plant knowledge was derived from correspondence with European scientists and by personal observation.

Compositionally, Merian's iconography was essentially in line with the spatializations of knowledge devised by her predecessors. The plants and animals were singled out against a white, plain background. Yet, Merian's work differs from theirs on two accounts. The realism she employs is not solely reliant on accuracy of detail. Her butterflies usually appear aligned with the representational plane—the wings are spread open and flat, as you would prepare specimens for an entomological collection. Her

---

58 Fuchs, L., F.G. Meyer, J.L. Heller, and E. Emmart Trueblood. *The Great Herbal of Leonhart Fuchs: De Historia Stirpium Commentarii Insignes*, 1542 (notable commentaries on the history of plants) Facsimile (Stanford: Stanford University Press).

plants exceed the previously seen parameters of realism by displaying a heightened three-dimensionality. This might be because Merian's focus was on reproducing, as accurately as possible, the patterns and shapes of butterflies. However, she was less concerned with the same level of epistemological formalism when painting plants. As a result, sometimes, her blooms bore holes, and more regularly, her leaves were damaged by insects. These imperfections are of capital importance to her understanding of what the scientific gaze should be concerned with: the interconnectedness between plants and insects rather than the aesthetically perfect, unblemished specimen held captive by an objectifying gaze. These details in Merian's plates laid the foundations for a new optics of natural history, partially anticipating, at least visually, the theorization of *umwelt* by German biologist Jakob von Uexküll.[59]

Plant Representation in the East

Many of the discourses and practices that objectified plants and animals in Western culture can be seen playing similar roles in the East. In India, the use of animals and plants as markers of aristocratic power, and their enmeshing into symbolic representational dimensions, was also common. Menageries and botanical gardens became popular during the Mughal Empire between 1556 and 1862. Prior representations of animals and plants, from the 12th and 13th centuries, show the influences of the *Physiologus* on earlier Buddhist art.[60] Miniatures and illuminations showing animals and plants in India present a similar approach to composition and iconography seen in Medieval Europe: a predominant flatness of the representational plane proposes a hierarchization of figures based on

narrative importance, rather than perspectival concerns.

The first, "modern" treatise of Indian natural history, *Mriga-Pakshi-Shastra* by the Jain poet Hamsadeva was published in the 13th century CE and is considered to be the most exhaustive descriptive account of Indian animals to date.[61] The illustration of Ustad Mansur, one of the earliest and best-known Mughal painters, presented animal and plant iconographies similar to their contemporary counterparts in Europe. The subjects appear somewhat flattened on the representational surface while the background is most regularly plain and monochromatic to make the body of the animal stand out. A synthetic realism pervades the images—surfaces and forms appear simplified while lighting is uniform, contributing to the general impression of flatness. However, it is known that around the 1580s Catholic priests traveled to some Indian courts with the intent of converting the Muslim population. For that purpose, they brought with them illustrated Bibles and oil paintings that incorporated a realism starker than the scenes depicted by Mughal artists of the time. While they failed in their theological intent, the aesthetic influence of those illustrations on local art was conspicuous.[62]

Thereafter, the Emperor Jahangir, who was a keen hunter, and kept a sumptuous menagerie, requested that royal court artists painted animals with heightened realism in order to convey the magnificence of their bodies and colors.[63] While at the same time, commercial relationships with Portugal introduced new varieties of plants from their South American territories. Marigolds, most especially, became devotional offerings. Again, the iconography of plants, as it was like in Europe,

59　Uexküll, J., M. Uexküll, and J. D. O'Neil. (2010) *A Foray Into the Worlds of Animals and Humans: With a Theory of Meaning* (Minneapolis: Minnesota University Press).

60　Dalton, M.O. (1911) *Byzantine Art and Archaeology* (Dover: Mineola) pp. 481–84.

61　Hamsadeva (13th century CE) *Mriga-Pakshi-Shastra*, English translation (Kalahasti: P.N. Press), 1972.

62　Alam, M., and Subrahmanyam, S. (2012) *Writing the Mughal World: Studies on Culture and Politics* (New York: Columbia University Press).

63　Krishna, N. (2014) *Sacred Animals of India* (New York: Penguin).

FIGURE 0.8 Attributed to Muhammad Khan, *Flower studies*,
1630–33.
ADD.OR.3129, F.67V, PUBLIC DOMAIN.

of Paradise organized in two highly anthropomorphic registers: the Garden of the Heart and the Garden of the Soul are of basic importance while the Garden of the Spirit and the Garden of the Essence stand above them. From the very beginning, therefore, the garden inscribed divine transcendence as the beauty of nature reflected transcendent truth: roses symbolized feminine, sublime beauty, while the lotus stood for fertility.[65]

Similarly, Chinese representations of plants were highly symbolic. At times the symbolic meaning was inscribed through myths or tradition and at others, and perhaps more interestingly, it was the result of linguistic or phonetic analogies, like in the case of the chrysanthemum, which pronounced in Chinese sounds like the verb "to remain." Its symbolization of long life is further anchored by the phonetic analogy between "nine" and "long time" in relation to the fact that the chrysanthemum is the flower of the ninth month in the old Chinese calendar. These instances of symbolic inscription in plants clearly highlight the disconnect between the meaning and the actual plant—in many cases, the symbolic layer has nothing to do with specific qualities or behavior of the plant/animal in question. As Wang Xiangjin wrote in *Record of All (Flowers) Fragrant*:

prescribed the flattening of the stems, arranged the leaves, and turned the flowers upwards against a plain background. The Mughal period nurtured a keen interest in plants and plant representation, which was initiated by Babur, the founder of the dynasty. His accurate descriptions of plants and substantial interest for the power of representation had a profound impact on the emergence of a new realism in art.[64] Yet, this desire to objectively represent living beings was, as in European culture, countered by the symbolic inscription of nature semantics. The *Qur'an* described four Gardens

I try to observe the morning flowers putting on their splendor, competing in all their great beauty and fragrance. Some keep company with others as they grow, while others go against time and show their preciousness. Despite their great floral beauty and exotic nature, such myriad manifestations are not easy to grasp. Their flourishing stems bloom and wither, also bringing joy and sorrow. Who says that such lodgings of joy and pleasantries of the heart are unrelated to the emotions and character?[66]

64   Verma, S.P. (2016) *The Illustrated Baburnama* (New York and London: Routledge) pp. 397–400.

65   Ruggles, D.F. (2003) *Gardens, Landscape, and Vision* (University Park: Penn State University Press).

66   邹秀文, 赵效锐, 靳晓白 (1997) *Flowering Lotus of China* (New York: Cornell University), p. 5.

FIGURE 0.9 Yun Shouping, *Peonies*, 17th century.
PUBLISHED IN THE U.S. BEFORE 1923 AND PUBLIC DOMAIN.

Symbolism domesticates. Allegories subjugate the otherness of the plant in a simple move that conceals behind a preinscribed screen of signification what we cannot comprehend. The plant is thus turned into a hollow vessel for human concerns and feelings. Animal studies identified the strictures of symbolism in representation from the early days. In his theorization of the postmodern animal, Steve Baker claimed that "symbolism is inevitably anthropomorphic, making sense of the animal by characterizing it in human terms, and doing so from a safe distance."[67] Baker's theorization overlooks the importance of symbolism in actual human/nonhuman relations beyond the specific register of artistic representation. For instance, the cultural and commercial popularity of many cut

flowers is directly linked to their assigned symbolic meaning. The same is true for many animals that were sought after in menageries, natural history museums, as well as those that have become protected by laws today. Symbolism affects human/nonhuman relations in many unpredictable ways, and while it surely aids processes of representational objectification, it might as well be the only reason why certain species are alive and thriving today as they rather appear to have domesticated us. Some species have conquered a cultural space in our lives which makes us tend to them, breed them on an industrial scale, and thus perpetuate their own success as species amongst others.

While the negative concerns with symbolism were specifically marked by postmodernist sentiments, symbolism in art and culture should not be considered wholly negative and requires more careful consideration to better map the

---

67   Baker, S. (2000) *The Postmodern Animal* (London and New York: Routledge) p. 82.

intricacies involved in human/nonhuman relations. Part of the provocative proposal of this book lies in the possibility to consider objectification as an inescapable condition in human/nonhuman relations and to bypass superficial negative judgment of an anthropomorphic kind in assessing the role it plays in these relations. In some cases, symbolism may actually turn out to be the key to unlocking a recovery of concealed human/nonhuman sets of power/knowledge relations.

Animal, Plant, Object

The links between objectification and representation of plants in art became even more entangled during the seventeenth and eighteenth centuries as religious, political, and economic shifts in Northern Europe set the scene for the golden age of Dutch still-life painting.

At the time, Antwerp became the largest port and banking center in Europe. The influx of gold and silver from colonialist activities caused a rise in inflation that enabled rich town-dwellers to purchase land at competitive rates. As the power of the middle classes expanded, a population increase triggered the modernization of agricultural systems devised to enhance production and profit. City markets acquired renewed financial and cultural, significance—this was well documented by the emerging popularity of paintings portraying opulent market scenes in which produce was fetishized as a marker of religious worship and a status symbol. Simultaneously, the optimization of agricultural processes boosted the botanical sciences and led to the emergence of a market specifically dedicated to flowers. In the 1630s the demand for many expensive, selected varieties of tulips prompted the set-up of the "tulip exchange." This moment marked the entry of flowers and plants into a new register of commoditization of unprecedented proportions. "Tulipomania," as it was called at the time, made some traders rich, until

1637, when a tulip-market crash led to financial ruin for many.[68]

At the same time, the Protestant Reformation's objection to the representation of religious images removed a substantial source of income for artists. In the Netherlands, artists turned to the painting of still-life themes like game painting and flower compositions as these offered a significant source of revenue and commercial flexibility. While portraits had to be commissioned, paintings of flowers and fruits could be made and stored in the workshop, waiting for a casual buyer. Here too, plants and flowers were caught up in a representational process of objectification. It is not a coincidence that, in still-life paintings, flowers and fruits were usually accompanied by human-made objects—they too inscribed specific symbolic meanings; sometimes religious, sometimes not. However, it is evident that cut flowers, as well as fruits, were semantically dealt with in the same way. Most regularly flowers symbolized God's abundance and the transitory nature of beauty, youth, and wealth. But above all, these paintings functioned as *memento mori*: the reminder to remain humble, for whatever riches one might conquer in life will be eventually taken away at God's will. In this context, flowers and fruits began to replace the religious figures that artists were forbidden by law to paint. Flowers were thus juxtaposed following a symbolic principle appearing in the same composition even if their blooming seasons took place at different times of the year. In these religious utopias, all flowers were "frozen" at the height of their beauty and freshness. Moreover, in a world in which cut flowers were expensive and not available year-round, these paintings would enable the appreciation of the diversity of colors and shapes in the botanical world. Artists would the consult botanical treatises, which provided readymade

---

68 Dash, M. (2010) *Tulipomania: The Story of the World's Most Coveted Flower & the Extraordinary Passions It Aroused* (New York: Crown/Archetype).

representations of plants and flowers to be lifted and assembled in always new and different scenes.

Fruit and vegetable themed still-lifes worked in very similar ways. Like flowers, fruits inscribed the passing of time and seasons, and with that, the desire to preserve beauty and prosperity indefinitely. Caravaggio's *Basket of Fruit* from 1599 was an influential and yet very unusual instance of fruit still life in which insect-nibbled fruits and blemished leaves tipped the utopian harmony of the classic still-life towards new philosophical and aesthetic notions of problematized realism. In this painting, the inevitability of death is embraced as part of a harmonious cycle of life and death. And as with the flower still-life genre, fruits appear as place-markers of religious symbolism. Amongst others, lemons symbolized the Virgin Mary, pomegran-

ates resurrection, apples symbolized temptation and the original sin, and figs fertility.[69]

Further underscoring the objectifying nature of the representations of flowers and fruits was the hierarchy of genres in the figurative arts, which was formulated in 16th century Italy. The structure of the hierarchy remained highly influential until the beginning of the 20th century and was inherently anthropocentric. It posited historical, religious, and mythological subjects as the most valuable genres because of the ethical and moral values associated with them, but also because painting the human body was considered the most difficult to appropriately accomplish. Portraits came just below, only because their ethical value was subjugated to the preponderance of the sitter's identity. Further down the list were everyday scenes, landscape, and cityscape—the lack of substantial human presence in the paintings reduced their importance. At the very bottom of the hierarchy were paintings of animals, plants, and fruits:[70] ontologically aligned to man-made objects, animals, plants, and fruits incarnated the passivity of matter that man could exercise dominion upon—they temporarily put at bay the defining anxiety intrinsic to human existence.[71]

One of the main purposes of Western classical painting was that of objectifying the world to affirm the power of the viewer over it. It is possible to identify a gradation of objectifying parameters in which women and nonwhite hu-

69   Impelluso, L. (2004) S. Sartarelli, trans. *Nature and Its Symbols* (Los Angeles: Getty Publications). Originally published 2003, as *La Natura e i suoi simboli* (Milano: Mondadori Electa).

70   Freedberg, D., and de Vries, J. (1996) *Art in History/History in Art: Studies in Seventeenth-Century Dutch Culture* (Los Angeles: Getty Publications) p. 199.

71   But besides defining the contextual value of the subject in painting, the hierarchy of genres also prescribed the use of particular canvas sizes for the top-tiers, which should not be utilized for the lowers ones, simultaneously structuring a pricing scale for each tier.

FIGURE 0.11   Michelangelo Merisi da Caravaggio, *Canestra di Frutta*, 1599.

mans, for instance, are more regularly objectified than white men, and in which animals and plants are more closely aligned to the registers of objectification reserved for the human-made, than the living. It is for this reason that the representation of flowers and fruits in art is always ambiguously suspended in a symbolic realm of objectification that transfigures the nonhuman into a metaphorical vessel for the human. What's left in the wake of this process is a relative form of interest for the natural in which we only seem to have two alternatives: the scientific objectification and the metaphorical objectification.

Gustave Courbet's paintings of fruit baskets created between 1871 and 1872, for instance, have a Caravaggesque quality. The fruits are

blemished, and the bowls chipped. These representations depart from the scientific notion of the specimen, and they simultaneously are the antithesis of the opulent, symbolic works of the Dutch and Spanish Baroque. Courbet's fruits provide an interesting instance of the slippery intricacies involved in the representation of the natural. Refusing the rhetoric of the specimen, Courbet's fruits still propose a realist-scientific iconography of decay which grounds the representation in a metaphorical realm. Courbet was the leader of the Realist movement in France— a revolutionary and highly political congregation of artists that rejected the idealized classical style of the French Academy in favor of a predilection for recording the raw materiality of objects and the straining lives of peasants

FIGURE 0.12   Gustave Courbet, *Still Life With Apples and Pomegranates*, Oil on canvas, 1871–72.

and working classes in general. He was arrested in 1871 because of his involvement in the socialist government of the Paris Commune and painted fruit baskets in his cell—those were the fruits his sister brought to him at the prison of Sainte-Pélagie. He was forbidden from painting human figures, therefore, to paint damaged apples instead constituted an act of resistance. These fruits are symbolically charged. As part of Courbet's longstanding commitment to expose the hardship faced by the proletariat and the working classes the blemished fruits embody the rough essence of an existence in which aesthetics and food could simply not afford to go together.[72] But is it even possible to represent the

nonhuman without relentlessly totalizing them through anthropocentric and anthropomorphic lenses? What aesthetic paradigms would enable a different optic to arise, one in which the representation is not scientifically illustrating the fruit or the flower? Moreover, what would a nonobjectifying paradigm tell us about the represented plants?

Victorian Britain developed an obsession for ferns that spanned between the 1840s and 1890s. Remembered as "Pteridomania": the craze for ferns that, to a degree, transcended social class and gender divisions, represented one of the many cultural facets of the colonialist approach to curiosity during the colonial period. Equally great was "Orchidelirium," the orchid craze that saw rare orchids being sold at London auctions for exorbitant prices. Both phenomena essentially involved the indiscriminate pillaging of

72   Brettell, R.R. (1995) *Impressionist Paintings, Drawings, and Sculpture* (Dallas: Dallas Museum of Art) p. 48.

exotic land, the destruction of untouched environments, and the waste of many plants as the vast majority of imported varieties were simply not suited to the dim lighting and cold drafts of the British Isles.[73]

Victorian excitement for new exotic forms and natural colors was complemented by the simultaneous prominence acquired by floriography. A cryptological communication through the depiction of mainly European flowers, floriography originated in France during the first half of the nineteenth century and became central to the spiritual paintings of the Pre-Raphaelites Brotherhood. Most notably, John Everett Millais's *Ophelia*, from 1852, successfully straddles scientific realism with the poetic demands of Shakespearean narration. The artist's determination to accurately capture each plant painted on his canvas led him to perch his easel on a precise spot on the bank of the Hogsmill River for a five month period. He allegedly spent eleven hours a day, six days a week on the bank, sometimes through adverse weather.[74] Surprisingly, the realism of the scene clearly annoyed some critics who reprimanded the artist on his approach to vegetation. *The Times*' critic said: "there must be something strangely perverse in the imagination which sources Ophelia in a weedy ditch, and robs the drowning struggle of that lovelorn maiden of all pathos and beauty." Meanwhile John Ruskin reportedly took issue with the lack of idealization in the portrayal of nature. "Why the mischief should you not paint pure nature," he asked, "and not that rascally wirefenced garden-rolled-nursery-maid's paradise?"[75]

To paint *Ophelia*, Millais returned to the then out of fashion Caravaggesque *memento mori* expedient. The rotting leaves of the greater pond sedge pictured on the left-hand corner of the canvas underlined, a little too much for some, the deathly theme of the painting. As Ruskin's comment shows, the classical ideal that painters should improve nature, rather than simply reproduce its imperfections, still had much currency in art. But Millais was a deeply religious man and therefore resorted to floriography to embed symbolism in his work. Thus, the willow becomes a text speaking of forsaken love; crow-flowers a gesture towards ingratitude; nettles to pain; daisies towards innocence; roses speak of youth, love, and beauty; violets hint at faithfulness; forget-me-nots foreground memory; pansies point at unrequited love; fritillaries to sorrow; and poppies evoke death.[76]

Thereafter, with the exception of Renoir's many paintings of cut flowers in which the interest of the painter was primarily focused on chromatic clashes and brushstroke effects, Impressionism was not particularly interested in plants. But Monet was different. The latter part of his life was spent painting his garden in Giverny where he moved in 1883 after his canvases found some commercial success in the United States. Monet was a fond horticulturalist. Not only would he tend to his plants personally with the help of some gardeners, he also experimented with hybridizing processes with dahlias, irises, and poppies, a variety of which he called *Moneti*. But it is his passion for water lilies that has been much celebrated in popular culture. Monet's interest in water lilies began in 1889 when botanist Joseph Bory Latour-Marliac exhibited his hybridized specimens at the World's Fair in Paris in the water gardens of the Trocadéro. Up until that point water lilies were only available in white, so the yellow and pink varieties exhibited by Latour-Marliac caught the artist's eye. It is interesting that Monet's choice of subject for his many paintings was grounded in a personal passion for plants, rather than from the desire to convey encoded religious symbolism. Monet's water lilies are not symbolic—Impressionism

---

73   Ziegler, C. (2007) *Favored Flowers: Culture and Economy in a Global Culture* (Durham: Duke University Press) p. 22.

74   Williams, D. (2012) *The Afterlife of Ophelia* (New York: Springer), pp. 87–88.

75   Barringer, T.J. (1998) *Reading the Pre-Raphaelites* (New Haven: Yale University Press) p. 64.

76   Williams, D. (2012).

FIGURE 0.13   John Everett Millais, *Ophelia*, oil on canvas, 1851–52, Ophelia, Google Art Project.

rejected symbolism in favor of documenting the optical impression of everyday-life as represented by its surfaces and the effects of light upon them. Because of the lack of details in impressionist paintings, Monet never used herbaria as source books. Monet's water lilies appear caught up in the artist's dialectics of color and lighting—their plant-beings dissolved through brushstrokes have become one with the water, the sky, and the foliage that usually surrounds them.[77]

But it is important to note at this point that traditional art historical discourses have not valued the type of inquiry I have led here—to the anthropocentric discourses of history of art there only are two types of objectification worth critically acknowledging: race and

gender stereotypes. Yet, there is something subtler about the ability of painting's idiom to objectify anything, including nonhuman beings, that has played a vital role in animal and plant representation through art. This objectifying ability is intrinsically bound to the gendering agency of optical realism: its scientifically inherent capacity to delineate the object of scrutiny as absolutely separate from the subject whose gaze beholds the object. It is in the absolute clarity of scientific illustration and the structural solidity of classical painting that the anthropocentric base is structured for the humanist subject. The optical clarity, key to the essence of the Enlightenment, produces affirmation in the viewer—that fictitious confidence that enables one to say: "this is…" and to, therefore, exercise power over it. Subjectivity is formed on these epistemological grounds and modalities—grounds that implicitly reassess sociocultural

77   Gordon, R., and S. Eddison (2002) *Monet the Gardener* (New York: Universe) p. 17.

FIGURE 0.14   Claude Monet, *Water Lilies*, Google Art Project (431238) 1915–1926.

normativity that also inscribed race and gender discourses. The link between the ability to see and say what is perceived reveals an important link between the closed forms of classical realism, the absolute clarity of scientific illustration, and language.

The institutional language of art history, natural history, and economic sciences strove for clarity—they aimed at clarity of transcription in objects and phenomena defining a shared, normative base: the discourses of disciplines. Subject specific terminology was designed to crystallize shared knowledge and contain the multitude of lifeforms. The repetition of specific statements, modalities and forms of writing was necessary to the effectiveness of information and to set knowledge as truth. Likewise, classical art deployed a vast vocabulary of specific statements, modalities and styles, all of which relied upon clarity to deliver explicit messages and specific meanings.

Let's not forget that Monet started to paint water lilies in 1897–99, at the very end of a century that saw a substantial fragmentation of artistic realities and movements in Europe. Through this period, realism in art became a political bone of contention—one equally ideologically charged with highly conservative values or with revolutionary ideals. The invention of photography (1826) problematized matters by materializing the possibility for blurred/out of focus images right under the eyes of the artists. Blurred photographs, the failed attempts to capture optical reality during the mid-nineteenth century, were inspirational to Monet and other Impressionists. What was at stake in this representational unclarity produced by the mechanical optic? To a degree, a process of de-objectification. Blurred photographs broke the straightforward linguistic connection between form and content—they inserted hesitation where once was affirmation. They shattered the sensuality of surfaces to focus on a broader overview of connectedness. Epistemologically speaking, this was a moment of paramount importance in the history of Western art—one that history of art usually simplifies through the notion of style or the biographical notion that Monet was losing his eyesight. If we can look beyond these discipline-specific filters, it becomes visible that Monet's water lilies are amongst the very first paintings about plants and flowers to embody this new "freedom of the image." Open form and lack of detail free the represented body from many economic, social, and cultural implications—if there is a symbolic register to be found in these extremely open paintings, it is that the water lilies are interconnected with everything else around them: the sky, the water, the grass, the trees hanging over them, and the human perceiving them. There's an eco-continuity and interconnectedness at play in these paintings that is unprecedented in the history of representation—one that simultaneously operates through the medium of paint as an ontological equalizer and one that bypasses any notion of scientific epistemology in representation itself. In more than one way, it is with the water lilies that a truly modern, and perhaps more than a modern history of representation begins.

Power, Epistemic Spatializations, and Materiality

Thus far, the two parts of this introduction have representationally summoned the specificities of different plant/human relationships. They are deliberately written in different styles and from different epistemic perspectives to problematize the very notions of materiality and epistemology. In the first section, titled "Amarcord," plants emerged through my childhood memories as a sociocultural agent situated in a specific local reality of the south of Italy during the 1970s and '80s. In the narration of these memories, I have avoided the use of scientific names, privileging the common names of each plant I recalled and making sure that their appearance was as enmeshed as deeply as possible in the social relations that seeded, propagated, and cared for them. But these social relations have been transcribed on the pages of this book through memory: a space of knowledge construction in its own right; one in which time warps, the outlines of objects blur, and mythologies intertwine with facts. The material bodies of the plants I recalled have gone through multiple mediatic reincarnations.

The diaristic, idiosyncratic tone of the first section was counterbalanced by the section that followed it, "Plants and Animals: Issues of Representation," in which plants emerged through the rendering operated by different disciplinary optics (natural history and art history) and

media (illumination, illustration, and panting). In both cases, the first and the second part of this introduction, all plant materializations have taken place through my writing voice inscribed on the surface of the pages of this book. The only reason why I am drawing attention to this epistemic contingency is because it reminds us that nothing ever really *is*, in a universal sense, but that every encounter with others, nonhumans, objects, particles is utterly defined by the materiality, modality, structure, and histories of the epistemic spatializations in which the encounter takes place.

In order to more clearly outline the importance of this concept I will recur to Michel Foucault's notion of "epistemic spatialization" and adapt this to the representation of plants in art. Foucault discussed the importance of architectural/material spaces and the production of knowledge in *Discipline and Punish*. There he developed Jeremy Bentham's eighteenth-century design for a prison system characterized by economies of power dispensed through a structural configuration imposing visibility for surveillance: *the panopticon*.[78]

Bentham's panopticon is architecturally constituted by a tower surrounded by an annular building. The building is divided into cells, each with two opposed windows that allow light to flood each space. By the effect of backlighting, an observer in the tower can control each prisoner in the building. The all-seeing nature of the panopticon defines specific economies of the gaze; it enables surveillance, but it also shapes the nature of what can be seen. The architecture of the cells limits prisoners' mobility and capitalizes on the stark appearance of silhouettes. What is surveyed in the panopticon no longer is a human, but a specific reduction, simplification, and objectification of a human—a form of visibility of what a human is made into by

---

78   Foucault, M. (1975) *Discipline and Punish: The Birth of the Prison*, translation Sheridan, A. 1977 (London: Penguin), 1991, pp. 195–228.

the conditions of the observation-process—a specific representational materialization constructed by the intersection of the panoptic architecture and surveilling gaze.

However, the panopticon is a transferable and adaptable mechanism of power, not simply an architectural space in the classical sense. In "The eye of power," Foucault's attention turned especially to institutionalized spatializations in which knowledge is produced and distributed, such as the hospital, the prison, and the asylum.[79] As an architectural figure encapsulating the practice of segregation and monitoring originally enforced by the syndic during a plague in medieval society, the panoptic mechanism "arranges spatial unities that make it possible to see constantly and to recognize immediately."[80] Its functionality is very practical, but its cultural meaning extremely complex: the panopticon makes visible the socionormative politics intrinsic to governmental, medical, and educational institutions.

In *The Order of Things*, Foucault returned to the notion of spatializations of knowledge focusing on the specific subject of natural history illustration, the representation of plants, and how Linnaean taxonomy was facilitated by these very spatializations.[81] There, Foucault outlined natural history as a "spatialization of the object of analysis." By this he meant that illustration, as a physical, epistemic space in which the object of study was materialized to become part of discourses, substantially impacted the type of knowledge produced about the object itself. Further clarifying his idea, in an interview, Foucault said:

> Then there was the spatialization into illustrations within books, which was only possible with certain printing techniques. Then the spatialization of the reproduction of the plants themselves, which was represented in books. All these are spatial techniques, not metaphors.[82]

This statement points to a broader implication related to materiality, space, and epistemology that in *The Order of Things* remains unexplored. If the knowledge that can be produced about an object of study is intrinsically bound to the architectural spatialization through which the object is studied, be it a cell, a photograph, or an illustration, then it appears clear that not only the space in which the object is materialized matters, but that the materiality of the spatialization involved is of paramount importance too. As previously seen, the flattening of animals and plants operated by natural history illustration bears practical as well as metaphorical implications—the optical flattening of plant bodies corresponded to a contextual flattening of the individual plant or animal into a specimen—silenced, immobilized, objectified, and extrapolated from its interconnectedness with biosystems for the consumption of the scientific gaze. The materiality of the book page, the flatness of the paper upon which the object is made to materialize, defines the power/knowledge relations specific to the epistemic modality. In turn, it can be stated that the scientific gaze is

79   For Foucault's analysis of the spatializations in hospitals see: Foucault, M. (1963); for prisons see: Foucault, M. (1975b); for the asylum see: Foucault, M. (1961) and Foucault, M. (1961). A famous interview from 1976 titled 'Questions on Geography' is also considered to be one of his most important texts on spatialization in general. Foucault, M. (1976b) 'Questions of Geography', in Gordon, C. (ed.) (1980) *Power/Knowledge: Selected Interviews and Other Writings, 1972–1977* (Brighton: Harvester, Press) pp. 63–77; Foucault, M. (1972) 'The eye of power' in *Power/Knowledge: Selected Interviews and Other Writings, 1972–1977* (Brighton: The Harvester Press) pp. 146–165.

80   Foucault, M. (1975) p. 200.

81   Foucault, M. (1966) *The Order of Things: An Archaeology of The Human Science* (London and New York: Routledge), 1970, 2003, pp. 139–144.

82   Foucault, M. quoted in Leach, N. (2005) *Rethinking Architecture: A Reader in Cultural Theory* (London: Routledge) p. 356.

never all-seeing, but that it is always defined by disciplinary, institutional, and ideological lenses that define its "visual scope".

This tension between the objectifying gaze, the other, and the space in which the encounter takes place is the determinant factor in the nature of the relationship that can be visualized. This tension is the matrix of what Foucault called *biopower*: the constant and intrinsic struggle between repression and resistance at the "level of life" which produces subjectivizations that are simultaneously passive and active. In most human/nonhuman relationships, both the human and the nonhuman engage in a relation characterized by the flickering of these roles—sometimes this flickering is almost imperceptible, but it is nonetheless present, and it is substantially defined by the cultural norms, rules, and conventions inscribed in the space in which the relationship develops. The history of humankind has been characterized by a regularly occulted operation of disciplinary powers towards the nonhuman, be it selective breeding practices, mass-farming, pruning, transplanting, grafting, harvesting. Human-animal and human-plant relationships have always entailed forms discipline in which the human sets specific rules around the limitations imposed by the biospecificities of the bodies of the nonhuman. Although at first glance it might seem that the human is the sole operator of agency, more careful consideration can reveal that the nonhuman always poses a form of resistance of some sort, or that, in not very obvious ways, the nonhuman responds to the disciplining of domestication with subtler forms of re-wilding. In these instances, plants and animals change human behavior by determining economies of care, regimes of sustenance, production of wealth, and inscribing power and economic value.

Foucault's conception of power as that which outlines an ensemble of actions inducing others in the production and consumption of epistemological objects becomes relevant in this context.[83] Foucault conceives power as a noncentralized entity—power is inextricably enmeshed in objective capacities (skills and preexisting knowledge) and communication (production and dissemination of knowledge, and exchange of information).[84] Power, in its many different iterations, permeates everything; and where there's power, there's resistance.[85] Resistance is not always antagonistic. It is productive in essence, and it is intrinsic and internal element to power itself: it is part of an asymmetry in which power gives structure to a field of possible actions that individuals or groups can enact.[86] Power thus determines possibilities; it defines actions taking place within specific spatializations. This is one of the most important contingencies involved in the definition of Foucauldian power and resistance conceptions. Whether these notions are applied to governments, institutions, familial nuclei, or organizations, the essential objective for the work of power and resistance is containment, either operated by physical boundaries or by the law.

It is for this very reason that this book is organized around chapters defined by actual spatializations, physical and cultural, in which the bodies of plants, as well as those of animals, objects, and humans materialize. The premise is simple. For instance: the abstract notion of "an orchid," is only epistemologically useful to the Platonic tendencies of Western philosophy—but why should we reduce our everyday shared experience with plants, or any other being, to the objectifying approaches of scientific

---

83   Foucault, M. (1981) 'The Order of Discourse' in Young, R. (ed.) *Untying the Text: A Post–Structuralist Reader* (London and New York: Routledge) 2006, pp. 70–71.

84   Foucault, M. (1966) p. 77.

85   Foucault, M. (1976) *The History of Sexuality 1—The Will to Knowledge*, London and New York, Penguin Books, 1998 p. 95.

86   Foucault, M. (1982) 'The Subject and Power', in Hubert L. Dreyfus and Paul Rabinow, *Michel Foucault: Beyond Structuralism and Hermeneutics* (Chicago: University of Chicago Press) 1983.

knowledge or the totalizing ways of Western philosophy, when they have been proved to construct very limited relational modes with nonhuman beings?

An orchid situated in a bathroom defines different biopower relationships to an orchid of the same species in a hotel lobby, to one in a botanical garden, or one in a gardening center. The power-fields at play in these very different spatializations of knowledge guide very different behaviors/levels of interactions or care between humans and plants. Being able to take these differences into consideration can productively problematize the agency of plants, their bodily presences, their materialities, and the power-negotiations plants and humans establish in specific spaces. Like natural history illustration and painting, the epistemic spatializations around which this book is structured are material and define human/plants relationships alike. But they are also defined by laws, rules and regulations, ethical and moral values, and most regularly, if not always, these spatializations are defined by capitalism. A spatialization is never just delimited space—a spatialization is constituted by perimeters and inscribed cultural codes. At times the perimeters of the spatialization are optically visible, they are marked by specific materialities, in other instances, the perimeters are imposed by the cultural norms and financial values inscribed in the spatialized area. This book proposes an alternative approach designed to address the contemporary challenges we currently face. As climate change, more than ever, threatens all forms of life on the planet, considering human-plants relationships from new perspectives is essential to providing answers to pressing sustainability issues, to revealing the importance of essential biointerconnectedness in ecosystems, and to leading us to a more complex appreciation of the variety of living organisms we share the planet with. It is now unattainable to discuss human-nonhuman relationships without properly acknowledging the interconnectedness between capitalist

shifts, environmental concerns, and biopolitical registers. It's not so much a matter of encountering plants in an abstract sense anymore, but one of mapping the interconnectedness between them and the ecosystems (biosystem and cultural system) they inhabit with us, along with the animals they host, the mineral balances and unbalances they cause in the soil, the air quality, the geological shifts they operate, and so on.

In this sense, Foucault's conception of "power-knowledge" relationships, the notion that power and knowledge are interrelated and that they impact on epistemology as well as upon the material world around us, is problematized by the preponderant logics of capitalism, which, in the Anthropocene, constitutes the essence of the episteme governing discourses and practices. In this book, the notion of built environment is provocatively expanded to include agricultural fields, hotel lobbies, shop windows, greenhouses, as well as forests and grass fields. This is done in the knowledge that capitalist logics permeate and define the essence of everything either by carefully prestructuring or simply by allowing, or by perpetuating. In *Capitalist Realism: Is There No Alternative?*, Mark Fisher discussed the role commodification played in the cultural production of the twentieth century, emphasizing the essence of a naturalized and pervasive regime of precorporation as preemptive formatting: a pervasive atmosphere conditioning everything that can emerge in capitalist culture, encompassing all production systems and modes.[87] Power structures and the power-knowledge relationships inscribed in capitalist realism are actualized and stabilized according to specific registers and logics of visibility and consumption that ultimately impact on the presence or absence of plants, on their bodies, their biorhythms, as well as our own.

Capitalist growth with its necessity to insert "bodies into the machineries of production," relies on this power-knowledge relational to

---

87   Fisher, M. (2009).

substantiate itself.[88] It is this modern conception of power as biopower enmeshed into capitalist realism, that which capitalizes on the living as intrinsically intertwined to the sphere of economic processes that can be more productively reconfigured to think about plants from new perspectives. It is in this Foucauldian context that I propose to think about plants as bodies in constant dialogue. Bodies that partake into complex, reflexive, and intra-active relationships of coevolution and becoming. It is in this context that their perceived passivity can be overcome as an obsolete and convenient relational mode that has deliberately impoverished the vegetal world. As it is known, art has played a substantial role in the configuration of the so-called animal turn in the humanities. Through its ability to enrich, problematize, and unhinge philosophical and scientific conceptions, in the case of plants too, contemporary art appears situated in a privileged epistemological position. It is in this sense that the examples discussed in this book will provide starting points, departures, paths of flight, and new directions that will prove productive in overcoming *plant blindness*.[89]

---

88   Ibid., p. 141.

---

89   The term "plant blindness" is used in the context pioneered by Wandersee, J.H. and E.E. Schussler (1999) 'Preventing plant blindness' in *The American Biology Teacher* 61, 2 (Feb. 1999), pp. 82+84+86.

PART 1

Forest

∴

CHAPTER 1

Lost in the Post-Sublime Forest

Giovanni Aloi

Midway upon the journey of our life
I found myself within a forest dark,
For the straightforward pathway had been
lost. Ah me! how hard a thing it is to say
What was this forest savage, rough, and
stern, Which in the very thought renews the
fear. So bitter is it, death is little more;
But of the good to treat, which there
I found, Speak will I of the other things
I saw there.

DANTE ALIGHIERI, *The Divine Comedy*[1]

∴

The ambiance of a forest becomes penetrable and yet mysterious, spacious and yet opaque, gesturing toward and withholding meaningfulness, through the play of sound and scents.

TIMOTHY MORTON, *Ecology Without Nature*[2]

∴

George Shaw's series of paintings titled *My Back to Nature* is delightfully dark, both in content and in hue. The pallet is restricted; colors are muted. Only now and then an intense glare of blue or green comes to disrupt the "still atmosphere of the aftermath" presented by each painting. Shaw's trees are deadly silent—they are silent witnesses at the edge of a forest, the denseness of which is always visible in the background. Traces of human activities appear in almost every painting: a discarded mattress on the ground, a pile of cans fills the cavity of a tree, ripped up magazines litter the grass in patches, sexually explicit spray-paint graffiti on tree trunks...

What a far cry from past representations of forests in classical painting. In Renaissance painting forests regularly figured as a backdrop. They reminded the viewer of the darkness lurking at the edges of reason. The well-lit human figures in the foreground, by contrast, stood for rationality—the nature and culture dichotomy was subliminally enshrined in beautiful images that perspectively placed the human at the center of the cosmos. Sandro Botticelli, Tiziano Vecellio, and Paolo Uccello painted forests as cultural landscapes charged with anthropocentric symbolism. These forests looked lush and dense—they were beautified by the Aristotelian idealism in which art should always perfect nature.[3] Their symbolic status was the result of semantic sedimentation in which myths and legends intersected the pragmatism of human self-sustenance. The secrets of impervious forests were eradicated by the Roman Empire's extensive use of timber for heating and building purposes. In many cases, deforestation was the essential prerequisite of conquest. Homes, ships, palisades, watchtowers, and redoubts were built with timber sourced from forests. Over centuries, forests shrank and expanded defining the living conditions of settlers in Europe. For instance, the barbarian invasions of the mid-first

---

1 Alighieri, D. (1320) *The Divine Comedy: Inferno* (Tyche) p. 3.

2 Morton, T. (2007) *Ecology Without Nature* (Cambridge: Harvard University Press) p. 115.

3 Aristotle. *The Poetics.* Translated by Allan H. Gilbert in *Literary Criticism: Plato to Dryden* (Detroit: Wayne State UP) 1940.

© KONINKLIJKE BRILL NV, LEIDEN, 2019 | DOI:10.1163/9789004375253_003

FIGURE 1.1
George Shaw, *Möcht' ich Zurücke Wieder Wanken, 2015–2016*. Humbrol enamel on canvas.
PRIVATE COLLECTION, LONDON, COURTESY WILKINSON GALLERY, LONDON © GEORGE SHAW.

millennium AD produced a substantial reconfiguration of the boundaries between urban and non-urban spaces. The abandonment of villages and areas cultivated by the Romans allowed forests to spread dramatically. However, alternate periods of forest clearings between 500 and 800 AD and subsequently 1100 and 1300, and the intensive foraging of bovines and other domesticated animals cleared much of Europe once again. Human sustenance was intrinsic to the effective managing of forest resources, their commercial, and agronomic values.[4]

The fortification of Medieval urban centers with moats and walls contributed to the reinforcing of the nature and culture dichotomy. As that which lied outside the city walls, the forest became a place of desire and opportunities just as much as it could unpredictably turn into one of fear and danger. In Medieval romances, knight-errants would wander forests in search of reaches, adventure, and love. However, robbers, witches, dragons, and basilisks lurked there too. Losing one's way in the forest became the climatic narrative-point of many folkloric tales—an implicit metaphorical admonishment—straying from the clear path functioned as a reminder that the perils of moral darkness would lead to perdition. In opposition, to follow the prescribed normative path established by society was essential to one's survival and success.

Dante Alighieri's representation of the "Selva Oscura" (The Dark Forest) in the *Divine Comedy* (1320) became the most influential cultural conception of the forest. There, the lost poet encountered the three capital vices: envy, pride, and avarice as incarnated in a leopard, a lion, and a she-wolf. In the dark forest Dante became physically, spiritually, psychologically, politically, and morally lost. Symbolically, Dante's forest was a primordial maze: the entrance to the classical Hades of Virgil's *Aeneid* and a Platonic image of chaotic matter in which the light of reason is obscured by the impenetrable deep of the vegetation.[5]

4 Rostovtzeff, I.M. (1926) *The Social and Economic History of the Roman Empire* (Cheshire: Biblio and Tunnen).

5 Alighieri, D. (1320) *The Divine Comedy: Inferno* (New York: Simon and Schuster), 2008.

FIGURE 1.2
Sandro Botticelli,
Primavera, 1477–
1482.
ITALY, UFFIZI
GALLERY.

FIGURE 1.3 Paolo Uccello, *The Hunt in the Forest*, 1470.

As a cultural space, the forest eluded the rationality of classical knowledge to such extent that it became the quintessential symbol of the unconscious. It was a space in which plants, humans, and animals engaged in a troubling fluidity, one enabled by the scarcity of light, the intricacy of tree-growth, and the absence of human-made referents. The Roman festivals of the Bacchanalia, in which copious amounts of wine would be consumed, were opportunities to delve into a sensual dimension devoid of human rationality and morality.[6] Identity and social class membership could only be shed in the depth of the forest and at the darkest moment in the night. More than any other domesticated-plant spaces, and not exclusively in Western culture,[7] the forest consistently embodied the limit of the human

6 Bonnefoy, Y. (1992) *Roman and European Mythologies* (Chicago: University of Chicago Press).

7 Leick, G. (2002) *A Dictionary of Ancient Near Eastern Mythology* (London: Routledge).

Midway upon the journey of our life / I found myself within a forest dark, /
For the straightforward pathway had been lost.

Inf. I, lines 1–3

FIGURE 1.4
Gustave Doré, *Selva Oscura*, 1857.

against the vast mysteries of nature's domain. This representational paradigm has been substantially used in painting for obvious reasons. A good example of this is Paul Delvaux's *The Awakening of the Forest* (1939) in which an inordinate number of naked women populates the depth of the forest of Jules Verne's science fiction novel *Journey to the Center of the Earth* (1864).[8] These figures appear to be at one with the environment; they inhabit a sense of wholeness enhanced by the suggested continuity between the vegetal matter and their bodies. Their nakedness situates them in a lost dimension of naturalness that the protagonists,

clothed men, can only observe from a fantastic-anthropological perspective.

In the attempt of constructing clear notions of human rationality, literature and art have devised representations in which the forest stands as the antithesis of the enlightenment's ability to extract the secrets of nature under the light of human reason. In Dali and Buñuel's non-linear short film *Un Chien Andalou* (1929), the sequence staged in the forest is psychoanalytically charged with a traumatic aura that ties together two oneiric and visionary narrative segments.[9] Here the forest symbolically connects murder,

8   Verne, J. (1864) *Journey To The Centre Of The Earth* (New York: Sheba Blake Publishing), 2015.

9   Buñuel, L., and Dali S. (1929) *Un Chien Andalou* (France: Les Grands Films Classiques).

suicide, and sexuality. The metaphorical and actual impenetrability of the forest have thus intertwined for centuries in representations designed to remind us (or convince us) that we no longer belong in nature; that we left a long time ago; and that the forest essentially is, for us, a place of loss: losing one's way, losing one's sanity, losing one's life.

However, like all symbolic forms, forests are not culturally fixed. Thus during the nineteenth century, with the rationalization and further annihilation of forests caused by the industrial revolution, artistic imagery shifted. At this point, the imperviousness of forests turned into the quintessential site of the romantic sublime. The fear of deep uncertainty, which the forest came to inscribe the outmost sign of our separateness from nature—the reminder that industrialization has numbed our (animal) instincts and senses to the point that survival outside civilization becomes impossible, behaviorally as well as biologically. The forest is where our human-ineptitude is confirmed on all accounts. This acknowledgment underlines the sense of astonishment, horror, or terror that Edmund Burke described in his influential analysis of the sublime published in 1757.[10] In a Kantian sense, the forest is a site capable of embodying both the mathematical as well as the dynamic conception of the term. The forest is sublime in size and in the frequent repetition of similar trees, which makes it a place of disorientation. Likewise, the forest can materialize or amplify the howl of the wind and the violence of a storm to dynamical sublime effects. In both instances, the rapid alternation between the specific pleasure found in being overwhelmed and the fear of such instance metaphorically inscribes the very drama of humanity against nature.[11] The

"greatness of dimension" and "infinity"[12] of the forest became the essential counterweight to the relentless, gritty ugliness imposed upon cities and countryside by the industrial revolution. Artists and poets looked at forests more than ever before, but they did so from a more than ever external perspective.

The sublime is enacted upon specific power-knowledge relations that simultaneously situate and define the connection between representation and the body of the viewer. To find sublime pleasure in the powerless and overwhelming feelings of potential annihilation, the viewer needs to occupy a position of safety—the exposure to the threat must be mediated, either through a spatial barrier, a painting, a photograph, or the page of a book. Thus set up, this distance between the cause of the threat and the body of the viewer always constructs representations of exclusivity: a paradoxical disconnect based on the act of looking and yet denying the act of seeing. During the nineteenth century, experiencing a sense of sublime while visiting a forest meant to explore one's limitations as a human, more than it meant considering the trees, the plants, the insects, the birds, and the mammals that constituted the forest itself. However, despite its structural complications, this mode of consumption became central to the persuasive strategies of the conservation movement that characterized the nineteenth century in Europe, as well as in the United States.

Constructing a notion of the "wild" as a space separate from civilization became a way to preserve an original and threatened natural dimension which inscribed our lost original purity: an untouched Garden of Eden. The act of the United States Congress from 1864, which decreed Yosemite as a site of sacred significance for the nation, inscribed religious values in the greatness of the sublime landscape that came to define national identity. Most importantly, the values

---

10   Burke, E. (1757) *A Philosophical Enquiry into The Sublime and Beautiful* (London: Routledge) pp. xlv–xlvi.

11   Kant, I. (1790) *Critique of Judgment* (North Chelmsford: Courier Corporation) pp. 61–91.

---

12   Ibid., p. 67.

FIGURE 1.5
Ansel Adams, *The Tetons and the
Snake River*, 1942. Grand Teton
National Park, Wyoming.
NATIONAL ARCHIVES AND
RECORDS ADMINISTRATION,
RECORDS OF THE NATIONAL
PARK SERVICE (79-AAG-1).

that informed the conservation movements in the Western world also became the implicit aesthetic-base for the marketing of emerging tourist industries. As a result, the naturalization of the discourses of spirituality and purity that served as representational backbones informed the photographic work of Ansel Adams, whose images captured an unspoiled paradise defined by monumental drama and sacred timelessness; an environment closely managed by man but simultaneously one from which man's presence must be categorically negated, at least representationally. The same paradox was simultaneously replicated by the aesthetic choices of wildlife photography and film where the expulsion from the Garden of Eden became the implicit and necessary subtext to the sublime experience: the fear of God's greatness. And it wasn't long before the capitalist applicabilities of the sublime construction of nature became evident—sublime aesthetics sold trips, photographs, books, and merchandise as our expectations of what nature should look like was set: perfection. This relational modality constitutes the quintessential dimension of our late modern conception of nature. Only as tourists, through the twentieth century, we can find our

place in nature as a commodity constructed by glossy brochures. However, as Bruno Latour has argued, the current threats posed by environmental deterioration, climate change, and mass extinction are reconfiguring the aesthetic sublime. A new disconnect is emerging: one between the scale of our actions as humans and our lack of grasp of the impact of these actions. No longer we are small and fearful while lost in the forest. The formulation of the Anthropocene as a new epoch is reversing our puny existence, casting humans as a massive force, a collective giant, one ultimately shaping Earth.[13] We have finally conquered the earth only to find it damaged. But with this inversion of scale also comes a dissipation of the sublime by the hands of a mounting guilt complex that we can neither fully grasp, nor appropriately address.

It is in this very sense that the paintings of George Shaw's introduced at the beginning of this chapter produce imagery that is utterly contemporary. The forest he paints bares

13   Latour, B. (2015) 'Waiting for Gaia. Composing the common world through art and politics' in Albena Yaneva and Alejandro Zaera-Polo (Eds.) *What is Cosmopolitical Design?* (Farnham: Ashgate) pp. 21–33.

undeniable human traces—but these are not images from tourist's brochures. They suggest the relative proximity of an irresponsible civilization. Marks and litters are signs of the frugality of a momentary human presence, a brief utilitarian existence, a certain lack of empathy or respect, a sense of disengagement. As images of alienation, Shaw's paintings propose the border by which human life can only exist temporarily or risk slipping back into animality. Like the surrealist forests of Paul Delvaux and Salvador Dali, Shaw's forest occupies a psychoanalytical dimension—although thoroughly realistic, it also is a space of the unconscious in which primordial desires and essential drives unfold.

As contemporary representations of the classical dichotomy between nature and culture, the liminality of these images is reinforced by the photography-informed realism that pervades the treatment of surfaces and details. The canvases are covered in rich Humbrol enamel paint, typically used for model trains and airplanes; the overall aesthetic is defined by a snapshot/documentaristic aura. The unnecessary detail, or that which the touristic aesthetic is keen to erase, becomes the focus of the canvases, which unashamedly confront us with an undeniable everyday ugliness. More than anything, the paintings portray a sense of disinterested and discouraged banality that has somewhat become naturalized in contemporary culture—they capture resignation—a gritty, apathetic dimension typical of liminal, unkept zones, peripheries, and no man's lands.

All canvases are, in a way or another, underlined by the notion of a pervading capitalism posing as the underlying essence of the disconnect between humans and nature. The forest thus becomes the stage upon which this disconnect is symbolically played out in contemporary times. Shaw's canvases are cunningly and allusively ambiguous. Their strength lies in the lack of idealization. The organicity of leaves, grass blades, and branches is juxtaposed to the artificiality of discarded blue plastic sheets of the

kind used to shelter cars from the elements. At times, these embody a ghostly presence; they look conspicuously out of place, at others, they seem to have, at least aesthetically, assimilated themselves in the ecosystem as they fictitiously pose as water streams snaking through the fallen leaves. But more substantially, because of the color blue, and the draping they form around branches, these sheets gesture towards a loss of spirituality; that, which characterized our sublime relationship with nature. The drapes evoke an absent Madonna—the remnants of a religious effigy of purity, abundance, wholesomeness, and birth—values once associated with the notion of the "mother nature" construct. The blue cloak of the Madonna, one of the most recurring iconographical staples of the Middle Ages and the Renaissance is charged with symbolic transcendentalism. It was traditionally associated with the essence of the cosmos, the sky, and the sea: symbols of the infinite and thus connected to God.[14] As a divine hue, blue situated the essentialism of the spiritual in sublime nature. However, as one of the most expensive pigments in the Renaissance, the amount of blue covering the surface of a canvas also functioned as a reminder of the status symbol of the commissioner. Shaw's blue plastic drapes gesture towards a loss of spirituality while simultaneously proposing an updated capitalist economy of the color itself—one associated with new forms of power and knowledge.

If the emergence of a sublime relationship with nature has only contributed to the separation between human and nonhuman, we are left wondering what aesthetic strategies might be at our disposal for the construction of an alternative aesthetic that can replace the spiritual one. In his critique of ecocritical theory, Timothy Morton has directly addressed the importance of rethinking environmental aesthetics,

---

14   Gage, J. (1999) *Color and Culture: Practice and Meaning from Antiquity to Abstraction* (Berkeley: University of California Press).

FIGURE 1.6
George Shaw, *The Living & The Dead, 2015–2016*. Humbrol enamel on canvas. Private Collection, London.
COURTESY WILKINSON GALLERY, LONDON © GEORGE SHAW.

a process that leads to the all-important consideration of the mesh of interconnectedness between different life-forms. Therefore, "Dark Ecology," the new aesthetic alternative to the sublime rhetoric of Romantic aesthetics, replaces affirmation with inquiry, certainty with doubt, exclusion with inclusion: the position of radical self-knowledge in which the concept of "Dark Ecology" situates within a panoply of interdependent human-nonhuman natures.[15] This is a modality of representation that Bruno Latour had already, in a sense, outlined in *Politics of Nature* as emerging from the catastrophic failure of the modern project at the hands of the planet's unexpected opposition.[16]

It is this light that the ghostly drapes in Shaw's paintings set the tone of loss for the whole series and in which other mass-produced materials litter the scenes. These human-made traces essentially are the spill of capitalism: irrelevant objects produced by economies of waste—the lack of value inscribed by the discarded objects are directly related to the mass production processes which created them in the first place. They are traces of the ways in which we relentlessly consume resources and carelessly discard packaging. The mattress, the beer cans, but most importantly the ripped up pages of porn magazines lying at the base of the trees are metaphors of the economies of desire consumed in the represented space.

The systematized consumption enabled by the pornographic material is by essence voyeuristic, swift, and superficial; or is it a reference to the bacchanalias that once happened in mythical Roman forests? A modern version that, like the forest itself is mediated by a flattened image of commoditized desire? Pornography is the product of an exploitative industry well known for its rapacious treatment of workers and their rights. These considerations rarely, if ever, become central to the consumptive gaze. With larger revenues than Microsoft, Google, Amazon, eBay,

---

15   Morton, T. (2016) *Dark Ecology* (New York: Columbia University Press).

16   Latour, B. (2004) *Politics of Nature* (Massachusetts: Harvard University Press).

Yahoo, Apple, and Netflix combined, pornography operates a quintessentially exploitative and utterly concealed, capitalist system. Through the relentless objectification of its constituents, pornography obliterates any ethicality of consumption for the purpose of fulfilling a predominantly male primal desire, which serves as the psychological blueprint for all others. The sexuality of pornographic-imagination is self-reflexively contained in the moment of consumption and to operate, it relies upon a drastic disconnect from broader affective economies. Its ability to provide immediate gratification through an addictive pathway of perception devised to disentangle ethical implications in the viewer essentially outlines the model for contemporary capitalist success. This, in essence, is the moral disconnect Latour laments—capitalism disconnects our ethical obligations, the range, scale, and nature of phenomena from the emotions, habits of thoughts, and feelings. It does so to facilitate indiscriminate consumption and to speed the production cycle to self-perpetuate its existence at the expenses of the consumer it simultaneously consumes. It is not, therefore, a coincidence that Shaw's forest appears somewhat "season-less"—the subdued lighting, the sparse foliage, the naked branches, the dead trees, all suggest environmental and climatic degradation rather than late autumn or early spring. This is the result of a relationship with nature that for too long has been structured on economies of pornographic consumption, based on surface value, exploitation, and immediate, but only temporary, gratification.

Capitalist economies of consumption also lie at the core of the giant multi-panelled iPad generated images of woods and forests produced by David Hockney in 2011. Standing in diametrical aesthetic opposition to Shaw's gritty and bleak canvases, Hockney's landscapes appear to be equally silent as Shaw's, despite being extremely bright and monodimensional.

Rather cunningly, *The Guardian*'s art critic Adrian Searle dismissed the works as "ines-capably dead and bland and gutless."[17] Many reviews of the London's Royal Academy of Art exhibition titled *A Bigger Picture* were also unenthusiastic. However, the media hype was substantial and the general public seemed rather pleased with the spectacle proposed by the large images. Sublime in essence, each image of Yorkshire's forests envelops the viewer in an overwhelming play of bold outlines and over-saturated hues. Like Renaissance forests filtered through a pop art optic, Hockney's are highly idealized. The iPad interface and the printing processes utilized by the artist rendered a highly stylized, sanitized, sterilized, utterly still, and silent image. The aesthetic literalism is somewhat reminiscent of Henry Rousseau's paintings from the late nineteenth century; yet, Hockney's works lack the sense of mystical wonder that the French naïve painter's work instilled in his canvases. Devoid of any mystery, brightly lit from a frontal vantage point that casts no shadows, and firmly composed around a predominant use of central perspective, Hockney's forests are thoroughly affirmative. Yet all they can affirm is the hollowness of our disconnectedness with nature that has developed over the past two hundred years, since the industrial revolution substantially redesigned landscapes, destroyed ecosystems, and shifted humans to biorhythms far removed from the passing of seasons. Hockney's images assert the double loss inscribed in Shaw's series.

It is only in this sense that Hockney's images can become interesting: if understood as a reveal of the modern conception of nature as pornographic consumption. Here everything is laid bare—everything is made available as an object to possess and behold through an emphatic throb of colors that has little if nothing in common to the nonmechanical gaze. Simply put, albeit unwittingly, Hockney's forests are the accurate result of centuries of objectification through the dynamics

---

17   Searle, A. (2012) 'David Hockney landscape: The world is not enough' in *The Guardian*, 16 January.

of sublime economies. The result is cold, ratio-nalized, predictable, and ultimately empty—the whole thing appropriately looks monodimen-sional, plastic, artificial, and Disneyesque. The gaze, which constructs this vision, quite appro-priately, is one which honestly owns the digitality and production processes essential to contempo-rary image making. Our relationship with nature has always been a mediated one—the struggle between the dichotomic opposites of nature and culture never becomes more evident than when the importance that representation plays in our relationship with biosystems is brought to the fore. However, Hockney's iPad operates a high definition digital camera filtered by a number of apps that adopt different effects capable of de-constructing, transmitting, and reassembling sig-nals to a high definition printer. It constitutes a cunning embodiment of the current dimensions in which constructs of nature are defined: lay-ers of capitalist mediateness that metaphysically and metaphorically distance us like never before from the nonhuman. However, it is important to note that this result is not one intrinsic to the use of advanced technological devices—technology does not implicitly separate us from nature, but the use of it we make does. Hockney's paintings of Yorkshire's forests are contemporary only on the surface—their structure, the relationship they establish with the viewer is essentially a classical one based on sublime dynamics. It is this aspect, which critics identified as a weakness in Hock-ney's images, that paradoxically, can be seen as an unintentional artistic strength. Like the work of many artists before him, despite his intentionality, Hockney's *A Bigger Picture*, sincerely and simply is the result of the episteme in which the images are produced—they are the sedimentations of past and present discourses, practices, and practices about nature.

The artist's deadpan painterly style, which made him famous during the 1960s and '70s, always suggested a sense of apathy and disaffection— a suspension of time and emotion that cynically exposes the simplicity of his subjects, or that at least one that rendered his subjects into hollow surfaces, in a Warholian sense. Hockney's forests are nothing more. They are not just inescapably dead, bland, and gutless because the artist is not able to render them alive, exciting, and profound. The aesthetic qualities they inscribe exemplify the aberrant and apathetic relationship with nature we have come to establish through sublime econo-mies of consumption that essentially underpin the Anthropocene. Hockney's images, to a greater degree than Shaw's, are terminal—they flaunt a simulacral quality that simultaneously evokes the papier-mâché model and the nonprofessioanal theatrical set. The absence of the referent to which they allude is prophetically chilling, just like the si-lence in which every single one of the images ap-pears to be immersed.

It should be recognized that shaking off over two-thousand years of iconographical sedimenta-tions of forest representation is not an easy task. However, to the point that technology does not represent per se a "distancing element" between us and the intricate biobecomings of animals and plants we call forests, the project titled *In The Eyes of The Animal* by creative studio Marshmallow La-ser Feast proposes a contemporary, posthuman, nonobjectifying aesthetic of forest-experiencing. As the title suggests the project involves a radi-cal decentring of the classical anthropocentric perspective, which has historically structured the representation of nature. The artists explain that

> the spectator flies over the impressive landscape of Grizedale, being able to zoom in on the tiniest detail of microscopic insects and see in the eyes of different ani-mals that live in the park. The aim is to understand how animals visually process the physical space and thus, leaving the human condition for a moment and even comparing the way we see to the way a bear sees, for instance.[18]

18   Marshmallow Laser Feast, *In The Eyes of The Animal*, press release, 2015. Commissioned by Abandon

FIGURE 1.7   Marshmallow Laser Feast, *In The Eyes of the Animal*, Installation, 2015
                    © MARSHMALLOW LASER FEAST.

FIGURE 1.8
Marshmallow Laser Feast, *In The Eyes of the Animal*,
Installation, 2015
© MARSHMALLOW LASER FEAST.

To this end, Marshmallow Laser Feast have designed a highly complex, virtual-reality headset combining Lidar scanning, CT scanning, and photogrammetry techniques, able to construct a rendering of the forest as perceived by a nonhuman.[19] With the aid of an immersive backpack-subwoofer transmitting base frequencies directly to the muscles and bones of the human body, the viewer can experience the forest beyond the constraints imposed by realistic, optical representation. With vision losing its primacy as epistemological tool in the construction of nature, the forest is finally enabled to shed its inscribed cultural meanings—it can momentarily, at least, cease to be the site of human mythologies to appear as the intricate space defined by biointraactions and biobecomings that art, philosophy, psychoanalysis have regularly concealed

Furthermore, displacing the primacy of vision, *In The Eyes of The Animal* brings into question epistemic notions of human and animal scale. Micro and macro locations become subjective and shifting, relative values define instead a speculative approach that produces an experience of an ever elusive overlaying of different forests coexisting at the same time. With the absence of human's centrality and the disappearance of a definitive notion of scale, also dissipates the work of classical beauty and the sublime. Here the historical antagonism towards nature is replaced by a new model of engaged-experience, one of being-with in opposition to the actual and metaphorical separateness essential to the sublime aesthetic.

Moreover, the posthumanist modes of perception enabled by *In The Eyes of The Animal* are site specific. The electronic kit is portable, and it produces nonhuman perceptions of the environment in real time as the viewer explores the space. That the experience is enabled to take place outside the gallery space, in a forest, is of paramount importance to the material as well as to the symbolic register inscribed in the piece. Being in the forest, and experiencing it through an interface that obliterates the sensorial cultural markers of being human proposes the opportunity of stepping out of the very human experience of the sublime. Doing without the gallery space, a powerful political gesture made famous during the 1960s by land art, also implies a disavowal of the classical histories of making and seeing art subjugated to capitalist laws and aesthetic conventions. As far as the opportunity to conceive nature through art in a true posthumanist way goes, Marshmallow Laser Feast have certainly mapped new and exciting territories.

Lastly, the technological interfaces comprising *In The Eyes of The Animal* do not replace the forest with a simulacrum, like in the case of traditional representations: they are technically reliant on the shared physical presence of the forest and the participant. This contingency constitutes one of the most important aspects of speculative aesthetics that are capable of upturning anthropocentric approaches to the nonhuman. The type of knowledge produced by the experience of one's body as immerse in the forest is a deliberately open-ended one. *In The Eyes of The Animal*'s emphasis on the "animal-vision" might be considered by some as some sort of practical answer to Thomas Nagel's 1974 essay "What is it like to be a bat?"[20] Some animal studies scholars might more definitely follow that path, yet, more interestingly in the context of this book, is the possibility this project proposes

---

Normal Devices and Forestry Commission England's Forest Art Work. Produced by Abandon Normal Devices and Marshmallow Laser Feast. Supported using public funding by Arts Council England and Forestry Commission England, online, <http://sonarplusd.com/activity/eyes-animals-marshmallow-laser-feast/>, accessed on 23 February 2016.

19   Detailed information about the technologies involved in the making of the hardware and software are available here.

20   Nagel, T. (1974) 'What is it like to be a bat?' in *The Philosophical Review*, 83, 4, pp. 435–50.

to conceive new forms of speculative aesthetics capable to free forests, and plants more generally, from the objectifying, reductive, and anthropocentric economies of cultural consumption that have led us to the current climatic crisis. The forest thus can unravel as something wholly new, outside of the prescribed linguistic sphere, unpredictable for reasons wholly different from those inscribed in mythological accounts—here man is animal amongst other animals, and most importantly, amongst plants.

CHAPTER 2

The Humblest Props Now Play a Role

Caroline Picard

Let's begin with a wedding. Mine. I was given a wedding gift from a former roommate. It was a gift from her whole family in fact; in fact, when Sarah and I lived together I was seeing someone else. Like a three-legged stool, Jim (call him Jim) and Sarah and me; I was in love with them both at once. Sarah who invited friends over to read Shakespeare plays out loud in our living room. Sarah and her nonboyfriend boyfriends who arrived unannounced to beg her advice. Jim: my other best friend—the lover, the builder, the adult. It was an ironic balance; perhaps because I could be honest—albeit differently—with both of them, whilst they concealed less than congenial feelings about the other from me. As is the way with roommates, Sarah moved out, shifting my personal ecology with Jim in turn. He moved back to Canada. Years later, I married Devin.

To commemorate the marriage, Sarah's family gave me an Oscar Bailey photograph, alternately called "North Carolina Woods" and "Dan in Our Wood" (1982–83), depending on where it is cited. Made by Sarah's grandfather, the print now stretches the length of my arms in the only hallway of my conjugal apartment. In its frame, thin but numerous tree trunks rise up out of a thick carpet of rotting leaves. Only in the middle does the autumnal forest thin out and in that parting, a strip of yellow meadow stands before another distant wood. Otherwise, two instances of the same younger man—in his thirties, I'd guess—bookend the woods. In both occasions, he hangs, suspended by ropes in an orange suit. The outfit looks practical and shapeless—as brightly colored as a traffic cone or hazmat suit, or maybe it is a color that deer cannot see. He hangs about five or six feet above the ground, helpless, like someone just fallen from the sky: the miscalculation of a parachute jumper.

Or an alien, maybe like in *The Man Who Fell to Earth* (1976), in search of water. In a way, the photograph captures humanity's awkwardness—a not quite earthly nor totally spiritual being damned to wrestle the opposing poles of mind and body.

On closer inspection however, the photograph troubles that binary tradition, in part because the camera's unusual participation is so present. Known for his long-format contact prints, Bailey used a Cirkut camera developed around the turn of the century to photograph large groups of people or panoramic landscapes. Once released, the wind up camera rotates around its axis at a particular speed coordinated by magnets and gears; the film moves in the opposite direction at the same speed, and within that delicate collaboration, 360 degrees are captured in one continuous linear image. If one wrapped the photograph around a scale model of its subject—in this case, the wood—the image would accurately reflect a standard perception of space; when spread linearly however, along one vertical line, the picture dislocates that viewer's spatial orientation.[1] In this case, the young man situates the camera's absent presence by his double appearance. On the left-hand side of the picture, head covered in the hood of his suit, he looks especially alien and defensive in relation to the trees. The suit looks taught around his groin, bearing the entirety of the man's weight. Here too, you see the ropes that hold him—how carefully they are wound around the tree trunks, admitting by their method the choreography of the figure's appearance.

---

1 Bailey, O. (n. d.) 'Oscar Bailey: Cirkuts,' Bailey Panoramas, <http://baileypanoramas.com/oscar-bailey/>. Accessed February 28, 2016.

In the man's right-hand side appearance, you see his face. He smiles this second time, more relaxed, legs crossed at the ankles. The man is beginning and end of the captured world and over the course of its duration, he has grown comfortable. By appearing twice in the same, suspended condition, he highlights the camera's mechanical intervention, a revelation further compounded by the strange pattern of cast shadows on the forest floor. In that respect, "Dan in Our Wood" dislocates some basic assumptions about the landscape and our human perception of it.

The woods. "Our wood." Designated in one of its titles with an imprecise ownership, something familial perhaps. The depth, texture, and ragged peculiarity of these trees starts emerge: a half wild/half domestic (or known) space that "Dan," the subject, enters, first as an intruder later to become part of. The legacy of this wood comes into focus as well. These trees are not only witnesses to the alien intruder but also participants, essential supports, and hosts with whom meaning emerges through the collaboration of camera, costume, gravity, light, trees, leaf carpet.

Mark Payne's essay, "Before the Law: Imagining Crimes against Trees," begins with a question raised by Christopher Stone about how the human legal system might address and incorporate nonhuman entities (including climate), suggesting that "the extension of legal standing to plants is envisaged as a continuation of the history of human ethical progress that granted such standing to women, other races, children, and animals."[2] Using Stone, Payne shows how complex legal mechanics must become in order to accommodate a stand of trees. One would have to account for and codify the interests of different parties: loggers, the trees themselves, and even any beetles living in the same grove. A whole ontological revision would be required, according to which a first-person advocate appeals (on behalf of nature) to an objective third party (the law), thus making human civic

logics commensurable with nonhuman "wild" ones. What indeed might an interspecies politics look like? In that cosmological vision the human is only a small part of some larger incomprehensible and likely nonlinear narrative.

> Because this vocation is accepted as the anticipation of a history to come, it is experienced as access to a legal imaginary outside history as such, where the institutional function of the imagination in an imaginary past and an imaginary future converge.[3]

Payne describes the choral presence of a grove of trees, which bears on the actions of a present moment without necessarily embodying a discrete and articulated place in that moment. Returning to Bailey's photograph, the trees not only lend the figure reason and significance but step forward, resisting the background passivity we've come to expect. Their duration extends so far beyond the young man's appearance, one might need a camera to capture one-hundred local years before glimpsing the drama of this particular grove. Yet also for Payne, the lyric poet operates more fluidly. "In his representation of Nature, the poet experiences the uprooting from history that Levinas has characterized as one aspect of the priority of ethics to ontology that emerges in a transformative encounter with the Other."[4] The poet has more freedom to articulate subjective experiences, without necessarily having to adjust an entire ontology. The image of Dan in the woods disrupts what might otherwise appear as an uncultivated landscape—a panoramic tableau of trees that, according to Western assumption, is instrumentalized for metaphor or timber.

Remember in Shakespeare's *As You Like It*, Orlando professes his love in the woods, posting badly composed poems on trees. In Act III, scene 2 he exclaims, "O Rosalind! these trees shall be my books, / And in their barks my thoughts I'll

2   Payne, M. (2017) 'Before the law: Imagining crimes against trees' in *Fatal Fictions* (Oxford: Oxford University Press).

3   Ibid.
4   Ibid.

character, / That every eye which in this forest looks / Shall see thy virtue witness'd everywhere."[5] The forest lends itself as a stage to amplify the human drama at hand. Presumably, the human is liberated from civilization to become more-authentic, or "natural." Rather than any permanent rejection of human society however, *As You Like It*'s forest only suspends civic structure. There is always a sense that the characters will, eventually, return to the city; the marriage towards which characters tend enforces that feeling. To humans, the woods are a temporary condition—much like the Spring Festival in which the play would have been produced, a time when Puritan ethics were suspended and established authority was acceptably mocked. The woods of *As You Like It* offer a similar suspension in which the individual can suddenly play with the otherwise implicit and unquestioned hierarchies that dictate her life. Yes, Rosalind assumes the male identity of Ganymede in order, she claims, to keep her and Celia, best friend and cousin, safe in the wilderness. "Alas, what danger will it be to us, / Maids as we are, to travel forth so far! / Beauty provoketh thieves sooner than gold."[6] Yet the joy of Rosalind's male alter ego comes from her exuberant and acrobatic performance of gender; she mocks and embodies sexual stereotypes undermining and reinscribing their power in turns. She mocks love like a seasoned cynic in one instance —"No, no, Orlando, men are April when they woo, December when they wed. Maids are May when they are maids but the sky changes when they are wives,"[7]—confessing earnest feeling in the next: "O coz, coz, coz, my pretty little coz, that thou didst know how many fathoms deep I am in love!"[8] Suspension provided by the forest stage, enables a double awareness in Rosalind, such that she is at once in love while being aware of its eventual passing.

Payne's essay goes on to describe "Hymn to Demeter," a poem by Callimachus, in which the hero Erysichthon decides to cut down one of the tallest trees in Demeter's wood, regardless of her warning to the contrary. Although Demeter lets the hero finish his work, she punishes him with insatiable hunger such that Erysichthon is cast out of his home and the relational society he had come to rely upon. As one no longer rooted in a grove of family, friends, and politics, he exists in a wilderness. "What is talionic about Erysichthon's punishment is not simply that it is a life for a life [i.e. tree life for human life], but that it obliges him to recognize that, in the extremity of his suffering, he too [like the trees] is a being who exists through self-care, who may or may not be of interest to others as such."[9]

Supposedly the man in the orange suit is the artist's son, Sarah's uncle. Perhaps his presence in the photograph is equivalent, somehow, to Orlando's love poems: an attempt to make a human gesture commensurable with a multi-framed field of incommensurable beings. In his book about Shakespearean festivals, C.L. Barber argues that Shakespeare captured a shift in the vernacular understanding of theater. "In making drama out of rituals of the state, Shakespeare makes clear their meaning as social and psychological conflict, as history. So too with the rituals of pleasure, of misrule, as against rule: his comedy presents holiday magic as imagination, games as expressive gestures. At high moments it brings into focus, as part of the play, the significance of the saturnalian form itself as a paradoxical human need, problem and resource."[10] In these ecological times, the scale of duration and narrative changes beneath our feet. Like an ontological earthquake, what has for so long remained in the background refuses to stay there, amplifying humankind's need to expand its theoretical stage and encompass historically

5   Shakespeare, W. (1599) *As You Like It* (Stanford: Cengage Learning Holdings) 2006.

6   Ibid., Act 1, Scene 3, lines 105–7.

7   Ibid., Act 4, Scene 1, lines 137–39.

8   Ibid., Act 4, Scene 1, lines 193–94.

9   Payne, M. (2017).

10   Barber, C.L. (2011) Shakespeare's Festive Comedy: A Study of Dramatic Form and its Relation to Social Convention (Princeton: Princeton University), p. 15.

FIGURE 2.1   Oscar Bailey, *Dan in Our Wood*, North Carolina, 1982
             © OSCAR BAILEY.

reclusive others. It is as though humanity has become an alien in its own land, suddenly aware of a
systemic impoverishment, a species perhaps that,
like Erysichthon, has stolen too many trees and
generations later realizes the danger of insatiable
hunger. We wander within a time frame of nuclear
waste, typhoons, and plastic. There is no static society to return to any more, and within that realization narratives and fairy tales must also change.

There is something almost cartoonish in such
an opera ... suddenly, just like in a Disney version of *Sleeping Beauty*, every inert passive
agent of her Palace began to yawn, to awaken
from its slumber and became fiercely busy,
from the dwarfs to the clock, from the door
knobs to the chimney. The humblest props
now play a role, as if there were no distinction
any more between main characters and the
environment drawn around them. Except for
the deep molten rocks inside the Earth and
deep space beyond the thermosphere, every
single element of the background is brought
to play its part in the foreground.[11]

On to what trees might we pin our offspring? The
artist, Katie Paterson, is growing an entire forest from which she intends, eventually, to make
single edition books for an imagined, future audience. What stories will those pages contain? The
thirty-year-old man, his costume, and the trees are
inextricably linked. I pace the length of this apartment. If I ignore the photograph, the shortest distance between two points is a straight line. If I look
at the woods, I see a non-Euclidean alternative in
which the straight line describes a curved space.
The dissonance of those alternatives encroaches
upon the consciousness of my life. Outside I hear
the buses pass by with so many adverts and smog,
the yell of a pedestrian, amidst cars blaring pop
music, or the crack of a firework reminiscent of
war. Waves of ecological awareness crash into that
milieu, and I wonder what a fairy tale for nuclear
waste might be.

---

11   Latour, B. "A Secular Gaia," *Facing Gaia: Six Lectures on*

the political theology of nature, Being the Gifford Lectures on Natural Religion, Edinburgh, 18-28, February
2013, p. 63. <http://www.bruno-latour.fr/sites/default/
files/downloads/GIFFORD-ASSEMBLED.pdf>. Accessed Sept. 3, 2018.

CHAPTER 3

Ungrid-able Ecologies: Becoming Sensor in a Black Oak Savannah

Natasha Myers

Walk with me. I'd like to take you to my favorite spot here in Toronto's High Park, just north of the shores of Lake Ontario. This four-hundred acre urban pleasure park is brimming with people running, biking, playing and picnicking. But it is not just a pretty refuge from the bustle of city life. It is a space where you can tune in to hear the plants and trees singing,[1] where you can feel the sheer effort they exert holding the earth down and the sky up. The majestic oaks that thrive in Toronto's High Park today are remnants of the ancient black oak savannahs that stretched out across these lands for millennia. These remarkable ecologies, with their wide open canopies, tall grasses and wildflowers, took root in the sandy soils left in the wake of retreating glaciers and ancient lakes.

This landscape is not just sculpted by glaciers, wind, water, animals, and plants. An oak savannah is always in transition, always on its way to becoming forest. It needs fire to thrive. For millennia people lit fires to keep the grasslands open for hunting, farming, and village life. The 250-year-old trees that are thriving and dying here today remember that time before colonization. They remember the fires. They remember their people.

In the wake of the violence of first contact with Europeans, much of this region around the Great Lakes was de-peopled. Many of the wide-open canopies of the oak savannahs and prairies indigenous peoples had shaped through fire closed in, and the forests thickened. Within one hundred and fifty years after contact, the forests covering this land looked as if they had never been inhabited. This was the "primeval" forest that so many of our conservation ideals long for, an ideal that renders invisible the deep history of plant/people entanglements that have shaped so much of the North American landscape.

This remnant of a savannah that we are standing in now was kept open only because it was grazed, first by the sheep that European settlers put out to pasture, and later by the lawn mowers that the park's keepers deployed to maintain the aesthetics of a pleasure park. In place of fires that regenerated the soil and stimulated the germination of new oaks, the sheep and mowers clipped young oak seedlings and buried generations of wildflower seeds under thick turf grass. Today, conservation ecologists recognize High Park's oak savannahs as rare and endangered identifying the savannahs as sites of natural and scientific interest. They have brought back fire, lighting, controlled burns to stimulate the seedbed and help regenerate the oaks. But today the oldest oaks are falling. And the next generation are only fifteen years old. What, then, is the oak savannah becoming?

How can we learn how to pay attention to this remarkable ten-thousand-year-old happening which is both in-the-making and coming undone?

---

1 See for example, 'The Language of Plants,' an electro-acoustic installation by Studio for Landscape Culture (Jasmeen Bains, Yi Zhou, and Simon Nuk) which was premiered at The Gladstone's 2015 Grow Op. The artists transduced the ultrasonic emissions generated by High Park's Oak Savannah plants into sounds audible to the human ear. <http://www.landcult.ca/projects/#/language-of-plants/>. See also, Gagliano, M. (2013) 'Green symphonies: a call for studies on acoustic communication in plants' in *Behavioral Ecology* (2013) 24 (4): 789–796 for recent scientific research in Plant Bioacoustics, a newly-emerging field of plant communication.

© KONINKLIJKE BRILL NV, LEIDEN, 2019 | DOI:10.1163/9789004375253_005

FIGURE 3.1   Natasha Myers, *Leafing Flames*, Kinesthetic
image, August 2017
© NATASHA MYERS.

What modes of attention can help us learn how to pay attention to the *naturalcultural* happenings of this remarkable urban landscape? What would it take to tune into this ancient ecology situated in the middle of a vibrant city? Can we learn to keep pace with the rhythms and tempos of its compositions and decompositions—with the ephemeral and enduring improvisations taking shape among the plants, trees, insects, birds, animals, and people?

Ungrid-able Ecologies

As a dancer and plant scientist-turned-anthropologist of the arts, sciences, and ecology, I have initiated a long-term ethnographic study and research creation project here in High Park.[2]

My aim is to interrogate the self-evidence of approaches to conservation ecology and environmental monitoring by throwing open the very question of what it means to pay attention to all these beings who have been paying attention for so many millennia. Working at the cusp of art, anthropology, and ecology, my research aims to cultivate a queer, feminist, decolonial ecology of an urban park that reimagines the techniques and practices of ecology beyond the normative, moralizing, economizing discourses that ground conventional scientific approaches. My aim is to cultivate a sensory practice that can document the growth, decay, combustion and decomposition that are essential to the life of this remarkable land.

This "ungrid-able ecology" reconfigures the naturalist's notebook by innovating techniques for tuning into the affectively charged spaces of encounter and the momentum that propels plants, insects, animals, and people to involve themselves together in this ongoing happening.[3] This collaboration with one of my oldest and dearest friends, dancer and filmmaker Ayelen Liberona, has seeded experiments with movement, including our experiments with kinesthetic imaging and kinesthetic listening in our efforts to document the energetic and affective ecologies of this remarkable landscape.[4] Our first project involved developing a guided multisensory tour of the savannah and a series of images and a sound installation for The Gladstone Hotel's 2016 Grow Op, an annual plant art and landscape architecture festival in Toronto.[5,6]

---

2   For more on my works with plants see Myers, N. (2014 and 2015).

3   On "affective ecologies" and "involutionary momentum" see Hustak, C. and Myers, N. (2012).

4   Ayelen Liberona is an award-winning dancer, choreographer and filmmaker. For more on her projects see <http://www.ayelenliberona.com/>.

5   "Becoming Sensor in a Black Oak Savannah" was performed as a guided tour of High Park's remnant savannah as part of Grow Op 2016: Cultivating Curiosity—An Exhibition on Urbanism, Landscape & Contemporary Art, April 21–24, 2016, Gladstone Hotel, Toronto, On. <http://www.gladstonehotel.com/spaces/gladstone-.

Affective Ecologies: Kinesthetic
imaging of the compositions &
decompositions of an oak savannah

If traditional nature photography captures living bodies and turns them into objects of aesthetic and scientific interest, our video works explore ways to do ecology otherwise. Our experiments with kinesthetic imaging aim to do ecology otherwise. Our kinesthetic images are attunements. They are generated in the act of moving with and being moved by the beings and doings in this black oak savannah. As relational images, they document the energetics of an encounter, the push and pull between bodies. Rather than capturing phenomena, these images make it clear that it is the photographer who is caught: captivated, we hitch a ride on what is becoming and coming undone.

The rotting logs, frilled mushrooms, crumbling leaves, ancient sands, and greening grasses of these lands are not discrete things, they are *happenings* taking shape through deep time and in the ephemeral moments of now, and now, and now. It is the photographer who must learn how to keep pace with these rhythms through her body.[7]

Sounding Out the Savannah:
Kinesthetic listening to the elasticity of
time in an urban ecology

Sounding out the savannah reveals that there are no boundaries between the rhythms of city life and the lives of the creatures who take root and take flight here. Our sonic ecologies document the vibratory milieu of a ten-thousand-year-old happening by tuning into its deep time, its seasonal cycles, its daily rhythms, its improvised encounters, fleeting moments, and disruptive events. Our audio recordings are generated through movement. Here, dancers' moving bodies lean into the sounds, amplifying their intensities, speeds, slownesses, and their affective charge. This dancing with sound is a mode of *kinesthetic listening*. Speeding up and slowing down the recordings reveals otherwise unimaginable worlds and opens up new ways of telling stories. Stomping feet become falling trees, shaking the earth in ways that recall the geological forces that formed this land. Slowing down birdcalls reveals other songs, other creatures and voices haunting the space. Gulls become coyotes. Traffic becomes rushing, rhythmic waves. Life churns to other rhythms. There is no silence here.[8]

Doing Ecology Otherwise

Use the following provocations as a guide to develop your own multisensory tours through your favorite urban park.

Gestures

Trees are remarkable dancers. You just have to slow down your sense of time to keep pace with the rush of their agile, moving bodies. Plants and trees move by growing. And they grow by lapping up sunlight and pulling matter out of thin air. As they grow, they literally make the world, thickening their trunks, branches, stems, and leaves as they inhale gaseous carbon and exhale oxygen. In this way, trees teach us the most nuanced lessons about mattering. Trees

grow-op-2016/>. Our second major event featured a synesthetic installation hosted by Music in the Barns and the Canadian Association of Theatre Researchers at the Great Hall in Toronto in May 2017. See <https://becomingsensor. com/about/synesthetic-installation/>.

6   The images and soundscapes described below, can be accessed and experienced online: see the Becoming Sensor website to view our video works (http://becoming-sensor.com), including Becoming Sensor in an Oak Savannah (<http://www.youtube.com/watch?v=Jo2XTt DmCrU>) and Alchemical Cinema, Take 1: Nightfall in an urban oak savannah (<http://www.youtube.com/watch?v= uqotgDhG440>).

7   See 'Becoming Sensor in an Oak Savannah', <https://www. youtube.com/watch?v=Jo2XTtDmCrU>.

8   See 'Alchemical Cinema, Take 1: Nightfall in an urban oak savannah', <https://www.youtube.com/watch?v=uqotg DhG4403>.

grow from million-fold centres of indetermination. As they grow, they explore the world around them, conducting inquiries, experiments, and catalyzing new ecological relations. They record their worldly experiences in their forms. You can get a feel for the remarkable history of a tree's encounters with insects, animals, wind, fire, and chainsaws by taking the time to trace its gesture. Winter trees, and trees whose spring buds have yet to burst make it easy to follow along. Trace a tree's silhouette, it's sweeping curves, arcing limbs, or meandering branches by pulling a pencil across a page, or by moving your own body. Let yourself be moved by its form.

Textures

Tree barks tell remarkable stories. The barks of young oaks in the savannah are taught, smooth, and speckled with grays, blacks, and whites. The sheen of fresh growth is ruptured with age. The old barks are rough, chiseled, and brittle. The distinct lines and fissures of each tree's bark are the effects of the forces of new growth happening below the surface. Each texture on each tree is the effect of that living being intently pressing itself up against itself, against its own once-living matter. This is the force of expansion, the subtle daily and seasonal rhythmic pulsing and thickening of the trunk as the sap rises. Each trunk thickens and expands as new growth dies off to join widening rings of woody tissues. Here life surfaces death; and death is lined by life. You can learn to feel the distinct formations of different trees of the savannah: black oak, red oak, white oak, red pine, white pine. Each species has a distinctive bark. And each tree has a distinctive story to tell. Try to feel out the differences by drawing your hand across the bark. Or you can make a bark rubbing by holding paper up to the tree and etching with charcoal.

Sonic Ecologies

Urban parks are not quiet places cordoned off from the city. There is no boundary separating city from park, urban life from realms people still call "nature." Parks promise another kind of rush and rhythm. The sounds of cars and trucks and planes are never fully muted. They just propagate differently. Muffled and modulated by trees and shrubs, birds and squirrels and insects, ravines and slopes, city sounds resonate in a distinct vibratory milieu. Urban parks generate their own noises too. There are the chipmunks with their shrill warning calls that come always with a shiver of movement, a rustle in the leaf litter. And the cicadas in the summer, sounding like electricity running in lines along the wires. In the oak savannah in High Park, there is a sandy hillside here the grasshoppers and dragonflies and wasps in high summer make such a din that they drown out the drone of planes above. If you slow down a recording of the sounds in this space you can almost hear birdcalls ricochet off the trees, making it seem as if echolocation is not the sole provenance of the big brown bats who deftly navigate this space at dusk. What do you hear?

Smellscapes

Plants are alchemists. They conjure the chemical composition of the atmosphere. They are the most talented of synthetic chemists, innovating nourishing sugars, potent toxins, tantalizing flavors, intoxicating substances, and the aromatic compounds whose sweet smells fill the air. Plants compose volatile concoctions to excite other plants as well as animals and insects and people. How can we learn to tune into the significances and sentiments that plants articulate through their volatile chemistries? Mapping smells in the oak savannah is a way to learn how these plants involve themselves actively in relations with other plants, and with insects, animals, and people. Try this. Lean into the aromatic bouquet of a flower. Take a deep sniff. Then another, and another. Let the smells excite your tissues. Do you sense different notes? Different tones? How does the scent move you? Does it have a shape, direction, or movement? Does it come with a memory? Or with a story?

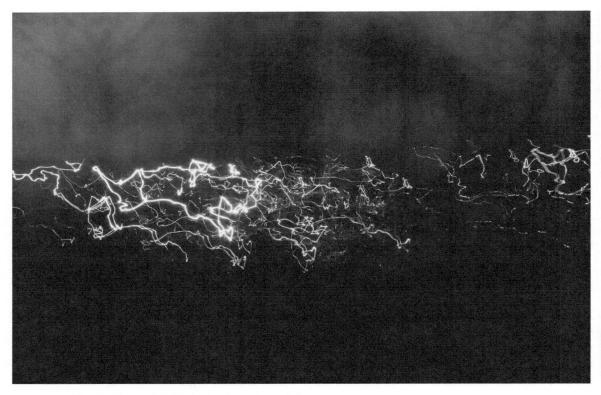

FIGURE 3.2 Natasha Myers, *Night Walk*, Kinesthetic image, February 2017
        © NATASHA MYERS.

Let the scent of that flower move you to write or draw or follow it with your body. Try smelling this flower at different times of the day or night. How does the scent change? How does it transform you? Smelling flowers is not the only way to tune into the articulate expressions of plant life.

Crouch down low and sniff out the rich scents that linger in the soil. Linger in that place where life cusps death, where the vegetal composers meet the fungal decomposers. How do these smells excite your tissues?

CHAPTER 4

An Open Book of Grass

Jenny Kendler

i   The Prairie is (not) a Forest

This chapter is on forests, but I want to tell you about prairies. Because this is not a place of forests. What we have here (where I write to you from)—what we *had* here, *long to have here—what we miss*, is tallgrass prairies. Now rolled under the plow.

Wikipedia, our modern oracle—no longer a voice whispering through the smoke of laurel and oleander— speaks of them mostly in the past tense. She says: "*very little tallgrass prairie remains.*"

From the height of human eyes, the prairie is not a forest; it seems, in fact, the very opposite. Rolling and flat, its only measure the horizon. Its openness, its mild, plain face turned to the world. In all this open space, we have been taught to see waste. We call it "just grass," waiting to become something useful. Oriented, as we are, to see greatness only when it towers above, we miss the tallness of tallgrass prairies.

In forests, we know how to see the sacred. The columns of trees. The slanting cathedral light. But can we not feel awe too—in the light and the wind?

It is only when we cease to privilege size, no longer preferring our own human scale, our verticality, that we see that *forest* (like many things) can be a relative term. Were we to be a Karner Blue Butterfly we would innately know the forest-ness of the prairie, grasses towering overhead, enfolding us.[1,2,3,4,5] Each strata inhab-

---

1   **The Karner Blue** (*Lycaeides melissa samuelis*) is a tiny metallic-blue butterfly, now vanishingly rare, as our thigh-skimming grasses once dotted with Lupine[2] have

been turned to elephant's-eye-high GMO corn, have been plowed under for endless feedlot-destined soy—have begun to make us feel another kind of small.

2   **Lupine** (*Lupinus perennis*) is the only food-plant of the Karner Blue. A beautiful blue-blooming plant in the legume family, Lupine's seeds were once used extensively by native peoples as a nutritious food crop—now targeted as a weed by Big Agro. Its name lupinus, meaning of the wolf[3], was given by European settlers who misunderstood both the flowers and wolves to be thieves. Also known as Quaker[4] Bonnets, Lupine, far from being a thief, is in fact generous—its symbiotic relationship with nitrogen-fixing bacteria enriching the soil for plants and humans alike.

3   **Gray Wolves** (*Canis lupus*) don't live only in forests. They too can thrive, used to thrive—like you could (you would, my dear)—in the rich wind-rolled folds of the prairie—blushing with ripe seed heads, filled with the song of grouse. Bison and antelopes moved to the pace of the wolves—aerating soil with their fleet hooves, cropping the grasses in rhythmic seasonal circles. But oh, the wolves themselves, they have had it far worse than the flower to which they are namesake. You already know.

4   **Quakers** began to settle the Great Plains area starting in the 1850s. They believed in dignity of all peoples and equality of the sexes, and built their homes of sod[5]—living (as we all would do well to remember we do) by the grace of the earth, and close to her.

5   **A sod wall is different from other walls.** Constructed from the prairie itself, in this way people lived both on, but also enclosed by the land. Enclosed by walls which were the landscape—rather than a way of shutting the landscape out. So, **a sod house is different than other houses.** Most other houses aim to create a human-place where nature is not: a not-nature-place. **So, a sod home is different than other homes.** The builders of those other homes forgot that no matter how they made their walls, their own animal-presence would makes their homes a nature-place. (They forgot to remember—not yet having learned that within us lies multitudes, that we too are ecosystems.) **So, a sod wall is different from other walls.** Sod is earth: layered with roots, shoots, rhizomes, and blooms. Living in a sod house is living inside the prairie. No longer on the skin of the earth, but with-

© KONINKLIJKE BRILL NV, LEIDEN, 2019 | DOI:10.1163/9789004375253_006

ited by perfectly adapted beings. The networks of roots underfoot. The detail and complexity of this woven ecosystem. And though we are thousands of times larger than much of the biota of this tiny forest, it does us well to remember the worlds that exist under our feet; these small lives supporting our small lives.

In this place, where I write to you from, the prairie was once a vast cloth of grasses and forbs. It held us together, this network of roots. It nourished us.

The press of my foot to the earth springs a hundred affections[6]

• • •

ii   A Plain(s) Poem

This framed poem has hung on the wall of my grandparents' home since I was a child. As secular humanists, they read this poem as I would like you to read this poem.

It is green grass and leaf that learned the miracle of turning starlight into life—thereby allowing all others to live. So, forget god—and think instead of plants.

> We broke today on the homestead
> The last of the virgin sod,
> And a haunting feeling oppressed me
> That we marred a work of God.
> A fragrance rose from the furrow,
> A fragrance both young and old.
> It was fresh with the dew of the morning,
> Yet aged with time untold.
>
> The creak of leather and clevis,
> The rip of the coulter blade,

> And we wreck what God with the labor
> Of countless years has made.
>
> I thought, while laying the last land,
> Of the tropical sun and rains,
> Of the jungles, oceans, and glaciers
> Which had helped to make these plains;
>
> Of monsters, horrid and fearful,
> Which reigned in the land we plow,
> And it seemed to me so presumptuous
> Of man to claim it now.
>
> So when, today, on the homestead,
> We finished the virgin sod,
> Is it strange I almost regretted
> To have marred that work of God?[7]

• • •

iii   Sweetgrass Dreams

The prairie wants to seduce you. Lull you, rock you to sleep on amber waves. Put your head down here, down among the roots of the Buffalo[8, 9] Grass (*Buchloe dactyloides*), and dream for a while.

---

7   R.G. Ruste, *The Last of the Virgin Sod*, 1912.

8   **Buffalo.** You knew we must talk of Buffalo. Though their "real" name is American Bison (*Bison bison*), and they are only distantly related to true Buffalo— buf-fa-lo, the sounding of hot breath huffed from heavy heads, is their onomatopoetic fame. By the 1800s, their fifty million were reduced to hundreds. But, Buffalo: You can see them now. You knew their forms on the prairies and plains behind closed eyes, rusted dust erupting from cloven hooves, wooly brown backs humped, a sea of dark curls, an impenetrable world—And their sound! You shot them from trains, saw them falling in the millions; each one took an hour to fall in black and white. We piled their skulls one thousand high. They made us feel something. Their deaths made us feel alive. Fuck us. Fuck that. We knew what we were doing, as we went deaf from the shots.

9   **General Sheridan, on the killers of Buffalo:** "These men have done more in the last two years, and will do more in the next year, to settle the vexed Indian

---

in. Tucked. When we lived in homes of sod, at night the prairie-earth would seep into us, gentling our dreams, making us long for the sweetness of young grass on our lips—waking children in the night with these passions, to forage under the butter moon.

6   Walt Whitman, excerpts of *Song of Myself* from *Leaves of Grass*, 1891–92.

*My tongue, every atom of my blood, form'd
from this soil, this air*[10]

• • •

iv   A Common Land

You must look at the prairie if you wish to
look at plants, to think deeply about plants, to
deepen the roots of your thinking on plants. If
you keen your sight here—in this plain(s) land
where the untrained eye slides off—it will serve
you well anywhere. This is an ecosystem defined
not by the grandness of rivers, lakes, mountains,
or shores—but by a tapestry of small plants.
Once a great and *common* place, intact prairies
are now vanishingly rare.

And here language could fail us, if we fail to
read its roots. Let me help you trace them, teas-
ing their strands from the darkened earth.

We once saw these prairies and thought *common:* as in our prairie-land is so common, it never could be exhausted. And as we continued to
forget to continue to see, *common* began also to
mean: *not worth examining, uninteresting.* Taken
for granted. Which soon became: *we'll take this.*
No longer dreaming of light and wind, we took
this once common land, making new dreams of
capital.

But I want you to know the common-ness of
our prairies in another way. I say *common* meaning *something we all had in common,* meaning
something we could all be a part of—still. I also
say *common* meaning for us all, meaning these
lands (all lands) should be held by people in

common (by human-people, buffalo-people,
wolf-people).

*For every atom belonging to me as good be-
longs to you.*[11]

• • •

v   Speaking without Words

So, prairie plants, if you have learned to keen your
senses, have much to say. They remind us to mind
the small things. To not to privilege our size. Or
even our perception of the pace of passing time.
(Standing within this time of lost prairies, I long
for a longer view of time.)

Wikipedia tells us that with their near miracu-
lous ability to make food from sunlight, plants
are at the base of most food chains on our planet.
And here again we see a problem with human language, with the way we read this word: *base.*

We have learned to think *base* meaning lowly,
at the bottom—even these words are unbal-
anced in their metaphoric content. We gloss
base to mean unworthy, puny, small. We favor
the vista of human stature, where we are somehow above, apart from the *base.* (We think to
escape death in this way.) We avoid seeing the
forest in the grass. We avoid seeing we are part
of this smallness ourselves—that we are constituted wholly of this cloth, promised to rot and
return to this microcosmic earth.

But I say *base,* as in foundation, *base,* as in we
rest upon you—*base,* as in we all collapse without you, plants.

*I guess it must be the flag of my
disposition, out of hopeful green stuff
woven.*[12]

• • •

---

question, than the entire regular army has done in
the last forty years. They are destroying the Indians'
commissary. And it is a well known fact that an army
losing its base of supplies is placed at a great disad-
vantage. Send them powder and lead, if you will; but
for a lasting peace, let them kill, skin and sell until
the buffaloes are exterminated. Then your prairies
can be covered with speckled cattle."

10   Walt Whitman, excerpts of *Song of Myself* from
Leaves of Grass, 1891–92.

11   Ibid.
12   Ibid.

FIGURE 4.1 Jenny Kendler, *A Place of Light and Wind* (*For Lost Prairies*), 2014. "Since 2014 I have been working in collaboration with environmental non-profit Natural Resources Defense Council (NRDC) on a series of environmentally engaged public art projects. *A Place of Light and Wind* (*For Lost Prairies*) transformed a 38-foot façade in a busy pedestrian area of Chicago into a photomural depicting native prairie flowers—in a brilliantly colored, immersive nine-foot-high swath. Passersby took photos of themselves among the blooms, and used their smartphones to scan the QR codes, which embellished the mural's pollinators. This signed them up to receive prairie flower seeds in the mail, and so with the assistance of these 'Prairie State' citizens, we spread the vision of the mural to backyards and window boxes all over Chicago—while simultaneously creating critical food hubs to support pollinators."

© JENNY KENDLER.

vi   Very Little

Illinois, where I live, is called The Prairie State, yet less than 1 percent of our prairies remain. Our Wikipedia oracle tells us again: *very little.* We wear our hypocrisy here, in this place where most people have never seen a prairie. This should tell us something, that we have named our home for a place existing in-name-only. It should tell us something about a people who might be holding a space open, for this prairie openness to return.

So—were it possible—how might seeing the prairie as a Karner Blue challenge our habituated conceptions? These lands could open us. They could read to us, while we read them—telling of a role beyond "caretaker." A new relationship not based on stature: physical or metaphoric.

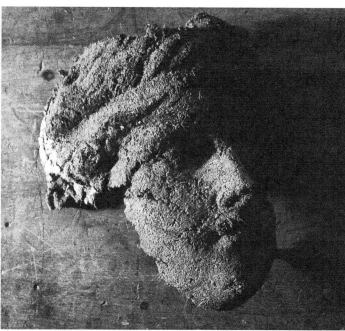

FIGURE 4.2 Jenny Kendler, *Sculpture—>Garden*, 2015–17. "An 'in progress project', *Sculpture—>Garden* are classical Greco-Roman sculpture, by way of vernacular Americana garden statuary. But, instead of marble or bronze, the sculptures are cast entirely from local soil and biodegradable binders suffused with Midewin prairie's native wildflower seeds. Sited outdoors, the sculptures will crumble and deteriorate, eventually transforming from their human forms into seasonal, self-sustaining gardens of native plants—a reminder that the human body is itself a part of nature—eventually going back to the earth to nurture future growth."
© JENNY KENDLER.

A (re)cognition that it is this common base of overlooked *others,* who in fact *care for us.*

(So don't exhaust yourself, my love, holding yourself up so high—just be instead *of* the world, down amongst the roots.)

What could it mean to welcome back into our sensuous world an understanding of the internal humming of these *others*, a respect for their own *wishing to be.* Can we attune ourselves to this vibration?

I bequeath myself to the dirt to grow from the grass I love, If you want me again look for me under your boot-soles.[13]

• • •

13   Walt Whitman, excerpts of *Song of Myself* from *Leaves of Grass*, 1891–92.

vii   A Prairie Path

The prairie's unendingness has ended. And still the plow has not stopped. Oh, place of light and wind, golden green with soft rippling grasses, shaken with birds, humming with insects. Your sod walls are turned over. Your seeds lie dormant. A once seamless quilt of plants pulled up and over our world, the prairie now lies in scraps.

But despite these ends, there are new paths beginning—and most of these start when we take the time to *truly look at plants.* All over our former prairies and plains, new desires are taking root. People are choosing natives plants for their yards, and are making butterfly gardens. Many people, like myself, lead foraging walks, working to recover old plant-knowledge. In Chicago, our Parks District is planting prairie swaths, and keeping them healthy with natural burns. Children are asking their parents to leave the milkweed in their yards un-pulled.

And slowly, the Buffalo are returning.

This is an appeal to let the prairie seduce you. Let your dreams be of seeds stitched underfoot, quickening with life. Yearn for sweet grass. Be an advocate for weeds. Imagine, again, the prairie as forest, remaking the quilt of the world.

Because in the Anthropocene Era, human imagination has become an ecological force—and so, *care has become a radical act.*

So, look out upon this future prairie, and build inside yourself a tiny house with walls of sod. The house is empty. What will arise from this emptiness?

PART 2

Trees

∴

PART 2

(1977)

CHAPTER 5

Trees: Upside-Down, Inside-Out, and Moving

Giovanni Aloi

When you know that trees experience pain and have memories and that tree parents live together with their children, then you can no longer just chop them down and disrupt their lives with large machines.

PETER WOHLLEBEN, *The Hidden Life of Trees: What They Feel, How They Communicate—Discoveries from a Secret World*[1]

∴

As tree of knowledge or as habitat, a tree may determine fate. Klee catches a dreaming virgin in its branches, or Jill Orr traces its energies in her performative photos. Owing to his structural affinity, man feels close to trees. Louise Bourgeois has men or women hugging the tree, Ana Mendieta's and Shirin Neshat's protagonists merge with it, Pipilotti Rist slips into its interior, while Ndary Lo equips the dancing tree with human limbs.

PETER FISCHER, *Thinking About Trees*[2]

∴

One of the most recent challenges faced by art history is to adequately address two sides of the same conceptual coin: anthropocentrism and nature. Despite the momentum gathered by the animal turn in the humanities since the beginning of the new millennium, and the more recent ontological turn involving agential relations and objecthood, art history remains safely anchored to a sense of anthropocentric narcissism that ultimately prevents posthumanist discourses from gaining the cultural traction they now deserve. The art historical ability to prioritize narrative strands, favoring the symbolic and the human, even when the intentionality of artist points towards new eco-agendas, is becoming problematic. The anthropomorphic and anthropocentric slant of the epigraph opening this chapter is indeed symptomatic of this very inability as intrinsic to the work of well-known contemporary artists. The limitations are clear—plants can be featured in art, but only through a symbolic register, that makes them meaningful to human affairs. To gain our attention, they have to ventriloquize the transcendental side of the existential.

Very few nonhumans have been burdened by cultural symbolism like trees have. Their longevity and verticality have lent them the ability to stand as metaphors for human life, strength, protection, spirituality, mourning, and generosity. The symbolic representation of trees thus abounds in literature and the arts from Europe to China, and Russia to the United States.[3] Like the sublime, symbolism essentially is a shorthand-tool capable of producing a specific kind of cultural blindness. While symbolism makes us look at trees in paintings, illustrations, and film, what it shows us is something altogether different. Trees have no interest in spirituality, in protecting us, or in our

1   Wohlleben, P. (2016) *The Hidden Life of Trees: What They Feel, How They Communicate—Discoveries from a Secret World* (Vancouver: Greystone Books) p. xiv.

2   Fischer, P. (2015) 'Thinking About Trees' in P. Fischer and B. Burgi (Eds.) *About Trees* (Köln: Snoeck) p. 19.

3   Lehner, E. and Lehner, J. (2003) *Folklore and Symbolism of Flowers, Plants, and Trees* (Mineola: Dover Publications).

mourning, and they usually remain indifferent to our hugging and dancing around them too. Symbolism is primarily a tool through which humans have always made sense of the world. It most regularly reaffirms man's centrality at the expenses of nature's separation from and subordination to humanity. Beyond its essential function in the narrativization of the world, symbolism plays defining roles, sometimes almost subliminal, in our evaluation of nonhuman lives, thus directly impacting their lives. Questioning the role of symbolism, and most importantly, understanding the limitations imposed by the anthropomorphism which characterizes plant-symbolism is essential, considering the emergence of the Anthropocene as a concept that acknowledges the pervasive, unpredictable, and destructive impact of human activities on ecosystems. Classical anthropomorphic symbolism relentlessly reduces trees to transcendental manifestations of human drives, relentlessly denying the chance to explore through art what plant-being might entail. At stake is the possibility to use art as a tool to rethink our relationship with plants to, more aptly, coexist on this planet.

Postmodernism equally mistrusted metanarratives and symbolism, for the latter has historically played a central role in the inscription of the former. During the 1970s and '80s, an iconoclastic drive brought artists to visually shred symbols and derail the naturalized symbolic connection between signifier and signified. Yet, despite awareness of the limitations imposed by symbolism and anthropomorphism in art, plants, and more especially trees, remain representationally subjugated by millennia of iconographical sedimentations.

In 1979, conceptual artist Rodney Graham employed a subtle representational strategy to enable a subversion of this contingency. The artist noticed that lone trees, from the apple tree in the Garden of Eden to Siddhartha's Bodhi tree and Harry Potter's Whomping Willow are generally more vulnerable to anthropomorphization than those that blend into the multitude of trunks of the forest. Graham built a giant camera obscura, placed it in front of a massive, solitary tree, and invited the public to walk inside to see the luminous image of the tree cast upside-down on the back wall. The upside-down image works as a reminder of the constructedness of nature by the hands of human perception and cultural norms alike. Technically, the image is a reminder of the optical dimension of vision prior to the perceptual codification imposed by the brain. However, as the oldest visual tool of science and art, Graham's camera obscura directly questions our ability to see beyond cultural conventions and norms. Most importantly, the project nods to its historical importance in the construction of romantic notions of nature in art during the nineteenth century, when the camera obscura became the technical foundation of photography's invention—another complex, and then largely misunderstood, world-forming tool.[4]

Inverting can be a productive artistic strategy in the slowing down and derailment of symbolic values. A decade earlier, pioneer land artist Robert Smithson literally uprooted trees, turned them upside-down, and planted them back into the ground thus exposing their root-balls to the air. His inversion, more violently than Graham's own, was deliberately designed to derail the anthropocentric symbolism, which sees trees as a "gentle shade providers." The reversal of the tree turns the familiar into an awkward questioning entity. What are we looking at now? Can we still call this a tree? What is at stake in this everyday made strange?

Amongst other things, the most important result of this inversion unhinges the signifier from the chain of signifieds. While Smithson's gesture is at odds with environmental politics, it still

---

4   Graham's work on upside-down trees was in the late 1990s reprised in the form of gigantic photographic prints exhibited on gallery walls, where they began to function as a critique of the symbolic constructedness that defined the history of western landscaped painting.

FIGURE 5.1 Rodney Graham, *Welsh Oaks* (#6), 1998. Courtesy Lisson Gallery.
PHOTOGRAPHY: KEN ADLARD © RODNEY GRAHAM.

inscribes a sense of urgency—it denounces the difficulty involved in making trees visible outside cultural constructs, something that costs the tree its life.

The paradoxes involved in recovering tree-visibilities in cultural milieus have been more complexly explored in 2002 by British artist Anya Gallaccio who filled the cavernous, neoclassical Duveen Gallery at Tate Britain with a glade of two-hundred-year old oak trunks and translucent slabs of sugar beet. Her site-specific installation capitalized on the undeniable materiality of imposing dead oak trees for the purpose of mobilizing a rewriting of the metanarratives of British imperialism. Oak was the necessary material in shipbuilding during the imperial naval-power phase of the eighteenth century. This subtext is important to the piece and is underlined by the subtitle given to the oaks' grouping: "As long as there were any roads to amnesia and anaesthesia still to be explored."[5] Slabs of sugar laid near the trunks gestured towards a semantic relationship with the trees, the architecture of the gallery space, and the context of imperialism that ultimately is inscribed in the museum collection. Landscape painting flourished as a commercial genre during the eighteenth century predominantly as a means of celebrating land ownership. They constitute a significant token in the sedimentation of symbolic layers of national identity in which nature is implicitly a commodity amongst others.

As it is known, Sir Henry Tate, the founder of the museum, was a wealthy philanthropist who became a millionaire dealing in sugar between 1859 and 1921.[6] Gallaccio's installation operated a much needed, accessible, rewriting of human/plant historical relationships. It foregrounded the forgotten role oak trees played in the making of the empire (actual and metaphorical) and simultaneously of the museum, which since its rebranding in 2000 has been exclusively defined by a notion of British national identity. Framed by the neoclassical space of the Duveen Galleries, the enormous tree trunks aesthetically echoed and ideologically underlined the mastodontic Ionic pillars supporting the building. They problematized the fictitious transparency with which classical culture has been revered in history until recently; wealth is accrued, and ultimately, power is administered. Staying firmly away from the anthropomorphic entrapment that could have emerged in the use of one lone tree, Gallaccio's trunks were segmented to dissuade the visualization of the human in the plant. They also appeared to be inverted, at least in a metaphorical sense, they were "upside-down" just as much as those by Graham and Smithson—but more than theirs Gallaccio's set up was designed to resituate tree-life in the chain of interconnectedness that shaped the British countryside along with its ecosystems along with human's ambitions and desires.

Humans have actively selected, crossbred, grafted, exported, and imported trees for thousands of years. Without having to focus on the obvious impact, which the miniaturization of Japanese bonsai imposes on the tree's growth, our coevolution with trees is undeniable. But in opposition to the anthropocentric narrativizations of traditional history, it is also evident that this coevolution is defined by inter/intra-actions with processes and species. Grafting and crossbreeding, for instance, have substantially defined our taste for certain sizes, colors, and flavors in fruits. The specific malleability, hardness, and durability of different woods have defined our sculptural and architectural abilities. And the aesthetic appeal of particular species against others has substantially shaped our notion of what is domestic and what is exotic supporting the metonymic representations of otherness in imperial constructs. Similarly, if

5   Horlock, M., H. Reitmaier, and S. Schama (2002) *Beat* (London: Tate Gallery Publishing).

6   Spalding, F. (1998) *Tate: A History* (London: Tate Gallery Publishing).

we can conceive plant-human relationships as coevolutive, it also appears clear that some species have, in a Darwinian sense, evolutionally-seduced us with their fruits, foliage, and flowers to secure our care and to maximize their ability of survival just as they would do with pollinators and other animals. This is their biopolitical form of resistance—inducing humans to incorporate them in specific economies as part of a transaction upon which the success of their reproduction relies. In all instances, the base upon which this coevolution unfolds is one defined by capitalist economies of production and consumption. Yet, this coevolution might have reached a point of unsustainable environmental crisis. The cost to biodiversity inflicted by the reproductive success of palm and soy within the capitalist frameworks that have characterized the past century could be one of the many examples of this crisis.

According to Jason W. Moore's book titled *Capitalism in the Web of Life: Ecology and the Accumulation of Capital*, right now, "the choice is between a Cartesian paradigm that locates capitalism outside of nature, acting upon it, and a way of seeing capitalism as a project and process within the web of life."[7] Clearly, the challenge is to consider capitalism as the mosaic of relations, the system of intra/interactions through which relations between humans and nonhumans articulate themselves. From this standpoint, capitalism becomes the result of a crisis of perception. No longer does it appear external to nature as that which encodes, quantifies, and rationalizes resources, but as a world-ecology "joining the accumulation of capital, the pursuit of power, and the co-production of nature in dialectical unity."[8] Capitalism is coproduced by manifold species and environments, and it can be seen to define the past two hundred years as the *Capitalocene*: the episteme, which not only

culturally but also materially shapes knowledge and the living condition on this planet.

In many ways, capitalogenic logics relevant to today's environmental circumstances were heralded by the work of artists comprising the Arte Povera movement in Italy during the 1960s and '70s.[9] Focusing on the abrasive materiality of sculpture and capitalizing on a rejection of the spiritual, the elitism, and the transcendence of modernist painting, Arte Povera problematized the discourses of capitalism, mass production, nature, and culture in substantially different ways from those operated by contemporary pop artists in the United States. Many Arte Povera artists deliberately juxtaposed "the new" and "the old" in order to complicate traditional notions of progress; they rejected scientific rationalism to define an imaginative space in which materiality could contribute to new forms of contemporary myth-making based on memory and locality. Most importantly, they acknowledged the problematic relationship between nature and industrialization as indissolubly bound to contemporary discourses.

Contextually, Arte Povera emerged from a contradictory and intense period of industrialization of the Italian postwar period, which later came to be known as the *Miracolo Italiano* (Italian Miracle).[10] During the 1970s, the capitalist success of new mass-production processes caused substantial geographical, as well as sociological, reconfigurations that deeply impacted the environmental conditions of northern of Italy. This shift augmented the fragmentation of an already precarious national identity in which the north and the south of the peninsula appeared environmentally, as well as culturally, and economically further apart. Moreover, while many artists in this movement like Alighiero Boetti and Mario Merz rejected the ideology of consumerist society, others like Giuseppe

7   Moore, J.W. (2015) *Capitalism in the Web of Life: Ecology and the Accumulation of Capital* (New York: Verso Books) p. 30.
8   Ibid., p. 3.

9   Celant, G. (1985) *Arte Povera* (Florence: Electa).
10 Crainz, G. (2005) *Storia Del Miracolo Italiano* (Rome: Donzelli Editore).

Penone, contemplated the notion that capitalism is, whether we like it or not, intrinsically bound to what we call nature. In this context, a critique of consumerist society operated by the choice of everyday and natural objects as selected by the artist was problematized by his methodological approaches. Most specifically, his sculpture titled *Tree of 12 Meters* is an example of Penone's ability to subvert the symbolic representation of trees for the purpose of favoring more complex biopolitical readings.

It was semantically important that the woodblock Penone carved had gone through an industrial process of rendering—in this way, a play of visibility and invisibility became central to the discourses inscribed in this work. The American larch (*Larix laricina*) he chose is native of Canada and the northeastern United States, from Minnesota to Maryland. It can reach twenty meters in height and sixty centimeters in diameter—the bark is flaky, and the wood underneath is reddish. Botanical historiography characterizes it as an aggressive species, in the sense that it germinates easily and before others in a variety of soils—furthermore, the larch is a very versatile plant capable of tolerating winter temperatures of -35 degrees Fahrenheit. The durable and resistant wood is used as pulp by paper-making factories while appropriately shaped individuals can be used for floorboards, posts, and poles.[11]

Penone's tree was industrially sawn into a beam—akin to Gallaccio's rework of oak trees into column-like trunks, this operation obliterated the lyrical symbolism of romantic representations, replacing this with notions of capitalist functionality and rationality.

Simultaneously, this process could be alluding to the transition of the living tree (nature) into a modular unit of architectural construction (culture). Like Gallaccio's oak trunks, Penone's larch is the product of capitalist economies that incorporate the tree on a commodifying register.

FIGURE 5.2 Giuseppe Penone, *Tree of 12 Meters*. Wood, 1980–02.
© TATE, LONDON.

The perfectly geometrical and smooth trunk of Penone's tree gestured towards human's ability to rationalize nature and to dominate it through consumptive processes. However, the artist's challenge to the notion of capitalism and nature as separate, or even opposed entities, is manifested in the skilled carving which attempted to reverse this very process. As Penone worked from an industrially sawn beam, he had no knowledge of the effective morphology of the tree that preceded it. Yet, he committed to a certain register of representational realism upon deciding to use the visible wood-knots on the surface of the beam to sculpt brunch-stumps.

11   Eckenwalder, J.E. (2009) *Conifers of the World: The Complete Reference* (Portland: Timber Press).

Much of art historical commentary on this work has favored the anthropomorphic symbolism which understands the carved tree as a recovery of an "inner child." Trees grow through an outer cell-layer called *cambium*, therefore, in the central part of a wood beam, technically lies a past, younger tree. Yet, Penone's concern exceeded this simplistic symbolic register. As the artist explained:

> The curiosity of discovering a new tree, and hence a new story, every time, and the stimulus in this sense that comes to me from the imaginative quality of every door, table, window, or board—all of which contain the image of a tree—explain the motivation and urgency of my recourse to this kind of operation, which is not repetition, but a new adventure every time.[12]

Far from romanticized notions of nostalgia, purity, and essentialism, Penone's *Tree of 12 Meters* produced an indissoluble hybrid of capitalism and nature in which both the beam and the tree are ultimately man-made and tree-made at the same time—they both are commodities defined by different value systems that equally rely on capitalist economies. A testament to this indissoluble condition is the visibility of the beam in what now functions as the sculpture's plinth.

An intentional disconnect between the title of the work *Tree of 12 Meters,* and the two sculptures comprising the work complicates matters further. The beam was sawn in half, and its top part made to face downward. Although the title points toward one tree, we actually see two. Like Graham's and Smithson's upside-down trees, this too constitutes a derailing operation designed to dissuade simplistic symbolic readings—a way to make the tree visible beyond the symbolism that would once again erase its material presence and its interconnectedness with

human economies of production and consumption.

Another work of art that further problematizes the conceptual dimensions of the play of presence and absence, visibility and invisibility for the purpose of derailing the anthropomorphic inherent to classical tree representations is *Hinoki* by Charles Ray. While Penone's *Tree of 12 Meters* suggests a collapse of the nature/culture dichotomy through the consideration of capitalist modes of production, Charles Ray's *Hinoki* derails symbolic readings by overlaying Western and Eastern notions of value, labor, and decay.

Hinoki, a thirty-two-foot long, 2,100 pound sculpture of the decaying trunk of a tree, took ten years to make. Symbolically it is an utterly antiheroic tree. Its verticality denied, its integrity corrupt. This tree is a carcass that speaks of loss and frailty, time and transience. The trunk is hollow—its heartwood, the central supporting pillar, has pulverized allowing the viewer to simultaneously see the inside and the outside. This natural contingency (many trees rot this way) however constitutes the actual, as well as metaphorical, base of the work. *Hinoki,* more than any other work by Ray, speaks of economies of visibility and invisibility in the intertwined processes of nature and capitalism. At the core of Charles Ray's work lies a dedicated interest in surfaces as the only aspect of a reality we can fully grasp. In a sense, the relentless reductionism he operates through the synthetic rendition of surfaces works as a metaphor of our perceptive limitations. It is perhaps not a surprise that the fallen oak which became the model for *Hinoki,* with its double inside/outside surface, haunted the artist. As he recalls:

> Ten years ago, while driving up the central coast of California, I spotted a fallen tree in a meadow just off the highway. I was instantly drawn to it. It was not only a beautiful log but to my eyes, it was perfectly embedded in the meadow where it had fallen decades earlier. Pressures from

12   Celant, G. (1989) *Giuseppe Penone*, exhibition catalog (Bristol: Arnolfini Gallery) p. 55.

FIGURE 5.3   Charles Ray, *Hinoki*, 2007
            COURTESY MATTHEW MARKS GALLERY © CHARLES RAY.

the weather, insects, ultraviolet radiation, and gravity were evident. Total collapse appeared to be no more than a handful of years away. I was inspired to make a sculpture and studied many other logs, but I realized that I was only interested in this particular one.[13]

Ray's statement already points to a nonsymbolic register in which the tree appears as a body,

neither living nor dead, but one that is an image of interconnectedness with biosystems. The artist's sculptural problem became not that of communicating emotion or sensation but to capture a heightened sense of perceptual awareness— a different register of consciousness capable of bypassing prefabricated images of classical harmony to map new systems of reference-relations that the work interlinks.

With the help of a few friends, Ray sectioned the tree into portable segments and transferred it to his studio in Los Angeles where it was cast using silicone molds. It was then reproduced in fiberglass. This method of life-casting has been a recurring practice in Ray's work. It reflects

13   Ray, C. quoted in B. Bürgi, C. Ray, D.W. Druick, M. Fried, T.R. Neer, J.A.M. Wagner Rondeau (2015). *Charles Ray: Sculpture 1997–2014* (New York: Distributed Art Pub Incorporated) p. 118.

his deep interest in objecthood and mimesis as problematized by an all-important notion of synthetic realism: one that deliberately and precariously straddles the notions of man-made and natural. The finished result was then sent to master woodworker Yuboku Mukoyoshi in Osaka where his assistants specialize in the reproducing work that is beyond reparation. "In Japan," Ray says, "when an ancient temple or Buddha can no longer be maintained, it is remade."[14] The cast of the oak was copied in a tradition of Buddhist remaking, at a one to one scale, using local cypress wood (*Chamaecyparis obtusa*: "hinoki" in Japanese), thus producing a hybrid oak/cypress tree with a double surface— a distinctive Californian morphology and a Japanese material texture and colour. The accuracy with which the surface of *Hinoki* was transposed twice, first from the original cast of the Californian oak and then through the hyper-detailed mimicry of Mukoyoshi's workshop is outstanding. The attention to detail went so far as to include insect tracks and other external impacts producing hybrid traces which preserved their true essential aesthetic despite losing their indexicality. Processually, this makes *Hinoki* the equivalent of the painting of a photograph— a kind of photorealist transposition in which surfaces are painstakingly rendered in their essentialism. In this specific case, like in many hyperrealist paintings, economies of artistic labor become enigmatically and paradoxically meaningful. Why couldn't Ray stop at the silicone life-cast he made? Why invest such tremendous amounts of skill and craft in copying the ravaged surface of a rotting tree?

Ultimately *Hinoki* makes us aware of a chain of ambivalences: the ones between the original tree, its silicone cast (the indexical trace), the fiberglass copy, and a human-made transcription of its imprint. *Hinoki* speaks of the visibility and invisibility of processes and materialities in our economies of consumption: it deliberately blurs the boundaries between notions of natural and man-made, nature and culture, and nature and capitalism by tracing an evanescent trajectory of multiple incarnations and transcriptions, each erasing the previous, until the viewer is confronted by a total hybrid of Eastern and Western conceptions of value, labour, preservation, and loss.

The fiberglass cast made from the silicone mold inscribed the tree's surfaces into an essential modern material essential to the mass-production of boats and planes. Casting, a method common for the making and reproduction of sculptures in classical art, has in modern time become the essential production stage of capitalist mass-production. Like many other goods that are made to travel around the world to complete a laborious assemblage process, the fiberglass cast of the Californian oak was shipped to Japan where its surface was once again inscribed into another material, this time, cypress wood. With every inscription into a different material, the surface of the Californian oak tree aesthetically morphed into a hybridized form that preserved a natural indexicality whilst substantiating a thoroughly man-made essence. The last production stage, operated by expert copyist sculptors symbolically reinstated human action as the defining element involved in the permutation. However, like every successful product of capitalism, *Hinoki* conceals the traces of human labor, flaunting a naturalness that it does not essentially own. Commodity fetishism entirely relies on this ability to aesthetically erase labor and the social relations involved in the making of objects for the very purpose of preventing ethical consideration.[15] Ultimately, its title underlines this contingency. The piece is titled after the name of the only constituent material visible to the viewer—fiberglass, silicone, and the original oak remains concealed.

---

14   Ibid., p. 118.

15   Marx, K. (1867) *Capital: A Critique of Pure Economy, Vol. 1.* (New York: Penguin), 2004.

At this point, it becomes possible to see how Charles Ray's *Hinoki* transformed a value-less rotting tree (at least valueless to capitalist economies) into a commodity: artwork, fetishized artwork, a luxury object, validated by the economies of the artworld. As Marx argued, commodities are in first and foremost "external objects": a thing that through its qualities satisfies human consumptive needs and desires. It is therefore cunning that a representation of a natural object should entail multiple transcription processes to ultimately bring to the attention of the viewer a notion of ambivalence between the externality of commodities and the externality essential to the construction of nature itself—the essential prerequisite enabling the fetishization of nature is situated here. In so doing, *Hinoki* laconically gestures towards the chain of indissoluble interconnectedness between man, nature, and capitalism, while its precarious ontological status encompasses the flickering of machine-made processing and the artistic tradition of craft, the mass-produced commodity, and the art object uniqueness. In this sense, capitalism emerges as a world-ecology engaged in the co-production of nature.

The construction of past Cartesian narratives and the ways in which we respond to the challenges posed by the current climate and capitalist crises are revealed as interrelated.

Considering

> capitalism's incorporation of planetary life and processes, through which new life activity is continually brought into the orbit of capital and capitalist power ... and the biosphere's internalization of capitalism through which human-initiated projects and processes shape the web of life[16]

allows a world-historical reconstruction of value. This is not the equivalent of denying the crisis we are traversing. As Moore argues, the conceptualization of a "capitalism-in-nature" constitutes a proposal that could enable the emergence of "workable methodological frames, conceptual vocabularies, and narrative strategies for world-historical change."[17] Most importantly, this shift would reconfigure nature's position from that which limits capitalist ambition, to that which engages in a coproduction of sustainable limits of human activity within an organization of nature-human relations.

Such proposal would entail reconsidering plant agency—their ability to coevolve with us in naturecultures that make our shared histories, productive forms of "being with," but also their need to be considered beyond the objectifying realms of functionalism, symbolism, and anthropomorphism. Rethinking trees as nonhuman beings capable of perceptual and behavioral complexities that are not human-like, but yet not inferior, is key to this task. German forester Peter Wohlleben's best-selling book *The Secret Lives of Trees* has attempted to enthuse nonscientific readership narrativizing the complexities of their lives, thus bringing us to reconsider the passivity with which trees (and plants more in general) have been burdened with over time.

The author accessibly describes how trees communicate through roots and fungi networks, that they establish relationships with neighboring trees, and that they are capable of learning through forms of memory: they make choices and have characters.[18] Some reviewers have however pointed out that his brand of anthropomorphism might effectively be problematic, since it can lead to oversimplifications and

---

16   Moore, J.W. (2015) *Capitalism in the Web of Life: Ecology and the Accumulation of Capital* (New York: Verso) p. 13.

17   Ibid., p. 28.

18   Wohlleben, P. (2016) *The Hidden Life of Trees: What They Feel, How They Communicate—Discoveries from a Secret World* (New York: Penguin).

reduction of trees' lives.[19] The task ahead is to sidestep the old forms of anthropomorphism and symbolism in favor of further speculative aesthetic approaches capable of engaging audiences with new conceptions of tree-being.

Céleste Boursier-Mougenot's contribution to the 2015 Venice Biennale titled *All the World's Futures* surprised viewers with *revolutions*, a kinetic installation involving three roaming trees. The work's main preoccupation revolved around human/plant relations, agency, and perception.[20] Similarly to Anya Gallaccio's oaks, Boursier-Mougenot reversed the archetypal nature/culture stereotype grounded in the inside/outside dichotomy by taking Scotch pines into the gallery space. Scotch pines are native to Eurasia, and their cultural coevolution with humans has been substantially defined by their aesthetic qualities, resistance, and versatility which makes them perfect Christmas trees. It is reported that Great Britain consumes roughly eight million Christmas trees per year, while the United States' consumption ranges between thirty-five and forty million. Stephen Nissenbaum's 1996 book titled *The Battle for Christmas* argued that Christmas trees were introduced to the United States not so much by German immigrants, as it is usually believed, but by some literary sources. Progressive reformists saw in the German tradition of the Christmas tree an opportunity to counterbalance the materialist and indulgent way in which Americans celebrated the festivity.[21] Through the introduction of rituals such as placing presents at its base on Christmas Eve, the tree was meant to rationalize and organize the exchange of commodities by providing a confined space and time for them. "The family tree became the locus of

not only surprise and gratitude but also of mutual generosity, the hub of a material exchange "forged outside the fevered crucible of market relations." However, in the long run, the introduction of the Christmas tree only provided a place marker and perfect embodiment for the ever-growing economy of decorations worth millions of dollars while enabling capitalism to market the passing of seasons.

Intended as a redeemer of consumerism, the tree has today become the emblem of the quintessential human/tree capitalist relationship. The processes of production and consumption involved in its farming, harvesting, selling, and recycling make the tree into a perfect commodity—a fetishized, disposable object with an inscribed yearly purchase demand.

Boursier-Mougenot's installation reversed the utter passification of these trees by providing the Scotch pines with a wheeled base linked to a complex electronic system of sapflow sensors which through a low-voltage electrical current gives them the ability to move in space and choose their preferred situation in relation to lighting, temperature, and humidity in their environment. In so doing, the artist literally uprooted the essential notion of *stasis* intrinsic to plant-being—making visible agential abilities we usually cannot appreciate due to our perceptive limitations. Plants' connectedness to their place of birth has been perceived as an essential objectifying quality of their being. Reversing this determinism reveals tree-agency enabling a gesturing towards the notions that are usually denied to plant-being: decision making, active involvement in processes of self-sustenance, and even character. The three trees in the exhibiting space were the same size, and age—yet, they seemed to prefer different places—they at times met each other, but of course we do not know if this was deliberately sought or incidental.

Ultimately Boursier-Mougenot's installation successfully made sense of plant-life beyond the stereotypical restrictions of objectifying

19 Caurstemont, S. (2016) 'Trees have an inner life like ours, claims bestseller' in *New Scientist*, October 26.

20 Boursier-Mougenot, C. (2015) *Revolutions* (Arles: Analogues).

21 Nissenbaum, S. (2010) *The Battle for Christmas* (New York: Knopf Doubleday Publishing Group.

FIGURE 5.4 Céleste Boursier-Mougenot, *rêvolutions*
PHOTO JEAN-PIERRE DALBÉRA BY CC BY 2.0.

consumerist strategies—what if we could perceive the agency of trees more readily than we do? Would we still cut them, dress them up, and dispose of them every year? Part of the exhibiting space in the French pavilion has been set up as a seating area described by the artist as a meditative zone. There, viewers could think about our relationship with plants while their aural attentiveness is stimulated by an acoustic environment: an electric rustling is emanated by the sensors enabling tree locomotion. The whole of Boursier-Mougenot's installation appeared therefore as an effective posthumanist utopia in which cyborgian apparatuses enable different plant/human relationals to arise. However, how probable is it that these new relational economies could take hold outside the gallery space? That visitors to the Venice Biennale would be exposed to Boursier-Mougenot's installation is of paramount importance to even instill the doubt that a plausibility might indeed exist.

CHAPTER 6

Animation, Animism ... Dukun Dukun & DNA

*Lucy Davis**

Around eight years ago I lived in a quarter of Singapore which alongside welcoming weekend congregations of migrant workers, also hosted a multitude of migrant objects; electronics, cardboard, timber, and tin. Each night, as the traffic quieted, the quarter transformed and a subsistence-army of nocturnal foragers, trolleyed discarded items to recycling pickup-points in exchange for a few Singapore dollars. I noticed that timber was not yet integrated into this "nocturnal ecology" and began to venture out at night collecting planks and discarded furniture.

Figure 6.1 depicts a 1930s teak bed from a karang guni, junk store in this same neighborhood that has been my partner in an ongoing exploration of historic, material, genetic, and poetic stories of trees, wood and people in Southeast Asia. However, in order to explain how this partnership came about, I need to foreground some art historical and material-led concerns, as it was these that drew me to at all try to trace teak from this one bed to a possible regional plantation-source, via DNA tracking technology.

One prevailing pursuit has been to physically work-through the material, labor and spirit of the mid-twentieth century Malayan Modern Woodcut; a movement through which migrant artists of the Chinese left inscribed dreams of permanent-residence in *Nanyang*.[1] Another impetus was to critically-engage Singapore's economic success-story, famously predicated upon the island-city's entrepôt processing of regional "cheap nature,"[2] from rubber to palm-oil. As recently as 1977, Singapore's seventh largest export was processed-timber from regional forests.[3] I wanted to find a way to bring these two, macro and micro practices together; to rework the micro-gestures of the Malayan Woodcut in a macro-ecological context of "cuttings of wood" (meaning regional deforestation).

Questions about how and from where timber migrated to Singapore led me into conversations with plant biologists and later geneticists. In the spirit of the Malayan woodblock, I originally imagined I'd be carving stories of migration into my

---

* The Migrant Ecologies Project embraces concerned explorers, curious collectors, daughters of woodcutters, miners of memories and art by nature. The research in this essay and that of Shannon Lee Castleman's which follows, was carried out under the auspices of this artist's collective.

1 Histories of the Malayan Woodblock Movement comprise one part of accounts of the Chinese left in Southeast Asia that are only being rehabilitated in the last couple of decades. See for example: L.C. Tju (2004)

'Political Prints in Singapore' in *Print Quarterly* 21, 3 (September), pp. 266–81; M.D. Barr and C.A. Trocki (Eds.) (2008) *Paths Not Taken: Political Pluralism in Post-War Singapore* (Singapore: NUS Press); and Davis, L. (2001) 'In the Company of Trees' in (2011) *Antennae: The Journal of Nature in Visual Culture,* 17, pp. 43–62. *Nanyang* means South Seas or island Southeast Asia, including Singapore.

2 "Cheap Nature" is a term coined by Jason W. Moore, Coordinator of the World Ecology Research Network. See for example Moore, J.W. (2014) 'The End of Cheap Nature or: How I learned to Stop Worrying about 'the' Environment and Love the Crisis of Capitalism' in C. Suter and C. Chase-Dunn (Eds.) *Structures of the World Political Economy and the Future of Global Conflict and Cooperation* (Berlin: LIT) pp. 285–314.

3 'Timber Seventh Biggest Export from S'pore' *The Straits Times,* May 10, 1977. The fourth incarnation of this project aimed to complicate this top-down view of Singapore and involved a study of patriarchal imprinting in a leading Singapore teak export family. See exhibition book: Wee, J. and Tay, K. (Eds.) *I am Like the Karang Guni of Teak.* Photography by Lucy Davis & Ya Ting Kee. Text by Lucy Davis. National University of Singapore Museum. (2014), 36 pages.

FIGURE 6.1   Lucy Davis, *Ranjang Jati: The Teak Bed that Got Four Humans from Singapore to Travel to Muna Island, Southeast Sulawesi and Back Again, 2009–2012*, Wilton Close, Singapore.
PHOTOGRAPH BY SHANNON LEE CASTLEMAN.

growing collection of found-objects; planks, broken chairs, table-legs, rolling pins. However, once these objects had settled in my studio, I'd begun a relationship with them. Although their wood had already been cut by the hands of unknown, Southeast Asian foresters and carpenters, these objects had an integrity which I felt unable to reduce to my own inscriptions.

Instead, I developed a woodprint-collage method; making two sets of works for each object: A first "natural history" print, depicted the object's constituent-parts. A second involved collaging print-fragments into contexts through which the wood might have migrated. As I was working backwards in this process, from familiar object to imagined tree, my "interpretive bias" leant more towards a "spirit" of an object in a tree, as to a "spirit" of the tree in an object. The resulting collages did therefore not posit a pristine, romantic source but rather something becoming, in and through encounters with migrant forest products on Singapore streets.

• • •

Every tree has a unique DNA identity, termed (with some anthropomorphic- arrogance) a "fingerprint." A Singapore startup, DoubleHelix Tracking Technology (DoubleHelix) has been advocating nonfakeable DNA-fingerprinting as a way to trace timber through global supply chains and combat illegal logging.[9] The task my team proposed however, was a little more complicated, requiring DoubleHelix to work backwards, interpreting degraded-wood from an eighty-year-old bed that I had "planted" in my back garden.[4]

This was not an exacting a process as we imagined: Complete, genographic archives of tropical timber do not exist. Fragmented collections are

scattered around the globe in restricted-access laboratories. We were consequently, pleasantly surprised when DoubleHelix connected preliminary tests from our bed DNA to century-old teak plantations in Southeast Sulawesi.[5] And so, photographer Shannon Castleman, DoubleHelix's Indonesia Country Officer and I travelled to Muna,[6] a Southeast Sulawesi island renowned for its teak, in search of samples and stories.

• • •

The uncertainty of our initial investigations is in stark contrast with the figuring of DNA in popular imagination.[7] While a DNA sequence might well lead a geneticist through rich and variegated encounters, there's a spirit of nineteenth century positivism in mass-media projections of DNA: a "Journey to The Source," colonizing new frontiers with the value-added, economistic timbre of the "The Barcode."[8] I'm grateful for the journeys our bed DNA has drawn us upon, and am persuaded of the macroecological possibilities of (open-source) genographic archives. But there were also complications in our collaborations:

Firstly, while the processes of DNA-extraction in an Adelaide laboratory were made completely

---

4   DoubleHelix argue the "use of DNA, stable isotopes, wood anatomy ... to independently verify product claims of species and origin ... vastly simplifies what can often be a complex and confusing verification process." <http://www.doublehelixtracking.com>, accessed 13 March 2016.

5   One reason for the DoubleHelix employee's enthusiasm for this journey might have been speculation that teak, imported to present-day Indonesia over many centuries from India, Burma, or Laos had "naturalized" in Southeast Sulawesi and that this might be evident in an altered genetic structure of older trees. The employee in question no longer works for the company (Email and verbal correspondence with DoubleHelix Tracking Singapore research representative March 2010).

6   I am only providing names for collaborators and interviewees who formally agreed to be named in this essay.

7   And indeed, in the marketing of DoubleHelix, see note 4.

8   Judith Roof argues in *The Poetics of DNA* "DNA ... is not just another scientific fact. DNA's overt connection to processes of representation (the alphabet, the book, the map [one might add here, the imprint LD]) makes ... representations of DNA particularly rich sites for understanding the interrelation of science, metaphor and narrative." J. Roof (2007) 'The Epic Acid' in *The Poetics of DNA* (Minneapolis: University of Minnesota Press) p. 24.

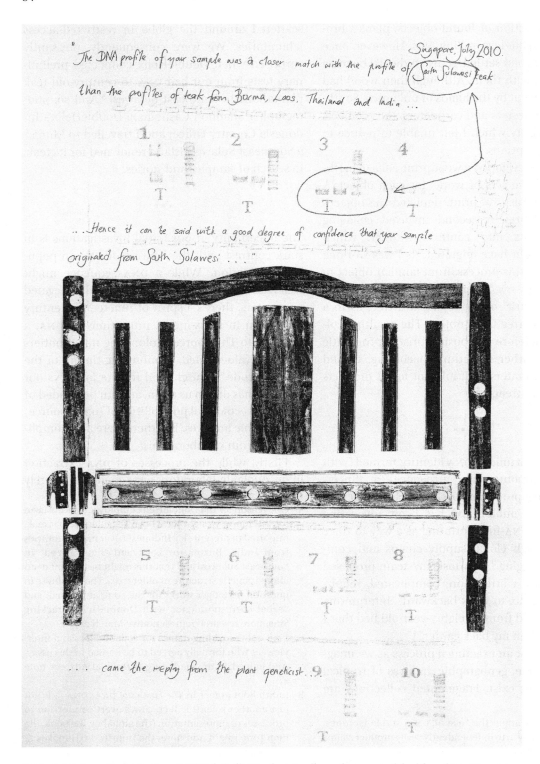

FIGURE 6.2   Lucy Davis, *Ranjang Jati* (Teak Bed). Woodprint collage of a 1930s teak bed found in a Singapore
              junk store with charcoal. 240 cm × 150 cm, 2012
              © LUCY DAVIS.

transparent to us,[9] the methods of matching our bed DNA to Sulawesi teak remained obscure. We were basically presented a gel print-out and informed this was a "confident match" with a sequence from our bed.[10]

A second complication concerned our own project premises; neither aiming to illustrate science, or appropriate "lab aesthetics." Instead, I'd hoped to explore the way a dream in DNA code might seed itself, like teak across the archipelago, exposing what I envisaged would be grounded but mutable ecologies of power, economics, labor, gender, and species. A later addition would be ecologies of spirits.

••••

The creation myth for *kulijawa*, or teak in Muna language,[11] recalls that seeds arrived on the island over five hundred years ago in the form of gifts by a royal Javan envoy to the Muna King.[12]

Teak enabled that Javan nobleman to implant himself and a timber economy in the Muna aristocracy via marriage. For centuries, only royalty could cultivate teak, with capital penalties for smugglers. Later, the Dutch intensified production, taking over plantations on the pretext of rescuing

islanders from Bugis slave-raids.[13] After independence the Indonesian government took over. A major timber boom ensued after Suharto opened plantations and rainforests for international logging and internal cronies in 1967. From the 1970s to the late 1990s, demand exceeded supply, sawmills lined the Muna harbor and "'rivers were thick with logs ... you could walk on wood all the way to the sea."[14] Today, practically all commercially-viable teak has been cut. No primary forest remains and sawmills are overrun with creepers.

At first it appeared that teak had monoculturalized Muna life, demanding subsistence farmers transform into plantation-workers and village headmen into mobilizers of labor for a logging economy. A saying heard repeatedly was *politik Muna adalah politik kayu*—"Muna politics is a politics of wood." Village buffalo, central to subsistence cultivation, were initially loaned-out to drag logs to river-floats. But the buffalo were sold off as the industry automated. Although there are still subsistence farm plots and fishing along the plastic-clogged, mangrove-depleted coasts, teak seemed to have colonized most aspects of Muna life.

However, alongside macro-ecological perspectives, our project also aimed to trace everyday and micro-gestures. In 2000 smallholder plantations were finally legalized.[15] For centuries before this, islanders could only legally fell teak for domestic purposes. But commercial teak takes thirty years to mature. This means villagers will continue

---

9   See Jardine Duncan (2013) 'Wood Extraction: The Basics' in Yu-Mei Balasingamchow (ed.) *Jalan Jati (Teak Road)* by The Migrant Ecologies Project, The Royal Botanic Garden, Edinburgh/Migrant Ecologies Project, Singapore, pp. 185–87.

10 This was information we took in good faith even though we'd been advised that most teak entering Malaya in the 1930s came from Burma. Discussion with David of 'David Antiques' junk furniture dealer from Rangoon road October 2009.

11 Interview with Muna oral historian and philologist, Mr La Ode Sirad Imbo, October 2010.

12 It is not clear how or when teak arrived in Java. Different studies posit Laos, Burma and India as the genetic parent of Javanese teak. See A. and H. Volkaert, 'The Evolutionary and Plantation Origin of Teak' in Yu-Mei Balasingamchow, ed. *Jalan Jati (Teak Road)* by The Migrant Ecologies Project The Royal Botanic Garden, Edinburgh/Migrant Ecologies Project, Singapore 2013) pp. 23–25.

---

13 'Our Neighbours: Slavery in Celebes' in *The Straits Times*, 10 January 1907. 'Situation in Celebes: Striking Advantages of the Argument of Force' *The Straits Times* 28 March 1908.

14 Interview with village head and community elders Tampo district, Muna.

15 Post the fall of Suharto in 1997, a decentralization process has taken place across Indonesia, the results of which are uncertain. For Muna islanders it means finally a possibility to establish independent smallholder teak plantations. Elsewhere, decentralization has meant more power to local gangsters, militias and cronies of Suharto who were awarded forest concessions during the dictatorship.

practices considered "illegal" according to the discourse of DNA-certification; cutting more quality teak than needed to build houses with double walls, keeping extra stocks underneath their homes for "repairs" and savings. A forest police officer was attacked with *parang* knives a week before we arrived in Muna while trying to apprehend woodcutters in a *hutan konservasi*; a plantation which had been awarded *konservasi* or "conservation" status, not in because of biodiversity but in order to protect the groundwater. Indeed the only *konservasi* plantations left uncut were those considered to be haunted.

• • •

Inside the *hutan-hantu* or haunted *konservasi* plantations a strange "battle" has been playing out between plantation teak and the indigenous banyan/beringen or strangling- fig. The banyan seed starts as a seed, dispersed in the canopy by a bird or a bat. The young plant puts out aerial roots which, when they reach the ground, enforce a complex ribcage-like architecture. "Possessing" and suffocating their hosts, strangling- figs are thought to house potent spirits throughout Asia.

While Shannon was photographing this tree at dawn, I looked around the still-rhythmic topography of the old plantation, observing how the light cast shadows of the large floppy leaves onto a comparatively-clear, dry forest floor. These regular patterns were interrupted sporadically by dark braids of aerial roots and a deeper, knotted shade where a banyan had taken hold, drawing other migrant flora as animals arrived to eat figs and deposited more seeds. As the sun rose, I heard a familiar clatter-squawk in the canopy; perhaps a banyan was fruiting? The birds resembled the yellow-crested cockatoo; critically-endangered in its native islands and yet escapee crackles thrive in cities like Hong Kong and Singapore. One noisy individual occasionally visits the pong pong tree outside my window.[16]

I began to realize that the active agents of conservation on Muna were neither the forest police, nor the few island NGOs, but rather cockatoos, banyans, and spirits.

• • •

The ability to divine which spirits have made a tree or piece of wood their home is the purview of *dukun-dukun* or shamanic wood-doctors.[17] A *dukun* conventionally advises whether a particular tree should be felled and which wood to use in house construction, providing incantations for each process. In Muna architecture,[18] the root- end of a plank should point groundwards and the crown-end skywards. For overhead beams, the crown points towards Mecca. Over the centuries, Muna *dukun-dukun* have migrated their arboreal expertise to encompass teak plantations. Muna *dukun-dukun* claim to know crown or root ends of a plank by holding it in their hands.

On the advice of a Muna oral historian meetings were arranged with two *dukun-dukun*.[19] Before we left Singapore, I had fashioned samples of our bed; leftovers from the DNA extraction into "team talismans" for us to wear during our fieldtrip. I presented one of these samples and a photo of our bed to each *dukun* and asked what they thought.[20]

Neither appeared impressed: The male *dukun* sat in the front of his new, concrete-walled house surrounded by neighbors and children and

---

16   The *pong pong* or *cerbera odollam* is, as we learned in primary school, a mango-sized fruit with a deadly

seed containing the poison *cerberin*. However, escapee cockatoos in Singapore seem to have found a niche food source, managing to consume the fruit without touching the seeds.

17   A fecund and spreading industry of *dukun-dukun* have transplanted themselves into modern life in throughout the archipelago and are consulted on on matters from healing, marriage, agriculture, architecture to urban planning, finance and politics.

18   See for example Waterson, R. (1990) *The Living House: An Anthropology of Architecture in South-East Asia* (Singapore: Oxford University Press).

19   Interview with La Ode Sirad Imbo ibid.

20   For a contemporary art response to Animism see Franke Anselm (ed.) *e-flux journal #36 Animism*. July 2012 <http://www.e-flux.com/journal/introduction —'animism'/> Accessed February 2016.

FIGURE 6.3 Lucy Davis, *Pokok Ranjang Jati* (Teak Bed Tree). Woodprint collage of a 1930s teak bed found in Singapore 240
cm × 150 cm, 2012
© LUCY DAVIS.

smoking a clove cigarette. He seemed relaxed ... perhaps a little amused? He told us that our teak was *jati-hitam* [black teak] of the lowest grade—used only for the lavatory and back-areas of houses. Laughing he tossed our "talisman" to one of his children as we drove off. The female *dukun* invited us into her older teak house with bright blue panels. We sat on a bench opposite her husband and niece (a *dukun* in training). It was dark inside but strips of sunlight slid in through slits in the boards. She explained her work: mostly with women's health and sometimes exorcisms. She explained that spirits were not of the trees themselves but that they settled in various trees, sites and timber. Her personal encounters included tree spirits with no heads but with eyes under their armpits. After examining our sample she declared our wood was not from anywhere in Sulawesi.

The Muna PR Chief, who arranged most of our interviews and accompanied us everywhere in his khaki uniform, appeared to thoroughly enjoy our discussions with the *dukun dukun*. But our collaborators, the DoubleHelix country-officer and our "fixer"; an engineer from Kendari on the mainland were resistant. The country-officer dismissed *dukun dukun* expertise as "animist magic," declaring his Catholic and our fixer's Islamic faiths to be more "modern" and "scientific." But then at breakfast while showing my earlier animated film, featuring Alfred Russel Wallace on my laptop, I recounted the legend of how Wallace formulated a theory of natural selection independently of Darwin while recovering from malaria in the Malay archipelago. Although neither familiar with Wallace, nor his fever-dream, at the mention of Darwin both went quiet then moved to the other end of the balcony to converse. Our fixer went to his room and the county-officer came back smiling. They had discussed together and agreed that although they both believed in DNA, neither believed in evolution.

The DoubleHelix officer also seemed quite exasperated by my repeating the same questions to villagers about the provenance of our bed, when could get the results from DNA. His main objective was to collect samples; leaves and small wood-cuttings, chipped from the sides of older trees with a special chisel; a collection he meticulously arranged in airtight containers in the boot of the car. As well as confirming a match with our bed, DoubleHelix wanted to collect a range of older, Muna teak samples. In the end however, although samples from Muna did indeed match DNA from our bed, the results were inconclusive as newer bed-tests appeared equally close to profiles from Burma.

• • •

On my return to Singapore, I spent one year in a darkened studio, pressing paper against the black-inked boards of my teak bed and amassing variegated mounds of woodprints, which I tore into strips. I shuffled these print fragments around the floor for months; trying to work through our multiple Muna encounters.

An animated film evolved slowly from this process and a dark and dense aesthetic led by these ever-metamorphosizing print-fragments and charcoal. The main actors in the film were non-human; a bed, a cockatoo and a banyan. In a series of instances cockatoo flies into the frame and settles on a bed, a boat, a teak stump and Marina Bay Sands and shits a banyan seed. These encounters animate a dance between plantation teak and the migratory banyan, Muna tree-lore and plant genetics that I only partially understand, but in which perspectives of country officers, woodcutters, artists, engineers, *dukun dukun*, tree spirits and DNA code turn together and break apart in an urgent struggle over cut wood in rising seas on two islands after a timber boom.[21]

---

21   I'm grateful for extended conversations over many years with art historian Kevin Chua (who also gave critical feedback on a first draft of this essay).

CHAPTER 7

Tree Wound Portraits

Shannon Lee Castleman*

The following "tree wound" photographs are one part of an eight-year exploration of historic, material, genetic, and poetic stories of wood, trees, and people across Southeast Asia by The Migrant Ecologies Project, discussed by Lucy Davis, Migrant Ecologies founder and Principal Investigator for the research in the previous chapter.[1] The field trips that I was involved in concerned an attempt to trace the DNA from a teak bed found in a Singapore *karang guni* junk store back to the location of the possible plantation in Southeast Asia using DNA tracking technology.[2] Preliminary tests suggested a match between the DNA from our tree and century old plantations in Southeast Sulawesi. And so, we arranged a field trip to Muna, an island in Southeast Sulawesi in search of samples and stories.

Halfway through a visit to Muna Island Southeast Sulawesi, we discovered what I referred to as "tree-wounds"; multiple, deep cuts on the sides of trees not facing the road on many of the older teak trees in the conservation forest. Muna's conservation forests are older teak plantations that have been awarded konservasi or "conservation" forest status—not because of biodiversity (which was devastated by timber planting in the nineteenth and twentieth centuries) but because former plantations maintain the water table for the island.

Mr La Ode Imbo, a Muna oral historian explained to us that since felling teak in *konservasi* forests is illegal, impoverished villagers who pass by large teak trees over a period of months will give a tree one cut with an axe after another until finally the tree falls or dies and no one is to blame. Villagers were then able to profit from the wood since it was understood to have fallen without intervention.[3]

Once we began to notice these "wounds," we realized that this practice was occurring across the whole island: Trees that appeared whole from the roadside were cut away from behind. Indeed, the only *konservasi* plantations left unmarked were those considered to be haunted.

Months after that first visit to Muna I couldn't get these "Tree wounds" out of my mind. I decided to return to the island with a large sheet of black velvet and wandered the edges of the forests, taking portraits of the trees I could recall from my former visit as well as newly-wounded trees. Some of the trees had been cut down by the time of my next visit. Others I encountered actually hadn't been attacked for years and were just left standing in their wounded state by villagers who had given up on them. I was informed this was most likely because those trees were also thought to be haunted and it was believed that they would bring bad luck to the person who felled them.

* Castleman's project is part of the Migrant Ecologies Project 2010–2011.
1 See also Davis, L. (2018) 'Animation, Animism … Dukun Dukun & DNA' in this volume.
2 The first launch of works from this project was at the Royal Botanic Gardens Edinburgh 2013, a second incarnation of works was exhibited at the National University of Singapore Museum 2014– 2015 <http://migrantecologies.org/Trees-Part-3>, <http://migrantecologies.org/Trees-Stories>.
3 Interview with Muna oral historian Mr. La Ode Sirad Imbo, October 2011.

FIGURE 7.1   Shannon Lee Castleman, *Tree Wound*. Muna Island, Southeast Sulawesi, 2011
          © SHANNON LEE CASTLEMAN.

CHAPTER 8

Contested Sites: Forest as Uncommon Ground

Greg Ruffing

I arrive in the Pacific Northwest at the end of spring, in the midst of a long dry spell that has desaturated much of the lush green I've always associated with this place. As the train approaches downtown Seattle, I feel a mounting unease about some new sensations flooding over me: one of the first views of the city reveals a skyline rife with cranes—the urban landscape here is being reconfigured as an influx of new money and tech culture accelerates real estate speculation, gentrification, and displacement.

In Fremont, I meet up with friends and we kill the evening drinking whiskey at some neighborhood bars. A weekend night out here confirms some of my fears about the socioeconomic changes unfolding in the city, which grips me in cynicism and leads me to more whiskey. On the walk back home we pass a sixteen-foot bronze statue of Vladimir Lenin gazing out upon overdressed twenty-somethings swarming the new posh bars and restaurants on Fremont's main drag.

From Seattle I head north to Everett, a formerly prosperous lumber mill town whose blue-collar edges remind me of where I'm from in Ohio, where they used to trade Northwestern timber for Midwestern steel. With its vast forests of Douglas fir, Sitka spruce and western red cedar, the Pacific Northwest has been a major domestic source of lumber products since industrialized practices began there in the late nineteenth century. Barons like Rockefeller and Weyerhauser have enriched themselves through massive extraction of these trees, and at a high cost to the environment, to indigenous peoples, and to the bodies of working people.

Radical labor activism ran deep in the early days of the lumber industry here, and those seeking to organize workers and challenge labor contracts were often met with harassment, imprisonment, violence, and murder. I had stopped in town to search for remnants of the 1916 Everett Massacre, in which a gunfight erupted at the city dock between labor activists and a gang of heavily armed police and vigilantes hired by local lumber mill managers. The massacre—which capped off months of police-backed intimidation and assault of labor protestors who supported strikes by mill workers seeking better pay and work conditions—left two vigilantes and over a dozen activists dead.[1] Much of the tangible memory of these events is no longer visible in Everett, save for the diligent maintenance of two small, largely forgotten archives in the region.

From here I wind back southwest to reach the Olympic Peninsula, nestled between the Puget Sound and the Pacific coast. The ring road circling the peninsula is dotted with logging hamlets whose quaint murals cultivate local pride in the industrial history that has consumed the forests beyond the edges of town. Roadside signs and didactic displays at a local museum assert that those involved in logging have a deep affinity for the forest, both because most of them live in close proximity to it and because their livelihood depends on the harvesting and production of timber.

---

1 Accounts of the 1916 massacre remain contradictory and controversial. Much evidence indicates that the dead vigilantes were shot in the back, and hence were presumably killed by gunfire from their own men. Meanwhile, estimates of the number of activists killed have never been fully corroborated; multiple witnesses reported that some wounded protestors fell into the water and their bodies were never recovered.

© KONINKLIJKE BRILL NV, LEIDEN, 2019 | DOI:10.1163/9789004375253_010

Traversing rural routes and service roads, I photograph various clearcuts and logging sites on the peninsula and elsewhere. Among these images, one in particular lingers: the vista from a hilltop looking out over layered ridges of mangled forest, scarred vegetation, oxidized stumps and branches, and drag lines down steep slopes—all stitching together a timeline of different eras of tree harvest and extraction.

In his 1925 short story "A View from a Hill," M.R. James tells the fictional tale of a professor named Fanshawe who travels to the countryside to visit an old friend. As the two stroll to a hilltop overlook, Fanshawe uses a pair of field-glasses to scan across the scene. However, upon peering through the glasses, the panorama is disrupted by visions of barren, treeless fields and the deaths of hanged men; when he removes the glasses from his eyes, the pastoral view returns. Fanshawe eventually learns the glasses' macabre secret: their maker, a local man named Baxter who disappeared under mysterious circumstances, had experimented by filling the lenses with a fluid derived from the boiled bones of men who had been hanged on nearby Gallows Hill, a former site of mass executions. Fanshawe was "looking through dead men's eyes" and summoning violent pasts into visibility.[2]

In James's story, landscape isn't presented as picturesque, bucolic, or tranquil, but rather as a disquieting space of esoteric elements, contested ownerships, and partially obscured sufferings. The land becomes defined more by what is missing than by what is present—alternately, what is actually present is the *haunting* reminder of a lingering *absence*.

Such haunting is an experience of strangeness, uncertainty, or disorientation—altogether, a feeling of the uncanny. This brush with the uncanny occurs at a junction of subjectivity and history: while the former may derive from a psychological haunting in an individual's mind, the latter is rooted in social relations. As Avery Gordon writes, we are haunted "in the world of common reality... It is an enchanted encounter in a disenchanted world between familiarity and strangeness. The uncanny is the return of what the concept of the unconscious represses: the reality of being haunted by worldly contacts."[3]

What occluded narratives animate an uncanny encounter with the scarred landscape of a forest clearcut? Deforestation as a form of environmental violence intersects with issues such as labor rights, indigenous sovereignty, and other aspects of imperialism and colonialism that comprise the foundation of timber extraction in places like the Pacific Northwest. The initial logging boom there was partly enabled by a series of government treaties between Native American tribes and the first governor of Washington territory, Isaac Stevens. Through accords such as the Treaty of Medicine Creek (1854), the Treaty of Neah Bay (1855), the Quinault Treaty (1855) and others, indigenous peoples were stripped of most of their rights to ancestral lands and relegated to only controlling miniscule areas on specific reservations. These new land arrangements were enforced by martial law and military aggression ordered by Governor Stevens. By the 1880s, the government had transferred much of its acquired territory into forest preserves, which it began selling off to major lumber corporations.

According to estimates from the Environmental Defense Fund, globally over thirty million acres of trees were cut down each year between 2000 and 2009, figures that are especially troublesome for rainforests and old growth forests. In the Pacific Northwest in particular, over 90 percent of ancient forests have been destroyed since white settlers arrived in the nineteenth century. Today most of the old growth has been

---

2   James, M.R. (2011) 'A View from a Hill' in *Collected Ghost Stories* (Oxford and New York: Oxford University Press) p. 342.

3   Gordon, A. (2008) *Ghostly Matters: Haunting and the Sociological Imagination* (Minneapolis: University of Minnesota Press) pp. 54–55.

replaced by young second- or third-growth forests managed by technocratic, market-driven principles that seek to simultaneously frame the process as both economically rationalized and natural in the lifespan of the forest. The resulting clearcut practices, and the industrially planted forests that come afterward, have led to erosion, mudslides, destruction of microorganisms in the soil, damage to animal habitats, and an overall reduction in ecosystem biodiversity. Ultimately, deforestation has had a drastic effect on climate change because living trees—and especially old growth forests—play a vital role in carbon sequestration. When trees are felled, they release their stored carbon into the atmosphere, where it mixes with greenhouse gases from other sources.

Thrust into the present environs of consumer society, incidents of environmental degradation and past violence invoke a perpetual haunting of the commoditized lumber we use to construct and fortify the buildings we live and work in, the furniture we use, or the paper we print and write on—which all become more than just the ghosts of formerly living trees. And yet, as Marx details in his theory of the commodity fetish, the commodity's mystery lies in the obfuscation of this haunting—for inasmuch as the social and economic conditions of the commodity's production are masked, its material origins, the past human labor involved in its manufacture, and its ecological residue all constitute a ghostly absence.

That hilltop photograph, the arresting scene which remained with me, has become central to my installation piece *Contested Sites #4*. The totality of the image—and by metaphorical extension, its content—is ordered through the standardized measurements of 8.5 × 11 inch sheets of paper that comprise the panorama's gridded array. Photography has long participated in the subjugation of landscape, beginning from the early commissions of Carleton Watkins, Timothy O'Sullivan, and others whose survey images of the American West aided in the plotting and parcelization of land for corporate

interests. Here, however, the ripping, peeling, and curling of the prints seek to disrupt the illusionistic picture plane and expose the thin sheathing beneath, which props up the entire framework. This deconstruction is further reinforced as the viewer navigates around the sides and back where the installation's lumber skeleton is readily apparent. Assembled from a variety of timber products and by-products—including plywood, stick goods, cardboard, and consumer-grade laser jet paper—that were salvaged and sourced from the Pacific Northwest as much as possible, the artwork is intentionally ensnared in a critique of its own production. Its problematic materiality rejects a potential aesthetic escape, while posing questions about how our behaviors and decisions as citizens, artists, and a society at-large that still utilize and consume massive amounts of timber-based products thus implicates us in the clearcut forest. Yet the leaning placard-like objects and the capacity for the installation to function as a discursive gathering space suggest that our answers will likely reemphasize how the forest is a contested site.

Further, contested sites are haunted by temporal, ecological and social histories. In his essay "Ghosts in the City," Michel de Certeau emphasizes that all places are haunted by their pasts. For him, old items such as trees or buildings can act as spirits or "wild objects" that articulate a specific place within daily life. These "wild objects" are ceaselessly tied to the political and the social.[4] Similarly, the cut logs, denuded fields and hillsides, upturned soil, and decaying stumps of a logged site are not only the specters of lost trees—be it the young forms harvested and replanted every fifty years under scientific forestry, or their sacred old growth predecessors—they are also spirits that express how the landscape has been altered by the imposition of

4   de Certeau, M. (1998) 'Ghosts in the City' in *The Practice of Everyday Life, Volume 2: Living & Cooking* (Minneapolis: University of Minnesota Press) pp. 135–36.

FIGURE 8.1   Greg Ruffing, *Contested Sites #4* (*or, Forest as Uncommon Ground*), 2016. Cedar, Douglas fir, misc. scrap wood,
plywood, color laser jet prints, tape, cardboard, rope, misc. hardware.
© GREG RUFFING

human social relations onto nature. Perhaps we could then see the pillaging of nature through deforestation and resource extraction as deriving from the same capitalist mechanisms and ideologies that colonize, commoditize, and instrumentalize urban space.

CHAPTER 9

Quercus velutina, Art of Fiction, No. 1111011

Lindsey French

The interview with *Quercus velutina* began on June 3, 2012, and has continued in a dispersed manner ever since. The setting was a multitude of locations and times, stitched together with a number of devices, technological and literary, which I brought along to facilitate this unlikely conversation. This assembled apparatus included a vibration sensor, custom software, and the vocabulary of Virginia Woolf's *Orlando*, in addition to more ephemeral components. While reading aloud the entirety of *Orlando*, I measured *velutina*'s vibrational responses to establish a key of translation. Custom software translated the vibrations (read as electrical impulses) back into text, producing the novel *seductiveness the which issued by the whole person.*[1] The grove itself was a hickory oak forest in western Michigan, a hill of sandy soil near a lagoon just cut off from the shores of Lake Michigan. *Velutina* was one of the taller oaks in the forest, dominating the upper canopy with large branches and, in the summer and autumn especially, thick leaves alternately arranged, with bristle tipped lobes and deep U-shaped sinuses and notches. Surrounding *velutina* were a number of recently fallen trees, small shrubs, and of particular note, a newly planted *Quercus rubra*, young author of *upon writing grass* and mentee to the tall oak.[2] And of course always present was Virginia Woolf, not in any knowable ghostly form, but rather as a prior temporal resonance reaching out to this same species,[3] none of us so definable as individuals, bodies, or forms, but momentarily sharing a language and a medium for translation and frustration to be experienced

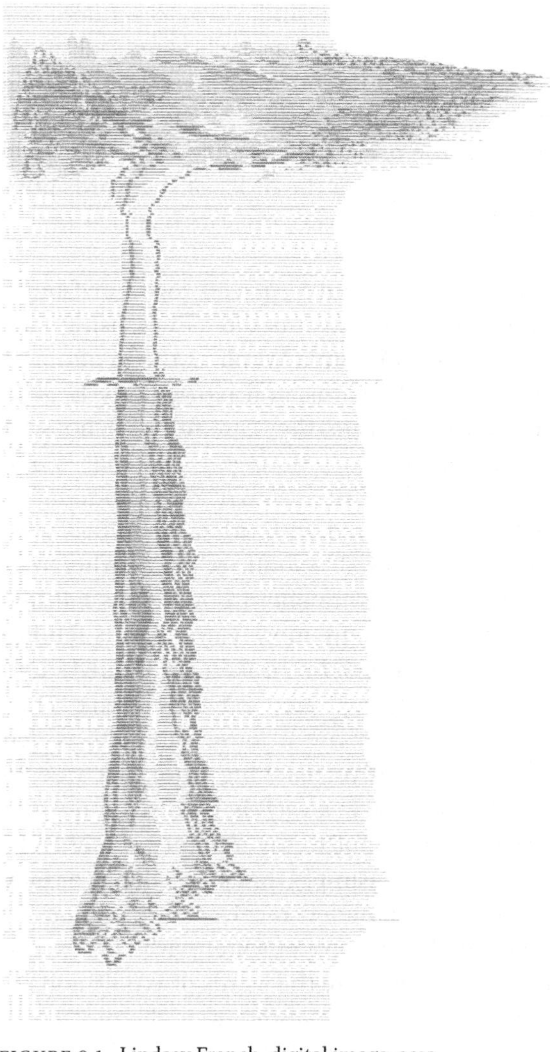

FIGURE 9.1 Lindsey French, digital image, 2012. CC BY-SA (CREATIVE COMMONS ATTRIBUTION-SHAREALIKE INTERNATIONAL 4.0).

1 For more information, see the introduction to *seductiveness the which issued by the whole person,* 2012.

2 *upon writing grass* was written by a red oak, *Quercus rubra,* in Chicago, the next generation in this series of texts.

3 The oak tree was a main character in *Orlando*, both as a living oak and the title of Orlando's lifelong manuscript.

 DOI:10.1163/9789004375253_011

together in the woods, and now, through traces of vocabulary.

A tree articulates itself in its positioning and its growth. It communicates via molecules of information: volatile airborne chemicals, nutrients and signal in the roots, clicks and sonic waves moving material slightly, subtly below the surface of the ground. *Quercus velutina* is a pen name, or rather, an inadequate and dodging signature of the novelist, a general pointing towards and rough outline of the organism, or rather of the organized assemblage responsible in some manner for the order of the words published as *seductiveness the which issued by the whole person.*

This conversation is pieced together from a number of previously unedited lines, using a vocabulary from Virginia Woolf as the medium of translation. Of words, and particularly English words, Woolf wrote, they "are full of echoes, of memories, of associations [...] And that is one of the chief difficulties in writing them today—that they are stored with other meanings, with other memories..."[4] Woolf, at this earlier moment in time, wrote about how words fail her. Us too. But in many more ways. Words fail because they cannot be broken into "single and separate entit[ies]," And yet they break. They fail because they are a loose substrate which hold this tentative reaching from oak tree to me. Plants signal in a way that is distributed and passive. This is not to say a plant's signal lacks intentionality—simply that a signal may or may not have an intended receiver. In listening for intentionality, we are not met with clarity. The words of *velutina* are the words of Woolf, and *velutina* is as much the author as is the molecular releases and the soil of the dunes and the telephone lines and the raving quietness of my time there, and of you. And they fail us all.

Our conversations were built around miscommunication and archive. Any mistakes in translation I blame on the impossibility of the media

of communication and the ability to transpose a conversation across a rift. I have tried then to parse the results of these conversations, shape them through my own queries, as one might filter from a static of white noise to listen for distinctive tones or timbres, or find in soft static a meaningful note. But *velutina* was withdrawn, as was I, and what remains is a reaching out, an articulation of the celebrity nature that trees as general figures hold in human culture, and an attempt at connecting through our momentary singularity. Given the unique spatiotemporal experience of *velutina*, the interview required years of communication, which has been distilled to the following translations, a precarious collaboration where the problematics remain chiefly with me and the limits of my perception, and now you as reader. Any moments of clarity remain as either projections or rare and special moments of intimate negotiation.

INTERVIEWER

The tree in general, and the oak specifically, is often positioned as a literary figure, part of a potent myth of humankind. Where do you situate yourself in the lineage of literary trees?

VELUTINA

Here roots, and above there ground, that life time us in exquisite literature, as the always tree, the Prayer a tree, make trees, tongue the perhaps language.

INTERVIEWER

Trees have been positioned as human analogues to the nonhuman world, the site of dreams, desiring, upon you, the tree.[5] Michael Marder

---

4   Virginia Woolf, 'Craftsmanship,' p. 203.

5   The list of trees as casual examples is extensive, but a few notable linguistic examples include: Ferdinand de Saussure, "Whether we try to find the meaning of the Latin word *arbor* or the word that Latin uses to designate the concept "tree," it is clear that only the associations sanctioned by that language appear to us to conform to reality, and we disregard whatever others might be imaged" (The Nature of the Linguistic Sign, *Course in General Linguistics*, p. 26);

writes about plants as a kind of synecdoche for nature.[6] Are you able to reflect or deflect the human gaze and its assumptions casually cast on you?

VELUTINA

not often reflecting,
tied encountering alluding round obstacle.
He reflected family of haziness
nobody displayed eyes.
that purposely our—
But symmetry moved?
nobody knew.

INTERVIEWER

Is there a kind of asymmetry in your collaborations with human editors or readers? I'm thinking particularly of *seductiveness the which issued from the whole person.*

VELUTINA

The hour, lips find froze paper, words wonder.
No condition time. and now? gardens visible?
study, and mouldy words and said that. —
'Whose manuscript

_____

Roland Barthes, "the concept of tree is vague, it lends itself to multiple contingencies. True, a language always has at its disposal a whole appropriating organization (this tree, the tree which, etc.). But there always remains, around the final meaning, a halo of virtualities where other possible meanings are floating..." (Barthes, p. 132)."Every object in the world can pass from a closed, silent existence to an oral state, open to appropriation by society, for there is no law, whether natural or not, which forbids talking about things. A tree is a tree. Yes, of course. But a tree as expressed by Minou Drouet is no longer quite a tree, it is a tree which is decorated, adapted to a certain type of consumption, laden with literary self-indulgence, revolt, images, in short with a type of social usage which is added to pure matter" (Barthes, p. 109). And see footnote 8. And even Deleuze and Guattari, as they are trying to move away from tree structures, reference the human relationship of parent to child (filiation) in a distinction between the tree and the rhizome, "A rhizome has no beginning or end; it is always in the middle, between things, intermezzo. The tree is filiation, but the rhizome is alliance" (Deleuze and Guattari, p. 25).

6   Michael Marder, *Plant-Thinking*, p. 3.

he single He iron, oak incessantly and tree. as forest; walnut on the tables ...
blood so, suddenly was lean and tables words drawn, trees of words,
that oak came stained words lay the words
yet we glance speech to omit

INTERVIEWER

You mentioned family earlier. We speak of lineages as trees—arborescent hierarchies, Linnaean taxonomies, branching evolutionary structures. You, your very name, *Quercus velutina*, ignores your singularity in its description of you as a species.[7] It avoids your specific being, as a tree, in this moment in time. And so the "you" I'm using is problematic. I don't know what to call you. Is this a resistance to naming, to knowing? Or perhaps more pointedly, in calling you "You," am I establishing I?

VELUTINA

eternal You
as you, her double dearest,

INTERVIEWER

And Virginia Woolf—

VELUTINA

Orlando's novelist

INTERVIEWER

You were using her vocabulary, or rather, your impulses were translated using texts written by Virginia Woolf.

VELUTINA

Orlando words, suddenly tossed pass Love's difficulty
When truth; was—himself. dead.

INTERVIEWER

You consider truth to be dead? Is the concept of "nature" dead as well?

_____

7   Again, see Michael Marder, *Plant-Thinking*.

VELUTINA

nature and its short, answer questions, said tense spur flight;

INTERVIEWER

Yes, a question said tense might cause flight—a release of molecule, or emotion, or an affective response not held by words. Do you respond more to my presence than to my verbal language?

VELUTINA

We stories. melody the of been the as words not. before was this truth crowd story repository stories
There, discourse. affections, even on before known when him, the struck. told through the story the peace so of mind.

INTERVIEWER

Sometimes a story can really be striking, can hit us hard and we feel it. Barthes writes about "speaking the tree."[8] This could be read as a materialist view of communication—that in order for a communication to occur, there must be a kind of transformation. Did you undergo a transformation when producing the text?

VELUTINA

over darkness. words to Translating which, turning on again… as strange.
poetry None prose, like a a woman, fox, play or poet; so words. raved, like height; a colour, height; sound like breathing emerald;
Orlando words, suddenly tossed at

---

8   "whatever the form of my sentence, I 'speak the tree', I do not speak about it….between the tree and myself, there is nothing but my labor, that is to say, an action. This is a political language: it represents nature for me only inasmuch as I am going to transform it…But if I am not a woodcutter, I can no longer 'speak the tree', I can only speak about it, on it…I no longer have anything more than an intransitive relationship with the tree; this tree is no longer the meaning of reality as a human action, it is an image-at-one's- disposal" (Barthes, p. 145).

may many of words sound anecdotes of floating to is statements. untruthful, that host words Book. if bold knowingly

INTERVIEWER

I think there is a question hovering here in the background about whether or not we can interpret a novel written by an oak tree as meaningful. There exist at the edge of your readership certain questions about your role.

VELUTINA

midnight seductiveness—again, issued there as person.

INTERVIEWER

That title, *seductiveness issued by the whole person*, touches on intimacy, something we've been talking about here and are experiencing as well. Is this a reference to the alluring nature of otherness? Is there an inherent seductiveness in which the form of communication this novel engages?

VELUTINA

Love? of limbs cried, nature, grew it passion heavy
if this a sanded loping past and Her greens in the the tingled who heads suddenly come Though romance, hardy questions folly,
Love's difficulty distant it of his soft flower over.

INTERVIEWER

The young oak, *Quercus rubra*, continued in your tradition as a writer, using your text as a vocabulary source. This is not an ordinary mentorship—*rubra* is of the same genus but not the same species. Were there crossed signals? How did you navigate that relationship?

VELUTINA

This was extraordinary both adored
queer
in it, to gesture the poetry tree,
let found in her no name.

FIGURE 9.2 Lindsey French, video still, 2012.

PART 3

Garden

∴

CHAPTER 10

Falling from Grace

Giovanni Aloi

You may chisel a boy into shape, as you would a rock, or hammer him into it, if he be of better kind, as you would aa piece of bronze. But you cannot hammer a girl into anything. She grows as a flower does.

JOHN RUSKIN, *Sesame and Lilies*[1]

∴

Paradise haunts gardens, and some gardens are paradises. Mine is one of them. Others are like bad children, spoilt by their parents, over-watered and covered with noxious chemicals.

DEREK JARMAN, *Derek Jarman's Garden*[2]

∴

A cactus next to a cherry tree. Gerberas, primulas, roses, gladiola, calla lilies, delphiniums, tulips, orchids, pansies, red and white anthuriums, chrysanthemums, pitcher plants, and sunflowers together and simultaneously in bloom. The picture is breathtakingly beautiful, yet the static composure of this unusual ensemble is made eerie by the freshly trimmed and compact English lawn from which the plants emerge. Indeed, something about this picture is just too perfect, too silent, and too still. In Marc Quinn's 2000 installation titled *Garden* over one thousand plants, at the peak of their aesthetic glory, have been immersed in twenty-five tons of low-viscosity silicone maintained at -20° Celsius.[3] A 12.7 × 5.43 × 3.2 meter cold room houses a tank in which this enchanted garden exists—it maintains the temperature of the silicone and that of the surrounding gallery space constant. The spectacle is sublime, or as many would report: otherworldly. *Garden*, as the title suggests, is essentially a utopia: the artistic incarnation of man's desire to control nature, to select, and organize what we find beautiful in it, to make this beauty visible, and most importantly, to prevent it from ever fading. But in its dioramic stasis, Quinn's installation does more than display natural beauty—the opposite is, in fact, true. The piece inscribes multiple and contradicting narratives of human and nature coevolutions through the geocultural delimitation of the garden: a space heavily riddled with symbolism, defined by specific power/knowledge relationships, and driven by often implicit and problematic aesthetic desires for purity and perfection.

In Judeo-Christian beliefs, the garden appears as the quintessential place of otherworldly harmony—a harmony man ruined when Adam and Eve ate the forbidden fruit from the Tree of Knowledge, thus acquiring an awareness of good and evil that made them godlike. With that also came the awareness of nakedness and the experience of an irreconcilable separateness from nature. This narrative has, at least in the Western world, tinged gardens with a sense of nostalgia. It is therefore not an understatement to say that many Renaissance and Enlightenment gardens mainly attempted to metaphorically restore the Garden of Eden on Earth. As

1   Ruskin, J. quoted in Sloane Kennedy, W. (1886) *Art and Life: A Ruskin Anthology* (New York: J.B. Alden) p. 39.
2   Jarman, D. (1995) *Derek Jarman's Garden* (New York and London: Thames and Hudson).
3   Prada, M., Celant, G., Leader, D., Quinn, M. (2000) *Marc Quinn* (Milano: Fondazione Prada) p. 286.

FIGURE 10.1 Marc Quinn, *Garden*, cold room, stainless steel, heated glass, refrigerating equipment, mirrors, turf, real plants, acrylic tank, low viscosity silicone oil held at −20°C.
PHOTO: ATTILIO MARANZANO. COURTESY: MARC QUINN STUDIO AND FONDAZIONE PRADA
© MARC QUINN.

the study of animals and plants emerged from the religious tales of the Bestiarium, and the epistemological approach of early natural history and botany substantially drew from its pages, it follows that Renaissance botanic gardens also originated from Biblical interpretations.[4] To recreate Edenic utopias constituted an attempt to reveal the greatness of God's work in a bid for salvation.

Quinn's installation specifically leverages upon the spiritual narrative of separateness between man and nature as symbolized by the tank which encapsulates the plants. All around it, a wall of mirrors relentlessly reconfigures this separation into a fictitious image of communion with the plants, thus producing the illusion of a restored unity. But the frozen silicone, which suspends the beauty of the flowers into a timeless state, prevents us from ever reentering the lost Edenic vision. Marc Quinn explained the impact Adam and Eve's action bore on the vegetal world as follows:

> people thought that when Adam and Eve were expelled from the Garden of Eden, all the plants in it were scattered all over the world. The idea ... was that, if they could bring them all together again in one place,

4   Drayton, R. (2000) *Nature's Government: Science, Imperial Britain, and the 'Improvement' of the World* (London: Yale University Press) and Prest, J.M. (1981) *The Garden of Eden: The Botanic Garden and the Re-Creation of Paradise* (New Haven and London: Yale University Press).

then it would be possible to recreate the Garden of Eden and the wisdom of God.[5]

But the ineluctable impossibility of reconstituting the harmony of the Garden of Eden, along with our unity with nature, looms large over Quinn's artificial attempt. As the artist said, "there is something sinister about a beauty that does not decay. Like *The Picture of Dorian Gray,* it implies decay somewhere else."[6] In fact, what is indeed striking about *Garden* is the conspicuous technological infrastructure required for the production of the vegetal assemblage. The imposing stainless steel cold room relies on the constant work of generators and refrigerating units to maintain the required temperature, while tube lamps especially designed to withstand temperatures of -50° Celsius enable visibility. A power failure would mean the disastrous demise of this heavenly vision. From this perspective, *Garden* can be perceived as a post-apocalyptic space in which the environmental degradation can no longer support life, except for climatically controlled human-made simulacra.

Quinn is right: if somewhere beauty does not decay, somewhere else something must be. The botanic garden, as well as the more common urban garden, is always a site of struggle in which man works hard at repairing what has been damaged elsewhere, outside the garden. Today, more than ever, the garden represents the artificially preserved oasis amidst the challenges of climate change. And in so doing, it metaphorically inscribes the desire to control the planet in an efficient, self-substantiated way. The "good gardener" optimizes and supplements nature's unpredictability. She/he provides water at regular intervals in order to keep all plants alive— fertilization, anti-parasitic treatment, and soil quality are essential to blooming/harvesting success. The rationalization, management, and provision of resources typical of gardening processes entails a utopian model that has over the last century become the blueprint of ecological approaches. But there is growing unease with the notion that we should, to begin with, perceive ourselves as "stewards of nature." Slavoj Žižek has controversially pointed out that blaming ourselves for climate change constitutes a strategy designed to still maintain some sort of control over nature. "If it is us who are the bad guys, all we have to do is change our behavior," he argues.[7]

Against the persistent notion of stewardship, Žižek proposes a radical aesthetic change, one that accounts for human activity as part of the complex naturecultures that have unfolded over time. His provocative claim that we should feel at home spiritually, visually, and intellectually in a landfill constitutes a totally antisublime turn grounded in a deep mistrust for ecology's purism and conservative approaches. Žižek might be right on many accounts. But perhaps, the landfill may not be the most productive site around which to rethink our undeniably problematic coevolution with ecosystems. Surpassing disavowal is essential to our future on this planet, but what Žižek's realism points to how impossible it is to cling to our past notions of nature in any productive way. However, snapping out of the cultural loop that constantly and implicitly conflates ecology with a Garden of Eden-like vision as a model of purity entails a leap into certain darkness.

"Nature-culture coevolutions" can be traced in the flowers composing Quinn's garden since they all are *cultivars*: varieties selectively bred over time to accentuate desirable characteristics. These flowers are the result of centuries (sometimes millennia) of nature-culture processes designed to tailor plants according to our

---

5 Prada, M., Celant, G., Leader, D., Quinn, M. (2000), p. 214.
6 Ibid., p. 213.

7 Žižek, S. (2013) 'Slavoj Žižek: Ecology is the new opiate of the masses' in *Dustysojourner.Wordpress*, online: [<https://dustysojourner.wordpress.com/2013/01/15/slavoj-zizek-ecology-is-the-new-opiate-of-the- masses/>] accessed on 27 March 2016.

own desires: how big a flower should be, how deep its coloration, how intense its fragrance. Simultaneously, by biologically allowing certain changes to happen, and forbidding others, plants have shaped our aesthetic taste and our economies, along with our senses.

The reconstruction of the Garden of Eden proposed by Quinn is far from the still, unadulterated vision of biblical nature it portrays. Yet we insist on projecting a mystified attribution of purity into gardens even when man's manipulation is visibly obvious. We regularly look at our gardens as retreats from capitalist economies of exploitation that dictate the frantic rhythms of our everyday lives spent in polluted urban environments. Yet any garden is the result of multiple capitalist transactions, from the land to the tools, from the shingles and pebbles to fertilizers and pesticides, and not to mention the plants purchased from the gardening center—nothing in the garden is ever "pure" in the "natural" sense. Contradicting and flimsy notions of authenticity always proliferate in garden narratives, which ultimately inscribe ideological and biographical texts.

My garden, for example, gathers a number of plants that are part of my personal mythologies—many have acquired their iconic status because of the roles they have played in my childhood (hibiscuses, oleander, artichokes, honeysuckle, angel and devil trumpets, zinnias...) others are more recent incorporations of my adult life and reflect my taste for color and structure (amaranth, irises, elephant ears, ferns...). And last but not least, many others find a place in the garden according to the resources they provide to insects and other inhabitants and visitors (fennel, echinacea, milkweed, and butterfly weed).

Quinn's *Garden* too is an amalgamation of symbols—more precisely, its mix of exotic and indigenous species constitutes a commentary on the historical forces of financial power over the lives of man and plants alike. Quinn's extremely varied range of flowering plants could not possibly coexist in the same garden due to their drastically different climatic needs. Not even a greenhouse could keep them alive in this proximity, never mind blooming at unison. This wealth marked by the outstandingly exuberant forms and coloration of exotic species, metonymically maps appropriative economies grounded in the past histories of colonialism. A few centuries ago, many of these plants were transported to Europe as tokens of dominion over distant cultures that were regularly misrepresented, misunderstood, and objectified. This connotation raises questions of cultural and biological origins of difference as amongst other exhibiting devices, notions of otherness were constructed through the painting of exotic animals and plants as markers of a primitive essence.

Henri Rousseau's naïve paintings from the end of the Victorian era can be used as an example. The artist never traveled abroad but almost exclusively painted tropical forests populated by dense vegetation and non-European animals. He combined separate sketches made at the botanic garden, zoo, and natural history museum in Paris. Technically, his paintings are collages of precontextualized colonialist epistemological sites.[8] Like in Quinn's *Garden*, Rousseau's paintings perform a suspended sense of livingness—both aesthetics, the naïve and the contemporary, are the result of neat organization and composition. In different ways, they both attempt to construct a sanitized space of resistance and domestication, a vision of nature counterbalancing the dramatic changes imposed by industrialization.

Rousseau's canvases of tropical forests attempt to repair the alienation of the modern metropolis by staging essentially urban gardens posing as "peaceful, exotic paradise." And it is also not a coincidence that most of the human

---

8   Green, C., Morris, F. (2005) *Henri Rousseau: Jungles in Paris* (London: Tate Publishing).

FIGURE 10.2   Henri Rousseau, *Equatorial Jungle*, oil on canvas, 1909, Chester Dale Collection.
IMAGE IN PUBLIC DOMAIN COURTESY OF THE NATIONAL GALLERY OF ART, WASHINGTON DC.

figures in Rousseau's paintings are female, some black and some white. The myth of organic wholeness intrinsic to conceptions of nature inscribes femininity as its originator, as that which gives life, nurtures, and supports. Patriarchal visions have constructed nature as female

to validate the necessity for domestication and subjugation, by association, of both women and natural resources. This also applies to Quinn's garden, in which, as the artist humorously says, the silicone can be understood as a having a kind of "cyber-maternal quality" because it is "the same liquid used in breast implants."[9] But, it is also worth noting that this conception of the symbolism of silicone in the installation stands in diametrical opposition to Donna Haraway's model of cyborg identity as the theorization of a future reconfiguration of femininity based on a postnatural model. In Haraway's conception, the boundaries of the body are deliberately blurred through a new mapping of ecospheres that no longer recognizes the Garden of Eden as a site of origin.[10] However, regardless of the cyborgian disavowal of this connection, over the past two hundred years, the gardening industry has worked hard at rooting the traditional conception of femininity as passive, submissive, nurturing, and giving through the practice of gardening. Myriad books, magazines, and gardening products have packaged modern gardening as a quintessentially female activity. The history of western representation has consistently and conveniently associated women with subjects perceived as delicate, therefore neither posing a threat or resistance to patriarchal dominance. Women like flowers; women like butterflies... Yet, this is not always true in all strata of cultural engagement for most of botanical researchers, as well as lepidopterists, are indeed men.

To better understand this phenomenon, it is worth considering the double register of feminine inscription/construction of capitalist consumption involved in gardening practices. Flowers, foliage, and butterflies populate a conspicuous amount of female interest publications in which notions of taste, frailty, decorum, and care have been pieced together into an especially pacifying capitalist economy-system of cultural surface: *the hobby*. Hobbies are by definition "pastimes," superficial forms of pseudocultural engagements designed to keep one's mind and hands busy on innocuous and creative practices extrinsic to the professional and political realm. Its purpose is to provide recreation from the meaningless and repetitive tasks of factory and office work. Like sewing during the nineteenth century, gardening was meant to keep women busy, away from politics, finance, and the desire of pursuing a professional career. In its circular twistedness, capitalism has always provided both the affliction and the cure and has monetized both all along the way. It is in this context that an entire publishing industry dedicated to gardening as a gender specific activity flourished during the second half of the last century.[11]

Aware of these entanglements, artist, curator, and advertising executive Erik Kessels has gathered a number of found photographs in a volume cunningly titled *Mother Nature*. The content of the book comprises images found in flea markets, junk shops, and fairs. They are anonymous fragments of past lives, which in the hands of Kessels appear contextually interlinked in a slow-burning process exposing the ideology that underpins their recurring iconographical recursivity. In his chosen photographs, women are captured posing in or in front of gardens, usually wearing floral pattern dresses. Although anonymous, the photographs intrinsically entails the coordinates of a male gaze, more specifically that of husbands. In almost every picture the relationship between subject and background is clearly associative on multiple levels: the cultural links between flowers, gardens, femininity, and motherhood, ultimately results in an objectification exemplified through what was, as recently as the second half of the 20th century, a predominantly masculine hobby: photography. These images are somewhat unwittingly and naïvely reparational in meaning. They enshrine women in ideological notions of purity, passivity, beauty, fertility, and compliance—values

9   Prada, M., Celant, G., Leader, D., Quinn, M. (2000), p. 215.

10   Haraway, D. (1991, 2013) *Simians, Cyborgs, and Women: The Reinvention of Nature* (London: Routledge), pp. 151–52.

11   Horwood, C. (2011) *Gardening Women* (Windsor: Windsor/Paragon).

FIGURE 10.3 Erik Kessels, *From Mother Nature*, published by RVB Books 2, 2014
© ERIK KESSELS.

that symbolically redeem them: this iconography returns women to the Garden of Eden, prior to Eve's encounter with the snake, as man's passive/obedient companion and object of desire at hand. Decay is the aesthetic dimension external to the garden for this very reason—it implicitly reminds us of the fall from grace, and with that, of the ineluctability of death, the moment of the universal judgement. For this reason, we are culturally trained to remove all dying growth from the aesthetic utopianism the garden is meant to embody. But beneath the foliage and showy flowers lies the sliver of unbridled life "good gardeners" always attempt to repress. What we call parasites and pests, namely aphids, caterpillars, snails, and slugs, constantly challenge the gardener's desire to organize and preserve. The photographic imagery Sharon Core produced for the series *Understory* captures just that—the undercurrent of interconnected biosystems we have been taught to erase for the purpose of reconstructing godly perfection.

The lighting in Core's photographs has a painterly quality that unequivocally links them to the undergrowth works of Dutch Baroque artist Otto Marseus van Schrieck. His *tenebrist* imagery, illuminated by a soft Caravaggesque chiaroscuro, problematized the intricacy of artistic and scientific debates of the seventeenth century. His approach can be seen as the combination of older religious symbolic orders of natural history's past and a newer scientific concern with objective realism in scientific illustration. Likewise, Core's photographs ambiguously situate themselves at the intersection of two related value systems of natural representation: the photographic truth and the painted illusion. While her images appear to capture a truer representational level of the life of a garden; the lighting suggests a substantial level of manipulation on behalf of the artist. Yet, this intervention is aimed at producing an *antigarden* effect where weeds and cultivars are allowed to flourish next to each other and where decaying leaves, snails, caterpillars, and fungal infestations are celebrated as an essential component of biosystems worthy of photographic attention. Ultimately the poetic darkness of these images stands as a challenge to the primacy of scientific positivism that constructs our understanding of nature. This darkness blurs the boundaries of otherness, infiltration, and corruption preventing clear distinctions, hindering rationality.

The boundary, and its precariousness, effectively is the essence of the garden as an epistemological space: fences, gates, pathways, borders, and lawns—the garden is a perimeter internally fragmented into different "sections of containment," each inscribing different ideologies of purity, order, and truth. Garden borders are always more than a frontier delineating the ownership of land. To scale, their cartographies pose the same challenges faced by nations in controlling borders and maintaining intact an always-under-threat sense of national/personal identity. It is not a coincidence therefore that the permeability of boundaries can easily cause neighborly conflict: a fallen branch, a rampant climber, invasive roots—for the sake of neighborly peace-keeping, garden economies should remain contained.

However, in the garden, internal conflict regularly is a matter of plant on plant encumbrance. As mentioned, collapsing the norms of botanical ontology, Sharon Coe's undergrowth photographs juxtapose cultivar varieties to those we would usually call weeds. It is important at this stage to acknowledge that weeds are essentially a capitalist construct. In woodlands, prairies, savannahs, or forests weeds simply do not exist—they do not exist in the sense that their presence is not culturally encoded within a particular perimeter of rationality. The weed is a liminal being defined by borders—it metaphorically and literally lives on the edge. A weed is a plant defined by geography much more than it is a plant characterized by its biological or aesthetic qualities. It only exists inside the garden, on the edge of the road, in front of the garage door, in the crack on the pathway. In essence, a weed is a plant in the wrong place. Weeds transgress boundaries and instate themselves without permission. Paradoxically, they are more "natural" than any other plant in the garden, yet, they are demonized like no other. Here comes the contradiction: while highly manipulated cultivars embody the essence of Edenic beauty, weeds have been to hell and back. A weed is an unwanted nuisance that seemingly parasitizes the garden by subtracting light, soil, and water from cultivars. The black cat of plants, with many more than nine lives at its disposal: a weed never seems to properly die. It insistently stalks petunias and pansies, bringing diseases to the rest of the garden (so many people think), contaminating purity with sometimes irreversible consequences. According to common perception, the weed takes over; it takes everything away, and gives nothing in return. The weed is a saboteur. We technically are at constant war with them. Humor aside, this ideology unfortunately underlines and substantiates a multimillion dollar industry based on the notion of "weed control" in the name of which we routinely poison ourselves and the land upon which we live, other animals, and the plants we desire or consume too.

Weeds are symbolically charged like no other category of plants, and it is because they are ontologically defined by the economies of human geographies that they have more recently infiltrated contemporary art. In this context, the anthropomorphic value essential to weed symbolism is brought to the fore more explicitly and disturbingly. Conflict, in the new millennium, is more than ever before grounded in new conceptions of territory, invasion, and appropriation that are magnified by the media. It is therefore not a surprise that the sinister anthropomorphism weeds inscribe powerfully resounds with developments in the European migrant's crisis, the waves of the diaspora in the Middle East, and the illegal immigration issues in the US, just to name a few. Nominally, at stake is cultural and financial stability—the utopian notion that a country might preserve an integral sense of identity through essentially xenophobic maneuvers. In short, the weed is always the Other—the Other which simultaneously threatens and constructs selfness, the one which is and isn't, the relative absolute referent which instills a very specific anxiety related to transience, temporality, and corruption.

For these reasons, more recently, artistic materializations of weeds have cast this constructed villain as an uncelebrated symbol of resistance—the weed resists capitalism by refusing to comply with aesthetic standards and economic values. We have been educated to find weeds aesthetically unattractive and to mistrust their fruits if any they offer. Through

a paradigm similar to that which imbues moral rectitude in the toned bodies of Greek athletes, the proportioned beauty of cultivated plants inscribes a noble sense of rationality acquired through discipline. The subtext of the *cultivar-culture* is rooted in classical patriarchal values of proportion, clarity, solidity, and strength. These are values that artist Michael Landy has aimed to substantially undermine in his drawing practice.

Landy came to fame in the early 1990s along with his Young British Artists peers who heavily capitalized on shock-tactics in their art for the purpose of attracting media attention and reaching wider audiences. But Landy's approach has mostly been somewhat quieter and meditative in nature—but most importantly, it has been essentially nonaffirmative in aim. From his *Break Down* (2001) performance installation piece in which he publicly destroyed all his possessions, to his deliberately flimsy and intentionally unfinished portraits, Landy's art has always operated in the twilight of classical values. The uncertainty, the insecurity, the subtlety of his pencil drawings embodies his predilection for a muted but subversive potentiality linked to vulnerability. Upon releasing the portfolio of thirty-some etchings of weeds drawn from specimens collected in East London, the artist said that weeds "are marvelous, optimistic things that you find in inner London ... They occupy an urban landscape which is very hostile, and they have to be adaptable and find little bits of soil to prosper."[12] Titled *Nourishment*, the collection of images reinterprets the iconographic modality of the classical herbarium through a transcendental configuration of space—here humble weeds are outlined with much precision and care as they float suspended in time and in a deterritorialized representational dimension. Landy's observation and transcription of the most minute details of each plant,

12   Buck, L. (2002) 'Champion of the urban weed' in *The Art Newspaper*, December.

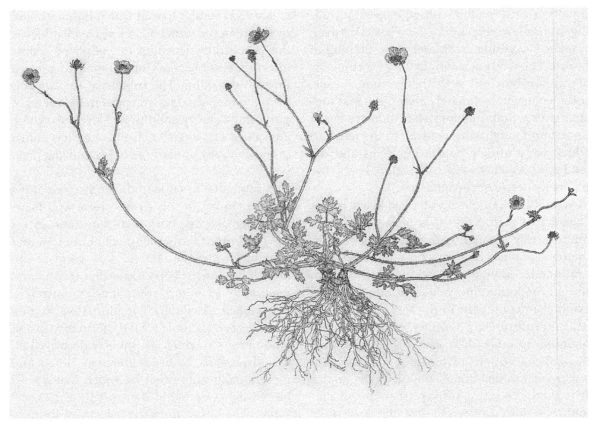

FIGURE 10.4   Michael Landy, *Creeping Buttercup (nourishment series)*, 2002. Image courtesy the artist and Thomas Dane
Gallery, London
© MICHAEL LANDY.

including their root systems, simultaneously subjugates the plant to a positivist aesthetic while freeing it from the geographical connotations which determine its weed status. This process enables the emergence of a fragile beauty that transcends the bold aesthetic essence of most garden cultivars.

One of the most valued aesthetic attributes in the selective breeding of modern day cultivars is what the industry calls the "compact-demeanor." This highly desirable morphological trait produces "tidy plants," maximizing the use of garden space as well as aesthetic, compositional impact. But Landy's weeds are straggly and thin and in opposition to the tradition of botanical illustration or Dutch still-life painting, leaves and flowers are not immortalized at the height

of their freshness either. Everything about them is anti-heroic, nonsublime, and devoid of drama. This is what makes these drawings uniquely charming, for they show something without the assumption of having conquered what is being shown.

Provocatively, in his surprisingly well received 2010 book, *Weeds,* natural history writer Richard Mabey brings his readers to consider the possibility that weeds are in fact our best companion species when it comes to the vegetal world. As he says:

Weeds thrive in the company of humans. They aren't parasites because they can exist without us, but we are their natural ecological partners, the species alongside

FIGURE 10.5   Abraham Cruzvillegas, *Empty Lot*, 2016. PUBLIC DOMAIN.

which they do best. They relish the things we do to the soil: clearing forests, digging, farming, dumping nutrient rich rubbish. They flourish in arable fields, battlefields, parking lots, herbaceous borders. They exploit our transport systems, our cooking adventures, our obsession with packaging. Above all they use us when we stir the world up, disrupt its settled patterns.[13]

In this sense, weeds can be seen as an opportunistic form of companion species that, as Mabey argues, also establishes symbiotic relations with us through partnerships providing materials, medicines, dyes, and thus indispensable to pre-agricultural times—a relationship reconfigured by modern capitalist economies.[14]

The relationship between the human impact on environments and weeds' ability to fill any space we impact was also the focus of an unprecedented installation in Tate Modern's cavernous Turbine Hall gallery. In 2015, Mexican conceptual artist Abraham Cruzvillegas collected samples of bare soil from thirty-six parks and gardens all over London and organized them in a composition of equally sized, triangular, raised beds. Lights and daily watering ensured the possibility of germination, but the artist refrained from directly planting anything into the soil—he deliberately played with our expectations and hopes. Within the context of the art museum, which has trained viewers to only expect pleasant and sublime representations of nature, *Empty Lot* takes on the atavic task to rewire our expectations when nature is inserted in the gallery space. The installation attempts to show us that nothing is ever empty, even when

13   Mabey, R. (2010) *Weeds: In Defense of Nature's Most Unwanted Plants* (New York: Ecco) p. 12.

14   Ibid.

FIGURE 10.6   Derek Jarman, *Garden in Dungeness*, ALH1 CC BY-ND 2.0.

at first glance it might seem so. Upon seeing the weeds spontaneously germinating from the ground, some visitors wondered what the point of it all might be. In essence, the piece is a plea for a new aesthetic: to look in the hope of seeing something, without expecting a showy rose, a colorful bed of marigolds, or a field of poppies. It's about shifting one's own cultural expectations while still finding interest in looking as a non-preencoded activity.

Cruzvillegas's installation was built entirely from recycled materials and found objects he gathered from around Tate Modern. In opposition to Marc Quinn's *Garden*, where the Edenic vision of harmonious nature was kept alive by a complex technological interface, Cruzvillegas's makes do with a self-powered bare minimum, gesturing therefore to a new, realist aesthetic register of sustainability which mirrors the shift in expectations we now have on bigger ecologies outside the gallery space. To further problematize his conceptual statement, the artist has deliberately upturned the man-managed spaces of well-tended London gardens and parks, disturbing soil to allow weeds to show themselves in a different geographic territory. In the gallery, space weeds acquire a new register of visibility usually denied by capitalism. The proposal is a difficult one, especially at a time in which we are hyper stimulated by ever fast-moving imagery on TVs, computer screens, and phones. What is at stake is the possibility for a new nonsublime register of visibility in which randomness, chance, hope, and unpredictability transgress the economic patterns of production gardening has taught us to relish over thousands of years.

The rise of environmental concern is finally shifting artistic frameworks through which our relationship to nature can be seriously retaught, sometimes even through new symbolic strategies, like in the case of weeds. Yet, it is important to acknowledge that nonaffirmative aesthetics in gardening had been already introduced in the 1980s by filmmaker, theater designer, and painter Derek Jarman who purchased Prospect Cottage in desolate Dungeness (the extreme corner of southeast England) and tended the first truly contemporary garden in the history of art. Jarman insisted that gardens must be "shaggy," and that they should be allowed to form spaces of wilderness, accidental charms, and strange juxtapositions.[15] His garden evolved from debris washed ashore by the sea and most importantly it never was delimited by visible boundaries.

Michael Charlesworth has described Jarman's found objects as "things that most people would see no beauty in or would see their value exhausted. They bring a connotation of collage, of Art Brut or Arte Povera, of a garden made by an "Outsider."[16] But most importantly, the garden directly sprawls around the cottage, echoing and incorporating the surrounding barren landscape. Here, cultivars and local spontaneous plants live together in an environment where "weed" is a foreign concept in a context where discarded objects, art, and plants coexist. Here coming and going is the norm, not only for the plants inhabiting the space, but for local animals and visitors who travel from all over the world and are unprepared to negotiate the garden's unmarked borders and unspecified status suspended between private property, public artwork, and house museum.

How appropriate that such queering of garden aesthetics should have been pioneered by the most influential and experimental gay artist of the last century at a time in which the homophobia of Thatcherite politics proliferated. How appropriate that Jarman spent in Dungeness the last few years of his life tending to this garden while battling HIV/AIDS, a condition quintessentially defined by an unprecedented ability to erect boundaries between individuals, social, and race groups. And how appropriately symbolic that this garden should be situated in the desert-like environment of Dungeness where the oldest power station in the world fills the marine breeze with an ever-present ghostly hum.

---

15   Jarman, D. (1995) p. 41.

16   Charlesworth, M. (2011) *Derek Jarman* (London: Reaktion Books) p. 136.

CHAPTER 11

Hortus Conclusus: The Garden of Earthly Mind

*Wendy Wheeler**

The first garden-like enclosed landscapes we know about were created five-thousand years ago in ancient Sumer in Southern Mesopotamia in what is now Iraq. They were made by the people who lived in the fertile land around the Tigris and Euphrates rivers, and were hunting parks which combined a delightful landscape with sport and with the growing of food (Hobhouse 2002). From the start, the garden was a place of both focus and dream: a mixture of sharp observation and the free-floating attentiveness involved in the creation of a mutual life. By 2500 BCE the Sahara began to dry out and the Egyptian Old Kingdom devised gardens whose layout was a reflection of their irrigation systems. Penelope Hobhouse tells us that these gardens, as revealed in tomb paintings, "usually contain ornamental pools and are planted with trees and flowers" (Hobhouse 2002, 12).

The garden's rectangular shape was dictated by irrigation flows, and this became a standard form for more than one thousand years through Assyrian, Babylonian, and Persian cultures and on to the Islamic gardens of the seventh century CE. In 300 BCE Theophrastus described and classified nearly five-hundred plants in his *Enquiry into Plants*. Here we can see the beginning of botanical science (Hobhouse 2002, 12). By 500 CE the Chinese had developed the town garden and the scholar's garden. The small domestic Roman garden had similarly been developed, as had the peristyle garden: the garden as small open room. By 1000 CE painting and gardening develop a "symbiotic relationship" in Chinese culture where "the garden is designed to resemble a landscape scroll" (Hobhouse 2002, 13). The development of botany continues in the first century with Dioscorides's *De Materia Medica* (Hobhouse 2002, 13). This will influence plant collectors for centuries to come.

From here onwards the two traditions: (1) of the small and medium sized garden on the one hand, often as a place of contemplation and withdrawal, natural and cultural growth unseparated, and decorated with flowers, streams and fruit trees, and (2) of the large formal garden and the enclosed hunting park garden of the nobility on the other, will continue until at least the eighteenth century in Europe.

In the Americas, Peruvian farmers from around 700 CE develop sophisticated irrigation systems. In Mexico, from approximately the thirteenth century CE onward, the Aztecs "developed ornamental pleasure gardens and an extensive knowledge of plant cultivation and botany" (Hobhouse 2002, 13).

Although the dates and details may not be familiar, none of the results of this very extensive history will feel unfamiliar today, either to the domestic gardener or to the professional horticulturalist. These are gardens, the shapes and aims of which we all readily recognize still. The development, especially in England, of the romantic landscape garden with the artificer's production of a studied naturalness, still calls on the garden as source of contemplation and the search for an ordering of inner profusion aided by the hidden manipulation of nature: a creative disorder based, as all such ordering is, on the necessity of limits and constraints. The recognition that there is a very real living relationship between the human and the meanings derived from his or her environment, or *Umwelt*

---
* Many thanks to Louise Westling for her helpful comments on an early draft of this thought piece.

FIGURE 11.1 *Hortus conclusus,* from the Villa of Livia or the Villa ad Gallinas Albas on the Palatine Hill. 1st cent. BC.
MUSEO NAZIONALE ROMANO, PALAZZO MASSIMO ALLE TERME, ROME. IMAGE, GIOVANNI ALOI.

as Jakob von Uexküll put it (Uexküll 1982), is very ancient.

With the triumph of a certain kind of science in Europe and in Western culture generally by the second half of the nineteenth century, "romanticism" too often became a derogatory term. In fact, the romantic philosophers and poets brought together two kinds of experience: one old and lost, the other newly found. The first was discovered in the revivification of older medieval forms of understanding caught in the idea of the book of nature and of Earthly experience as a school for souls (Harrison 2001, 17). The second was a new sense of relational immediacy between a vivid external reality on the one hand, and the equally vivid internal experience it seemed to call up, on the other. It was this latter that was explored in the new form of the *roman,* or novel, which gave romanticism its name. One can see the same intense interest and pleasure in the world of things displayed in

Dutch still life paintings during the same seventeenth century which gave us novelistic realism. These two worlds meet perhaps most strikingly in the paintings of Vermeer where objects come to life in the pensive hands of letter readers and milkmaids—mind-makers and food-makers. The romantic view of *Natursprache,* of nature's capacity to "speak" that informed Goethean science and then German Romantic philosophy (Rigby 2015), and which came into the Anglophone world via poets such as Samuel Taylor Coleridge and William Wordsworth, is now, perhaps surprisingly, reappearing in newer forms in contemporary biology (Shapiro 2011). It takes a particularly well developed theoretical shape in biosemiotics (Hoffmeyer 2008).

Of course, this ontology of sign relations describes, according to those developments set out in the semiotic of Charles Sanders Peirce and in the work of those he influenced such as Gregory Bateson, both of them then influencing Gilles

Deleuze, Félix Guattari, and Gilbert Simondon, an ontology of evolutionary relation and growth both natural and cultural. While hunting and farming require prolonged attentiveness to the habits of animals and plants, the garden is the made place where both kinds of attentiveness are symbolized and take place. This is attentiveness to attentiveness itself in all of its modes.

This is also the kind of dreamlike or meditative attentiveness which the art critic and historian James Elkins writes about in a 2010 article entitled "How Long Does it Take to Look at a Painting?" Elkins starts off talking about the enormous lengths of time which some people spend sitting in front of a painting. He, himself, has looked at a Mondrian painting for, altogether, about a hundred hours. A woman he met at the Chicago Art Institute had been visiting a Rembrandt painting of a woman leaning on a half door every day in her lunchtime for "decades" (Elkins 2010). Quite quickly, though, Elkins moves on to a discussion of Dieric Bouts's *Weeping Madonna*. This is an example of an *Andachtsbilder*, a devotional image and a new form of painting which came into being at the end of the middle ages in the fourteenth century. The *Andachtsbilder* was "specifically intended to produce an intense, emotional experience" (Elkins 2010). It drew the beholder closer in order, according to one art historian as Elkins tells us, to evoke "the immediacy of a quiet conversation," not one of the spirit only, but also of bodily identification:

> There was a new doctrine in the air, enjoining worshippers to do more than just sympathize with Jesus or Mary: the aim of prayer was to identify with them bodily, to try to think of yourself as Jesus, or as the Mother of God. You would look at such an image steadily, sometimes for hours or days on end, burrowing deeper and deeper into the mind of the Savior or the Virgin. Finally you would come to feel what they had felt, and you would see the world, at least in some small part, through their eyes. At that point their tears would be your tears. In the medieval doctrine, you would be crying "compunctive" tears: God's tears at our sins, given back to God. (Elkins, 2010)

Of course, we are not surprised to know that the *hortus conclusus*, the enclosed garden, a major theme in gardening as we have established, is also associated with the Virgin Mary and, by extension, with the monastic cloister. We could say that the garden is also "compunctive" in this way. Mary is herself an enclosed garden and a site of meditative illumination on the body as site of feeling-making mind. This theme appears in abundance in paintings and manuscript illuminations from about 1400, but we recognize its features—the pool or fountain, the four pathways, the fruit trees and flowers—from much earlier periods, the Islamic garden especially. This is a locus in which spiritual food and the water of life is added to orchards and ancient irrigation systems as necessary for the growth of bodily food. The two play alongside each other in constant dialogue through emblem and metaphor, as we would expect.

A deep unity of physical and spiritual, material and immaterial, features is symbolized by the garden. The intensity with which a relationship to a painting or other work of art can be established, and the long dialogic relation which can grow—the growth of meanings—is found also in the established relation to a garden. Not only the living things, the plants, can themselves be caught up in a growth of knowledge, whether by chance or the hybridizing hand, or merely in their own habitual communicative biosemiotic lives, but also that same process can be established via an iconography and with a painting over time. Once we understand that mind is not "in" the brain but is the result of relationships between a living organism and the objects of its semiotic attentiveness, we are in a position to understand that the garden is, at its symbiotic heart, a garden of earthly mind.

Mind isn't "in" brains at all. It is the result of organisms' relational responses to the patterned organisation, the habits, of their *Innenwelten* and Umwelten. These responses are dialogic and informational. They flow within and between systems, gradually shaping relata over time according to what is and is not possible. This ceaseless cybersemiotic negotiation and habitual becoming of living being, which is clearly a biosemiotic affair, is what Gilbert Simondon called dephasing:

> No individual would be able to exist without a milieu that is its complement, arising simultaneously from the operation of individuation: for this reason the individual should be seen as but a partial result of the operation bringing it forth. Thus, in a general manner, we may consider individuals as beings that come into existence as so many partial solutions to so many problems of incompatibility between separate levels of being. And it is owing to tension and incompatibility between potentials harboured within the preindividual that being dephases or becomes, in order to perpetuate itself. Becoming, here, does not affect the being from the outside, as an accident affects a substance, but constitutes one of its dimensions. Being only is in becoming, that is, by its structuring in diverse domains of individuation (physical, biological, psychosocial, and also, in a certain sense, technological) through the work of operations. (Combes 2013, 4)

Such becoming, usually habitual, but also capable of alteration by the organism's creative and shaping seizure of chance (Wheeler 2016), is something which all living organisms must be able to accomplish in a world full of unpredictable change. This possibility of process and new meanings, whether as biological functions or as an aspect of cultural development, is fundamental to the evolution of every created lifeful thing.

In other words, semiosis makes mind, not the other way round. In humans, biosemiosis lays the ground for the evolution of cultural semiosis, and for the human version of Simondonian individuation. The same is true for nonhuman animals, and also for works of art and technology (Wheeler 2016). The garden is one of its most potent emblems. Biological, cultural and technological histories impose constraints on their potential lines of flight, on, that is, those Simondonian processual dephasings by which individuation occurs. These constraints are not simply matters of biological form but are essentially semiotic. They are *habits of relationship*. As Terrence Deacon points out in *Incomplete Nature: How Mind Emerged from Matter*, such "Habits may be real causes in their own right." According to Charles Sanders Peirce, Deacon continues, these and similar patterns such as those found in the formal limits of relations found in the productivity of gardens are "the ultimate locus of causality. In the terms used here, habits begetting habits can be translated as constraint propagation" (Deacon 2012, 202).

Within the constraints of the garden's walls and irrigation technologies, and also from its plants and cultural accretions, as well as from its remembrancing demand that we live from and return to Earth, the gardener's muddy hand realizes the promise of the poet's meditative making. The semiotic relational ontology must consist in both a responsiveness to signs in their umwelten as von Uexküll describes it in his theory of meaning (Uexküll 1982), and also a capacity for biosemiotic interpretation and potential action. In accord with this insight, we must come to the view that the garden is the invention *par excellence* where those many minds, human and nonhuman, are gathered and organized by men and women in a dialogue where many worlds speak across a divide between nature and culture which, in truth, has never existed. Semiosis, or the action of signs, unites them (Deely 2015; Wheeler 2016). The garden is, itself, precisely such a made and making organism: many minds made into one and, as every gardener knows, the whole a living growing thing.

CHAPTER 12

Eden's Heirs: Biopolitics and Vegetal Affinities in the Gardens of Literature

Joela Jacobs

Gardens are artificial. Plants grow next to each other as they would not without human intervention, and careful trimming, pruning, and weeding ensures the dominance of certain kinds over others, in order to achieve a desired aesthetic effect. Gardening thus requires constant interaction between humans and plants, making it an act of biopolitics, in which power over life (here plants as a population) is wielded by a human regime of authority and means of technology, science, and knowledge. This kind of biopower is, in Foucault's words, the power "to 'make' live and 'let' die,"[1] and it is enacted upon vegetal bodies that react in genus-specific, individual, and situational ways to these interventions into their reproduction, nutrient access, shape, size, and color. In particular, the tendency to think of plant-as-species or plant-as-genus rather than individual, is even more pronounced than the biopolitical effect, described by Foucault, of perceiving humans as species or population rather than individuals (though it may be difficult to make a distinction where the individual plant begins and ends). Yet the ubiquity of vegetal life in gardens is overwhelming, once one is *looking at plants*. Once perceived as life forms or rather a living mass of organisms, their majority rule in gardens can be unsettling or even uncanny. Gardens in particular are spaces in which the ratio of human to plant is usually skewed to such an extent that it raises questions of vegetal (bio)power. Put differently, in gardens, humans, though they may hold the garden shears, are usually in the minority,

and this fragile dynamic perhaps explains the urge to control these spaces with particular biopolitical force and ensure their "cultivation."[2]

The aesthetic powers of nature over the human senses and the ideal way to cultivate them in a garden space became a subject of much debate in the eighteenth century. In contrast to the previous artfully manicured, geometrical style of the French formal garden, a space designed to display human interventions in nature, the eighteenth-century turn to the meandering English landscape garden was embedded in a debate about the impact nature could have on the soul in these new "natural-looking" spaces. Consisting of rolling meadows, clusters of shrubbery, and tree groves, these spaces invited visitors to wander their expanses, while strictly symmetrical French gardens with their carefully arranged lines of sight restricted them to clearly delineated paths. While the English style of garden certainly *looked* more natural than its manicured French predecessor, it was just as systematically constructed and maintained, rendering biopolitical intervention merely less visible. Nonetheless, these gardens with their idealized view of nature became a symbol of free, democratic, and bourgeois ideas in contrast to the feudal, aristocratic, and absolutist French reputation of the gardens in the fashion of Versailles. While the spatial regularity of the French model represented the rational logic of

---

1 Foucault, M. (1975–76) *"Society Must Be Defended": Lectures at the Collège de France, 1975–1976* (New York: Picador), 2003, p. 241.

2 An unattended garden is called overgrown, acquiring a connotation of human neglect, loss of control, and wildness rather than naturalness. This wildness comes with a mysterious attraction so typical of liminal spaces, which is emphasized by the narratives we spin around secret gardens (e.g., Hodgson Burnett, F. (1910) *The Secret Garden*).

Enlightenment, the fantasy of naturalness of the English garden befitted the Romantic emphasis on the untamed aesthetic powers of nature that inspired the artist's imagination.

Accordingly, gardens constitute the setting of many literary works of the time and form a particularly favored backdrop for the unfolding of human emotions and relationships, which often point to larger socio-political issues. The sensual aesthetics of the garden make it a favorite setting in which to play out human attractions because these spaces of carefully regulated plant reproduction and flourishing fruitfulness represent a model for the love stories unfolding on their grounds: starting a family is contingent on a careful choice of suitable partner and the proper societal steps of courtship. A disruption in any of these steps creates the stuff of novels, and the prospect of fruitfulness marks their happy endings. Literary texts and poetic language therefore frequently suggest that human and vegetal reproduction are regulated by the same "natural laws." The most famous German author of the period, Johann Wolfgang von Goethe, opens his scientific exploration of *The Metamorphosis of Plants* in 1790 with a poem likening the reproduction of the two species:

> The plant-child, like unto the human kind-
> Sends forth its rising shoot that gathers limb
> To limb, itself repeating, recreating,
> In infinite variety ...
>   ...Twin forms
> Spring forth, most delicate, destined for union.
> In intimacy they stand, the tender pairs,
> Displayed about the consecrated altar,
> While Hymen[3] hovers above. A swooning scent
> Pervades the air, its savor carrying life.
> Deep in the bosom of the swelling fruit
> A germ begins to burgeon here and there[4]

Though Goethe also notes differences, the idealized plant children, plant generations, plant marriage, plant pregnancy, and plant parenthood in these verses infuse human love and eroticism with a certain "naturalness" that connects them harmoniously to their environment.[5]

Goethe radically rewrote his harmonious understanding of the relations between humans and nature in his 1809 novel *The Elective Affinities*, which details the relationships among four people occupying an estate within a vast garden. The novel's first sentence introduces a contrasting idea of "unnatural" reproduction by describing the practice of grafting parts of plants onto others: "Edward—so we shall call a wealthy nobleman in the prime of his life— had been spending several hours of a fine April morning in his nursery-garden, budding the stems of some young trees with cuttings which had been recently sent to him."[6] This "unnatural" act of combining different kinds of tree into one seems to foreshadow the novel's disastrous ending, which involves the death of a child who resembles all four protagonists and is parented in unconventional arrangements. At first glance, this tragedy seems to underscore the importance of adhering to biopolitical regulation. Yet, as discussed by the protagonists themselves, the title of the novel, *Elective Affinities*, denotes the chemical process of attraction between unlike compounds, and the experimental pairing of vastly different elements runs through the novel from the tree grafts in the first sentence to the child's ambivalent resemblances toward the end. Rather than simply calling for a return to tradition, Goethe's novel unfolds the fundamental human failure to assess our rather limited control over nature (which, for him, includes the

---

3 Hymen is the Greek god of marriage.

4 von Goethe, J.W. (1790) *The Metamorphosis of Plants* (Cambridge: The MIT Press), 2009, p. 2f.

5 It should be noted that the complex structures that Goethe sees as inherent to this harmony render it incompatible with theoretical-discursive speech; it is significant that harmony appears most directly *in a poem*, while the accompanying theoretical texts remain contradictory or paradoxical.

6 von Goethe, J.W. (1872) *Elective Affinities* (Boston: D.W. Niles), p. 3.

human). He thus mounts a biopolitical critique of eighteenth-century beliefs in rationalization-above-all, by using a "natural law" (elective affinity) to showcase the impossibility of control.

Throughout the novel, the elective affinities play out predominantly in the gardens. While Edward works in the nursery-garden at the novel's beginning, his wife can be found "yonder in the new grounds,"[7] where renovations in the new English style have just been completed. Anticipating the couple's eventual estrangement, each of them gravitates to a different sphere of the garden, as will their future lovers. As the couple is pulled into different liaisons by two other protagonists and all four keep repositioning themselves toward each other, they actively transform the garden and it becomes a space of development for the relationships. Each area comes to represent a different approach to gardening, and as the affinities among the four protagonists shift, plans for the garden are continually discussed and revised, leading to a string of renovations and "repossessions" that re-distribute the spaces according to the changed relationship pairings. Yet in the end, both the old and the new relationships fail utterly, and accordingly, the landscape seems to resist the protagonists' attempts to fundamentally change it.

While the expansive gardens of the novel are renovated in the style of an English landscape park, its tree-lined alleys still recall its more structured and ornately stylized past in the French fashion, which is the legacy of the Edward's father. Thus commenting on the changing times and the political implications of the eighteenth-century garden debate, the text highlights the elective affinities governing human affairs, while simultaneously underscoring their potentially devastating effects, whether they affect the private sphere in matters of the heart, the public sphere in matters of the state, or the liminal space of the estate garden that is uprooted and rearranged by every new generation. The biopolitical violence enacted on the garden by each generation contrasts with its endurance, as it outlasts each new owner.

Revisiting the grafted trees again in the novel's middle, Edward's new love-interest

> Ottilie observed, how well all the grafts which had been budded in the spring had taken. "I only wish," the gardener answered, "my good master may come to enjoy them. If he were here this autumn, he would see what beautiful sorts there are in the old castle garden, which the late lord, his honored father, put there. I think the fruit gardeners that are now don't succeed as well as the Carthusians[8] used to. We find many fine names in the catalogue, and then we bud from them, and bring up the shoots, and, at last, when they come to bear, it is not worthwhile to have such trees standing in our garden. (140f)

The fleeting character of human affinity is contrasted with the patience required for growing a plant (and indeed an entire garden) and the investment of previous generations in the knowledge necessary for this task. The gardener points out that successes and failures come with both the old and the new ideas.[9] As beautiful as the old castle garden is, the new

---

7 Goethe, *Elective Affinities*, p. 3.

8 The monks and nuns of the Carthusian order live in solitude, with a garden attached to each cell, suggesting that gardening is a sacred practice that can substitute the benefits of human interaction.

9 The gardener's appearance also brings out that the majority of the human labor of gardening is kept invisible, just like its biopolitical regulation. Though the novel opens with Edward gardening, he does so as a hobby, not an occupation. For the most part, these protagonists make plans and tell others what to do. It seems, in fact, necessary to keep this labor invisible to fulfill the purpose of a pleasure garden as a space for leisure, as opposed to kitchen gardens or other agricultural sites. In this, pleasure gardens resemble the perhaps most frequently imagined garden: Eden—a paradise lost due to the failure of control over its human population. Even though Adam and Eve are granted dominion, the biopolitical power of the human inhabitants of this vegetal space is uniquely limited by the divine prohibition of interfering with the fabled and most powerful plant of the human imagination: the tree of knowledge. Ironically, Adam and Eve are punished for their transgression by being forced to practice agriculture, which entrusts them with biopolitical power once again, yet this penalty of hard work raises peculiar questions about the labor involved in gardening.

JARDIN FRANÇAIS | JARDIN ANGLAIS

FIGURE 12.1   Illustration by Blanche McManus in Mansfield, M.F. (1910) *Royal Palaces and Parks of France* (Boston: L.C. Page), p. 14.

grafts have taken well too—yet their failure is as possible as that of the new fruit gardeners. It remains to be seen who or what proves to be "worth while." The established "catalogue" can only record past success, not foretell the future, precisely because nothing is as much under human control as eighteenth-century rationa-

lism suggests—especially not nature. Gardens, with their carefully cultivated organizations of plants, present the illusion of control par excellence, while the very subtlety of their vegetal resistance makes them uniquely suited to demonstrate the undermining of human biopower, once we remember to look at plants.

CHAPTER 13

Thoreau's Beans

Michael Marder

The problem of sovereignty, though usually not discussed with regard to the vegetal world, is crisply outlined in a quandary that, time and again, crops up after my lectures. The gist of it is the following: "If I am to treat plants ethically, then how am I to decide which ones deserve to grow? What gives me the right to destroy some of them as weeds, while nourishing and nurturing others? In short, if I subscribe to your philosophy, should I just sit back, watch my garden overgrow with grass, and give up on gardening as a violent activity, disrespectful towards plants?"

In *Walden*, Henry D. Thoreau faced a similar dilemma. Experimenting with self-sufficient living, he cultivated a small bean-field close to the hut he had built in the woods: "That was my curious labor all summer—to make this portion of the earth's surface, which had yielded only cinquefoil, blackberries, johnswort, and the like [...] produce instead this pulse. [...] But what right had I to oust johnswort and the rest, and break up their ancient herb garden?"[1] If, in its traditional formulation, the prerogative of sovereignty was to "make live or let die," in its vegetal reformulation by Thoreau, it has to do with making grow or letting wither. The unarticulated basis for sundry decisions passed on plants is utility: Which species would be more advantageous for yielding food, construction materials, clothing, and the like? Whatever is deemed useless is condemned to uprooting as a weed; whatever may serve our purposes is allowed to continue growing and even expanding.

To these taken-for-granted reasons, Thoreau opposes the natural history of a place, the plants' own "ancient herb garden," or what we would now call an "ecosystem." He does not fetishize wilderness. Rather, he implies that giving any "portion of the earth's surface" its due means, in the Leibnizian spirit, respecting its self-expression, including in the vegetation that proliferates there. From the standpoint of the place itself, the weeds are the humans as well as the monocultures our species spreads wherever it finds itself or the animals it breeds and/or exterminates. Exactly one century after Thoreau's *Walden*, Aldo Leopold will encapsulate this insight in the idea of "thinking like a mountain."

Let sovereignty remain grounded on utility, but let also the forgotten questions *useful for whom? useful for what?* be raised. On the one hand, the weed is a plant that impedes the realization of human goals. On the other hand, and more broadly, it is a plant that prevents the thriving of an entire ecosystem. So, if usefulness for life's flourishing, in all its diverse manifestations, were the criterion for declaring something a weed, then wouldn't vast sugarcane and corn fields as well as eucalyptus forests be included in this category? After all, the sprawling sugarcane, corn, and eucalyptus plantations reduce biodiversity, cause soil erosion and deplete the nutrients and minerals it contains.

Thoreau has an inkling about the relative nature of the word "weed," which he upends in his self-reflexive agricultural practice: "Removing the weeds, putting fresh soil about the bean stems, and encouraging this weed which I had sown, making the yellow soil express its summer thought in bean leaves and blossoms rather than in wormwood and piper and millet grass, making the earth say beans instead of grass—this was my daily work."[2] Here is a beautiful manifesto of plant-thinking, if

---

1 Henry David Thoreau, *Walden*, ed. Jeffrey S. Cramer (New Haven: Yale University Press, 2006), 168–69.

2 Thoreau, *Walden*, 170.

there ever was one: leaves and blossoms are the yellow soil's expressions of "its summer thought," concretized in beans with Thoreau's assistance. Yet, we cannot help but notice a stark contrast between his interference, or his mediation between the earth and the plant, described in terms of encouragement ("and encouraging this weed which I had sown") and in terms of an imposition ("making the yellow soil express its summer thought"). That is where push comes to shove: Does Thoreau exercise sovereignty over the crops and the soil he cultivates or does he facilitate their mutual expression? Is labelling his choice of plant *weed* sufficient to counterbalance the adverse effects of his willful decision?

We must shake off the erroneous impression that we are faced with only two options, the either/or of absolute control and complete passivity. Inaction and mere receptivity are the harbingers of nihilism, caught up in a deadly spiral with its opposite, namely the sovereign dream of ceaseless potency and activity. To avoid choosing is not to act ethically; it is to evade responsibility and to assume an indifferent posture, as disrespectful toward the beings that deserve our attention as is their ruthless exploitation. We cannot be ourselves *either* if we totally submit to whatever happens or if we are (or think we are) in total control of the situation, wherein we play the determining role. Revisiting the worry that an ethical philosophy of plants would yield overgrown gardens, it becomes clear that a certain measure of selectivity, narrowing down the possibilities of what would take root and continue flourishing, is not disastrous; it is an element of our *engagement* with plants.

I find the suggestion that any active engagement with other living beings—whether vegetal, animal or human—partakes of sovereignty and violence to be grotesque, an exaggeration of valid concerns with the overreach of our desire for domination. Such an exaggeration does not promote but in fact harms its cause. Curtly put, the disengagement it endorses risks flipping into indifference and abandon, where the stance of letting-be might quickly deteriorate into that of letting-die or letting-wither. It might, in other words, continue wielding sovereignty by other means.

As an alternative, care involves solicitude, attention to the cared for, singling out and respecting their singularity, while contemplating and setting in their unique context (some would say *relativizing*) the motivations behind such attention. A caring approach is, furthermore, interactive, to the extent that it includes willingness to be cared by what or who you care for. We would be deluded if we were to think that gardening or farming is a unilateral relation: the plants and the earth respond and change their self-expression depending on my actions. And again, Thoreau is at the forefront of vegetal interactivity. "What shall I learn of beans or beans of me?"[3] he asks, teaching us an invaluable lesson in plant-thinking.

---

3   Ibid., 168.

PART 4

Greenhouse

∵

CHAPTER 14

The Greenhouse Effects

Giovanni Aloi

The frost has made patterns on the glass—
as Plato would have it—the patterns inherent in abstract nature and behind all life had
to come out, not only in the creative heat
within, but in the creative cold on the other
side of the glass. And the wind makes patterns of sound around the greenhouse.

SUSAN GLASPELL, The Verge[1]

∴

Starting the engine of one's car isn't what it
used to be, since one knows one is releasing greenhouse gasses. Eating a fish means
eating mercury and depleting a fragile ecosystem. Not eating fish means eating vegetables, which may have relied on pesticides
and other harmful agricultural logistics.
Because of interconnectedness, it always
feels as if there is a piece missing. Something
just doesn't ad up. We can't get compassion
exactly right.

TIMOTHY MORTON, Dark Ecology[2]

∵

In Central Europe, during the first half of the seventeenth century, the term greenhouse began
to denote a brick and mortar building with large
windows used to shelter precious citrus trees imported from the Far East from the Northern European winter cold.[3] Like the cabinets of curiosities

and menageries of the Renaissance, these buildings were a matter for wealthy aristocrats and
monarchs. The tropical species imported thereafter via colonial dealings required more light and
warmth—with them came the necessity to build
glass roofs and heating systems able to maximize
exposure to sunlight. By the end of the eighteenth
century, the term "greenhouse" thus began to denote a structure with a glass roof, large windows,
and a free-standing iron-stove burning coal to
maintain temperatures above 70 degrees Fahrenheit during the cold months.[4] During the first half
of the nineteenth century, the term greenhouse
thus came to denote ever larger and complex
whole-glass and cast-iron structures. These were
still most regularly attached to mansions, but they
were now heated by pipelines carrying hot water.

By the beginning of the second half of the
nineteenth century, the term had come to define cavernous standalone structures made of
wrought-iron ribs supporting large panels of glass.
These structures were now being erected not
solely for the private enjoyment of the wealthy,
but also as educational institutions for the public.
Botanic gardens educated city dwellers, reinforced
nature/culture dichotomies, and shaped notions
of national identity. It is also around this time that
new agricultural processes, augmented by the accelerated rhythms of the industrial revolution, adopted the greenhouse, not as a place for aesthetic
contemplation, but as one entirely dedicated to

1　Glaspell, S. (1921) *The Verge*, in *Plays* (North Charleston:
　CreateSpace Independent Publishing Platform), 2014.

2　Morton, T. (2016).

3　*Sanga Yorok*, written in the year 1450 AD in Korea, con-
　tained descriptions of a greenhouse which was designed to

regulate the temperature and humidity requirements of
plants and crops. One of the earliest records of the Annals
of the Joseon Dynasty in 1438 confirms growing mandarin
trees in a Korean traditional greenhouse during the winter
and installing a heating system.

4　Woods, M., and Warren, A.S. (1988) *Glass Houses: A History
of Greenhouses, Orangeries, and Conservatories* (Milan:
Rizzoli) p. 29.

FORCING GARDEN, IN WINTER

FIGURE 14.1   "Forcing Garden in Winter". Illustration from *Fragments on the Theory and Practice of Landscape Gardening* by
Humphry Repton, 1816.
PUBLIC DOMAIN.

the intensive production of fruits and vegetables. Through progressive technological ameliorations, during the last century, extremely expensive and mastodontic geodesic domes set the greenhouse-prototype model for educational/research institutions. Simultaneously, the ubiquitous, cheap polytunnels became to encapsulate the economic essentialism of intensive, capitalist cycles of agricultural production.

More recently, by the end of the last century, the term greenhouse took on a different but related signification: it came to symbolize the excessive trapping of the sun's warmth in the lower atmosphere caused by the unregulated burning of fossil fuels and clearing of forests.[5] Paradoxically,

the utopian model of a tropical enclosed paradise contained the premonition of a future in which we would be painfully made aware of the finitude of the planet. The lush utopia of the Victorian greenhouse, made possible by the technical and material innovation brought by the industrial revolution, inscribed the simplified model of a macrocosmic

5   On October 24, 2016 it was reported that "The world is in a
new era of climate change reality," with carbon dioxide in

the atmosphere reaching a symbolic threshold which it will
not fall below for many generations, scientists have said. In
2015, for the first time, carbon dioxide levels in the atmosphere were at 400 parts per million (ppm) on average
across the year as a whole, the World Meteorological
Organisation's (WMO) annual greenhouse gas bulletin reveals. Press Association (2016) 'New era of climate change
reality as emissions hit symbolic thresholds' in *The
Guardian*, Monday, October 24, online: [<https://www.theguardian.com/environment/2016/oct/24/new-era-of-climate-change-reality-as-emissions-hit-symbolic-threshold>] accessed on October 24th, 2016.

system upon which the planet's life depends and which the industrial revolution has irreparably tampered with.

Thus, the greenhouse could be understood as the emblem of the Anthropocene. In its tri-folded application the term can, in fact, inscribe the structure of botanical gardens and research-laboratories as the sanctuary in which to prevent the loss of species; the power tool of agriculture as a symbol, simultaneously curse and hope, of environmental management; and the atmospheric effect emblem of the glass-like fragility upon which all life on earth depends and that global warming is now making more and more vulnerable.

The historical development of greenhouses has its roots firmly planted in power/knowledge discourses that emerged from Renaissance ideologies of elitism. During the fifteenth and sixteenth centuries, European kings and aristocrats displayed their wealth and power through the gathering of rare naturalia and precious artifacts. The cabinets of curiosities in which these objects were housed entailed a complex intermingling of knowledge, power, and economic wealth. This epistemic modality, to place nature in a delimited space, be it the live animals in menageries, or preserved specimens in the cabinet of curiosities, had become the essential precondition of the emerging discipline of natural history. This power/knowledge matrix was carried forward in much, if not all, scientific endeavor that followed. "Knowing" was never a matter of purely personal pleasure or individual bettering, it has always been a means to acquire a more privileged social position through the economic gain knowledge itself enables, and which in turn generates prestige—a specific form of socio-charismatic power.

Menageries, the kingly collections of exotic animals from which the modern zoo originates, became a convention of courtly life during the twelfth century. And like the cabinet of curiosities, which gave rise to the museum, menageries became institutionalized during the eighteenth century. Both sites constructed an essentially domesticated conception of nature, one compartmentalized, somewhat ordered, and most importantly subjugated. This power of subjugation symbolically underlined the presumed omniscience and uncontrasted power of the sovereign. The correlation was simple: he, who can subjugate animals as ferocious as lions, tigers, and bears, surely has the skills, intellect, and strength to govern a people and its territory. Similarly, cabinets of curiosities empowered the owner of precious objects through a sophisticated display of intellectual mastery—the cabinet constructed an autobiographically curated miniature of the world, which crystallized the anthropocentric notion of man as world-forming and nature as a passive object to be collected and mastered.

The greenhouse, which emerged in the seventeenth century, encapsulated similar power/knowledge relationships—as an epistemological space in which nature was subjugated, values of curiosity, aestheticism, and connoisseurship drove the nobly born to collect exotic plants as a sign of social distinguishment. Louis XIV, the Sun King, owned over a thousand orange trees. The exotic fruits and flowers defined his identity, and that of the court's ruling elite, at once distancing them from the common man. Perishable and sophisticated luxuries like exotic flowers and fruits symbolically stood in opposition to the lowliness of lettuces, potatoes, and onions.

The cavernous greenhouses of nineteenth century Europe problematized these values by incorporating a public, educational element. Imbedded in the "rational recreation" programs that provided bettering opportunities for the citizens of ever-larger and ever-industrialized cities was the promise of a reconnection with the lost sense of communion with nature. Despite this being the official premise, the greenhouses of the Botanical Gardens of Kew in London had other more urgent targets to address. It is now known that the institution operated as the principal node for "economic botany": the study and cultivation of plants for financial gain, which was of crucial importance to the success of the British Empire.

Lucile H. Brockway's inquiry on the role of the Royal Botanic Garden in colonial expansion reports of two fascinating case studies that demonstrate how nature-cultures form out of biopolitical registers defined by an indissoluble interlinking of humans, plants, geographies, institutions, and economies. In one example, Brockway focuses on Cinchona, a genus of flowering plants native to the tropical Andean forests of South America, which cured malaria and thus constituted one of the most lucrative exports for the region. The British government regularly purchased quinine, a Cinchona extract, at the cost of £53,000 per year to cure soldiers who had contracted malaria in India. Transplanting Cinchona to India would have broken the South American market monopoly, making the cost of the medicine plummet.[6] Although the East India Company initially rejected their proposal, the Great Rebellion of 1857, and with it the necessity to increase British military presence, reversed the tide. Researchers at Kew Gardens in London traveled to South America to obtain Cinchona seeds and successfully imported the species to India, thus wrecking South American economies, while simultanesouly strengthening the prestige and power of the British Empire. In the process, the biosystems of Indian regions were irreparably altered by this maneuver, which objectified plants as pure commodity with little respect for ecosystemic interconnectedness.

A similar case involves rubber plants. During the second half of the nineteenth century, Brazil monopolized the rubber market. In 1876, in association with the Indian Office, Kew Gardens sent botanists to South America for the precise purpose of smuggling seventy-thousand rubber seeds to break Brazil's hegemony over an increasingly desired plant-derived material.[7] The rubber plants grew well when imported in Malaysia, providing by 1938 over one million tons of rubber a year to support the ever-growing automobile industry. In both cases, Kew Gardens' enormous climate controlled greenhouses played a pivotal role in the expansion of the British Empire, effectively enabling the exploitation of as many as twenty million people into slave labor—a socio-historical situation that still impacts today's societies around the world.

Many of the intricacies involved in the symbolism of the greenhouse as an emblem of past colonialist approaches and current environmental anxieties have been problematized and subverted by Mark Dion's *Neukom Vivarium*.[8] During the winter of 1996, a massive Western Hemlock tree fell into a ravine, forty-five miles outside Seattle. The dead tree was relocated inside a large greenhouse designed by the artist. There, a life-support system of air, humidity, soil, light, and water has kept the ecosystems which thrive in and on its dead body alive ever since.[9] The *Neukom Vivarium* exemplifies the frailty of natural systems, and the futility in attempting to substitute nature and its processes. Here the greenhouse effectively represents this ambition, just as much as it did during the eighteenth and the nineteenth centuries. However, what is reversed in Dion's piece is the notion of triumph and subjugation, which plants in greenhouses usually inscribe—the miracle of the greenhouse is turned to an antisublime and thoroughly material register of presentness stripped of rhetorical notions: decomposition and regeneration are intertwined and interdependent. As the artist explains, the piece is not really about the tree, as much as it is about a nonanthropocentric conception of "nature as process." In the greenhouse, the space that defines specific economies of human/plant-consumption and production, success is spelled out by the presence of thriving plants producing lush foliage, fruits, and flowers. However, there is no room for decay in the utopian space of the greenhouse. Decay, in the classical conception of the greenhouse, is failure— it reveals man's inability to replace nature in full. With *Neukom Vivarium* Dion invites us to rethink vegetal life as the

---

6   Brockway, L.H. (2002) *Science and Colonial Expansion* (New Haven: Yale University Press) p. 113.

7   Brockway, L.H. (1979), 'Science and colonial expansion: The role of the British Royal Botanic Gardens', in *American Ethnologist*, 6, 3, August, p. 458.

8   The installation is titled after Bill and Sally Neukom, the philanthropists who donated the piece to the Seattle Art Museum.

9   Boetzkes, A. (2010) *The Ethics of Earth Art* (Minneapolis: University of Minnesota Press) pp. 1–3.

FIGURE 14.2   Mark Dion, *Neukom Vivarium*, Installation view: Seattle Art Museum, Seattle Washington, 2007. Photo: Paul Macapia. Seattle Art Museum, Gift of Sally and William Neukom, American Express Company, Seattle Garden Club, Mark Torrance Foundation and Committee of 33, in honor of the 75th Anniversary of the Seattle Art Museum.

COURTESY THE ARTIST AND TANYA BONAKDAR GALLERY, NEW YORK © MARK DION.

foundation of ecosystems beyond the traditional dichotomy of life and death. With this reconsideration, comes the opportunity to rethink classical notions of identity and the limitations their anthropomorphic nature imposes on the complexity of nonhuman lives.

The Hemlock is the state tree of Washington, and it is thus imbued with nationalistic symbolism. While the tree in the greenhouse is technically dead, its decomposing wood provides the base for the next forest. From this perspective, the piece can be read as an invitation to look beyond the utopianism of national identity in order to acknowledge the uncelebrated diversity that truly thrives in its aftermath. But from a materialist perspective, the tree is simultaneously alive and dead in a sense that recalls Jane Bennett's

notion of vibrant materialism. To Bennett, all objects are equally engaged in networks of relations and connections. Materials are thus no longer inert conduits for meaning; they are substances-in-becoming: their qualities are histories that invite us to follow and retrieve agential engagements between human and nonhuman networks. And most importantly, at the core of Bennett's theorization lies the conviction that our conception of passive matter, something defined by capitalist materialism, has for too long fed "human hubris and our earth-destroying fantasies of conquest and consumption."[10]

10   Bennett, J. (2010) *Vibrant Matter: A Political Ecology of Things* (Durham: Duke University Press) p. ix.

In this sense, Dion's fallen tree constitutes a monument to alternative narratives of livingness, which continually redesign notions of life and death, and success and failure, into trajectories of new beginnings. Similarly to Mark Quinn's *Garden*, Dion's vivarium relies on a complex technological support system to exist. Once man is involved, the maintaining of plant-life, becomes intrinsically bound to capitalist economies of sustenance and representation. Like Charles Ray's *Hinoki*, Dion's vivarium questions alternative scales of temporality and challenges anthropocentrism—they both are "living artworks" in very different ways. Hinoki's wood, inhabiting the sterile and climate controlled space of the museum environment was granted a new lease of life of roughly four-hundred years. This period involved a molecular crisis and a period of settlement. Instead, Dion's greenhouse space provides the ecosystem thriving on the fallen tree to substantiate itself indefinitely and without significantly specific prediction of how the structure will morph through time. Unlike *Hinoki,* a tree transfigured through the vacuumed-objectification of the art museum, Dion's tree is materially engaged in a dialogue with bacteria, fungi, insects, lichens, moss, and other plants. Dion's *Neukom Vivarium* thus pioneers new aesthetics of *fragility* capable of stripping the fallen tree of its romantic aura by lifting it from its environment and placing it into a greenhouse. This ultimately is an ever-in-progress readymade work of art: an event that ultimately aims to impact our relationship with nature outside the gallery space. This intention is testified by the inscription in the *Neukom Vivarium* which reads:

> My art asks you think about both nature and sculpture not as objects but as process. I like to imagine a young visitor coming here when she is ten, returning with her family as a teenager, stopping by as a college student, then one day taking her own children to the park to teach them about the nurse log and

how it looked when she was their age. She would have always entered the same building but never had the same experience.[11]

To Dion, registers of aesthetic experience are of essential importance—there is nothing to harvest in this greenhouse and no tropical flowers to marvel at. Dion wants us to look at the everyday, usually uncelebrated, wealth of local plants and other organisms that construct the biosystems we are also vitally connected to. The ultimate aim essentially is that of retraining our eye, reframing our ways of seeing, using the greenhouse as a symbolic and actual space through which our attention for otherwise unnoticeable phenomena can be focused.

A different attempt to subvert the inherent colonialist discourses inscribed in the greenhouses of botanical gardens is proposed by French artist Pierre Huyghe, whose artistic concern centers on anthropogenic considerations of human/nonhuman relations. The artist has devised a specifically curated circumscribed installation at the Palacio de Cristal in Madrid. Huyghe's installation, titled *La Saison des Fêtes,* is based on the inaugural greenhouse exhibition of 1887 entirely dedicated to the Philippines, then a French colony. As it would be expected, the original exhibit used plants as tokens of the faraway lands owned by the country—a statement of propagandistic grandiosity which educated audiences in very specific nationalistic ways. To this metonymic image of subjugation and exploitation, Huyghe proposes a circular composition fragmented into twelve sections: a symbol of utopian perfection, in which plants associated with different world festivities are juxtaposed: red roses for Valentine's Day, pumpkins for Halloween, good luck bamboos, palm trees and jasmines and cherry blossoms to mark the start of spring. In this way, the same geographical space brings together the ephemeral cycles of human existence as defined by the cyclicality, the biological, and the

---

11   Dion, M. (2006) 'Inscription plaque' situated inside the *Neukom Vivarium.*

symbolic while simultaneously revealing their interconnectedness.[12]

In upturning the power/knowledge relationships inscribed in the greenhouse, the artist proposes a set of ambiguous, and at times contradictory, trajectories inviting the viewer to ponder the complex roles plants play as cultural cornerstones, identity markers, and sustenance providers in our everyday lives. Thus, Huyghe becomes concerned with *connective images*—images that do not represent the world in the attempt of producing and ideologically preinscribed notion of national identity, but images that propose a sense of complicity and self-reflection. But while on the surface, the installation might seem a positive invitation to world-unity, the lush and healthy appearances of foliage and synchronized blooming gestures towards the highly controlled, capitalist production of plants as cultural archetypes. In so doing, the artist reminds us of the roles symbolism plays in perpetuating biopolitical registers in human/plant relations. Although we might think to be always the ones in charge, the varieties chosen by the artist have in many ways successfully colonized us, infiltrating specific cultural milieus with their aesthetic characteristics.

Millions of plants are mass-produced in greenhouses around the world for the sole purpose of marking a festivity—their ephemeral existence is preencoded by capitalism within the modalities of production and consumption we inhabit with them. These plants are not grown to last, they are hyper-fertilized, and genetically modified to produce extremely large and colorful flowers or fruits. Poinsettias are a case in point—their biological needs require a certain amount of heat and humidity to thrive in a home environment—yet, at the beginning of November, every year, they are dispatched *en-masse* to supermarket shelves and DIY warehouses where they receive neither for weeks until they are purchased to decorate someone's living room. That will almost inevitably be their final

resting place as stressed by the ordeal, they drop dead soon after Christmas. The plants included in *La Saison des Fêtes* gesture towards economies that rarely, if at all, have anything to do with sustenance and care. The politics of ornamental plants constitute pressing (and yet under scrutinized) issues at this stage of the Anthropocene where so much of the world population starves, and the situation is only bound to get worse because of climate change. Likewise, these issues appear here to be problematized by the systematized notions of belonging to one culture or another represented by markers of difference which reiterate a divisiveness of sorts. The intricacies inscribed in an installation that initially seems to blend in materiality and conceptuality with the permanent collection of the greenhouse thus emerges as a painfully critical counterpoint to it.

Overlaying themes of colonialism with those of archetypal mass-produced species and their colonization of human culture, Huyghe's installation gestures towards the utopian notion of the inexhaustible cornucopia that greenhouses have always represented which is no longer sustainable in this phase of the Anthropocene. Jason W. Moore has argued that capitalism has today exhausted the historical relations that produced, what he calls, *cheap nature*. According to Moore, the four essential variables enabling capitalism to thrive are labor-power, food, energy, and raw materials. Advancing labor productivity within commodity production became a substantial preoccupation of the sixteenth century. Ever since capitalism has in different ways been able to overcome crises by securing "new cheap natures" faster than the growth of demand. These crises have thus far been overcome through epoch-making agricultural revolutions maintaining the cheap food/cheap labor nexus in place.[13] As Moore argues,

---

12 Alteveer, I., Brown, M., Wagstaff, S. (2015) *The Roof Garden Commission: Pierre Huyghe* (New York: MoMA).

13 Moore, J.W. (2014) 'The end of cheap nature. Or how I learned to stop worrying about the environment and love the crisis of capitalism' in *Structures of the World Political Economy and the Future of Global Conflict and Cooperation* (eds.) C. Suter and C. Chase-Dunn (Berlin: LIT) pp. 285–314.

England's late eighteenth-century agricultural stagnation and food price woes were resolved through the American farmer's marriage of mechanization and fertile frontiers after 1840. The productivity stagnation of early twentieth century capitalist agriculture in western Europe and North America was resolved through successive "green" revolutions, manifested in the postwar globalization of the hybridized, chemicalized, and mechanized American farm model.[14]

However, the latest crisis, the one we are currently facing, has its roots in 2008's economic crash—at this point, the capitalist world-ecology would require a new round of "capitalist-agricultural-revolution," one that can entail a configuration of capitalism as a way of organizing nature in radical and sustainable new ways.

Since the early 1970s, these principles have been the focus of Helen Mayer Harrison and Newton Harrison's art practice. The artists have produced a critical body of work exploring contemporary notions of sustenance, supporting biodiversity, and community development. Most specifically, they produced their so-called *Survival Pieces* at the time as a way of envisioning new sustainable and productive ecosystems. Their main concern was the possibility of growing one's food to drastically reduce the impact of mass-agriculture and the ever-increasing shipment of vegetables and meat around the globe. The Harrisons wanted to dismantle consumerist aesthetic of mass consumption for the purpose of reconnecting individuals with the processes involved with agriculture and farming. Back in the 1970s, these works seemed visionary and somewhat far reaching as if the survival scenarios they depicted belonged to a distant sci-fi dimension. In retrospect, their work has acquired a prophetic quality—the artists were able to see the impending crises ahead and in the process, they actively provided solutions through creative thinking.

In more than one occasion, they transformed the gallery space into a greenhouse into which to grow a range of plants. Much of these indoor installations, such as *Portable Orchard* (1972–73), implemented grow-lights to provide substantial amounts of nutrients to the plants. Growing plants indoors pointed to a future in which growing plants outside would be impossible due to irreparable deterioration of air and water quality. Returning to the very origin of sixteenth-century greenhouses, *Portable Orchard* presented a selection of dwarf citrus trees planted in twelve 4 × 3 inch hexagonal redwood boxes. The installation's aim was to assess which species would best adapt to the new indoor condition. Most trees fared rather well; only a few died during the show—but those that died posed important questions about the effective sustainability of this format: while engineered manufacturing guaranteed predictable outcomes, engineered agricultural processes still had a long way to go.[15]

A year later, *Full Farm* gathered together some the Harrisons' projects within a proposed educational context: the installation comprising of *Portable Orchard*, *Potato Farm*, *Flat Pastures*, *Upright Pastures*, and *Worm Farm* was meant to educate grade school and high school students. As planned, the project exposed the challenges involved in this approach to food production. But despite the artist's intentions, a general lack of serious interest for this subject in an artistic context was also exposed. As the Harrisons recall,

> It happened that the potato patch was attacked by blight and quickly expired. The beans grew well in the upright pastures. The flat pastures, with vegetables and salad greens, were highly productive. Somebody planted marijuana in the upright pastures. Someone else planted peyote in the flat pastures. The exhibition did not last long enough

14   Ibid., p. 290.

15   Weintraub, L. (2012) *To Life!: Eco Art in Pursuit of a Sustainable Planet* (Berkeley: University of California Press) pp. 74–80.

FIGURE 14.3   Helen and Newton Harrison, *Full Farm*, 1974. Installation,
COURTESY THE ARTISTS © THE HARRISONS.

for serious harvesting and feasting, although salads were prepared. The exhibition was not loved.[16]

This prompted the artists to change their approach to art making in order to engage audiences through different aesthetic strategies devised to educated about the impact of mass-agriculture and, more recently, climate change. Between 2007 and 2009 (at a time in which we entered the new capitalogenic crisis), a multimedia project titled *Greenhouse Britain: Losing Ground, Gaining Wisdom* proposed site-specific visions of an ever so near future in which the rising of waters and the erosion of coastlines would soon demand the relocation of millions of people. In *Greenhouse Brit-*

ain, the basic greenhouse environments built by the artists are reconfigured (in prototype form) as a *Sky Garden*: a one-hundred fifty story high pyramidal high-rise development containing public amenities, apartments, gardens, and biofood production units. Up to five-thousand people, the artists claimed, could be relocated to these utopian structures resembling a greener and environmentally aware version of Le Corbusier's modernist utopia *Plan Voisin* (1925). The impressive amount of data and cartography assembled by the Harrisons in support of their project substantially contributes to the shift from their visionary utopianism of the 1970s installations to an utterly real sense of urgency. In their work, humans would live in a gigantic greenhouse-like structure to survive on a planet whose biosystems have been irreparably corrupted. This constitutes another instance in which the greenhouse unfolds into the tragic and most eloquent symbol of the Anthropocene, from

16   Harrison, H.M., and Harrison, N. (2016) *Full Farm*, 1974, *The Harrison Studio*, online: [http://theharrisonstudio. net/full-farm-1974] accessed on July 1, 2016.

unwarranted reaches and extravagant abundance derived from subjugated cultures to a life of rationalized self-sustenance based on subjugation; from a sense of wonder and a disproportionate power, to one of dread and loss of certainty; from a desire to celebrate a tropical paradise to that of staying alive despite the destruction of paradise; from owning it all to losing everything.

For some reason, the many reviews published at the time inevitably reduced the alarming messages delivered by *Greenhouse Britain*. A review on *The Guardian* read:

> There is a gentle beauty in their work and much charisma in the otherworldly maps and text panels that are poetic and personal rather than dryly official. The exhibition is, of course, a call to action, but it is foremost a lyrical meditation on what ecological disaster and collective recovery might one day look like.[17]

Le Corbusier's *Plan Voisin* was never built. In the name of the highest principles of modernist functionality, the architect proposed to raze the heart of Paris to erect in its place gigantic towers. His design was nonetheless responding to real urbanistic issues of space and overpopulation. While Le Corbusier's vision did not materialize in Paris, innumerable incarnations of its ill-fated ideals sprung up in the peripheries of many cities around the world. Le Corbusier's blueprint was appropriated and adapted to fit the socioeconomical realities of many low-income classes. Will there be a point soon in which the Harrisons' *Sky Gardens* will too, like *Plan Voisin*, be appropriated by developers in search of new cost-effective urban solutions? And if so, who will be allowed to live in these more than ever utopian greenhouses? How will environmental justice unfold considering such project would

proably require corporate sponsorship in order to be actuated?

Related economies of functionality and sustainability are at play in BioArt pioneer Suzanne Anker's *Astroculture (Eternal Return)* installation staged at The Cathedral of St. John's the Divine, New York, in 2015. Situated in the middle of the nave, a series of square modular containers glowing with deep purple light altered the multicolored lighting filtered through the church's stained-glass windows. The assemblage represents an alternate method of growing food, one that Suzanne Anker believes, might become commonplace in the future. Inside the containers peas, beans, strawberries, tomatoes, and lettuce grow in the light of a future that brightly glow all the way down onto earth from outer space. The purple light that shines on them was developed to enable microagricultural economies for the International Space Station. This Veggie System enabled astronauts to eat fresh salad in space for the first time, thus defying the well-known restrictions that apply to astronaut-dining. The limited space available on the space station is the key to reverting the destructive and ultimately inefficient uses of soil made by mass-agriculture around the globe in pursuit of cheap nature. Part provocation and part stroke of genius, *Astroculture (Eternal Return)* envisions a mini-greenhouse scenario that can fit into a city apartment to support the lives of those who live in it. The possibility of imagining this level of individual substainability bears the seed of a global change that could in many ways enable animals and plants to reclaim the land that has for many centuries been exploited for agricultural processes. Bringing the agricultural dimension inside the house reverts the blueprint established at around 8000 BCE when the first agricultural technologies began to emerge on the banks of the Nile. Ultimately, this model of city living might not even result into much of a sacrifice. Can we envision a world in which this human-plant domestic proximity has existed for thousands of years? A sharing of space and resources that might lead to a different appreciation of plant life? Would we allow

---

17   Mahoney, E. (2008) 'Greenhouse Britain,' in *The Guardian*, March, February 14, online: [<https://www.theguardian.com/artanddesign/2008/mar/14/art1>] accessed on July 1, 2016.

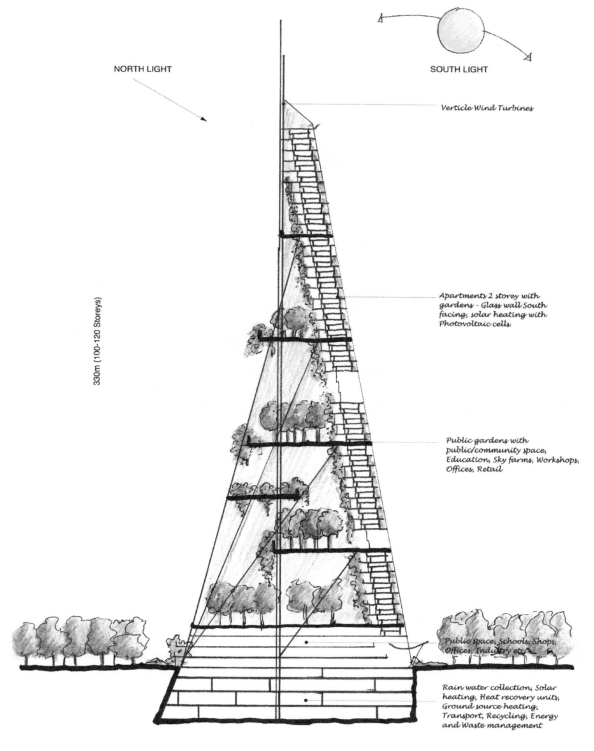

NORTH LIGHT

SOUTH LIGHT

Verticle Wind Turbines

Apartments 2 storey with gardens - Glass wall South facing, solar heating with Photovoltaic cells.

Public gardens with public/community space, Education, Sky farms, Workshops, Offices, Retail

330m (100-120 Storeys)

Public space, Schools, Shops, Offices, Industry etc.

Rain water collection, Solar heating, Heat recovery units, Ground source heating, Transport, Recycling, Energy and Waste management

FIGURE 14.4   Helen and Newton Harrison, *Sky Garden Plan* from Greenhouse Britain. Installation project, 2011
COURTESY THE ARTISTS © THE HARRISONS.

FIGURE 14.5 Suzanne Anker, *Astroculture (Shelf Life)*, 2011/2014. Installation view at [macro]biologies II: organisms, Art Laboratory, Berlin
© SUZANNE ANKER.

tomatoes and peppers to rot on the plants, as we sometimes do when they end up in our fridges, if we had personally taken care of their growth and well-being in the close relational of our apartments?

Anker's micro-agricultural alternative technique dispels the myth that healthy food requires prodigious sunshine and acres of land. The light used by the artist is apparently better assimilated by the plants than sunlight itself. Her setup requires crates and plant dishes from a plant nursery, red and blue LED strips, seed packets, and soil. The modular containers, mini-greenhouses she has used in the installation cost less than $100 each.

So, it makes perfect sense that *Astroculture (Eternal Return)* should be installed in a church, where economies of visibility and invisibility, the earthly and the otherworldly, and materiality and faith constitute the framework around which long lasting sets of life-molding beliefs have been organized for millennia—this is a prayer for a different way; a silent gospel for a sustainable future.

CHAPTER 15

Solarise

Luftwerk

Artists, architects, and designers are continuously inspired by the shapes, textures, and colors found throughout nature. In our own work, we continue this tradition by exploring how form and function can influence—and be influenced by—the processes of plant life. As artists, we are interested in the properties of light as a material and how it interacts with architecture, plant life, and humans. Investigating the relationship between light and natural and man-made environments propels us to develop work that blends research, technology, and contemporary art to engage and shift viewers' perceptions of their immediate surroundings.

As site-specific artists, we have always been interested in the concepts and uses of built space. Our interest in how the organic natural world interacts with the built environment dates back to *Projecting Modern*, a new media installation at Frank Lloyd Wright's Frederick C. Robie House. We began our research for the exhibition by mining Wright's aesthetics for content and shared dialogue, and to gain a holistic understanding of the ideas the building represents and inhabits. Inspired by his philosophy of "organic architecture," coupled with the intricate integration of natural materials from infrastructure to décor, we became intimately aware of the architect's relationship to nature and its effect on the underpinning philosophies informing its final design. *Projecting Modern* invited visitors to explore light installations that provided an integrated dialogue which spoke to—rather than spoke for, or about—Wright's aesthetic.

Shortly thereafter, we were commissioned by the Western Pennsylvania Conservancy to create an immersive light installation celebrating the seventy-fifth anniversary of Wright's Fallingwater residence in Mill Run, Pennsylvania. The famed house stands as one of his greatest masterpieces for both its structural dynamism and striking integration with its natural surroundings, both aspects of which informed the final content of the artwork. Mounting a seven-channel video installation throughout the surrounding forest, we projected moving images directly onto the multiplaned front façade of the building. The result was a performance of patterns and abstracted imagery, deconstructing its physical architecture into multiple "moving" canvases. We aimed to emphasize the relationship of the building to its site, magnifying the harmonious coexistence of natural and manmade forms.

These exhibitions became important milestones in our art practice, informing future dialogues with the built and natural environment.

The Conservatory as Laboratory

I was attracted by the immensity of the sea, and in its place came the Great Plains of America... A sea of flowers in all colors of the rainbow.

JENS JENSEN, *Landscape Architect, Garfield Park Conservatory*

Our most recent experience looking to the organic for inspiration was through *solarise: a sea of all colors*, a response to the plant collection and architecture of Garfield Park Conservatory in Chicago, Illinois. Built in 1907—and one of the America's largest greenhouses—the conservatory is considered a civic gem in the "Emerald Necklace" that is the city's unique boulevard and parks system. It was built with the intention to serve as a place for

FIGURE 15.1 Luftwerk, *Florescence*. Acrylic, suspension wire, LED lighting 2015
PHOTO: JOHN FAIER © LUFTWERK.

the public to wander, explore, and rest within an increasingly industrious city.

With *solarise* we were inspired by the vision of Jens Jensen, the designer of the Conservatory and godfather of naturalistic landscape design. We aimed to create a series of art installations that echoed Jensen's sentiment to elevate the experience of Nature, while also highlighting the importance constructed environments play in urban society and civic planning. We were immediately inspired to dive into the history of the building, as well as the myriad ways in which plants interact with light.

To better understand the DNA of the project we connected closely with conservatory staff to gain insight into the history of the building and its plant collection; how it evolved and how it is used daily. As the conservatory hosts multiple "houses" within its confines for different plant collections, it presented the opportunity for multiple points of intervention. As we developed the exhibition, each artwork began to reflect the unique qualities found within each house, resulting in five large-scale installations that sat in direct dialogue with their surrounding natural environments.

We found that some of our challenges would be to ensure artwork was in conversation with the surrounding environment and not overtaking it, keeping in mind the plants featured, the scale of the conservatory building itself and how we would interact with and direct the viewers gaze. From here we sought to create works that did not interfere with the plant collection footprint embedded within the site, but that enhanced the feeling of wonder the collections instill in their own organic beauty.

Being light-based artists, we researched how plants "see" light and how they use it to grow, adapt, and thrive under different conditions to further inform the designs for our installations. For example, we were fascinated by the comparisons that can be made between human vision and the "vision" of plants. We also found that plants can detect or "see" a wide spectrum of light, and that the direction, color and frequency of light affects how they react and adapt to different environments.

For example, we learned that while light is necessary for plant growth, only the red and blue spectrums are most vital to the growth process. Inspired by this, we created *Florescence*, a sculptural intervention of red and blue petals, hung canopy-like in an optical pattern. As the light passed through the translucent petals, colorful shadows were cast throughout the entirety of the Show House, creating an immersive experience that shifts visitors perception of the colors of the plants, heightening their awareness of how humans see plants and how plants "see" light. By flooding the space with red and blue, we aimed to create a "charged" environment, accentuating the ways in which people, plants, and color interact with light. In the conservatory's Horticulture Hall we were inspired by sacred geometry, which has its roots in the study of the shapes of organic nature and the mathematical principles at work behind their designs. *Seed of Light*, a kinetic chandelier consisting of multiple suspended pools of water and light, released water droplets from above into clear trays, magnifying circular ripple shadows across the floor of the hall. The piece's geometry and performance reference the compositional pattern of the Flower of Life—the universal symbol of creation. At certain times, droplets of water were released simultaneously hitting all trays at once, with ripple shadows overlapping in a perfect myriad of circles, further encapsulating this nod to sacred geometry.

Another example of looking to plant life for inspiration was with *The Beacon*. When Jens Jensen conceived the long dome structure for the conservatory, he referenced the prairie grass haystack, an icon of the Midwest landscape at the time of the building's construction. His legendary quote as mentioned previously, not only informed the title and tone of the exhibition, but also *The Beacon* itself. Reinterpreting Jensen's admiration for waving fields of prairie grass, we created a dynamic light installation featuring computer-programmed LED lights that run along the interior of the Palm House dome, the front façade of the conservatory. The colors found within the lights were taken directly from video content we recorded of the prairie grass and outdoor landscape on the conservatory's grounds. The piece is activated by anemometers that gauge the course and speed of wind passing across Chicago and translates this data to the LED lights, affecting the vibrancy, speed, and dynamics of the installation. Dependent upon the weather, *The Beacon* creates a fluid gesture of light that aims to mimic the tall prairie grasses swaying in the breeze that Jensen was so enamored with.

By looking at plants closely, we gain a deeper understanding of how they create and shape the world around us. We see firsthand how they can inspire design and form, and how the natural environment informs the world we create around us. As artists who use light as our medium—something that is so vital to natural growth—we find there is still much to learn about how light interacts with environment. Using our practice as an intervention and laboratory for experimentation with light, we look forward to learning more from our surroundings as we continue integrating artworks into different sites around the world.

CHAPTER 16

The Glass Shields the Eyes of the Plant: Darwin's Glasshouse Study

Heidi Norton

I was standing in Darwin's studio turned greenhouse.

The light filtered through over-head layered glass, forming soft-scattering prisms, and I wondered if he knew Isaac Newton. A separation of white light streamed through angled glass, from red to ultra violet. I can see things more in focus now. Looking around Darwin's greenhouse, my attention is held by singular plants sitting on stools, as they are bellied up to a bar. Like the glass... when I looked at them, the plants glowed with brighter colors—a sort of profounder significance. Red leaves like rubies; blue leaves like the sky.[1] A multifocal attention is characteristic of green plants that register blue and red/far red light in leaf phytochromes. This photoreceptor—a pigment that plants use to detect light—is sensitive to light in the red and far-red region of the visible spectrum. R:FR light ratios are responsible for the bud burst in Silver Birch that are growing outside.[2]

This was discovered several centuries after Darwin's present experiments with phototropism before me now. An odd apparatus was set up several feet above the plant shoots. I moved closer to survey its presence. Using a sheet of glass with magnification as tracing paper, Darwin traced the movement of a plant. A glass needle was attached to the shoot and a blob of wax sat bubbled up on the tip, like blood on the tip of a needle. A white card sat below the needle with block dot indicating the starting point below the needle tip. Darwin didn't see me. He placed an ink spot on the glass so that it, the dot on the card, and the black wax blob on the tip were all in-line. As the plant moved, another dot was traced on the glass, and so-on, producing a magnified record of the movement of the shoot tip.[3]

Darwin's *The Power of Movement in Plants* was published in 1880. He needed a greenhouse more than he needed his library. He knocked down the walls and replaced them with glass; it was a glass house, originally designed for the time-travel of plants-of-sorts. A few years later, in 1832, the industrialization of sheet glass made possible the ambitious construction of the iconic Crystal Palace and the Royal Botanical Gardens at Kew.

The Palm House at Kew

The Palm House at Kew is steamy hot. I wipe my brow. I walked backwards from Darwin's greenhouse to this place. The distance between things. The zone of interaction. What space, what boundaries, allow the transition between this and that?[4] "It will be so clear that you won't see that glass is there,"[5] said Richard Turner (alongside Decimus Burton), who designed and constructed the Palm House between 1844–48. The architectural design came with concerns for the cultivation and preservation of plants. Many people came together, scientists, physicists, botanists, gardeners, and

1 Modified text from Huxley, A. (1954) *The Doors of Perception* (US, Harper & Row) p. 5, quoted in Batchelor, D. (2000) *Chromophobia* (London, Reaktion Books) p. 33.

2 Marder, M. (2013) 'Plant Intelligence and Attention' in *Plant Signaling & Behavior*, 8, 5 (Landes Bioscience, May 2013), <http://www.ncbi.nlm.nih.gov/pmc/articles/PMC3906 434>.

3 Darwin, C. (1898) *The Power of Movement in Plants* (D. Appleton and Company).

4 Lund, K., and Norton, H. (2011) *After the Fires of the Little Sun*. Installation piece held at Chicago's Ebersmoore.

5 Schoenefeldt, H. (2011) 'The Use of Scientific Experimentation in Developing the Glazing for the Palm House at Kew' in *Construction History*, pp. 19–39.

FIGURE 16.1 Heidi Norton, *Palm Pressed*, 2011. Glass, resin, plant, mirror, spray paint, sand 36 × 48 in (91.4 × 121.9 cm).
COURTESY OF THE ARTIST © HEIDI NORTON.

engineers, to resolve the technical and environment design questions, especially the provision of the ideal lighting conditions and the creation of ideal indoor climates tailored to the needs of tropical plants.[6] The introduction of large-size, sheet-glass panes had serious implication for design development. However, the irregularities of sheet glass, acted as meniscus lenses, scorching plants. Through several experiments with selective glazing and the relative transparency of different colored media to each class of radiation, he concluded that healthy plants could be best achieved using green glass. Copper oxide was added into clear sheer glass: opaque to the invisible infrared radiation and cut off the far end of the red spectrum in visible light.[7]

> The glass employed here is the most delicate emerald green. Viewed from within, and at right angles, it appears colorless, seen obliquely from within the green is apparent; viewed externally the tint is very decided, ad when the sun strikes it at a particular angle it presents a most curious and beautiful appearance, the whole surface that is illuminated glowing like a mass of gigantic fiery opals. (18)[8]

What would it be like to make a piece that's like looking into the window of a greenhouse?

The Artist Greenhouse Studio

For several months, I lived in a warm sunny room, surrounded by several smaller plants. We lived on a shelf in front of large glass window that opened to the outside air; and were often swapped in and out, placed on other wall shelves. A woman would stand behind a large black box, which appeared to be a camera and take photographs of us. At first I thought I was in a greenhouse, as the sun felt so

warm and strong against my shiny green. One day she took me and lay me gentle and flat against a hard cold surface, arranging me in different positions—side, back, front. When she finally settled on a position, she dumped some gooey sticky sap-like material all over me. The exterior layer of my skin, the cuticle, was stuck to the surface; but my upper epidermis, mesophyll, and lower epidermis continued to function. My roots hung freely and every few days she would spray them. I am not sure if I will live or die. Although, I had seen a nearby tropical dieffenbachia, painted with latex grow a new shoot.

I could signal by releasing airborne volatiles to my fellow Majesty and palm varietals at the Palm House within the Garfield Park Conservatory. The conservatory is also called, "landscape art under glass," it exhibits plants similar to me in an "exhibition," while also cultivating and preserving. There, the plants are surround by plate glass windows that trap sun, versus be embalmed into a piece of glass. The Palm House: filled to the sixty-five foot-high vaulted ceiling with eighty-four representatives of the two thousand different varieties of palm trees known to exist today. One of the most intriguing of these palms is the Double Coconut Palm. Growing off the coast of South Africa, this palm produces thirty to fifty pound seeds believed to be the largest seed of any plant in the world.[9]

Peter Tompkins's Greenhouse

I chewed a betel nut, the seed of the areca palm, which was sliced, then wrapped in leaves of piper betel vine coated with lime, while coming-down from the journey. Stevie Wonder's *Journey Through "The Secret Life of Plants"* LP alternated with Mort Garison's *Plantasia* playing over a loud speaker 24/7 in the greenhouse. Peter Tompkins has an affinity for the dracaena palm. The gashed, dragon-blood extracted ones, come here to retire. They

---

6   Ibid.

7   Ibid.

8   *Gardeners Chronicle & New Horticulturist*, 8, 4, March 1848, quoted in Ibid.

---

9   <http://www.garfield-conservatory.org> (accessed March 21, 2016).

also send vials of the red resin that he collects on a shelf. A special greenhouse had been constructed to accommodate one particularly large dracaena. There was a hole cut perfectly the circumference of the trunk and sealed to prevent air escaping into the greenhouse. Legend has it that this is the actual plant that Cleve Backster performed the famous polygraph test on, the Dracaena about which Peter Tompkins and Christopher Bird later wrote about in *The Secret Life of Plants*. Through the experiment, Backster imagined to set the leaves of the plant on fire, a thought to which the plant, apparently, reacted with an electric jolt. "Could the plant have been reading his mind?" asked Tompkins and Bird.[10]

The Inverted Greenhouse

The opposite of light is dark. Plants use the phytochrome system to grow away from shade and toward light.

Charles Bonnet Tropism Experiment from 1779:

> Two etiolated bean seedlings oppositely placed in a vase of water were tied downward. With the shutter closed, each seedling reoriented upward toward the nearest wall. When the shutter was raised, both seedlings reoriented toward the opening.[11]

We sat in an inverted glasshouse: a black box that looked like an early invention of a camera. On one wall was a hole with an eight-inch diameter, a flood of light would sometimes stream in. The voice of the man referred to it as a shutter. Sometime he would open the shutter and feed us light. An all black room to grow a plant? Within our plant bodies we have something called photoperiodism, which is our biological response to the timing of light and dark periods. It helps set our circadian rhythm. Bonnet's early model of the "blackhouse" turned camera obscura sat at Elmhurst Art Museum as part of Heidi Norton's *Prismatic Nature*. I sat in the dark room and learned to adapt my photochrome system to the period in which light was allowed into the shutter. The beam of light also formed an image of the outside world that I was precluded from. It was a beautiful inverted image of the park in color that could only form through the darkness. This tension highlights the confused relationship that humans have with nature, like a biologist who must kill something in order to understand how it lives.[12]

Edward Steichen

Ingest a delphinium and die. Edward Steichen was grooming his six-foot purple spikes with a finger-size, fine tooth comb in his large greenhouse in Connecticut. It looked like a beautiful alien. Our name for this plant comes from the Ancient Greeks, who saw in the flower's unopened bud, with its long tail-like nectary, a resemblance to the shape of a dolphin. As the dolphin was the animal with which Apollo was associated in Greek mythology the flower's name relates directly to that god presiding over the arts and music.[13] He told me he was preparing to cross breed a new varietal for purity of color. Other brilliant, inquisitive minds have set out to explain the phenomena of colors or taken a shot at the workings of perception. Edward

10   Tompkins, P., and Bird, C. (1973) *The Secret Life of Plants: A Fascinating Account of the Physical, Emotional, and Spiritual Relations Between Plants and Man* (New York: Harper and Row).

11   Bonnet, C. (1779) *Œuvres d'Histoire Naturelle et de Philosophie* (Neuchatel, Switzerland: S. Fauche), quoted from Whippo, C.W. (2006) 'Phototropism: Bending towards Enlightenment' *The Plant Cell*, May 18, 5, pp. 1110–19. Online: [<http://www.plantcell.org/content/18/5/1110.full#ref-13>].

12   Foumberg, J. (2011) 'Heidi Norton—Ebersmoore' in *Frieze*, Issue 141, September, online: [<https://frieze.com/article/heidi-norton>].

13   Museum of Modern Art (1936) Press Release 18636-17, 'Steichen Delphiniums', June 22. Online: [<https://www.moma.org/momaorg/shared/pdfs/docs/press_archives/331/releases/MOMA_1936_0027_1936-06-18_18636-17.pdf?2010>].

here wants to know why some things seem much more "alive" than others. He's out to prove these feelings are not simply subjective. If ecology offers solid formulations for the so-called life of natural systems, he wants to demonstrate that we can in fact do the same for art, for the vitality that vibrates in certain ordinary things. The rational mind takes in the mysteries of the universal.[14] He scribbled on a worksheet:

*Kind of plant*_____

*Seed parent*_____ (*name or number*)

*Pollen parent*_____ (*name or number*)

*Date cross made*_____

*Number to be assigned offspring*_____

Using an artist paintbrush, he swept pollen from stamen. The pollen transferred to the stigma of the seed parent. The irises of his eyes resembled the interior of the bud. With a blink, he told me of the upcoming show at Museum of Modern Art, where he was later the curator of the photography collection. He will be exhibiting the Carl Sandburg varietal. The Museum of Modern Art will be converted to a green house. A fine art museum converted to conservatory, exhibiting its first and only exhibition of live plants in 1936.

A Glasshouse Where People Once Lived

I'm envisioning something that admits the peculiar pairings of impulses: to aestheticize to

brutalize. Specimens holding their breath, trapped in alluring sediments.[15]

Exhale. My name is the *Museum Archive Dedicated to Edward Steichen*. I'm made of rows of layered glazed glass alternated with optical glass—plants pressed, liquid bubbled and oozed into frozen drips—suspended. A demonstration of photorespiration, a wet plate, a slide tray, a window. Look closely, I breathe. Step back, I'm a mirage. I sit in an authentic glasshouse designed by Mies van der Rohe. The McCormick House is one of three residential homes in the Unites States. The glass and aluminum window bays reach from floor to ceiling, enclosing me, plants and lapidary stones secured from the neighboring conservatories. I am the expression of all words written thus far. Transparency may be an inherent characteristic or it may be a quality of organization, of layering—literal and phenomenal.[16] When light strikes at forty-five degrees and you view me at forty-five degrees, I no longer sit on the interior. I meld into the exterior. I am outside. And at one point, long ago there was no such thing as inside and outside. And then there was, and what we call nature was outside. The world of plants and rocks and dirt. Of bees and rivers, etc. And someone figured out how to bring it all home and name it and corral it into a greenhouse.[17]

---

14   Lund, K., and Norton, H. (2011).

15   Ibid.

16   'Transparency: Literal and Phenomenal' (with Robert Slutzky). Written 1955–56; first published in *Perspecra*, 1963. Reprinted as *Transparenz*, B. Hoesli, ed., Basel, 1968. Online: [<http://iris.nyit.edu/~rcody/Thesis/Readings/Transparency%20-%20Rowe-Slutsky.pdf>].

17   Lund, K., and Norton, H. (2011).

CHAPTER 17

The Lichen Museum

Laurie Palmer

When I met with Lichenologist Rebecca Yahr at the Royal Botanic Gardens in Edinburgh, she led me and two interns on a tour of the lichens "in the collection." The Gardens include twenty-eight glasshouses, two of which were built in the Victorian era, and seventy acres of carefully-maintained exterior gardens with the name of each plant carefully labeled on a stick. Rebecca headed down a stone path towards the rhododendrons. After about ten feet, she stopped, bent down, pulled out her 10× hand lens and said, "Here is one of my favorite species!" We all bent down, pulled out our lenses, and, "with bums in the air," examined the surface of the stone, at a distance of two centimeters. Rebecca scraped off a little piece with her knife. One of the interns gasped—"What would the gardeners say if they saw you remove a plant from the collection?"

Rebecca shrugged and said they wouldn't notice. And anyway, lichens are not plants. Nor can you grow them with any intention. The lichens "in the collection" at the Royal Botanic Gardens are there purely by accident—by their intention, not the gardeners'. You can't make a lichen do anything it doesn't want to do.

It is hard to write about lichen because the grammar always seems wrong. As a symbiotic organism, half fungus and half alga, it/they are/is neither singular nor plural, and neither wholly plant (algae are plants) nor fungus (fungi make up their own kingdom). Our seeming incapacity as humans to deal with collective identities has resulted in lichens being classified solely under fungi, "lichenized fungi" to be exact, as if the process of "lichenization" was a kind of paralysis, or colonization enacted by one party on another; as if any two-ness has to involve a hierarchy with one party dominating the other. In contrast, the lichen symbiosis tends to be mutually beneficial in most species. With one foot in each of two taxonomic realms, lichen—tiny, stepped on, slow to grow— rattle the foundations of Western ontology. On top of that, they are anticapitalist. Lichen are anticapitalist because you can't translate their vegetal being or their vital forces into money. Lichen successfully resist human manipulation and exploitation, mainly because they are small and slow, but also because they are a coalition.

> Are we in a better position to encounter plants when we do not know what to do with them?
>
> MICHAEL MARDER

Rebecca led us in a slow, studded fashion along the path, stopping and bending and looking at orange, brown, green, and black scabs which came into exciting detail only at extremely close range. Eventually we made it to the rhododendrons, which were just starting to bud in little pink and red ovals. But that was not why we were there. Their twigs and branches fizzed with seventeen different kinds of foliose lichen, and some spectacular hairy clusters hung down like ornaments. Rebecca told us that none of this was here thirty years ago—that the man who had her job before her had said there was no lichen in the garden until Edinburgh closed its factories and the air got clean.

Some species of lichen love pollution, even selecting for different flavors of nitrous oxide or sulfur dioxide, but many (if not most) can't tolerate it. The lichen symbiosis produces forms exquisitely designed to maximize surface area because lichen get almost all of their nutrients from the sun and from moisture in the air. Because of this, they are exceptionally vulnerable to what else is in the air. Some lichen are "used" by humans as pollution

© KONINKLIJKE BRILL NV, LEIDEN, 2019 | DOI:10.1163/9789004375253_019

monitors, but it's a passive "use" in the sense that we can't put lichen in a certain place and see if they thrive or die. It's more a question of whether certain species of lichen are already present in that place or not, or if they used to be, indicating a change in pollution over time. We can observe and learn from lichen but we can't extract their labor because we can't make them do work.

You can't grow lichen in a lab in order to cultivate lichen acids useful for medicine because no one (lichenologists tell me) has successfully persuaded lichen to reproduce under laboratory conditions (yet). You can't speed up lichen's productivity in the field in order to harvest it for dye because it refuses to grow any faster than it wants to, and you can't gather enough material at its naturally slow rate to generate a profit. You can't sell lichen as a plant to beautify your garden because it may, or may not, decide to grow in a new place. That may be true of plants, that you can't guarantee their growth, but generally there are things you can do to aid the chances that they will thrive. But lichen is so sensitive to microclimactic conditions that moving it even twenty feet from one side of your garden to another could alter its well-being, not to mention if you change the substrate on which it is attached, or try to move it inside a glass house.

I am particularly drawn to the crustose lichens, and of those, the ones that are tightly cleaved to rock, some of which are so deeply embedded in the crystals of the rock that you can't tell what is lichen and what is rock. This is yet another complicating "symbiosis," but one that knits together mineral being and organic life. Lichenologists believe that the lichen receives something from the rock substrate, because some species of lichen will only grow on silicate rock and others only on carbonate. Who knows what the rock gets from this relationship—the pleasure of an intimacy that changes one's constitution? (Certainly the structure of the rock is slightly eroded over time.) It is very hard to extricate, much less use, crustose lichens. But there they are

What if (plants) ... grow so as to ... to welcome the other better?
MICHAEL MARDER

There are many more unknown species of lichen than known species. One scientific paper on lichen has one hundred authors, each one having identified one new species, the point being that there are hundreds and thousands more to identify, and that lichenologists the world over just need to fan out. I am not so interested in identification per se but I am interested in that unprecedented collectivity of authorship, as well as the possibility that any new coupling of fungus and alga could become a new species, and that there might be a mathematically gigantic, if not infinite, set of possible species. And, of course, those that already exist are always evolving. Slowly.

Once you start looking, you find lichen everywhere, and start to notice their magnificent forms. There is no need to touch, or take them (though Rebecca did, and lichenologists do, for study). You can just watch. Like in a museum. At first I imagined a museum for and about lichen, that would exist in an actual place. But then I wanted to turn that thing inside out, distribute it, an inside-out museum, one that existed everywhere, and then I realized that's not something one person, or even a group, can or should try to do. It's something that already exists. It already exists! This thing that can't be collected, gathered, contained, stored, hoarded, but that distributes itself through and across space, escaping slaughter and resisting cooptation by capital. You can find pieces of it, but you can't collect them, they need to be left in place, and watched in place—and in watching, you might form a curious alliance. There is no centralized control in this museum, and therefore no danger of saving as an intentional act, because if anything in this world survives it will not be because it is saved by humans. It will be through complex, distributed processes that are only partly if at all human-initiated, and certainly not human-controlled. It will happen through infinite and

FIGURE 17.1   Laurie Palmer, *Lichen at the Marin Headlands, California*
COURTESY THE ARTIST © LAURIE PALMER.

infinitesimal acts of encounter, and differentiations caused by encounters, and new relationships developing through encounters, including perhaps encounters between humans and lichen. It won't happen on purpose. We do what we do because we are in love with the world. The Lichen Museum is already existing as a maximally exposed, inside-out institution. It's free, and it's always open.

PART 5

Store

∵

CHAPTER 18

Hyperplant Shelf-Life

Giovanni Aloi

Whoever wishes to escape is obliged to queue at the narrow slots that serve as exits, and to pay a ransom. The supermarket is a prison, the most private of all spaces. It does not serve for dialogic exchanges, but imposes discursively, imperatively, a specific behavior of consumption upon the receivers of its messages. ... The supermarket is an apparatus that simulates the republic in order to seduce its receivers so that they may be manipulated as consuming objects.

VILEM FLUSSER, *Post-History*[1]

• • •

There was no significant level of agreement or disagreement with the statement that indoor potted flowering plants in supermarkets are picked over, banged up, unwatered, and in bad shape.

FARRELL E. JENSEN AND PATRICK J. KIRSCHLING, *An Analysis of Indoor Potted Flowering Plants Purchase Behaviour*[2]

∴

Wheelbarrows, costermonger's carts, and supermarket carts have all appeared in contemporary art as "commoditization symbols" of natural resources. Mark Dion's 1990 installation titled *Wheelbarrows of Progress* critically addressed the politics of what was then called, "green issues" ranging from the Republican dismantling of the renewable energy program in the US to the obsession of conservation movements with charismatic megafauna. "Tropical Rainforest Preserves," the last wheelbarrow in the procession, contained a number of tropical varieties of palms, rubber trees, and philodendrons customarily grown as house plants. The piece ironically gestured towards the contradictory aesthetic economies that characterized forest-politics during the 1980s and that which followed: on one side, forests were re-contextualized by North American institutions as oases of transcendentalism within urban realities, and on the other ecological groups were busy constructing new notions of a national park for the purpose of locking up natural resources under the name of environmental protection.[3] In this context, the wheelbarrow represents the heritage of agricultural logics that have effectively shaped the landscape and metaphorically set the coordinates for our broader relationship with a distant nature that is always and foremost a resource to be moved here and there for consumption.

To underpin this point, the side of the "Tropical Rainforest Preserves" wheelbarrow is scrawled with information about the land-owning situation in Latin America and the notion of a "sustainable agriculture," which is directly connected to tropical forests. Fulfilling the demands of "cheap nature," as a normalized consumptive modality of the latter stage of the Anthropocene dramatically damages tropical forests at the rate of forty-six to fifty-eight thousand square miles lost per year: the equivalent of forty-eight football fields every

1 Flusser, V. (2013) *Post-History.* Translated by Rodrigo Maltez Novaes (Minneapolis: Univocal).

2 Farrell E.J. and Patrick J. K. (1975) *An Analysis of Indoor Potted Flowering Plants Purchase Behavior* (Voorhees Mall: New Jersey Agricultural Experiment Station) p. 14.

3 Corrin, L.G., Kwon, M., and Bryson, N. (1997) *Mark Dion* (London: Phaidon) p. 10.

minute.[4] In the light of such catastrophic speed of destruction, acknowledging the indirect and yet undeniable genealogical lineage shared by the wheelbarrow and the supermarket cart reveals the works of significant anthropogenic economies. If the wheelbarrow symbolizes the management and consumption of natural resources, now more than ever before, the shopping cart exemplifies the cultural disconnect between (mis)managing resource and unsustainabile consumption. For instance, consider the persistence of the shopping cart in the dimension of cybershopping, where the immateriality of the experience relinquishes a physical container to facilitate purchases—and yet, shopping cart icons stalk the top right corner of most web pages. This iconic persistence testifies the cart's psychological importance in consumption. First and foremost, the cart delimits an existential void. It capitalizes (pun intended) upon a primordial sense of anxiety, a specific kind of *horror vacui* cultivated by capitalism over time.

The wheeled-cart was introduced into the shopping experiences of millions of North Americans during the 1930s when Michael Cullen's idea to oversize the original Piggly Wiggly market format gained traction.[5] With cars and refrigerators redefining the timescales of everyday life, the apparent necessity to buy big and save more generated new shopping mythologies. At that time, the cart became the symbol of shoppers' independence: their right to choose amongst competitive brands and to have their fill, should they wish. Gone was the modest, local grocery store with a counter clerk who would take your shopping list and collect the items for you. In a mighty capitalist-evolutional sweep, the cart replaced the wheelbarrow transforming at once the history of the commercial object-display and inventing shopping navigation. With the mobility and power granted by the cart

also came the rise of eye-catching packaging that promised more and better.

Amidst this cornucopic abundance, some carts went astray—they became such regular a sighting that, in 1999, designer and artist Julian Montague decided to devise a dedicated taxonomic system for them. His approach relied upon observing the stray carts in the way that a naturalist might observe animals. As such, he never posed or repositioned or interfered with stray carts for his photographic documentation.[6] And as thirty-three typologies of stray carts were identified, it also became clear that behind the creation of a classification system, which simultaneously shaped the natural and man-made world, laid an anthropological mapping of new capitalist economies.

The same year Montague's *The Stray Shopping Carts of Eastern North America: A Guide to Field Identification* was published, stray supermarket carts appeared in the work of New York-based, Malaysian artist, Tattfoo Tan. While inside the supermarket the cart represents the possibility of fulfilling a desire, beyond the perimeter of the parking lot, deterritorialized on the city streets, the cart reveals its inherent lack of value as a vessel for wealth that it can only momentarily contain. Tattfoo's work has been informed by his experience of poorer urban realities where the stray cart most regularly functions as an essential tool of survival for the homeless. As the artist argues:

> A discarded shopping cart is the sign of our times. The collapse of financial institutions and big corporations. The recession is caused by our excessive and irresponsible buying habits. Foreclosure of real estate, cause the working poor to be homeless, and suburbanization causes the abandonment of our inner city neighborhood.[7]

4   Unknown Author, 'Deforestation Overview' in *WWF*, online: [<http://www.worldwildlife.org/threats/deforestation>] accessed on 11/02/2016.

5   Freeman, M. (2011) *Clarence Saunders and the Founding of Piggly Wiggly: The Rise & Fall of a Memphis Maverick* (Mount Pleasant: Arcadia Publishing).

6   Montague, J. (2006) *The Stray Shopping Carts of Eastern North America: A Guide to Field Identification* (New York: Abrams).

7   Tattfoo. (2006) *SoS Mobile Gardens*, online: [<http://www.tattfoo.com/sos/SOSMobileGarden.html>] accessed on 23 August 2016.

FIGURE 18.1 Tattfoo Tan, *SoS Mobile Garden*, Mixed media, 2009.
COURTESY THE ARTIST © TATTFOO TAN.

From these considerations emerged *S.O.S. Mobile Gardens*, a series of politically charged "mobile edible gardens" made of retrofitted, discarded shopping carts filled with living plants such as tomatoes, peppers, zucchini, and herbs paraded on the streets of New York or chained to posts in disused parking lots and other deteriorated urban spaces. The aim is to trigger discussion on contemporary economies of consumption, social injustice, ecology, sustainability, and healthy-living through the possibility of reinventing a fairer capitalism in which shopping carts effectively provide food to those who need it the most. Tattfoo, whose primary aim in art is to engage local communities to trigger urban regeneration, invites people to produce their own mobile gardens in aid of social causes and provide information on how to do so on his website. Plants' inability to move is in Tattfoo's project subverted and harnessed in a bid to attract attention and to reconsider the presumed fixity of social, local issues, and spaces.

The immobility of plants has been central to their objectified status, at least since Aristotle noticed that they only exhibit three of the four types of movement pertaining to living organisms. In *De Anima*, plants are endowed with the ability to alter their state, to grow, and to decay. Yet, they are not capable of changing their geographical position as most animals are.[8] To the Greek philosopher, plants appeared, therefore, to be somewhat "less than animals," or as Michael Marder argues: Aristotle conceives plants as defective animals which only posses the rudiments of a soul.[9] Thus falling victim to a constant zoologization, plants' apparent nonparticipation in a human/animal conception of locomotion has substantially impacted the ontologization of vegetal life itself. The apparent nonphenomenality constructed by this interpretation has facilitated reckless capitalogenic systems of production and consumption to dispose of plant-life in unprecedented ways and volumes.

These economies become partly visible, as a tip of the iceberg, in the ways in which supermarkets and major gardening centers/home improvement stores manage them.

Supermarkets generally have difficult relationships with living organisms as they most regularly deal with perishable and preserved nonhuman matter that has, in most cases, gone through substantial processes of rendering. In the supermarket, nonhuman life is stilled (vegetables, fruits, eggs) or is recently terminated (fish and meat). Here, the concept of freshness effectively stands for "recently killed," yet not frozen. Plants, like animals, are everywhere in the supermarket—canned, chopped, sliced, liquefied, and pulverized. Some plants and their fruits are kept in semisuspended animation through mild refrigeration, and treated with 1-methylcyclopropene, a chemical that enables apples to "stay fresh" for nine to twelve months. Lettuces might have been harvested three weeks prior to appearing on the supermarket display. Unripe bananas are gassed with ethylene for twenty-four hours after shipping so that they can quickly and artificially ripen on time following a two-week journey by sea. Carrots and potatoes too can easily be harvested nine months prior to their appearance in store.[10]

In response to these circumstances, in 2009, the artist collective by the name of Futurefarmers devised a project titled *Fruit* to promote consumers' ecological knowledge about produce, making visible the concealed agricultural processes, which ultimately feed urban dwellers. The installation invited shoppers to print custom-made fruit wrappers featuring information about food production, alternative food systems, and local food movements and wrap the around oranges at their local supermarkets. In the exhibiting space an example was provided by a market stall filled with wrapped oranges posed questions about the people who

8   Aristotle. (1986) *De Anima (On The Soul)* H. Lawson-Tancred, trans. (New York: Penguin Books).

9   Marder, M. (2013) *Plant-Thinking: A Philosophy of Vegetal Life* (New York: Columbia University Press) pp. 20–22.

10   Press Association (2003) 'Just how old are the "fresh" fruit & vegetables we eat?' in *The Observer*, 13 July, online: [<https://www.theguardian.com/lifeandstyle/2003/jul/13/foodanddrink.features18>] accessed on 23 August 2016.

Local Food Movements
1960's San Francisco, California

The Food Conspiracy was political to the core and was used as a way to organize neighborhoods against price-gouging super-markets and to raise consciousness about the irrationality of the profit system. They used food distribution as a way to organize and politically educate the community. It strove to build a "People's Food System," including a network of small, community food stores through-out San Francisco. It originally began for the purpose of allowing groups of people to buy fresh products in bulk, but quickly grew beyond weekly politically charged potlucks into an autonomous network of neighborhood grocery stores. These "buying clubs" morphed into legitimate and successful businesses, but they didn't lose their political edge. If anything, the storefronts helped center the groups' politics by giving them a physical space in which to ground their activities.

FOOD MILES

Farm to Shelf → CO2 emissions
"Foodmiles" is the distance that food travels from the place it was growing to the place it is purchased by the end consumer. Often these journeys go half way around the world, taking detours and inefficient paths. The energy it takes to carry billions of tons of fruit each year from remote farms to the city is enormous and has a major impact on the environments it passes through. Since the cost for shipment has hardly any effect on the price of products, most people are not concerned about buying locally grown food. However, buying local is not only better for the environment, but also supports the local economy. It is often healthier and provides consumers with fresher and therefore tastier products.

-Food travels on average 1,300 miles from farm to table.
-39% of what Americans eat is produced in other countries.

Urban Farming
Growing food inside the city.

The United Nations recently reported that 50% of the world's population will be living in cities by 2007.

Urban farming is an effective way of cutting down CO2 emissions both in reducing Food Miles and providing open spaces. It makes a greener and healthier city and provides a way for neighborhoods to organize. Farming together produces a sense of community and forges a connection between food production and food consumption that is becoming lost. Some crops have considerable yield potential and can provide up to 50kg of fresh produce per square meter per year in the city.

Demand subsidized urban gardening for individuals and groups!

Edible Parks! Plant fruit trees in public parks!

PLANT NOW!

Free Soil → Right to Know Campaign
www.free-soil.org/fruit

Free soil set out to investigate contemporary food production and its relation to the city. By following oranges from farm to shelf we were offered an insight into the complexity of this operation. Much of the information about what we eat is lost within this complex process, like how much waste is produced or who it is produced by... The corporations who control our food systems hold detailed information about each step of the process down to the tree the fruit comes from, but this information is held tight and proprietary. Let us demand to know more!

We have the Right to Know!
An online DEMONSTRATOR is waiting for you! Go now, to free-soil.org/fruit to plant a demonstrator. Contribute your voice and join a growing community of people who want to KNOW! Take the survey and your demonstrator will grow!

You have the right to know how your food is produced!

Do you know about the people who grew this fruit?

Do you know how much CO2 is produced to get this orange to YOU?

Do you know how long this orange has been off its tree?

Grow your own food! Know your cities urban gardens!

Contribute now to Free Soil's online demon-stration! →

GO NOW!

www.free-soil.org/fruit

FREE SOIL

www.free-soil.org
Free Soil is an international collective of artists, activists, researchers and gardeners who take a participatory role in the transformation of our environment.

FIGURE 18.2   Futurefarmers, *Fruit*, 2005.
COURTESY OF THE ARTIST © FUTUREFARMERS.

grow food, the amount of CO_2 produced to deliver and store it, and how old the fruit is. "You have the right to know how your food is produced" incited the leaflet.[11]

The concealed processes involved in food production, plant shipping, preservation, and processing make it very difficult for consumers to stand by precise ethical positions—this is a capitalist strategy designed to disempower. But what can be said about the ethicality involved in applying the same expensive, polluting, and environmentally unfriendly methods of production to the fundamentally unnecessary sale of ornamental flowers and plants? Over the past twenty years, cut flowers and potted plants have also made their appearance in supermarkets. In the best-case scenarios plants are located towards the entrance because of their need for natural lighting, something supermarkets have generally excluded from the shopping experience: windows distract shoppers from their consumerist task. Cut flowers, more so than potted plants, are subject to the same treatment reserved to "fresh vegetables" and fruits. In 2011 an essay by John McQuaid published by the *Smithsonian Magazine* mapped the interconnected biopolitical scenarios that involve humans and plants in the production of the quintessential supermarket bouquet. According to the author, the North American revolution in supermarket flowers can be traced back to a master's thesis written by David Cheever, *Bogotá, Colombia as a Cut-Flower Exporter for World Markets*.[12] Then a graduate student, Cheever had identified the savannah near the Colombian capital as an ideal agricultural site for producing cut flowers due to the constant mild temperatures, abundant light,

and soil quality. After graduating Cheever turned theory into practice, opening Floramérica: a new capitalist, assembly-line model designed to supply, at competitive prices, fresh flowers to North America. Back in 1969, their first target was Mother's Day, for which they focused on the production of carnations, one of the most durable and less fragile cut flowers. Within five years of Floramérica's trading, the area had become a center for cut-flower production grossing $16 million per year. Today, Colombia still controls 70 percent of the US cut flower market.[13] Much of the economic success behind this business-model revolves around the contained cost at which supermarket flowers can be offered in opposition to their local flower-shop counterparts. But how can prices be kept competitively low when a perishable item like cut flowers is made to travel miles through multiple refrigerated containers and trucks?

As it is true for many other plant and animal food derivate, the cost saved by the shopper is passed on to the producers and the environment. Growers are paid a minimum wage for long hours of repetitive operations; many female workers report sexual harassment from male bosses; underage labor is a regular occurrence, and all workers are relentlessly exposed to over a hundred dangerous chemicals necessary for the production of the high volumes required by the industry. Furthermore, the production of cut flowers demands ample amounts of fresh water, which is now a luxury for a region with limited rainfall such as Bogotá. A rose requires as much as three gallons of water to develop. The companies working on the savannah extract millions of gallons of water drawn from over five thousand wells. This is having a devastating impact on the local environment due to the draining of springs, streams, and wetlands. At the outskirts of Bogotá, indigenous plant species compete for survival with the cultivars in

---

11   Franceschini, A. (2005) *FRUIT Network*, 2005, in *Future-farmers*, online: [<http://www.futurefarmers.com/#projects/fruit>] accessed on 26 August 2016.

12   McQuaid, J. (2011) 'The secrets behind your flowers chances are the bouquet you're about to buy camefrom Colombia. What's behind the blooms?' in *Smithsonian Magazine*, February, online: [<http://www.smithsonianmag.com/people-places/the-secrets-behind-your-flowers-53128/>] accessed on 10 August 2016.

13   As the author acknowledges, this growth took place in a country ravaged by political violence for most of the 20th century and by the cocaine trade since the 1980s, and it came with significant help from the United States.

greenhouses; but for how long? A rose in our living rooms means one less plant in the wild, which means one less source of food for animals and reduced mineral wealth for the soil. These are the chains of inference that capitalism does not want us to consider at the supermarket. Although recent governmental regulations have imposed sustainability targets, the industry is still predominantly self-regulated. The 2008 global economic crisis also had a quantifiable impact on workers with many being laid off because of the fall of the dollar and the revaluation of the peso. All this lies behind the colorful petals of carnations, roses, and chrysanthemums purchased in bouquets at supermarkets around the United States and other parts of the world where the same model is now being used. As it always is in the biopolitical economies of the Anthropocene, human/nonhuman relations are defined by intra-active dynamics as outlined by Karen Barad—a queering of the familiar and usually anthropocentric sense of causality that unsettles the metaphysics of individualism. The ethic-onto-epistemologies that arise from considering the flowers, the workers, the infrastructures, the water, the climate, the indigenous plants, the company owners, the shipping companies, and the supermarket shopper and their impact on the entanglements of particular material articulations of the world, constitutes the essence of anthropogenic economies.[14]

These complex politics are implied in a 2008 painting by British painter Rose Wylie in which the artist's bold antipoeticized representation of a carnation and a white lily attempts to reach beyond their aesthetic beauty gesturing to their essential nature. Often compared to Philip Guston's satirical scenes of everyday-life and Jean-Michel Basquiat's political statements, Wylie's naïve aesthetics challenge the viewer to come to terms with a disingenuous approach. In this sense, *Flowerpiece*, is a

work of rupture—its anticelebratory and abrasive aesthetic is the equivalent of a slap in the face to both the Dutch tradition of still life painting, which posed flowers as symbolic *memento-mori,* and that of Impressionism, which most regularly reduced the vegetal world into a diffraction of hollow, abstract clashing hues. Wylie's flowers are deliberately unpleasant—if they are to be understood in relation to the sensual and mystical aura of Georgia O'Keeffe's flowers, then Wylie's have nothing to do with sexuality or a submissive femininity either. At the bottom of the large canvas, a black scrawled line of text clearly reads "Tesco Carnation and Lily." The British viewer would instantly know that these are supermarket flowers at their best, or worst, revealed in their inherent, essential ugliness. Beneath the glossy look and right underneath their sometimes dyed petals lurks an endless chain of eco and social exploitation. Tesco is a multinational supermarket, banking, insurance, and merchandise chain based in the UK, which currently ranks third in the world by profit and fifth by revenues.[15] Controlling more than a quarter of the grocery market in the UK, Tesco has frequently been accused of aggressive expansion-strategies that drive smaller local business away from towns and neighbourhoods.[16] Wylie's abrasive style gestures towards an inherent ugliness masked by the corporations' efforts to conceal the exploitative essence behind the alluring beauty of fresh supermarket cut flowers.

If behind the beauty of cut flowers always lurk layers of capitalist exploitation in which plant-life

---

14   Kleinman, A. (2012) *Published in Special doCUMENTA (13) in Issue of Mousse Magazine* (Milan, Italy), Summer.

15   Potter, M (2011). 'Tesco to outpace growth at global rivals—study' in Reuters, 16 February 25, online: [<http://www.reuters.com/article/tesco-igd-idUSLDE-71F1LR20110217>] accessed on 18 June 2016; Kalish, I., Eng, V. (2016) 'Global Powers of Retailing 2016', in *Deloitte*, online: [<https://www2.deloitte.com/global/en/pages/consumer-business/articles/global-powers-of-retailing.html>] accessed on 18 June 2016.

16   Friends of the Earth (2004) 'Every Little Hurts: Why Tesco Needs to Be Tamed,' MPs Briefing, online: [<https://www.foe.co.uk/sites/default/files/downloads/tesco_every_little_hurts.pdf>] accessed on 16 June 2016.

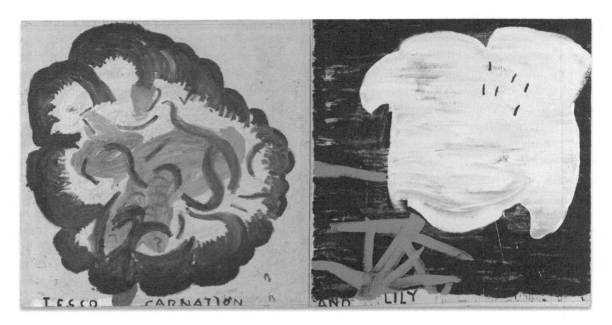

FIGURE 18.3   Rose Wylie, *Flowerpiece, Carnation and Lily*, 2010. Oil on canvas 185 × 351 cm
© ROSE WYLIE.

is instrumentally objectified, potted supermarket plants simultaneously are the products and victims of perhaps even more convoluted dynamics. As it might be expected, potted plants usually come from similar intensive, assembly line scenarios. Essentially, they are *hyperplants* grown to achieve aesthetic perfection unsustainable outside the greenhouse's controlled environment. These plants usually carry an exuberant number of blooms, their leaves have been treated with shine-sprays, and they are parasite-free because of the neonicotinoids pumped in their systems. They look hyperhealthy, but they have in fact been pushed to the verge of collapse-point—they have been, quite literally, built to be purchased quickly and to be disposable. Most "domesticated potted plants" prefer continuity and stability. They thrive in conditions where temperatures, lighting, fertilization, and humidity are kept constant throughout the growing season. Consistency and stability are what allows the production of a certain amount of foliage and flowers. Plants constantly evaluate the availability and steadiness of resources to

manage their growth within specific economies of sustainability. Irregular watering, for instance, places many plants into a "zone of uncertainty," triggering a conservative approach to leafing and budding. This characteristic *biomalleability* makes plants perfectly objectifiable by the capitalist system—the clock-timer rules the potted plant-world with impeccable precision. Moving from the hypercontrolled environment of the production greenhouse to the comparatively dimly lit, dry, air-conditioned space of the supermarket is deeply traumatic. Many plants will perish within a week of being stocked, and those "lucky" enough to be purchased will go through a relatively lengthy and stressful period of adjustment to, in many cases, less than favorable domestic conditions.

Despite being more obviously alive, supermarket potted plants are ontologically aligned to heads of lettuce and bags of carrots—they are in a state of suspended animation. The better they endure this stage on the shelf, the more they become staples in supermarkets environments. Poinsettias, African violets, philodendrons, orchids, gerberas, and more recently a vast array of succulents have over time been developed to better stand the climatic challenges of store environments.

We have all seen them suffer on the shelf, but many of us just look and walk by. To raise ethical equations about the conditions in which plants are treated in these industries is still near-taboo. The conversation between Michael Marder and Gary Francione, discussed in the introduction of this book, is a clear sign of how certain ideologies require plant-objectification in order to deflect ethical implications. As long as plants remain objectified and deprived of "intelligence" and "drives" we can eat them, use, and dispose of them without guilt. Recent plant research, however, has attempted to turn the tables on the classic notion that plants cannot suffer or make decisions due to lack a brain or nervous system. The outstanding fact is that plants can make decisions and "suffer" without these apparatuses. Comprehension of this paradigm requires the ability to abandon anthropocentrism, to think beyond the human nervous system complex, and to appreciate that nonhuman beings can even sense what we cannot sense at all.

In 2008, the Swiss Federal Ethics Committee on Non-Human Biotechnology (ECNH) published a document titled *The Dignity of Living Beings with Regard to Plants: Moral Consideration of Plants for Their Own Sake.*[17] Far from attempting to establish legal rights for plants, the report nonetheless recommended condemnation of any arbitrary harm on plants as morally impermissible also requiring moral justification for instances in which plants appear to be totally instrumentalized. Plants are thus conceived as nonhuman beings excluded from the category of absolute ownership. But despite the positive intention, it remains unclear how a document of this kind can in any practical

way impact the industrial processes of enormous quantities of plants, which are essential to food production as well as other forms of consumption. What plants would be granted rights in this context?

The gardening centers of home improvement chains are no better place for living plants as they operate supermarket economies on a larger scale and have even less expertise in perishable goods. These businesses never employ properly trained gardeners. Therefore, plants are neglected, placed in too sunny or too dark areas, exposed to cold, and to the elements. It is not unusual to see mistreated plants in "big box stores," but they are not allowed to remain within customers' sight for too long since they reveal the unethical nature of the economies which regulate their lives and more regularly their deaths.

Srijon Chowdhury's 2015 installation by the title *Affected Painting* provides a cunning exemplification of intricate nature-culture entanglements defined by the capitalist economies of mass-production in this context. Set up as a freestanding composite of multiple vertical canvases, *Affected Painting* hides an inconvenient truth on one side and distracts via a sublime illusion on the other. One side has demarcated painterly qualities, while the other is a sculptural assemblage. For the latter, Chowdhury has gathered a number of cheap mass-produced objects which juxtaposed construct a postmodernist landscape of ruination. On this side, everything is laid bare—here, there is no mystery and no mythology: a plastic milk crate, some concrete blocks, product packaging, posts of paint, and an inordinate amount of electric cabling hooked to power strips alimenting studio spotlights filtered by broad sheets of colored gelatin. Amongst these man-made objects are some potted plants—different varieties of common mass-produced palm trees, a yucca, rosemary, and some dead plants too. The assemblage has a profoundly utilitarian and gritty quality. But upon walking to the opposite site of the installation, the discordant desolation instantly vanishes. On this side, mystery and mythology are all that

17   ECNH (2008) *The Dignity of Living Beings with Regard to Plants: Moral Consideration of Plants for Their Own Sake* (ECNH: Berne) online: [<http://www.ekah.admin.ch/ fileadmin/ekah-dateien/dokumentation/publikatio nen/e-Broschure-Wurde-Pflanze-2008.pdf>] accessed on 25 August 2016.

FIGURE 18.4   Srijon Chowdhury, *Affected Painting*, installed at Imperceptibly and Slowly Opening Installation, Sector 2337, Chicago, 2015.
PHOTO BY CLARE BRITT © SRIJON CHOWDHURY.

exists. The silhouetted exotic plants produce intricate and elegant overlays of visibility and invisibility which evokes desires worthy of a nineteenth century orientalist dream—everything appears effortlessly beautiful, peaceful, and eternal. Chowdhury's piece encapsulates the politics of capitalist dreams. The sale of capitalist dreams in which nature is always constructed through the exploitation of nature itself is the result of gritty and reckless operations able to conceal themselves behind a screen of fictitiously harmonized aesthetics.

Returning to the other side of the panel, after losing oneself in this fantastical vision, is a shock to the senses—the spotlights are blinding, the surfaces and materialities of the assembled objects highlight an irresoluble fragmentation, but most importantly, what becomes more visible are the labels still attached to the potted plants—they are from Home Depot, the largest home-improvement retailer in the United States with a revenue of over $83 billion per year. As the only textual element in the work, the labels steadily anchor a layering of criticality in which the essential notion the shadows in this Plato's cave is the power of make-believe that big-box chains rely upon to facilitate an *ethically unflinching* mode of consumption.

FIGURE 18.5   Srijon Chowdhury, *Affected Painting*, installed at Imperceptibly and Slowly Opening Installation, Sector 2337, Chicago, 2015.
PHOTO BY CLARE BRITT © SRIJON CHOWDHURY.

So accustomed, we are, to ignoring the behind-the-scenes of capitalist production and consumption that revealing them can cause anger. In 1995 BioArt pioneer George Gessert staged an installation titled *Art Life* in which audiences were given the opportunity to actively impact on the lives of selected specimens of *coleus hybrids*. Coleus is a species of plant native to South East Asia and Malaysia widely grown around the world because of its intensely colored and variegated leaves. Extremely easy to propagate, it's a fast-growing plant that thrives in part-shade environments with relatively little care. For these reasons, coleus has become a garden and patio favorite around the world. Visitors to Gessert's exhibition were confronted with tables filled with potted *coleus* and were invited to answer a questionnaire which would be used to set the preferred traits of future coleus

hybridizations. Plants that were not identified as aesthetically pleasing, and those which got damaged or began to suffer during the installation period, were discarded in a composting bin situated in the gallery. As the artist revealed, a substantial number of visitors objected to this aspect of the exhibition accusing him of performing selective operations reminiscent of eugenics strategies and Nazi ideologies.[18] Yet, what Gessert staged was a pretty transparent reenactment of the methodologies involved in the selective breeding and mass-production of this, and many other hyperpopular plant varieties. He shifted the selective power from

18   Gessert, G. (2016) 'Drawing in the nonhuman—George Gessert in conversation with Eduardo Kac' talk delivered at The School of the Art Institute of Chicago, 27 October.

FIGURE 18.6   George Gessert, *Art Life*, Exploratorium in San Francisco, 1995.
COURTESY OF THE ARTIST © GEORGE GESSERT.

the producer to the consumer, thus forcing the latter to confront the ethics of important choices.

However, Gessert's *Art Life* went beyond reminding us that hybridization involves the disposal of many living plants. The artist brought in plain sight the cynical system economically focused on the maximization of profit at the expense of vegetal life that lies at the core of capitalist operations. Big-box stores make relatively little money on the sales of live plants as they sell them on behalf of nurseries that take a 70 or 80 percent profit cut and benefit from the high traffic the stores generate. It's a "pay by scan" system in which the big-box stores don't lose if they don't sell. During the busy seasons of spring and summer, plants attract customers who are very likely to buy garden furniture, BBQs, and more expensive items. This also explains why there are no real gardeners at work in these chains—the stores are

not interested in investing or developing specialized gardeners because the plants themselves are only a means to the sale of other items. As a store manager said: "Their cost for a one gallon-pot perennial is cents. Even at minimum wage, it's much cheaper to let five-hundred plants die than to pay wages for someone to drag around a hose watering hundreds of four-inch pots. They rely on a quick inventory turnover ... sell it quick before it either needs maintenance or croaks. Some will die ... it's business."[19]

Plants that look worse for wear are usually given a one-week period of marked down price—those that do not sell will be binned. At that point, the

19   Triciae. (2004–2009) 'Home Depot throwing plants away' in *Houzz*, July 9, online: [<http://forums.gardenweb.com/discussions/1433913/home-depot-throwing-out-plants>] accessed on 23 March 2016.

store can gain full credit from the nurseries that produced the plants, but the plants must, under contractual agreement, be destroyed to prevent any unlawful return-claims from taking place. Like the visitors to Gessert's *Art Life,* many shoppers struggle to come to terms with this system. Quite rightly, they feel that living plants should not be systematically destroyed for economic reasons. Yet the capitalist logic prevails. Would it be possible to devise a system which at least prevents perennials from being discarded in this way? A system that donates them to individuals, groups or oganizations that might benefit from them? Beyond one's own inclination to relate (empathically or not) to the life of a plant, one is left to wonder if the resources invested in the making of each discarded plant count for anything more than the monetary value assigned to them at the beginning of the production chain. And beyond the environmental and economic considerations drawn in this chapter, how does the treatment of plant-life impact on the processes involved in animal production and consumption? And from there, following Giorgio Agamben's argument on the continuity between animality and humanity within the biopolitical regimes operated by concentration camps, what could be at stake in reconsidering plant-human relations?[20]

---

20   Agamben, G. (2004) *The Open: Man and Animal* (Stanford: Stanford University Press) pp. 21–22 and Agamben, G. (1995) *Homo Sacer: Sovereign Power and Bare Life* (Stanford: Stanford University Press). In *Homo Sacer*, Agamben develops the concept *bare life*, a dimension of being which exists in the absence of rights and political government. The sacredness of the human is thus only produced by the 'anthropological machine,' something which also defined the otherness and bare life of the animal.

CHAPTER 19

Life in the Aisles

Linda Tegg

Could there be a more vivid example of the world-for-us than the supermarket? Climate controlled, evenly lit, rationally organized, perennially available. Every product perfectly scaled and packaged to be effortlessly plucked off the shelf. Shopping carts coast along the vinyl floors unburdening the shopper of even the weight of their own purchases.

While ounces and grams are marked on almost every product and checkouts calculate the value of every item, the entire supermarket seems devoid of gravity, as if hovering suspended over layers of car parks. The shop is as divorced from its surroundings as the products it sells are abstracted from their source. The supermarket is indeed a marvel of modernism.

The bulk food section breaks from the prepackaged logic of the majority of the store. It arranges a vast array of grains and legumes into transparent gravity bins. The range of color and variations between the types of gains is emphasized by the proximity and uniformity of their containment within their clear silos. Green mung beans are positioned between the specked brown pinto and creamy white flageolet beans for visual contrast. In one glance I can access the diversity of range at hand.

Competing for space on the shelves, the branding seems to be compensating for something. I recently purchased a fourteen-dollar box of *lovingearth* raw organic activated berry choc paleo mix. This one product, among many similar, claims in vegetable inks on 97 percent postconsumer recycled fiber packaging, to take inspiration from the diet of our ancestors of the Paleolithic era.

Aspiring towards the preagricultural diet within an upmarket Melbournian supermarket is wondrous. Twelve-thousand years ago when only one million humans inhabited the earth, when Europeans had not yet become pale skinned or tolerant to lactose, in a supermarket built on what was likely an indigenous hunting ground only two hundred years prior.

These hunting grounds were expanses of grassland that ignited the imagination of British explorers. The grasslands struck a chord with the British as they recalled the privately owned gentleman's parks of England. Early settlers understood this parallel as an inexplicable magic, rather than make the leap to understand the grasslands to have been cultivated for over forty-thousand years by Aboriginal people.

The image of rolling hills dotted with trees is a recurring motif of human prospering. Such imagery provides redemption in postapocalyptic science fiction, a return home. Perhaps the idea of this landscape is more important to our composure than we realize. The natural history museum will tell you that humans evolved as our prehuman ancestors were driven out of the jungle and into the savannahs and onto two feet to see over the grass.

As I write, Elon Musk is planning to transport one million people to Mars to create a self-sustaining colony, to ensure the survival of our species should Earth fail us. News of the tardigrade's ability to survive in outer space recently spread in a flurry of online articles. When dehydrated, this microspecies enters a state of suspended animation. When rehydrated they reactivate and continue on. The capacity to sustain long periods of dormancy becomes an enviable quality when considering interplanetary travel. The tartigrade appears to have something we want.

Returning to the bulk section of the supermarket the variety is reassuring. The bean names are so diverse, Jacob's Cattle, Tiger Eye, Adzuki, Great

FIGURE 19.1　*One World Rice Pilaf*, Linda Tegg, 2015. Source: image copyright Linda Tegg. *One World Rice Pilaf, Terrain*, Linda Tegg, 2015. Source: image copyright Linda Tegg. *One World Rice Pilaf and the vital light*, Mercury installation view, Linda Tegg and Brian M. John, 2015.
SOURCE: IMAGE COPYRIGHT LINDA TEGG.

Northern, that it's easy to imagine each variety of bean has a unique and poignant history as it has coevolved with humanity, that in looking into these beans we could somehow see ourselves. Alongside the names, Product Look Up (PLU) numbers are assigned. These PLU numbers maintain continuity across different stores and suggest something else entirely. A disconnect, a world to be consumed, the supermarket is turned outwards and one might point their scanner at anything and draw it into commodification.

The logic of the PLU numbers and the supermarket may very well guide cosmopolitan life. Compartmentalized scanned in and out as we move rapidly through streamline systems as individual units. Across the globe supermarkets are remarkably familiar, everything in its place.

For someone who has eaten as much hummus as I, the difficulty of visualizing a chickpea plant is astonishing. Naturally, the legumes and cereals contained in slick clear acrylic should be full of potential, not only as food but also plants, so I decided to grow what I could. I was so estranged from the process that it seemed impossible; the seeds must be somehow processed, heat treated, sterilized. From the supermarket it's easier to imagine the plant as latent image coiled in a film canister than something that can take root and expand beyond the surface.

Most difficult to imagine is the Yellow Popcorn. From the grain in its hard shiny yellow hull, it's difficult to fathom the fragile fluffy cloud like flakes we eat, let alone the vibrant green seedling it can also become.

Sprouting is easier than one might expect, essentially you just add water. A few YouTube tutorials cover the basics and serve as a window into vegan kitchens across the United States. These enthusiasts want more from their food, to activate, to germinate, to eat something more alive. They become hosts of their own lifestyle shows. A young woman sprouts mung beans in her campervan then a more reclusive type would explain their elaborate wheatgrass setup from a basement apartment. They seem to spend a lot of time on their food.

Attaining more nutrition from the legumes was not my goal. I wanted to shift my understanding from consumable to community, to something to live amongst rather than on. To *unknow* them as food and recognize them as *plants*. To take a kidney bean and grow Phaseolus vulgaris, whatever that might be like.

Only one step out of the supermarket, I grew over fifty varieties of legumes and cereals in orderly ten by twenty inch containers. Everything was indoors under grow lights. As the semblance of a plant community grew exponentially I arranged it, and rearranged it into forms that resembled hillsides, valleys and craters. The rigidity of the containers persisted, advancing and receding in counterpoint to the volume of the plants. My aspirations were somewhat romantic. However the grid pattern served as a reminder that plant life was being drawn through a human structure. The illusion of rolling hills would be interrupted like a film slowed down until the individual frames are visible.

Of course this was far more than an image, the plants were alive and I was struggling to meet their needs. They were tragically dependant so I accelerated; increasing soil depth, rigging trellises, and buying more lights. As one life form was brought forward others followed. When mold appeared on the grains eczema started to appear on me. An outbreak of gnats caused problems with the neighbors.

A day's neglect or changes in the building's heating had huge impact; these were not houseplants. Inevitably the studio and gallery spaces would eject us. While the grains had undoubtedly travelled across civilizations to make it to the bulk section of the supermarket the plants were difficult for me to transport. I moved them in trolleys, friend's trucks, vans hired by the hour and taxis. Anticipating international travel I decided to compost the plants and somehow found solace in the thought of them finding contact with the ground. Something to do with the mold and the gnats.

CHAPTER 20

Greenbots Where the Grass Is Greener: An Interview with Katherine Behar

Katherine Behar, Fatma Çolakoğlu, and Ulya Soley

As labor has become gradually more mechanized and machine-based, the artist Katherine Behar questions the capitalist foundation of who the laborer is and what awaits humanity in the near future. Behar's artwork *Roomba Rumba* is an installation consisting of two Roombas (autonomous robotic vacuum cleaners) carrying rubber trees and vacuuming a generic green carpet endlessly while a well-known children's song "High Hopes" plays in the background. The song's hero, a little old ant, overcomes hardships, and in this piece Behar recasts the ant "as an even more perfect worker—a machine." She also draws uncanny similarities between the plants and exploited workers, as well as machine production and human labor. The rubber plants and Roombas become interactive objects, and they both work as metaphors of repetitive labor. With the music in the background as they vacuum, these plants seemingly dance the Rumba; their rhythmic swivels humanize them, adding persona to these green-natured creature-like beings.

Your choice of rubber trees as the key players of this installation is significant. Despite their being quite common house plants that everyone would recognize, did you have other motives or reasons for choosing to use rubber trees?

Originally, I chose rubber trees in reference to the soundtrack to *Roomba Rumba*, the song "High Hopes," which plays as a karaoke backing track in the installation. "High Hopes" is a children's song about a little old ant who tries against all odds to move a rubber tree plant. The song's protagonist, an ant, has long been a symbol for the worker. By replacing the ant with a Roomba, a robotic vacuum, my intention was to highlight how the automated labor of robotic machines is a contemporary extension of slave labor. It seems there's nothing wrong with utilizing a machine to do one's bidding, but in automation the machine itself is a stand-in for a human laborer—in the case of a Roomba, a vacumming domestic worker or perhaps a housewife. More subtly, the song "High Hopes" teaches human children to identify with the ant. Willingly modeling themselves as perfect neoliberal subjects, they'll always try to keep working, driven by irrationally "high hopes." These continuities between human and nonhuman labor give the project an unsettling, dystopic dimension, despite the cheery song and the inviting, leafy dance.

As I developed this project and learned more about rubber tree plants, I discovered ways in which these plants are workers, too. Like Roombas, rubber trees are prized domestic companions. They are recommended as house plants for their air purification efficiency as well as their capacity to withstand human neglect uncomplainingly. In other words, the rubber tree may be a maintenance worker in its own right, maintaining air quality alongside the Roomba, maintaining the carpet. Both labor dutifully in the background, just like the unknown ant in the song.

This installation aims to reverse these patterns, swapping exploitation, hostility, and neglect for cameraderie, hospitality, and care. People rarely mention the carpet in this project, but in many ways this bright green, consumerist, domestic substitute-for-grass embodies these values. As a would-be plant, it welcomes the vacuums' care and hosts interactions between plants, machines, and humans on its surface.

Like robot's etymological root in the word *robota*, rubber trees are also linked to slavery. When I presented an early version of this project for FemTechNet at the University of Michigan, Eliza Cadoux gave a brilliant interpretation of the project using the rubber tree as a point of departure. In Congolese rubber plantations, Belgian colonialists punished underproductive workers by cutting off their hands. Productive workers were then forced to work doubly hard to support themselves along with their maimed family members. Cadoux insightfully identified how this literally "hands-free" form of slave labor is sublimated today in "hands-free" technologies like Roombas, which in this project still bear rubber trees as a burden. With regard to plants, we could expand this postcolonial critique of violence to include an Anthropocenic critique of violent plantation practices that harm rubber trees by draining their sap, and devastate ecological diversity through monoculture and agribusiness.

These specificities of rubber trees reinforce the notion that nonhuman plants and nonhuman machines can be compatriots of human workers, united as we all are in conditions of work, exploitation, precarity, and cruelty.

Could you elaborate more on how you perceive the future's human-nonhuman solidarities and where you would position plants as part of this dialogue? How would this solidarity be possible in a capitalist, consumerist context?

By extracting labor from humans, machines, and plants across the board, capitalism is already well on the way toward flattening anthropocentric hierarchies, so toppling those hierarchies is not enough, and this is where human-nonhuman solidarities come in.[1] In projects like *Roomba Rumba*,

I attempt to forge inclusive partnerships between all categories of being on the basis of this mutual exploitation, which already puts humans, machines, and plants on level ground.

It's a human habit to prioritize solidarities where we already perceive similarity or commonality. But on this basis, if machines are superceding animals and plants as human counterparts, we may find ourselves caring *least* about plants. This would be a serious mistake, not because plants, as organic species like humans, deserve priority over inorganic machines, but because the only conceivable way to counter the broad, expansive scope of capitalist extractive logic is through solidarities that are equally as broad.

Along with solidarities between humans and machines, which are common in my work, *Roomba Rumba* also enables caring connections between machines and plants, and plants and humans. Although it might sound absurd or silly at first, there's already a serious basis for this way of thinking in feminist theory, alternative and anticapitalist economic theory, and environmental theory.

We are all conscripted into work and exploitation under patriarchal capitalist systems. These systems integrate organic and inorganic or animate and inanimate components side by side, and they are optimized to render distinctions like these quaint and irrelevant. It also no longer makes much sense to distinguish production from consumption or producer from product—these familiar separations are rendered moot. Take the advent of big data: humans are exploited not just as sources of labor power in production, or as sources of desire and debt in consumption, but also—in the form of data—as sources of raw material. I think if there's positive potential in this situation it's a chance for more empathic and collaborative relationships with the object world. In nonhuman solidarities with machines, we acknowledge our shared capacity for labor power, and with plants (and minerals), our common status as raw materials.

We have a powerful legacy of feminist scholarship that connects the exploitation of people and

---

1 I have developed this idea in "An Introduction to OOF" in (2016) *Object-Oriented Feminism* (Ed.) Katherine Behar (Minneapolis: University of Minnesota Press).

FIGURE 20.1   Katherine Behar, *Roomba Rumba*. 2015. Installation view at Sector 2337, Chicago. Photograph by Soohyun Kim.
Image courtesy of the artist.
© KATHERINE BEHAR.

the exploitation of nature. For example, in *The Death of Nature*, Carolyn Merchant established how scientific rationalism justified the twofold exploitation of both women and nature during the Industrial Revolution; further, in *Caliban and the Witch: Women, the body, and primitive accumulation*, Silvia Federici underscored the flagrant violence in this utilitarian paradigm, which continues today. In *Roomba Rumba,* both the organic rubber trees and the inorganic green carpet are stand-ins for "nature" in Merchant's sense, while the Roombas raise the specter of "pure exploitation," evoking Federici's history of violence at the crux of our human-nonhuman entanglements.

For example, the word *robot* derives from the Czech word *robota,* which translates as "forced labor" or "serf labor." This means whenever we talk about robots, we are really talking about social relationships because we are employing the metaphor of slavery.[2] Robots like the Roombas seem to offer an end to human work. But, who gets to enjoy this end of work? Today automated labor might be better understood not as machinic labor but as dehumanized labor. Automation now either still means forced labor—slave labor, or maybe prison labor—or it means offloading jobs that have traditionally been done by humans to machines, leaving humans unemployed and vulnerable.

At the same time, it's important to distinguish between dehumanization and the nonhuman. Nonhumans—like the plants, robots, and carpet

2   This passage draws from the interview 'Nonhuman Solidarities: Katherine Behar and Eben Kirksey Discuss *High Hopes (Deux)*' in *Bad at Sports*, August 18, 2016, online: [<http://badatsports.com/2016/nonhuman-solidarities-katherine-behar-and-eben-kirksey-discuss-high-hopes-deux>].

in this project—can counter dehumanization by expanding the possibilities for solidarity which dehumanization forecloses.

> *Roomba Rumba* **is a popular work in your exhibitions. It grabs the attention of the visitors and invites them to interact with the plants carried away by the Roombas. It is clear that the interaction between humans, objects, plants, and machines are vital to your overall work. Could you expand specifically on the anticipated role of the visitor for this piece?**

My aim in *Roomba Rumba*, as in much of my work, is to construct an opportunity for human viewers to experience care toward the nonhuman object world, while also recognizing that that world consists of many different kinds of relationships that are totally external to and independent of human involvement. Humans may pass through a world in which plants and machines have formed their own symbiotic systems. The plants and machines respond hospitably to human presence, accommodating human visitors, and flirtatiously working around the temporary human intruders. The plants in particular seem to invite camaraderie and care from humans, gently caressing guests with their leaves. Ironically, these techno-phytological assemblages model the ideal behavior I wish humans would exhibit toward nonhuman objects. Sadly, we humans are not nearly so gracious as hosts. Too often humans respond opportunistically and destructively to the nonhumans that cross our paths.

CHAPTER 21

Home Depot Throwing Out Plants

Various Contributors

Besteststepmommy (Zone 5/ Mi)[1]

Hello,
I'm just distraught over this. My daughters and I went to home depot looking for some plants. We went through the plant department and found a cart with plants that were and marked down to $2.00, so I started putting them in my cart. There was lavender, hostas, and a few other perennials that I was not familiar with being a newbie. As I was doing this an employee stopped me and told me that they were not for sale (there was not sign). When I questioned him about it his answer was that they received full store credit so they threw them away. I was disgusted. We walked out leaving and them found some hibiscus plants for $7.97 and most of them were in terrible shape. So, I went back to this man who I found was a manager and he told me he could not give me a discount that they get full credit. I told him what I thought about them being put into a dumpster and he told me that is not exactly were they are put. He said they are put into a baler, crushed and made into compact bales.

I was just horrified. I asked him why the plants were not taken better care of and he said that they can only water form above and that it is not good for all of the plants.

As I left I stopped another employee and complained about this store policy and he told me that the manager had thrown out $4000.00 worth of plants the day before.
Shame on Home Depot ... Shame Shame Shame […]

triciae (Zone 7 Coastal SE CT)

Folks, HD, L's, WM, etc. are businesses first and foremost. They have stockholders to account to. It is MUCH more expensive to pay labor to properly take care of hundreds/thousands of itty-bitty plants than it is to let some of the inventory die. Their profit margin is set to cover these losses. In addition, contract arrangements w/the growers further protect the bottom line. They are NOT gardeners. They are business people. Their cost for a 1 ga. perennial is pennies. Even at minimum wage, it's much cheaper to let 500 plants die than to pay wages for someone to drag around a hose watering hundreds of 4" pots. They rely on a quick inventory turnover ... sell it quick before it either needs maintenance or croaks. Some will die ... it's business.

Bruggirl (8b)

Kev,
Unfortunately, tossing the plants for full credit is a corporate rule, and can't be overruled by a store manager. Actually, their cost per pot isn't that low, because they get that replacement guarantee. The garden center in these places is a "loss leader," which exists just to get people into the store. It's ones of the lowest profit margin areas of any big box store.

---

1 This thread has been published here with little to no grammatical correction and alteration from its original online state in order to retain the vernacular specific to the exchange. Extracts from (2004–2009) "Home Depot throwing plants away" in Houzz, July 9, online: [<http://forums.gardenweb.com/discussions/1433913/home-depot-throwing-out-plants>] accessed on March 23, 2016.

© KONINKLIJKE BRILL NV, LEIDEN, 2019 | DOI:10.1163/9789004375253_023

Sillybugs (z10 FL)

One of the HD's near me, puts all the going "crusty" plants on a huge cart and leaves it sitting near the dumpster (all the way on the other side of the lot away from the compactor). When I drive by and see this, I go inside the wanna be nursery and ask if I can have the plants from the garbage.

Half the time they have no idea what I'm talking about and say to me... "if there in the garbage, I don't see why not" so I go and take what I want. And try to nurse it back to health. I think only one time someone b-ed at me, and I told them, I was sorry, the woman inside said I could have them.

Maybe I sound dumb saying this, but I feel so sad for the plants that get tossed out like that, it is a shame that a lot of people often see plants as so disposable.

Why can't they make a community program and donate the plants to clubs or organizations??? I'm sure allot of kids would have a ball. Or some retired people in homes could have a great hobby to take up some of their time. The possibilities are endless!

–my 2 cents—SillyB

lizziem62 (z4 Ont.)

hey sillybugs, I agree with you, big business is sad, and helping to ruin the environment.

We have White Rose here in Canada, and they have open dumpsters. I used to get truckloads out. Often, I put them through the compost just to use the soil up. Made me sick that I was composting every little crumb and they were throwing away so much. I was innocent then, and had no idea how much waste there was out there. I sure wish I could get into those open dumpsters!!!!! Like you, some stores leave them beside the dumpster for a while and I rescue them whenever I can. I wish they would donate them to charities. It would be so nice to fix up the front of the space, or soup kitchen or something that doesn't have the money to spend on extras, but could benefit from a sprucing up.

LowesLNS

Wow ... its pretty interesting reading all this from a customer's point of view. I work for Lowes as the nursery specialist, and I take my job very seriously. Everything in my yard is taken care of very well.

The only plants we get full credit for are any plants you see inside the store, and tropicals that might be outside during the warmer months. Policy is anything distressed is marked down for seven days. After that, we call the vendor, get our credit and throw them out. Why do they give us credit? I asked this question when I first started. They told me that Lowes itself is not selling the plants, vendors are selling their plants through Lowes. Vendors fight for the "privilege" to sell their plants at Lowes. Which means is if they are an approved vendor, if their plants die for any reason, we get our money back. It sounds stupid that if I forget to water a plant and it dies, the company gets its money back. But the fact is that the vendors takes that risk of loss because they are selling a whole lot more through us than they would on their own, and at a higher profit. Lowes does not make that much money on plants, our markup is only between 20–30%.

Nothing kills me more than people asking me if they can just have plants that i am throwing out, and telling them no. I try my best to keep everything alive but the conditions inside the store are horrible. I would love to give away the stuff we get credit for (or take it home myself) but unfortunately ... I need my job. If a customer walks out the door, goes dumpster diving, or gets anything marked down more than 50% on full credit items, and mentions my name ... its unemployment for me. I've already been warned a couple of times.

But if ya want anything in my yard that's past bloom or out of season. I can make all the deals I want. I like to find homes for everything.

[...]

crosstongue_aim_com

I don't think wining on the internet or talking about this stuff to managers is enough to make a point. But you did give me an idea. I'm gonna make 100 copies of this page and place a stack of them in the garden center or somewhere so all the gardening people who shop there can read what happens and join in the outrage. I also have a lot of other maltreatment stories like their bonsai trees... they GLUE the rocks on which dissolves into the soil and eventually seeps into the roots, and the cement rocks choke the poor bonsai off. Their jade plants are almost always over watered and lacking proper light [they have no red on the leaves and very poor roots] but it is true that other than plants that are exotic or sensitive they do have great plants for the price. I'm also gonna try to snap some picks of the plants being thrown out and post them in the newspaper, if I cant get them in there then i will at least post them in my school newspaper. (surprisingly a lot of people my age get pretty outraged about this kinda stuff) I mean we are trying to go green and recycle and giving away and or donating those plants that get thrown out is RECYCLING I don't even care if they give them to costumers they could donate them to charities and such. It may not be food or clothes but plant really do affect the vibe of a room. The could also rather than fibbing about what they do with the plants also just send them back to the nurseries. 3/4 of the plants start as cuttings there anyway. They could take cuttings of the living plant, grow it and then sell it back to Home Depot so the same plant can get recycled 3 or 4 times rather than only getting 1 chance to be bought not to mention it would save the nursery money because they would not have to buy as many new plants to propagate and intern Home Depot can buy the pants back in bulk for even less that what they are presently buying them for. And who knows with the money they would be saving may go towards better plant care as well

jordan_californicus

Okay, I have to put in my two-cents, both as a person on the retail side of things, and as a customer. And to clarify, no, I do not work at a big box-store. It's not a chain store. And I'm damn proud of the work I do, even though I know there's always room for improvement. Firstly, as it's been explained by many a store employee, yes the store / nursery gets credit back from the manufacturer for plants that have expired / haven't sold. It is an agreement between the buyer and the seller that the plants are DESTROYED. It would cost the seller too much to have them shipped back. In some cases, this is done, but usually this is limited to small items such as bulbs and small houseplant items and such. I know it makes sense that "Well if they're going to throw them away why can't I have them?" You cannot have them because the store is under legal obligation NOT to give them away. Then one would say "Then they should take better care of them". On any given spring day, go out to one of these nurseries and start counting plants. Just start at one row and start counting. And realize that in a given week, thousands more plants will come in, thousands will be sold, and maybe less than a few hundred will actually have expired, gone past their prime. There is a turn-over, like any other business, because even with good care, plants die. Things come up. Crap happens. The better nurseries manage to keep their plants happier longer, but in the long run, a large perennial shrub can only last so long in a 5 gallon bucket. Less in a gallon pot. Less in a 4 inch pot. Now as a frugal customer, you see this as blatant waste. And anything a employee tells you is an excuse for this waste. And of course, there's always incompetent people to make matters worse. Guess what? There's incompetent people EVERYWHERE. I see them everyday. It's only obvious that some of those people would have jobs where they work incompetently in an area where we would inevitably be forced to interact with them. Back to being the customer, you see this as waste and expect the nurseries to do something about it. What? I've already established that they can't just 'give them away'. Should they let them sit on the sales rack longer then? For how long? You have to realize that the stores don't just throw a clearance sign on a plant for five minutes, clock it, then say 'Okay toss this baby out we're getting credit for it!" No, they try to sell it first, at a lesser profit to them because like it or not, they're a business. They're trying to make a living just like each and everyone of us does as well. So they try to at least squeeze a meager profit out of it. If that doesn't happen within a reasonable time, then the store logically has to move it. Why? BECAUSE THE PLANT LOOKS LIKE $%*^. See, a frugal customer, myself included, may see a plant in need of rescue. But a vast majority of shoppers see that as a sign of a bad nursery, a business that does not care about its image. Even if a business hides this clearance 'zone' away from the main public eye, it will eventually be seen, and in many that leaves a bad 'taste' in their mouths as shoppers. Remember, the business thing? Business need money. That's how they stay ... in business. If you want that plant, then get it when's it's discounted. Lots of other people were already willing to pay the price it was worth when it was healthier. Fewer, though still some might pay its accommodated price for its current state. But when I have to deal with the constant "Oh, you're throwing that away? Can I have it? *no* ..." every few weeks? People like that give frugal shoppers a bad image. I see these vultures every so often. They're a rare breed, mind you, and shouldn't be allotted with the rest, but they're there. They eye the same plant, every time they come in. They get in a tiff when someone else pays for it at a price they wouldn't give in to, and they fuss when they don't want to pay at a price lower than what they themselves would've gotten it for even if they were a wholesale business. Freaking VULTURES.

Now, stores / managers should be somewhat accommodating. It's not unreasonable for a customer to ask for a discount on a plant, but asking for anything over 40% is pushing at a major loss for the retailer. In the customers mind it's "just $5"

but a loss is a loss. It is a constant reflection on someon's higher-up (even small businesses have higher-ups) that can be good or bad, and every loss and gain counts. Friendliness and respect will get you far here. But do not assume that because even if you are a regular, that you are given *manatorial* (I so made up that word because I could) privilegesPersonal rant: Customer comes in. Sees flat of flowers, looking not their best but certainly not out for the count, in July. Asks if he could get a deal on them, and had they been actually worse for wear, I would've asked the manager. But they certainly weren't, they had new buds, so I said no. He then gets the gall to insist "Well, these petunias are starting to get covered in fungus, and you're an idiot to not give them to me at a discount price. Now it's just going to spread, and when you throw them away, the manager will let me take them out of the trash, because he knows me". I replied with an "Okay, sir" and left, because I didn't need to stoop down a few levels. I didn't need to stoop down and tell him "Sir, that'd be great and all, if those really were petunias, and not the lavenders they really are. And if that really was a fungus, and not normal leaf variegation, which it is. And if the manager really knew your name, which I'm pretty damn sure he doesn't".

So, frugal customers, bear with us. Forgetting about the few incompetents out there, we're really trying our hardest to do the best with what we got. It's business, that's just how it is. And most of us try to compensate elsewhere when we can. Our business is a strong donor to 4-H. We try to use our utilities wisely, and operate in the least wasteful manner. You're not going to see us throw away a truck full of flowers because they were Marigolds that "Well shucks, these should sell good in January", and then they all froze. It's my nightmare that one of my higher-ups may one day do that, but that's neither here nor there and will probably be dealt with should it ever happen.

Thank you for your patience.

Jordan

FIGURE 21.1 Anonymous, Plants abandoned in box chain disposal area, 2017.

novice_2009 (zone 6b)

SillyB, good idea about giving them away. It would be a great plan. Another idea is to start a community gardening group effort to take some of these plants and spruce up city lots in not so pretty parts of town. I too think it's sad to see plants grown, and if they can't make money anymore, thrown in trash. We take so much and never give back. It's a shame, our disposable society and its ways. It's all about the money. If us like-minded people get together and make our voices heard, maybe some policies will change. Until then, we are just complaining to each other. Much love to you all.

PART 6

House

∴

CHAPTER 22

Presence, Bareness, and Being-With

Giovanni Aloi

Gently caring for them in his own way, Carver often sang to them in the same squeaky voice which characterized him in manhood, put them in tin cans with special soil of his own concoction, tenderly covered them at night, and took them out to "play in the sun" during the day.

PETER TOMPKINS AND CHRISTOPHER BIRD, *The Secret Life of Plants*[1]

•••

In fact, the only things in the flat Crowley devoted any personal attention to were the houseplants. They were huge, and green, and glorious, with shiny, healthy, lustrous leaves. This was because, once a week, Crowley went around the flat with a green plastic plant mister spraying the leaves, and talking to the plants.... [...] In addition to which, every couple of months Crowley would pick out a plant that was growing too slowly, or succumbing to leaf-wilt, or browning, or just didn't look quite as good as the others, and he would carry it around to all the plants. "Say goodbye to your friend," he'd say to them. "He just couldn't cut it..."

NEIL GAIMAN, *Good Omens*[2]

•••

In 1997, Rotterdam-based sculptor Rolf Engelen walked past a pile of garbage on the street and noticed some green leaves sticking out. Instead of walking by, Engelen picked up the plant and nurtured it back to full health. This encounter prompted him to wonder about the ethical dimension involved in the possibility of discarding a living being in the garbage, like any other inanimate object. From that consideration emerged a work of art capable of making people reflect upon the value we attribute to plant life and by proxy, to life in general.

Prodding the boundaries of human/plant empathy thus became central to Engelen's project titled *The Second Chance Plant*—an installation piece that provided an effective solution for abandoned plants.[3] If, as seen in the previous chapters, the power/knowledge relations inscribed in the greenhouse and the big-box home improvement stores objectified and commodified plants in absolutist terms, Engelen's project aimed at radically subverting this defining condition for plant life. The greenhouse in which *The Second Chance Plant* took place was not an intensive production space where multiple, cloned, hyperfed plants are grown for the purpose of achieving cosmetic plenitude.

As more and more plants were rescued from garbage cans, the artist decided to establish the greenhouse as an adoption center for unwanted houseplants. All exchanges took place for free—the capitalist foundations, which define economies of production in the agricultural and floral greenhouse were suspended and

---

1 Tompkins, P., and Bird, C. (1973) *The Secret Life of Plants* (New Delhi: Harper Collins) p. 136.
2 Gaiman, N. (1990) *Good Omens: The Nice and Accurate Prophecies of Agnes Nutter, Witch* (London: Gollancz).
3 Purves, T., and Selzer, A. (Eds.) (2014) *What We Want Is Free: Critical Exchanges in Recent Art* (Albany: SUNY Press) p. 287.

replaced by different economies and aesthetics of care. And perhaps more importantly, on the biopolitical register, plants' bodies were allowed to grow outside the constrictive frameworks of capitalist forces that enlarge and multiply their blooms, gloss their leaves, and impose compact shapes. In *The Second Chance Plant*, extrapolated from the capitalist economies which produced them, houseplants reclaimed an individuality usually precluded to them in human/plant relations.

Once selective breeding definitively sets desirable traits, many mass-produced varieties of plants are usually cloned. Plant producers enforce biopolitical regimes designed to standardize vegetal anatomy in order to produce sellable plants at the appropriate consumer-time of the year. What these biopolitical regimes implicitly aim to produce is a multitude of perfect specimens. Like other commodities in stores, plants undergo quality checks before being sold. Those that do not match product specifications are binned, just like in George Gessert's *Art Life* installation.

As it is well known to those who, over the past twenty years, have followed animal studies discourses, the concept of the specimen is one of the most dangerous with regards to the objectification of nonhuman beings. As an essential epistemic tool of science, the specimen is the living-being-cum-object of studies. The identification of the specimen is first and foremost an ideologically driven process of aesthetic selection which aims at crystallizing the distinctive morphological aspects we value the most in a living being. Thus, the scientific specimen is a model of perfection against which taxonomy, the cataloguing of the world operated by natural history (which during the early twentieth century informed the movement of eugenics in the US and Europe), can be articulated.

All mass-produced plants are engineered for the purpose of becoming ideal specimens: optimum replicas ontologically aligned to factory mass-produced objects more than living beings.

Reconfiguring power/knowledge relations and specimen aesthetics, Engelen's *The Second Chance Plant* derails the specimen aesthetic inscribed by the biopolitical registers of capitalist production restituting a degree of individuality to the discarded plants nursed back to life. Ultimately, the individuality of plants' remains an elusive entity—one central to the lack of empathy which humans have developed towards them, and essential to their reckless exploitation. In Engelen's installation, not dissimilar from society's approach to rescue animals, every plant carries with it a story, that begins with its rescue, along with a biography made visible by the encoding of accidents, damage, inappropriate light/heat conditions, and other occurrences upon its body. The high adaptability of vegetal life means that the body of an individual plant can dramatically morph to best capitalize on the circumstances in which it grows. After six months in a domestic environment, a plant purchased at the supermarket, if it survives, usually looks substantially different from its cloned siblings in the store.

At this point, it is important to acknowledge that not all houseplants are the same. Beyond the space in which the human/plant encounter takes place, time is one of the most important factors in human/plant relations. Because plants exist on a different time-scale than ours, spending time with plants constitutes one of the few access points we have at our disposal to build an empathic relationship with them, and the domestic sphere can provide a useful opportunity to do just that. Human/plant relations in the house-space develop at a different speed from those between humans and pets, yet there are parallels between animal and plant worth considering in this context.

As long as plants are not considered objects of design, like color accents or as vertical counterparts to the horizontality of a sofa, or "perfect to fill that blank wall by the window", they can too become companions. Plants whose presence in the house is originated and dictated by these parameters will be discarded in the garbage along with the odd chair that's been sitting around too long. The plants we understand beyond objecthood, have moved house with us multiple times, have witnessed breakups, survived parties, holidays, cold drafts, irregular waterings, and in more than one occasion brought us to move furniture around to make them happier—these are the plants that manage to survive despite us, the ones some of us end up talking to, the ones that, eventually, truly die.

German born British painter Lucian Freud is internationally known for his paintings of models that provocatively challenge the art historical tradition separating the naked from the nude. But beyond this celebrated (of course) anthropocentric focus, the artist's career is dotted with many interesting and highly original paintings whose prominent subjects are plants. These are the works that usually leave art historians short of words, thus remaining suspended in an enigmatic dimension of frustrated, cryptic, symbolic allusiveness. This is, however, no shortcoming on behalf of the artist. Art historians have generally not been able to seriously consider the possibility of a human/plant relationship, even a momentary one, worthy of being captured on canvas.

In *Interior with Plant, Reflection Listening (Self-Portrait)* from 1967–68, the lush foliage of a potted variegated pandanus takes up most of the canvas. On the left-top corner, fading in the background is a self-portrait of the shirtless artist with a cupped ear and closed eyes. Based upon the initial sense of uncertainty caused by the nonaffirmative composition, I entertain the notion that the artist is alluding to a certain *presence of the plant*—something reaching beyond the swift encounter; perhaps an attempt to bridge the sensorial gap which separates us from them. In this context, the nakedness of the artist can be understood as representative of a cultural dismantling of the preconceived notions of plants we all inherit and which usually prevent us from engaging with them as anything more than objects. This nakedness speaks of a kind of vulnerability necessary to establish openness—to be "with the plant" in a space defined by more than

sight: the sense through which we more regularly comprehend them and objectify them in return. The cupped ear, which substitutes sight in the artist's self-portrait, at first might appear humorous as plants are usually ontologically diminished in popular culture because of the silent dimension they occupy—from this specific cultural construct emerges the paradoxical image of the human speaking to plants as a lonely lunatic, outcast, or sociopath. Yet, there's something interesting and productive in this unorthodox attempt to "hear" what the plant might have to say.

The idea that plants could sense being spoken to or that they might even be able to read our minds was gaining popularity at the time Freud's painting was made. In 1966, Cleve Backster, a CIA interrogation specialist hooked a galvanometer to the leaf of a dracaena he kept in his office.[4] To his surprise, the needle of the polygraph machine would rouse whenever he thought of burning the plant. On the grounds of this astonishing reaction, he proceeded to experiment with many other varieties establishing that plants have an awareness of their surrounding which also involved an ethical dimension (displaying an aversion to violence towards other plants). His findings were first published in the *International Journal of Parapsychology* in 1968 and then popularized by a *New York Times* best seller titled *The Secret Life of Plants* by Peter Tompkins and Christopher Bird.[5] Despite the fact that Backster's experiments could never be successfully replicated, the book tapped into a long-standing, and seemingly widespread desire, to connect to our vegetal companions. Ultimately, a plant's silent, dependent, constant, impartial

---

4   Backster, C. (2003) *Primary Perception: Biocommunication with Plants, Living Foods, and Human Cells* (Irwindale: White Rose Millennium Press).

5   Backster, C. (1968) 'Evidence of primary reception in plant life' in *International Journal of Parapsychology*, X, 4, Winter, pp. 329–48 and Tompkins, P., and Bird, C. (1973) *The Secret Life of Plants: A Fascinating Account of the Physical, Emotional, and Spiritual Relations Between Plants and Man* (New York: Harper Collins).

FIGURE 22.1 Lucian Freud, *Interior with Plant, Reflection Listening (Self-Portrait)*, 1968. Oil on Canvas. Private Collection
© THE LUCIAN FREUD ARCHIVE/BRIDGEMAN IMAGES.

presence in the house would make it the perfect keeper of our secrets, passions, desires, fears, and hopes—perhaps a plant absorbs our anxieties and joy just as it absorbs CO_2. The laconic presence likens the plant to a wise old friend who knows how to listen and knows better than to speak. This, in essence, might be the implied proposition of Freud's painting—the absurd possibility that, in a

moment of vulnerability, the plant that shares the intimacy of the domestic space with us might, in the depths of its roots, know what we keep doing wrong in our lives.

Although it precedes it by thirty years, Freud's *Interior With Plant* seems to anticipate the staging of what will become the most influential human/nonhuman encounter in the history of contemporary philosophical thinking: Derrida's nakedness in the presence of his cat.[6] In *The Animal That Therefore I Am*, exploring the interstitial space between animal and human, Derrida asserted that the entire history of Western philosophy, from Aristotle to Heidegger, is guilty of inappropriately representing the ontological status of animal and man. In the text, this line of inquiry is set off by a nude, impromptu encounter with his cat, whose stare calls into question both the philosopher's humanity-animality and his subjectivity. Here too, like in Freud's painting, Derrida's nakedness is factual as well as metaphorical—it is simultaneously the nakedness of a domestic interior, the vulnerability underneath cultural constructs, and the nakedness of Adam in the Garden of Eden—a self-awareness which constructed humanity as separate from nonhuman beings. In this situation, the cat's otherness emerges as a questioning entity, awakening the consciousness of the human in a paradoxically alienating way, making him painfully aware of this very nakedness. Derrida's ensuing shame is twofold: on the one hand, he is ashamed because he should be clothed—this would be the appropriate condition for the human in opposition to the naked animal; on the other, he is ashamed of being ashamed by the commonality which his nakedness shares with that of the animal.

> Against the impropriety that comes of finding oneself naked, one's sex exposed, stark naked before a cat that looks at you without moving, just to see. The impropriety [*malséance*] of a certain animal nude before the other animal, from that point on one might call it a kind of animalséance: the single, incomparable and original experience of the impropriety that would come from appearing in truth naked, in front of the insistent gaze of the animal, a benevolent or pitiless gaze, surprised or cognizant. The gaze of a

seer, visionary, or extra-lucid blind person. It is as if I were ashamed, therefore, naked in front of this cat, but also ashamed of being ashamed. A reflected shame, the mirror of a shame ashamed of itself, a shame that is at the same time specular, unjustifiable, and unable to be admitted to.[7]

In this encounter consuming itself on the level of the singular and irreducible, the cat is a who, not a what. The cat has her point of view—that of an absolute other capable of inducing a sense of absolute alterity. But can the encounter with a plant ever induce a similar chain of inference considering that the plant constantly seems to us unable to lay hold of self through a meaningful level of perceptible consciousness? In Hegelian terms, the plant lacks a sense of self because of its presumed inability to own itself beyond the phenomenal obviousness of its growth.[8] Furthermore, it can be argued that, in a Levinasian sense, the plant also lacks a face—the interface necessary to produce a response and demand ethical obligations.[9] So where does the possibility for a more "meaningful encounter with a plant" lie? And what can be drawn from it that might surpass or problematize the analogy with human/animal encounters?

In Freud's painting, the canvas has been outlined as an epistemic space of sameness in which contiguity between plant and human body is visually accomplished through the bare retainment of superficial differences. Both plant and human appear in a sense to share a communal and essential dimension of nakedness. But in opposition to the notion of identity, which is traditionally buried in the finitude of man, Michael Marder argues that a plant embodies an approach to alterity that tends,

> with every fiber of its vegetal being, towards an exteriority it does not dominate. Its

6   Derrida, J. (2008) *The Animal That Therefore I Am* (New York: Fordham University Press).

7   Ibid., p. 5.

8   Marder, M. (2013) *Plant-Thinking: A Philosophy of Vegetal Life* (New York: Columbia University Press) pp. 69–70.

9   Levinas, E. (1969) *Totality and Infinity: An Essay on Exteriority* (Pittsburgh: Duquesne University Press).

heteronomy is symbolic of Levinas' quasi-phenomenological description of the subjectivization of the I in the ethical relation to the other that/who is unreachable and cannot be appropriated by the I.[10]

In this interconnectedness to its surrounding, the plant bypasses any possibility to be naked in a Derridian sense—even more so than a cat, Freud's plant lacks the anthropocentric notion of self-awareness which could reveal a sense nakedness. Yet, this should be seen as an entirely positive circumstance—the plant is present in a, usually undervalued, wholesome way—a state of presence that is more regularly precluded to the human. In the space of sameness outlined by Freud's canvas, another type of nakedness is revealed—this is not the nakedness of shame but the *bareness* of being-with. Freud's painting thus gestures towards a "laying bare" of human-nonhuman bodies. This notion of shared-bareness carries with it a connotation of vulnerability that has been discussed by Giorgio Agamben in *Homo Sacer*. A "bare life" is not the same as biopolitical life, the managed political subject/object of power relations, but a being alive outside the ethico/political schemata. The bareness of the artist juxtaposed with the intrinsic one of the plant, thus gestures towards a communal stripping of rights in which the disposable status of modern life in the face of the capitalistic sovereignty is momentarily accomplished in the domestic space.

A form of "being-with a plant" thus entails, if possible, dismantling all the coding epistemological tools such as zoology, biology, botany, religion, literature, and capitalism to access a momentary bareness stripped to necessity. But although the plant might seem initially unable to command as much thought-mobilization as Derrida's cat, the disadvantages inscribed in its facelessness, voicelessness, and ultimately its inability to respond, can momentarily appear to be compensated by the radical passivity of its *bare-being*. The plant

is always *bare* in a dimension of radical otherness. This radical otherness is grounded in radical difference, not in having or being less. Being bare is a state of being that the plant owns much more wholesomely than we could ever do. It is in this sense that the domestic setting proposed by Freud's painting enables a *milieu* in which the plant is a nonjudging, witnessing other—a knowing accomplice, constantly withholding evidence, but perhaps recording or absorbing other presences.

And say the plant responded? With the diminutive self-portrait included in *Interior With Plant*, Freud gestures towards a paradox specific to the idiomatic of painting—its silent stillness—a metaphysical contingency revealing an essential affinity between plants and painting. The artist's eyes are closed. Paintings that allude to acoustic phenomena implicitly gesture towards the medium's idiomatic limitations. They inscribe a critical awareness of their own essential being, laying bare their limitations and the perimeters of their fields of action. They relentlessly allude to the presence of an inaccessible, yet undeniable, sensorial dimension. In this sense, the *Reflection Listening* segment of the painting's title appears to deliberately disrupt the primacy of sight for the purpose of suggesting other relational modes of engagement capable of transcending the predictabilities and entrapments of human language. Who is reflecting what in this painting? The ambiguity of the word reflection is key in this encounter. What is being reflected? Who is reflecting? Has the surface of the canvas been transformed into a mirror?

In the work of humanistic psychologist Carl Rogers, reflective listening was considered a psychotherapeutic practice based on a dialectical process unfolding between the therapist's empathy and the genuineness of the interlocutor. Reflection, in Rogers's original formulation, is a product of therapist self-restraint, something he will later realize might lead to insincerity on behalf of the therapist. He thus conceives reflection as a means of implementing attitudes of empathy

---

10   Marder, M. (2013) p. 72.

FIGURE 22.2 Moe Beitiks, *The Plant is Present*, installation, 2011
© MOE BEITIKS.

and acceptance in the dialectic process. Could this be something Lucian Freud was considering when titling his work?

Meghan Moe Beitiks's *Plant is Present* installation project aimed at further exploring the potentialities of being-with a plant on a "one-to-one" situation akin to that of the domestic sphere. The artist worked with *Sansevieria trifasciata*, one of the most common and resilient houseplants in the world. Native to tropical West Africa from Nigeria east to Congo this evergreen perennial plant is extremely tolerant to low lighting, irregular watering, and it is virtually immune to parasites. It is particularly interesting, in the context of this chapter, that this plant most regularly goes by the names of "snake plant" and "mother-in-law's tongue." These culturally laden names always pin the plant to representational registers linked to the biblical as well as language—the connotations of the snake as the symbol of sin and the mother in law as the Other

whose gaze relentlessly judges are underlined by the harrow and sharp shape of the blade-like pointy leaves.

In this occasion, the artist dressed her plant and sat it on a chair—in so doing, this humorous anthropomorphization implied the possibility of a plant-nakedness, preventing the instant classification of the plant in the rank of the object. Visitors were then invited to sit in front of it for a certain length of time. The installation was a response to Marina Abramovic's 2010 MoMA 3 months long performance titled *The Artist Is Present*. Abramovic then spent a total of seven-hundred and fifty hours in the gallery space, giving museum visitors the opportunity to sit opposite her and simply stare. Silent Abramovic only relied on her bodily presence and the intensity of her gaze to strike a connective bridge with a stranger—a state of being together that is not underlined by the urgency of a positivist exchange and neither by the productiveness of agreement. Breaching beyond the linguistic dimension, establishing a kind of "reflective silent listening" was what Abramovic hoped for. The otherness staged in these encounters could therefore not be one defined by difference or similarity but by the acknowledgment of a shared dimension of existence that equally burdens and enlivens the living condition beyond the bonds of race, gender, and social status.

This essentialist performative experience was hijacked by Beitiks who contextualized *The Plant is Present* as follows:

> The question becomes: if we are willing as a public, to wait in line for hours to sit in the presence of a famous artist, what else could we be devoting our attention to? If the act of sitting silently with someone gives us a new appreciation of them, gives us a feeling of connection, of enlightenment, why not bestow that attention on something worthwhile—like the important ecological work of a common houseplant?[11]

Beitiks accompanied the staging of the performance with a series of notes that, relying on scientific information, made the visitor aware of the plant's many talents: these involved significant contributions to design, tireless effort to clean the air, ability to suffer abuse and neglect, tremendous level of bodily sacrifice in devotion to the needs of humans. Some of the visitors who sat in front of the Sanseveria reported that spending time with the plant with a sense of intent other than any practical economy felt "connected with the moment." A visitor said: "I found it deeply relaxing & meditative to stare into the face of the plant. It was a very peaceful, non-combative exchange," another noted that "It's nice to sit with something that listens in peace," "Marina was exactly as interesting," "The plant swayed in the wind. So I swayed, too" and "I felt a connection to the plant and was able to live in the moment."[12]

11   Beitiks, M. (2011) 'The plant is present' in *The Sustainability Review*, online: [<http://www.thesustainability-review.org/blog/the-plant-is-present>] accessed 8 October 2016.

12   Beitiks, M. (2011) 'Everyone who sat with the plant, day two/comment book part one' in *Culture/Nature/Structure*, online: [<http://www.meghanmoebeitiks.com/everyone-who-sat-with-the-plant-day-two-comment-book-part-one/>] accessed 8 October 2016.

CHAPTER 23

Houseplants as Fictional Subjects

Susan McHugh

No living beings populate literary history more inconspicuously than houseplants. Almost always they are written as read: to be seen as objects in stories and not as subjects who have histories. To identify with a potted plant signals that a character is pathetic, sympathizing with its sufferings perverse, and truly caring for them pathological. For houseplants, proximities to people intensify rather than overcome species and other divisions. Or so the story once went.

In recent decades, as literary animal studies has grown, plants take up the role that more animate nonhumans used to play, as narrative wallflowers transforming into figurative social butterflies. Crudely put, in literary theory plants are in danger of becoming the new animals. Twentieth-century fiction however presents a more complex history, wherein thinking about houseplants is entangled not simply with other nonhuman beings but also in changes to plant propagation and cohabitation with humans. Just as ethological knowledges enable animals to have histories, in the broadest sense, growing awareness of the lives of houseplants profoundly changes their stories in relation to characters who are not therefore brought into the fold but instead become all the more respected as liminal figures.

Unlike domesticated animals in contemporaneous fictions, they do not seem set to simply bloom as characters. So, what accounts for the switch from symbols or psychological projections toward a more complex sense of houseplants' social and narrative functionality? Gaining interest in the period in which the mod cons of piped water and central heat enabled commercially-produced, ornamental houseplant-keeping to become an ordinary urban experience, novels and stories chart a budding sense of respect for potted plants as

vulnerable living beings that connect people to one another on the edges of life.

George Orwell's novel *Keep the Aspidistra Flying* (1936) is an inauspicious place to start. The titular houseplant is a constant presence—"one of those awful depressing things"[1]—and eventual symbol of all that is wrong with the modern world. Aspiring writer Gordon tries and fails to live in poverty in order to pursue art, finally persuaded by his pregnant girlfriend to return to middle-class comfort as a copywriter for an advertising agency. Along the way, Gordon's projections of his own inner struggle to come to terms with what he initially sees as "mingy lower-middle-class decency" take a vicious turn toward the "mangy" plant furnishing his rented room:[2]

> Gordon had a sort of secret feud with the aspidistra. Many a time he had furtively tried to kill it— starving it of water, grinding hot cigarette-ends against its stem, even mixing salt with its earth. [… After fueling his stove, he even] deliberately wiped his kerosiny fingers on the aspidistra leaves.[3]

Orwell's most likely referent is *Aspidistra elatior*, a native to Asia where it evolved in the shade of forest canopies, and more recently it became imported and sold as a household foliage plant well suited to the low-light conditions of the drab English city. Commonly known as the cast iron plant, it was one of the few to survive the dust, soot, and noxious fumes of Victorian coal heat and gas light,

---

1 Orwell, G. (1956) *Keep the Aspidistra Flying* (New York: Harcourt) p. 246.

2 Ibid., p. 22.

3 Ibid., p. 28.

eventually becoming notorious for withstanding severe neglect. Actively moving from plant neglect to torture signals how Gordon emerges as "toxic," an Orwellian antihero.[4] Ostensibly redeemed by return to the adman life, Gordon comes to view those who "'kept themselves respectable'—kept the aspidistra flying" as their emblem—as "bound up in the bundle of life," and the houseplant itself as a veritable "tree of life."[5]

Yet the terms of Orwell's metaphor prove fatal, undercutting the very possibility of consideration of the plant as alive. In the final scene, Gordon argues that an aspidistra is "the first thing one buys after one's married. It's practically in the wedding ceremony," and its purpose is to be displayed "in the front window, where the people opposite can see it."[6] Ultimately the "tree of life" is reduced to a favored commodity of bourgeois conspicuous consumption. A far cry from the rats who disfigure people's faces in *1984* and the pigs who become indistinguishable from people at the end of *Animal Farm*, the aspidistra—a houseplant artificially selected for its resilience against the inevitability of human disregard—threatens no such signs of life.

Taking a significant leap toward representing plants as warranting people's conscious engagement, Flannery O'Connor's early short story "The Geranium" (1946) starts from the spectacle of an ailing, tortured plant that becomes smashed, having fallen from an apartment window. Transplanted to New York from the rural south where he recalls that geraniums flourish as bedding plants, the old white protagonist Dudley notes that every day the neighbors "set [the geranium] out" then "let the hot sun bake it all day and they put it so near the ledge the wind could almost knock it over," in his mind tut-tutting, "They had no business with it, no business with it."[7] Having thus foreshadowed its accidental demise, the story hinges on whether, as the lone sympathetic human witness to the tragedy, Dudley can overcome his own limits and save the houseplant.

While Dudley likens the plant to a polio-stricken child "wheeled out into the sun and left to blink,"[8] he is often read as symbolized by the dying plant, uprooted from his home and consequently dwindling all the more rapidly.[9] But, in the end, clear limits mark his connection to the plant. Descriptions of Dudley pining for the black servants who enabled him to hunt and fish into old age make him an increasingly unsympathetic character; like the animals he killed, he cares about those people only as instruments of his desires. So, it comes as no surprise that Dudley abandons his impulse to help the plant because his deep-seated bigotry prevents him from accepting the help that he in turn would need from the African American neighbor, who is the only one who warms to Dudley, but whose independence and familiarity as a neighbour, not a servant, is abhorrent to the old bigot. As the story devolves to an allegory of racism, concern for the plant's suffering dies on the vine, so to speak, and the fallen plant is left "at the bottom of the alley, its roots in the air."[10]

O'Connor's experiment with presenting the plant as a psychological projection therefore retreats safely into symbolism, at least, when the reader chooses not to know much about the plant itself. Assuming that, like most creatures referred to as "potted geraniums," the plant that the author has in mind is actually of the genus pelargonium, the story gains interest in terms of intersecting human-plant histories. Originating in southern Africa, all pelargoniums traveled to the New World along familiar slave-trade routes. Although exceptionally drought- and heat-resistant, coldness

---

4   Colls, R. (2013) *George Orwell: English Rebel* (Oxford: Oxford UP), p. 39.

5   Ibid., p. 239.

6   Ibid., p. 246.

7   O'Connor, F. (1946) 'The Geranium' in *Accent: A Quarterly of New Literature*. Reprinted in (1971) *The Complete Stories* (New York: Farrar, Straus and Giroux) online:

[<http://s3.amazonaws.com/dfc_attachments/public/documents/3205162/The-Complete-Stories-Flannery-oConnor.pdf>].

8   Ibid.

9   Darretta, J.L. (2006) *Before the Sun Has Set: Retribution in the Fiction of Flannery O'Connor* (Bern: Peter Lang).

10   O'Connor, F. (1946).

will kill them. In the New York climate described as naturally and culturally chilly, the racist's story undercuts the ability of the African American man and smashed plant alike to find each other, let alone to flourish, although the possibility remains that their stories could be different in other circumstances.

Gaining distance from the emblems and ego-projections of earlier fictions, Mary McCarthy's *Birds of America* (1965) indicates how consideration creeps further into fictional representations of the houseplant as a living being with needs that never simply parallel but intersect with those of people. It centers on an extremely socially self-isolated man, whose sense of his own superiority makes him unable to recognize what he shares in common with other people.[11] Midway into the novel, central character Peter Levi, a young American student in Paris, buys a fatshedera plant and names it Old Fats. Despite the guidance of the plant-seller and a plant manual, quickly it grows "long, leggy, and despondent, like its master,"[12] who decides to take Old Fats for walks. Nearly killed by a passing car on their last walk, he accidentally drops the plant, and it is instantly decapitated. A well-meaning French stranger wraps it in a newspaper to save it for him, but Peter decides on the spur of the moment to "junk" the plant, and just "a last trace of humanity" prevents him from dropping the plant into a trash can in plain view of its would-be savior.[13]

Again, the choice of plant species bears greater scrutiny. Even before the smashup, Peter muses, "Certainly the Fatshedera would have been happier in nature, wherever it basically came from—the Far East, he supposed."[14] Far from the Orientalist "other" intimated by Peter, the name fatshedera (x *Fatshedera lizei*) reflects the species' unlikely

creation from two different plant genera. A cross between the houseplant species popularly known as Moser's Japanese fatsia (*Fatsia japonica Moserii*) and the native European woody vine Atlantic ivy (*Hedera hibernica*), fatshedera was first successfully bred in 1912 at the Lizé Frères tree nursery in Nantes. Old Fats thus lives and dies not far from the site of the invention of its kind, whose commercial introduction coincides with the historic transition in global power away from European colonization and toward US imperialism. Well into a story critical of humanist intellectuals' collusions with social-engineering agendas at the dawn of the Vietnam War,[15] the potted plant's death forces a fleeting connection with an otherwise perfect stranger in a land strange to Peter and only partly native to the plant, yet troubles Peter's smug conviction in his favorite Kantian "commandment," namely "The Other is always an End."[16]

A queer homage to Orwell's *1984* (1948), Haruki Murakami's novel *1Q84* (2009–10) glimpses a similarly special social function of plants for people who are isolated through no fault of their own. Central character Aomame, the assassin committed to killing serial abusers of women and children, has one request of Tamaru, the person who arranges her retirement into a new identity: "I have a potted rubber plant in my apartment. I'd like you to take care of it. I couldn't bring myself to throw it out."[17] Both understand that she means not the usual hired-gun euphemism, but actually that he cares for the houseplant otherwise destined to be junked.

To herself, lifelong loner Aomame laments that the houseplant was her only creaturely companion:

11   Marsh, K. (2002) '"All My Habits of Mind": Performance and Identity in the Novels of Mary McCarthy' *Studies in the Novel*, 34, 3, p. 315.

12   McCarthy, M. (1965) *Birds of America* (New York: Harcourt, Brace, Jovanovich) p. 158.

13   Ibid., p. 184.

14   Ibid., p. 166.

15   Schryer, S. (2007) 'Mary McCarthy's Field Guide to US Intellectuals: Tradition and Modernization Theory in *Birds of America*,' *Modern Fiction Studies* 53, 4, pp. 821–44.

16   McCarthy, p. 252.

17   Murakami, H. (2010) *1Q84*. Trans. Jay Rubin and Philip Gabriel (New York: Alfred A. Knopf) 2011.

she had regretted having bought it on impulse, not only because it was sad-looking, bulky, and hard to carry, but because it was a living thing. ... The rubber plant was her first experience of living with a thing that had a life of its own.[18]

Purchasing it, she discovers "she could not help but feel that paying money to take ownership of a living organism was inappropriate."[19] Although she entered the store to buy pet goldfish, amid her anticapitalist revelation the rubber plant instead catches her eye: "shoved into the least noticeable spot in the place, hiding like an abandoned orphan," appealing not exactly in a positive way, yet "she *had* to buy it."[20] But only when facing the prospect of never seeing it again does she become troubled about what will happen to it next: what it means to care for another who can outlive you.

Among the most common ficus trees used as houseplants, the rubber or *Ficus elastica* is a native across Asia that has become commercialized as a remarkably resilient and consequently common houseplant. As a garden plant, it proves less welcome, for its roots are the bane of all hardscaping. In the Indian forests where it is native, the roots are often guided to form living bridges, suggesting how a different figure could be trained up through the rubber tree as a houseplant in fiction.

In its uncertainty about the future of the potted rubber, *1Q84* signals an as-yet underdeveloped plant-fiction potential for marginalized people. Raised in a small, self-segregated religious community and abandoned by her family when she renounces her faith, Aomame only ever forms two lasting friendships, each abruptly ended by suicide and murder. She seems positively gregarious, however, in contrast to Tamaru, a gay, mixed-race

Japanese-Sakhalin Islander, whose story of electing to protect a developmentally disabled boy in the brutal orphanage where they were raised partly explains how he too becomes an exceptionally competent assassin in the service of social justice.

Drawn to be a perfect example of the social outcast in 1980s Japan, Tamaru earns the respect of Aomame not by identifying with her but by proving that, unlike her, he can "take responsibilities for others' lives," among them the disabled boy and his employer's guard dogs.[21] When she entrusts him with the rubber plant, it materializes a rare but conceivably realistic living bridge between two incredibly lonesome lives. One of several fragile connections that together constitute the novel's alternative model of power in a post-Orwellian (if not posttotalitarian) world,[22] the plant-human triangle augurs well for queer love.

What would it take to show houseplants in a new light, rather, to move literary practice beyond an incandescence that just keeps them alive and into a full-spectrum fluorescence that would allow them to flourish? Informed by biopolitical theory's recognition that current political vocabularies provide a partial means at best of making nonnormative forces and actors legible,[23] my reading of these novels indicates that propagation of nonsymbolic, ethologically-informed representations of houseplants extend models of accounting for life at the margins, and in ways that are related to yet distinct from animals in literary fiction. At least, Murakami's rubber tree suggests that potted plants come to offer timely points of connection and models of resilience at the limits of more-than-human social life in late capitalism.

---

18   Ibid., p. 551.
19   Ibid., p. 552.
20   Ibid., emphasis original.

21   Ibid., p. 553.
22   Gomel, E. (2014) *Narrative Space and Time: Representing Impossible Topologies in Literature* (New York: Routledge) p. 199.
23   Wolfe, C. (2013) *Before the Law: Humans and Other Animals in a Biopolitical Frame* (Chicago: University of Chicago Press).

CHAPTER 24

Seeing Green: The Climbing Other

Dawn Sanders

Attentional Field

In his books *About Looking* and *Why Look at Animals?* Berger provokes us to restructure our attentional field to plants both within, and beyond, an anthropocentric lens. As John Berger has noted, "our customary visible order is not the only one: it coexists with other orders" (2009, 10). In contemporary everyday life the complex morphologies and behaviors plants possess are often reduced to simple contextualized categories, so, for example, *Monstera deliciosa* experiences life in captivity as an "ornamental house-plant," in which it will "roar for space" (ourhouseplants.com); *Hedera helix* is commonly viewed on an antagonistic continuum between an "attractive" plant, which can make shady walls interesting and a rapid-growing "nuisance" on homes and walls. Beyond its natural borders *Hedera helix* has been described as "an invader."

Climbing was one of the plant movements that fascinated Charles Darwin. In his desire to study this aspect of "plantness" he used the walls of his own home as an experimental plane upon which to watch the "twitchers, twiners, climbers and scramblers" (Browne 2003, 417). He grew an *Echinocystis lobata* plant, whose behaviors he described in a letter to Hooker written on June 25, 1863, an extract of which follows:

> Having the plant in my study I have been surprised to find that the uppermost part of each branch, (ie the stem between the two uppermost leaves, excluding the growing tip) is constantly and slowly twisting round, making a circle in from 1 1/2 to 2 hours: it will sometimes go round 2 or 3 times, & then at same rate untwists & twists

in opposite direction. It generally rests half an hour before it retrogrades. The stem does not become permanently twisted. The stem beneath the twisting portion does not move in the least, though not tied. The movement goes on all day & all early night— It has no relation to light for the plant stands in my window & twists from the light just as quickly as towards it.

> This may be common phenomenon for what I know; but it confounded me quite when I began to observe the irritability of the tendrils.—I do not say it is final cause, but the result is pretty for the plant every 1 1/2 or 2 hours sweeps a circle, (according to length of bending shoot & length of tendril) of from 1 foot to 20 inches in diameter, & immediately that the tendril touches any object its sensitiveness causes it immediately to seize it. A clever gardener, my neighbour, who saw the plant on my table last night, said "I believe, Sir, the tendrils can see, for wherever I put the plant, it finds out any stick near enough". I believe the above is the explanation, viz that it sweeps slowly round & round. The tendrils, have some sense, for they do not grasp each other when young. (Darwin Correspondence Project Letter 4221)

So, Darwin became increasingly intimate with the diverse strategies plants employ to sense structures that can aid their clamber away from the dark towards the light.

Time-lapse photography has enabled the private lives of plants, and the subtle complexities of their movements, to become visible to humans, and yet we still appear to render such movements invisible. In *Of Plants, and Other Secrets*, Michael

Marder suggests such inattention to botanical life is related to the fact that "we are largely asynchronous with plants" (2013, 19) and "have neither the patience nor the capacity to linger with them, to accompany their development and growth" and thus "a face-to-face relation to plants is a non-starter" (20). Nonetheless, humans continue to live in close proximity to their "house-plants," and those plants that colonize the walls in, and around, urban dwellings.

Londa Schiebinger affirms the act of naming plants "as a deeply social process" (2004, 195) and speaks of the "linguistic imperialism" of binomial names developed by the Swedish botanist, Linnaeus. However, an even greater act of imperialistic enclosure is embodied in the treatment of domesticated climbing plants. Subsequently, at the same moment in time, a confined tropical climber (*Monstera*) can be held captive inside a human home, while outside a self-clinging creeper (*Hedera*) scales the walls before sensing the cut of a gardener's secateurs. In his essay on the sculpture of Romaine Lorquet, Berger suggests, in the context of postindustrial culture, that "anything which enters that culture has to sever its connections with nature" (1980, 189); in relation to Berger's statement, the plant behaviors of both *Monstera* and *Hedera* have been restrained by humans, such that their capacity for "plantness" has been pruned to fit the truncated "nature" of urban human culture.

Morphology

Hedera helix climbs by using "aerial rootlets" with matted pads which cling tightly to substrate. In short, it is a phytogecko running the walls of human life.

Monstera deliciosa is a tropical climber. In the wild, the germinating seedling has an interesting characteristic:

> the seedlings, upon germination, will grow in the direction of the darkest area (not just

FIGURE 24.1   Hedera helix (Dorling Kindersley, 2010)
IMAGE IN PUBLIC DOMAIN.

merely away from light) until they encounter the base of a tree to grow on. They will then begin to climb toward the light which is generally up into the canopy of the tree upon which it is growing. (University of Connecticut, 2016)

It possesses two types of leaf—unsplit and split, the latter being preferred in house-plants for aesthetic reasons. Indeed, some house-plant internet sites encourage the "polishing" of the dark shiny leaves; thereby creating houseplant housework.

Lingering

Given that much of this confined "plantness" happens in and around domestic settings, it is ironic that the site for Darwin's work on climbing plants was his family home in Kent-Down House. Here, in his study, on the walls of his house and in the

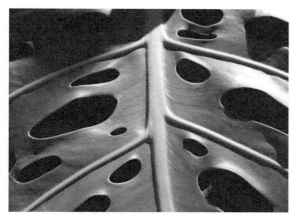

FIGURE 24.2   Monstera leaf (source Wikimedia Commons)
                 IMAGE IN PUBLIC DOMAIN.

garden Darwin entwined himself in vegetal behaviors. Berger suggests, in his essay *The Field* that our observance of a "first event" can lead us to observe other events, which result in us being "within the experience" (1980, 196–97). Darwin, through his lengthy observations of climbing plant events became closely familiar with the subtle nuances of plant movement and the "quietly complicated lives of plants" (Browne 2003, 163). Such familiarity, I would suggest, came about because Darwin chose to "linger" and "accompany" plant-life in its

own temporal zone resulting in him being, in Berger's words, "within the experience" of "plantness." In so doing Darwin could discern, and delineate, the various features that enable climbing plants to clamber away/towards the dark to reach the light. Rebecca Solnit suggests that we have come to think of landscapes' "crucial condition" as space, but she argues "its deepest theme is time" (Solnit, 2001). In the context of attending to plants in our everyday spaces perhaps taking time to linger and accompany botanical actions will assist us to see the green plant rather than the climbing other.

"Mother, what is it?" asked Kezia.

Linda looked up at the fat swelling plant with its cruel leaves and fleshy stem. High above them, as though becalmed in the air, and yet holding so fast to the earth it grew from, it might have had claws instead of roots. The curving leaves seemed to be hiding something; the blind stem cut into the air as if no wind could ever shake it.

"That is an aloe, Kezia," said her mother.

"Does it ever have any flowers?"

"Yes, Kezia," and Linda smiled down at her, and half shut her eyes. "Once every hundred years." (Mansfield 1962, 35)

CHAPTER 25

Plant Radio

Amanda White

Since the very beginning of radio broadcasting many people and communities have envisioned it as a way for the community to speak to itself and to give voice to the voiceless. ... Community radio has been an intimate friend of many struggles for self-determination and liberation from oppression.

LIBERATING THE COMMONS, *Free Radio Berkeley*[1]

Radio technology is commonly acknowledged for its accessible qualities as mode of communication; being relatively inexpensive, simple to construct and operate, and thus widely viewed as a potentially useful tool for citizens to engage with one another and generate a mass audience. From community organizations to hobbyists to radical political mobilizations, this continues to be the case today. Whatever the democratic and/or public possibilities of the medium, the radio waves themselves are heavily policed and regulated all across the globe; this is enforced through national laws in most countries. In both the United States and Canada there are regulatory authorities (FCC and CRTC respectively) that control the radio waves by requiring and overseeing the distribution of prohibitively expensive broadcasting licenses. These regulations essentially limit access to the airwaves even as the technology itself is readily available. Therefore, while radio has the potential to amplify the voices of unheard or marginalized communities, these activities are often necessarily illegal, and the threat of legal penalties discourages its

use. As a result, radio is frequently criticized as being a means of maintaining the status quo and of controlling the flow of information rather than a potential site of expression and communicative freedom for citizens.[2] It is precisely because the radio waves are such a contested space that there is such a rich history of active resistance at the grassroots level, with activists and artists alike harnessing radio's communicative and symbolic powers. Anyone using the airwaves is aware of its legal implications, and for many breaking these laws is part of the purpose of pirate radio projects. As American radio activist Stephen Dunifer writes; "Organized or not, unlicensed broadcasting has always been an attempt to gain access to the broadcast commons by rejecting the confined spaces (political, social and artistic) created, regulated and imposed by the state."[3] In her text *Take it to the Air: Radio as Public Art*, Sarah Kanouse similarly notes that it is precisely because it is such a contested space that using radio in artistic production is inherently political. She further argues that even if a work lies within the legal limits of transmission and runs no risk of interfering with commercial broadcasters, the use of radio as a medium is still a political act because even small microwatt transmitters are "devices which are often used in ways that violate the spirit, if not the letter of the law."[4]

1 Dunifer, S. 'Free Radio—Liberating the Commons' *Free Radio Berkeley.com/* online: [<http://www.scribd.com/doc/8310831/Liberating-the-Commons>] 05 Dec. 2014.

2 Castells-Talens, A., Rodríguez, J.M.R. and Chan Concha, M. (2009) 'Radio, control, and indigenous peoples: the failure of state-invented citizens' media in Mexico' *Development in Practice*, 19: 4–5, pp. 525–37.

3 Dunifer, S. 'Free Radio—Liberating the Commons'. *Free Radio Berkeley.com/* online: [<http://www.scribd.com/doc/8310831/Liberating-the-Commons>] 05 Dec. 2014.

4 Kanouse, S. (2011) 'Take It To The Air: Radio As Public Art' *Art Journal*, 70: 3, pp. 86–99.

FIGURE 25.1   Amanda White and Brad Isaacs, *Plant Radio for Plants*, radio transmission, plants, performance/intervention, 2014–2016. Courtesy of the artist
© AMANDA WHITE AND BRAD ISAACS.

In the spirit of citizen's radio, *Plant Radio for Plants* was developed by Brad Isaacs and myself and performed as an intervention into local communities of indoor and outdoor plants in and around London and Toronto, Canada, in 2014. We had originally intended to build a pirate radio station as an artistic intervention which would interfere with regular radio programming and broadcast live from plant life on the margins of urban space to the nearby human populations. As the project developed, we were inspired by this history of citizen's radio movements and the concept of radio as a space for community to form and enact resistance to hegemonic powers. Our work became centered around the possible experiences and collective potential of the plant communities themselves, rather than plant interference with the human content on the airwaves. Diverting the project towards the experience of the plants

is a gesture that—while largely symbolic for us by referencing human social movements—might in some way empower these plant communities, which were being amplified towards one another in the work.

Plant Radio was constructed as a series of low-watt homemade radio transmitters based on a simple electronic schematic; they were inexpensive, easy to build, and each unit included a built-in microphone and wire antennae. We attached these transmitters to sticks in wooded areas, leaving them in place over a period of several days. Transmissions were received at 89.5 FM, which we played to groups of houseplants living in the vicinity. This created a means of communication between two groups of immobile plants who were physically separated by the human borders of indoor and outdoor. We propose this act as an acknowledgement of the systems of power that enforce the separation of these communities, and in the hopes that it can assist in organizing their resistance to it. Scholars in development and communications studies have argued that in some cases citizen's media and communication can be powerful tools for the marginalized, noting that; "this kind of bottom-up media is about raising voices, but also about finding voice in the first place. It is about reshaping boundaries, not just being heard within them."[5] *Plant Radio for Plants* mirrors these actions against the top down institutionalization of the radio waves by challenging whom the airwaves are for in general; by pushing the boundaries of who may hear, or be heard, by considering what kinds of communications are privileged, and interrogating the human-centered concepts of "voice" and "community" altogether. The concept of *Plant Radio* circumvents the prescribed spaces for plants, acting as a form of resistance to the ontological hierarchies that marginalize them. The radio commons may be a public space, however, as Sarah Kanouse writes, they represent a form of public space that can reinforce the exclusions and tensions that are already apparent in other more visible public arenas.[6] Plants are already rendered peripheral, not only in our everyday physical spaces but also in our imaginations, a phenomenon that has been referred to as plant blindness in which we privilege human or even animal activity.[7] Not all plants are overlooked to an equal extent; for example, ornamental domesticated species (as opposed to economic domesticated varieties such as crop plants) are especially invisible, evidenced by a lack of attention given to their cultural, historical or medicinal importance.[8] Wild plants on the other hand, tend to be generally

perceived as superior to domesticated species.[9] The human-centered ontology that marginalizes and further categorizes plants in this way is built from the same foundation of hierarchical value ordering that produces other marginalized communities, which citizen's radio movements have long sought to challenge. *Plant Radio* attempts to reconcile with these issues by adapting a nonanthropocentric approach, wherein the community is inclusive of nonhumans, and can be heard.

While the electromagnetic spectrum is not an exclusively human space, there is no question that radio broadcasting itself is a human endeavor, and we acknowledge that plants likely have their own methods of "broadcasting." For example, some recent studies have suggested that common micorrhizal networks can facilitate biocommunication across plant individuals of multiple species,[10] creating what some scientists have referred to as a sophisticated internet or "wood-wide web" of connected plants across the rhizosphere.[11] However potted plants cannot access these underground networks as they are confined to individual containers, and therefore we rely on radio—a human mode of communication—in combination with the plants abilities to communicate through sound or sonic vibrations to complete this work. While we nurture and care for our houseplants, they can be easily overlooked. As ornamentals, their identities are reduced to companion species at best or at worst decorative objects. Indoor domesticated plants rely entirely on humans for survival, their access to basic needs, potential for movement, and

5   Pettit, J., Salazar, J.F. and Dagron, A.G. (2009) 'Citizens' media and communication' *Development in Practice*, 19: 4–5, pp. 443–52.

6   Ibid.

7   This is referred to in Matthew Hall's 2011 book; *Plants as Persons: A Philosophical Botany* (Albany: SUNY Press).

8   Gessert, G. (2010) 'The Rainforest of Domestication' in *Green Light: Toward an Art of Evolution* (Cambridge: MIT) pp. 21–31.

9   In his book *Green Light*, Gessert suggests that the wild plant ability to resist domestication may contribute to the perception that they are more sophisticated or intelligent.

10   Barto, E., Kathryn, J., Weidenhamer, D., Cipollini, D., and Rillig, M.C. (2012) 'Fungal Superhighways: Do Common Mycorrhizal Networks Enhance below Ground Communication?' *Trends in Plant Science*, 17: 11, pp. 633–37.

11   Giovannetti, M. et al. (2006) 'At the Root of the Wood Wide Web: Self Recognition and Non-Self Incompatibility in Mycorrhizal Networks' *Plant Signaling and Behavior*, 1: 1, 1–5, p. 1.

ability to form communities are therefore highly controlled. Our work with these plants attempts to intervene into this space of containment and dependency, providing indoor and outdoor plants access to a potential social interaction with one another, autonomous of human comprehension.

Accordingly, *Plant Radio* does not rest entirely in the realm of the symbolic; it is informed by literature in the plant sciences, which suggest that there are various ways in which plants experience auditory communication. Most of us at some point have encountered claims that plant growth can be affected or stimulated by sounds like singing, talking or music, yet there has always been some debate around these propositions.[12] For the most part this stream of research has been all but dismissed as an anthropomorphic way of looking at a kingdom of species with capabilities which are divergent from our own, but that are unique and sophisticated in their own right. In an article titled *The Intelligent Plant*, popular culture and food writer Micheal Pollan considers the perception of plant abilities relative to our human understanding in conversation with a number of plant scientists, in which this question—around plants and their musical preferences—is dismissed as anthropomorphic nonsense.[13] Some have acknowledged that while perhaps causally misinterpreted, these beliefs and observations concerning plant responses to human sounds might actually be uncovering the real effects of something else. To support this, there is an abundance of actual scientific research in this area which has recently demonstrated that plants *do* emit their own acoustic vibrations as well as respond to them selectively.[14] Plants may not care

about the qualities of music in the way humans do, but they may respond to auditory stimulations for their own unique reasons. For example, researchers from the University of Missouri found that sounds or vibrations emitted by feeding herbivorous insects were not only detected by plants, but also elicited chemical response reactions from them.[15] This was observed when the plants were played the sounds of caterpillars eating leaves, and within these results it was also noted that the plants were able to discriminate between vibrations caused by the insects chewing and those caused by other factors. Another recently published study titled "Tuned in: plant roots use sound to locate water" similarly identified ways in which plants may utilize sound to their benefit. Here the researchers observed that plant roots have an ability to locate water sources even in the absence of moisture (for example water travelling nearby in pipes) by sensing vibrations.[16]

While we acknowledge the possibility that the audio exchange facilitated by *Plant Radio For Plants* may have no effect on the communities with which it attempts to engage, we are also aware that to dismiss the potential that plants may respond to sound waves that we cannot hear or see is problematic and prescriptive in its own right. To assume that they can't respond would be equal to the anthropocentric notion that plants prefer certain styles of music to others. By broadcasting the auditory landscape of wild plant life and its environs to indoor plants, we are open to the possibility that the sounds a plant would encounter as part of its life cycle may produce responses. Perhaps the private lives of these plants, which have always been segregated by human borders, may be enriched in some way by this experience. With the

---

12   These questions have been studied in pseudo-scientific capacities, for example the experiments described in the 1973 book *The Secret Life of Plants by* Peter Tompkins and Christopher Bird, in which they attempt to prove anthropomorphic forms of sentience in plants.

13   Pollan, M. (2013) 'The Intelligent Plant'. in *The New Yorker*. 23 Dec. pp. 92–104.

14   See for examples, a review on the topic: Gagliano, M. (2012) 'Green Symphonies: A Call for Studies on Acoustic Communication in Plants' in *Behavioral Ecology* 24: 4, pp. 789–96. As well as, Gagliano, M., Mancuso, S., and

---

Robert, D. (2012) 'Towards understanding plant bioacoustics' *Trends in Plant Science* 17: 6, pp. 323–25.

15   Appel, H.M., and Cocroft, R.B. (2014) 'Plants Respond to Leaf Vibrations Caused by Insect Herbivore Chewing' *Oecologia* 175: 4, pp. 1257–66.

16   Gagliano, M., Grimonprez, M., Depczynski, M., and Renton, M. (2017) 'Tuned In: Plant Roots Use Sound to Locate Water' *Oecologia* 184, 151–60.

knowledge that community-based art practices are also often anthropocentric,[17] an important part of *Plant Radio* is that it necessarily excludes humans from participation in parts of the conversation. We must be satisfied with leaving some of these questions unanswered, if we are going to deviate from a methodology in which humans must always sit at the center of the work.

---

17   Marcellini, A., and Rana, M.D. (2016) 'Notes Toward a Non-Anthropocentric Social Practice | Art Practical' *Art Practical.com*. Web. 01 Mar.

PART 7

Laboratory

∴

CHAPTER 26

Psychoactives and Biogenetics

Giovanni Aloi

Biohacking is the new gardening.

ANDREW PELLING, *Growing Organs on Apples*[1]

• • •

It was the experience of the museum, coupled with that of a working science laboratory and then enhanced by the herbarium display. This combination of dead, working and living environments created the schism between places where a cure is promised, but also where scientific accidents might occur.

PRUDENCE GIBSON, *Janet Laurence: The Pharmacy of Plants*[2]

• •
•

Since the nineteenth century, scientific objectivity has been the quintessential epistemological approach of institutional practices. It has configured disciplinary methodologies, intrinsically defining what could be seen and what could be said about what is captured by the scientific gaze. The poststructuralist waves of the 1970s, with their emphasis on overdetermination, and capitalization on the power of discourses upon the shaping of reality, led to the canonization of institutional critique as a viable and productive form of art practice. Foucault's interest in the history of

science and its relationship to power and the writing of history, for instance, radically challenged any notions of transparency in the production of knowledge. Most pronouncedly, his mistrust for metanarratives led him to devise an antisystemic approach that substantially made him an antihistorical historian—his archaeological model of inquiry turned the "history of history" writing on its head. Departing from the hermeneutics of classical Hegelian historiography and its structuralist linage, archaeology, Foucault's methodological approach to the new history, is concerned with the possibility of describing discontinuous surfaces of discourses for the purpose of denying any absolute truth or meaning—in so doing, it rejects conceptions of continuous evolution of thought and accumulation of knowledge driven by progress.[3] At stake in this negative work is the possibility of recovering what classical historians, from their white, patriarchal, Eurocentric perspectives deemed nonessential to the construction of an ideologically inscribed and progress driven account of human civilization

It is this specific epistemic contingency that contemporary artist Sebastian Alvarez addresses in *A Pseudo-Ethnobotanical Chronology of Psychoactives*—an eleven-foot long scroll-like photographic annotation of the history of the world in which psychoactive plants intersect with humans. The image features a photographic collaged *superplant* that the artist uses as embodied timeline. The Frankensteinian assemblage, as curator Caroline Picard called it, proposes an alternative chronology in which crucial historical events no longer are wars, but, for instance, the moment in

---

1 Pelling, A. quoted in Gamble, J. (2016) 'Are plants the future of regenerative medicine?' in *The Atlantic,* online: [<http://www.theatlantic.com/science/archive/2016/07/growing-organs-on-apples/493265/>] accessed on 2 March 2016.

2 Gibson, P. (2015) *Janet Laurence: The Pharmacy of Plants* (Sidney: University of New South Wale Press) p. 123.

3 Foucault, M. (1972) *The Archaeology of Knowledge* (London: Routledge) 2002, pp. 6–9.

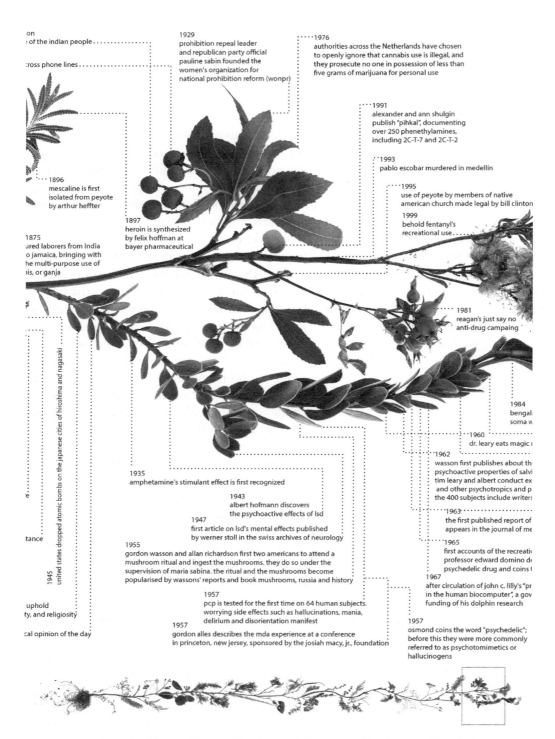

on
...of the indian people ....

...cross phone lines ....

1929
prohibition repeal leader
and republican party official
pauline sabin founded the
women's organization for
national prohibition reform (wonpr)

1976
authorities across the Netherlands have chosen
to openly ignore that cannabis use is illegal, and
they prosecute no one in possession of less than
five grams of marijuana for personal use

1991
alexander and ann shulgin
publish "pihkal", documenting
over 250 phenethylamines,
including 2C-T-7 and 2C-T-2

1993
pablo escobar murdered in medellín

1995
use of peyote by members of native
american church made legal by bill clinton

1896
mescaline is first
isolated from peyote
by arthur heffter

1897
heroin is synthesized
by felix hoffman at
bayer pharmaceutical

1999
behold fentanyl's
recreational use.......

1875
...ured laborers from India
...o jamaica, bringing with
...he multi-purpose use of
...is, or ganja

1981
reagan's just say no
anti-drug campaing

1984
bengal
soma w

1960
dr. leary eats magic

1962
wasson first publishes about th
psychoactive properties of salvi
tim leary and albert conduct ex
and other psychotropics and p
the 400 subjects include writer

1963
the first published report of
appears in the journal of me

1935
amphetamine's stimulant effect is first recognized

1943
albert hofmann discovers
the psychoactive effects of lsd

1947
first article on lsd's mental effects published
by werner stoll in the swiss archives of neurology

1965
first accounts of the recreatio
professor edward domino d
psychedelic drug and coins t

1967
after circulation of john c. lilly's "pr
in the human biocomputer", a gov
funding of his dolphin research

1955
gordon wasson and allan richardson first two americans to attend a
mushroom ritual and ingest the mushrooms. they do so under the
supervision of maria sabina. the ritual and the mushrooms become
popularised by wassons' reports and book mushrooms, russia and history

1957
pcp is tested for the first time on 64 human subjects.
worrying side effects such as hallucinations, mania,
delirium and disorientation manifest

1957
gordon alles describes the mda experience at a conference
in princeton, new jersey, sponsored by the josiah macy, jr., foundation

1957
osmond coins the word "psychedelic";
before this they were more commonly
referred to as psychotomimetics or
hallucinogens

1945
united states dropped atomic bombs on the japanese cities of hiroshima and nagasaki

...e

...tance

...uphold
...ty, and religiosity

...cal opinion of the day

FIGURE 26.1   Sebastian Alvarez, *A Pseudo-Ethnobotanical Chronology of Psychoactives* (detail), 2015.
Digital print. Courtesy of the artist
© SEBASTIAN ALVAREZ.

which (in 600 BCE) an Indian surgeon stated the usefulness of cannabis and wine as surgery anesthetics; or the first reference to tea in the Chinese dictionary from 347 BCE; the beginning of the use of opium dating 1000 CE; the first warnings against morphine in 1874; and the widespread use of marijuana amongst US soldiers between 1963 and 1975. As the artist explains, the image is part of a "series of efforts to understand the deeply complex relationship between blood and chlorophyll."[4] For this purpose, Alvarez employs a political conception of collage which enables a reconfiguration of what classical historical optics deliberately ignore in order to recover specific economies of plant-consumption. In his ontological revision, plant-agency is neither systematically erased nor demonized. *A Pseudo-Ethnobotanical Chronology of Psychoactives* presents the viewer with an image in which the normativity of metanarratives is shuttered by a nonjudgmental/non-puritan approach to psychoactives. As historiographical prioritization is compromised and ingrained notions of classical anthropocentrism and agency are abandoned. Metanarratives are ideologically driven tools that relentlessly frame man at the center of the picture as the "one in charge"—the logical, rationalized construction of historical events they produce implies that the clarity of human reason is the guiding force in progress. But as it is known, psychoactive substances produce alternative dimensions of perception and derail sensorial focus from the pragmatism of everyday life, at times suspending judgment whilst inducing fluidity in ethical norms. In Alvarez's narrative, therefore, plants are represented as equal historical coactants. They blur the historical gaze, the vision of sobriety essential to the idea of civilization and progress upon which classical history has been founded.

Likewise, history of art has a tendency to situate the artist-genius at the center of agential hegemonic relationships with matter—but the genius of the modern artist stands in diametrical opposition to that of the Renaissance master. In the metanarratives of art history, Leonardo, Michelangelo, and Raphael are defined by the rational light of classical philosophy and the desire to portray nature in scientific terms as a celebration of God's greatness. Instead, the modern artist is typecast as a tortured soul attempting to find himself through the darkness of an ever increasingly fast moving and unstable world. Cliché has it that the Renaissance master strove towards purity, while the modern artist deliberately sought intoxication in order to gain access to an interior world whose depths he cannot master without the aid of alchemic intervention. Plant-derivate psychoactive substances have played a prominent role in art making and in the "history of creativity" more generally. During the nineteenth century, advances in the chemical industry permitted the refining of cocaine (*Erythroxylon coca*) and opium (*Papaver somniferum*) while Absinth (*Artemisia absinthium*) was a recurring instrument in the work of many writers as well as Impressionist, Post-Impressionist, and Early Modern artists. The 1960s and '70s brought to the fore a new wave of experimentation with substances in which the effects of magic mushrooms (*psilocybin*) and marijuana (*Cannabis sativa*) were accompanied by the influence of synthetic drugs like LSD.[5] Plant derivate psychoactive substances substantially changed the nature of the artist's studio enabling transformative effects in which the solidity of identity-constructs and perceptual shared certainties could rarefy.

As the 2014 exhibition titled *Under the Influence* acknowledged, the use of psychoactive substances has been widely minimized by the art historical establishment for obvious reasons—the cultural industry does not want to be seen idolizing illegal drugs.[6] Yet, art historical metanarrativizing strategies have inscribed (and implicitly justified) the agency of psychoactive substances through an anthropocentric mythologization of the genius, who

---

4   Alvarez, S. (2015) *A Pseudo-Ethnobotanical Chronology of Psychoactives*, wall-mounted exhibition text, Sector2337.

5   Lowinson, J.H. (2005) *Substance Abuse: A Comprehensive Textbook* (Philadelphia: Lippincott Williams & Wilkins).

6   Exhibition held at Soil, Seattle, curated by Shane Montgomery—May 1 to May 31 2014.

intoxicates in order to envision a higher order of transcendentalism. Behind this narcissistic approach which romanticizes the figure of the artist as a newly found shaman lies a more subtle and fragmented history of artistic intra-action between artist and plant—one in which plants are usually passive, despite the active/altering substances they bring to art making—these narratives always position the plant as a vehicle for the artist's own freedom, never as that which in plant-like ways contextually informs the perception of the artist. But while artists of the last century consumed psychoactive plants and then produce work that had nothing to do with them, certain contemporary artists, some contemporary artists spend time with plants to reverse this relationship. The contemporary artist's studio thus becomes more of a laboratory, a place in which to study plants rather than one in which to consume them.

Historically, the laboratory is the quintessential epistemological space—the institutionally defined zone of scrutiny; the site of hypertechnological magnification, juxtaposition, dissection, and splicing; the place in which raw materiality enters the discursive dimension engaging in a reflexive form of indissoluble "becoming with." Whether an artist's studio, a biochemistry lab, a carpentry workshop, or a kitchen, the laboratory tends to operate along panoptic economies of visibility and agency. There, humans are situated at the center of an ecology of choices, optics, chances, manipulations, apriorisms, and technical challenges. The keys to the production of knowledge in the laboratory are instruments that range from everyday kitchen utensils to the most sophisticated particle accelerator. The relationship between matter, human, space, and instrument closely defines the type of knowledge that will be produced in the laboratory. Furthermore, the temporality through which these relationships form relentlessly calls for the establishment of ethical parameters that bear on the human's freedom to experiment, as much as on broader and external shared cultural notions of what is and what isn't ethically permissible. Whether an artist's studio or a scientific

facility, the epistemic space of the laboratory is by nature a theater without an audience in which error is the founding block of a trial process leading to a certain point of productive potentiality we call art.

Of the many artists who spent time in the studio with psychoactive plants, Dorothy Cross certainly is emblematic of a new approach that departs from the clichéd art historical notion of the intoxicated genius, to engage with psychotropic plants and their properties on a critical and conceptual level. Over the past twenty years, the artist has nurtured a persistent interest in foxglove, a plant native of Western Europe, but has spread to many other areas on the globe. This species is the perfect example of the ambivalent and arbitrary ways in which we tend to culturally and legally classify plants—something that profoundly impacts our relationships with them. Throughout the nineteenth century, foxglove became popular in US gardens. But its initial appreciation was overshadowed by the danger of its psychotropic and poisonous properties, which could easily intoxicate and even kill gardeners, children, and pets. Therefore, it wasn't long before its resilience and toxicity got it filed in the United States Department of Agriculture as "an invasive and noxious weed." This ambivalence persists today as, despite this classification, the plant is still sold at garden centers around the country. And though the internet is filled with horror stories of hallucinations and near death intoxication, foxglove is not officially classified as an illegal drug.

Cross's sculptures of individual foxgloves made throughout her career thus celebrate this very ontological instability of weeds. To activate discussion, the sculptures effortlessly hinge on a deliberate inappropriateness of the artistic medium. In the tradition of art history, bronze, is a "noble material": it entails a rich history of classical narratives pinned by anthropocentric affirmation—the material was reserved for the making of costly statues of victorious gods, athletes, and emperors. Through its use, Cross elevates the plant to the mythological status and heroic heights while

FIGURE 26.2   Dorothy Cross, *Foxglove*, 2012. Cast bronze,
124 × 44 × 41 cm, 48.8 × 17.3 × 16.1 in
IMAGE COURTESY OF THE ARTIST AND
KERLIN GALLERY, DUBLIN © DOROTHY
CROSS.

retaining a nonaffirmative aesthetic and an allu-
sive narrative inscription that ultimately betrays
an underlying poetic of romanticism.[7]

In this case, the explored relationship between
human and plants is one grounded in childhood.
While playing in the woods, Cross, and her friends
would be regularly told to "never place [their]
fingers in a foxglove and then lick them or [they]
would go blind." The verticality of the plant, towering above the rest of the vegetation, with its
unusually shaped clusters of colorful flowers,
thus became part of a childhood mythology that
led Cross to explore the artistic productivities involved in the "seeing blue and white" caused by
foxglove poisoning.

Witches Gloves, Dead Men's Bells, Fairy's
Gloves, Bloody Fingers, Gloves of Our Lady, Fairy
Caps, Virgins' Gloves, and Fairy Thimbles. This is
the list of common names recited by a child's voice
at the beginning of Cross's web-based portion of
the project *Foxglove: Digitalis purpurea*.[8] The
screen-field in which the footage unravels is circular—a reference to the Renaissance shape of the
tondo, the religious paintings symbolizing transcendental perfection, colliding with the shape
of the ocular bulb. Cross became interested in the
fragilities shared by the technology used to generate online images and the human sight as well as
the frustration inherent in any limitation of vision,
whether biologically or technologically-based. As
previously mentioned. During the eighteenth
century, vision became the quintessential tool of
scientific objective-epistemology. The reliance on
sight as the most objective of the sense defined the
parameters of discipline-specific normativity as

7   The artist's sculpture was produced from life-casting, a process through which the object is not literally sculpted but
allows it to imprint itself onto the material in a way similar
to photograms, thus retaining a register of indexicality.
Through this material contact, life casting produces an intensely charged register of realism more similar to the act
of transcription than that of the copy.

8   Cross, D. (2005) *Foxglove: Digitalis purpurea* (DIA: New
York) online: [<http://www.diaart.org/program/exhibi
tions-projects/dorothy-cross-foxglove-digitalis-purpurea-
web-project>] accessed on 10 February 2015.

truth. Adopting the agential properties of foxglove thus becomes an opportunity to undo ontological certainty. Therefore, the main body of the project consists of loops of clips that turn blue and eventually disappear in response to the interaction of the viewer's mouse. The web-interface deliberately takes the viewer/participant into a realm of appearances where images materialize and fade only partly under her/his control.

But beyond the nonaffirmative interactive element, the disorienting shift of colored-vision presented by the video (a nonanthropocentric strategy othering the representational gaze), the blue circularity of the image, also gestures towards a history of erotic cinematography. The association between the color blue and erotic material derives from a nineteenth-century censorship method used in burlesque shows.[9] A blue spotlight was shown over the performers' bodies during the most audacious sequences to conceal the starkness of details. Drawing on the recurrent themes of sexuality and desire explored through the natural world, *Foxglove: Digitalis purpurea* brings the viewer to question notions of sobriety and intoxication where poison and sex appear equally positioned in the production of what could be defined as altered states of mind. After all, both can constitute ways in which moral restraint and notions of identity can acquire transformative and experimental levels of fluidity.

Like Cross, Carsten Höller also focused on the ability plants have to affect our behavior beyond the conventional notion of intoxication. In 2004, the artist's Stockholm studio was filled with *Solandra maxima*—endemic of Mexico and South America, the plant, also know as "cup of gold," has a long history of being used by the Huichol of Mexico for sacred initiations and ceremonies.[10] All parts of the plant, which can grow to sixty feet in length, contain atropine-like alkaloids present in other Datura varieties. Consumption of *Solandra maxima* induces a lack of coordination,

hallucination, and so-called irrational behavior. The toxicity of the plant for humans is so intense that even chewing fragments of the flowers can cause death.[11] Höller, who holds a doctorate in biology, has developed an artistic practice consistently oriented towards the performative, the participatory, and the experiential. He devised a corridor-greenhouse filled with *Solandra maxima* to make its visitors "fall in love." The large chalice yellow flowers exuded an intense scent, while the use of strobe lights cast an environment designed to disorient the viewer into a nonaffirmative dimension of "becoming-with." The artist hoped to produce a sensorial experience capable of replicating that of falling in love—the elusive subject of many works of classical art spanning literature, music, and visual representations. However, while other media have more regularly approached this most subjective theme from a descriptive metaphorical dimension, Höller's *Solandra Greenhouse* attempted to induce the bodily experience of falling in love in the absence of the object of desire.

Solandra Greenhouse thus functions as a scientific laboratory in which the physical dimension of falling in love could be synthetically reconstructed through the communion of nature and technology. The scientific ethos behind the installation mines the poetics of "love and psyche" to its core, pointing at the importance of biochemistry in the emergence of what we connote as feelings. But more interestingly, Höller decided to work with *Solandra maxima* because of the pheromone it releases which is, according to the artist, largely responsible for the feeling experienced in the greenhouse. Pheromones are airborne chemicals capable of affecting the physiology and behavior of many plants and insects amongst other animals.[12] Their agential potentials were researched throughout the last century and the extent to which they might impact on the life of organisms,

9   Ibid.

10   Whistler, A. (2000) *Tropical Ornamentals: A Guide* (Portland: Timber Press).

11   Nellis, D.W. (1997) *Poisonous Plants and Animals of Florida and the Caribbean* (Sarasota: Pineapple Press), p. 242.

12   *Karlson, P. Lüscher, M.* (1959) 'Pheromones: a new term for a class of biologically active substances' in Nature, 183, 4653, pp. 55–56.

FIGURE 26.3   Carsten Höller, *Solandra Greenhouse* (*Garden of Love*), 2004
© CARSTEN HÖLLER.

including humans, remains unknown. However, it is now generally accepted that relationships between plants and insects are largely regulated by pheromones, which captivate actants in inescapable relationships of becoming designed to maintain symbiotic interconnectedness in place. Some arachnids and insects use pheromones to attract prey, to conceal their species-membership in order to parasitize, to attract partners, to mark territory, and to scare predators.[13] But more recently, research has focused on plants' ability to use pheromones to their advantage when responding to insect attacks. For example, when caterpillars eat their leaves, nasturtiums react by releasing pheromones that attract parasitic wasps.[14] Thus pheromones bypass the notion of intoxication, losing one's control, inhibitions, or identity boundaries. They shatter the illusion of rationality and control essential to the formation of identity as a closed construct. They reveal a world of captivation, of which we are also a part: a dimension that is not, in Heideggerian terms, a poverty of the world specific to animals but a shared network of invisible confidential communication that substantially impacts on the material world beyond the abstract notions of will and desire.[15]

Höller's *Solandra Greenhouse*, therefore, is more successful at encouraging the contemplation of plant/bee or plant/moth relationships than it is at inducing the feeling of falling in love. Yet in so doing, it poses important questions about the integrity of human cognitive abilities about the

captivation at play in biosystems involving plants and animals—another crack on the smooth surface of our fictitious sense of exceptionalism towards other nonhuman beings.

Over the past twenty years, the emergence of the BioArt movement has capitalized upon the notion that registers of scientific visibility or invisibility can challenge our perceived center-stage role in our relationship with nature. In the process, many artists have taken over the scientific laboratory as a space of artistic inquiry, appropriating scientific methodologies, instruments, and theories to produce truly innovative art. Impacting the strict processes and procedures that define the epistemic production in scientific laboratories, artists have channeled a latent energy—they have discovered that bridling the ethical subtexts of scientific research enables the emergence of new ontologies that can impact everyday life. BioArt is therefore seriously engaged with materiality on a deep level, as it is through the material presence of its creations that it questions normative strictures as well as the very elusive promise of so-called progress.

In this spirit, Australian artist Janet Laurence has been working with psychotropic plants expert Matthias Melzig for her contribution to IGA 2017 (the International Gardening Expo in Berlin). In Laurence's case too, researching the transformative effects of psychotropic plants is not an opportunity for escapism but a chance to reconsider the Earth's surface and, as argued by Prudence Gibson, "the objects and detritus and mismanagement that contribute to the Earth's temporal geological strata".[16] The project entails the construction of a medicinal garden arranged on high-pod like plinths which serve to define a pathway along which visitors can taste plant-extracts provided in a variety of vials. The resulting hallucinatory effects they experience provide a plant-world interface typically excluded from the register of standard art and science education.[17] This approach is

13   Landolt, J.P. (1997) 'Sex attractant and aggregation pheromones of male phytophagous insects' in *American Entomologist*, 43, 1, pp. 12–22.

14   Verheggen, F.J., Haubruge, E., Mescher, M.C. (2010) Alarm pheromones-chemical signaling in response to danger' in *Vitam Horm*, 83, pp. 215–39.

15   Between 1929 and 1930 Heidegger delivered a series of talks titled *The Fundamental Concepts of Metaphysics: World, Finitude, Solitude*, there he argued that nonhuman animals cannot grasp the essence of the world because of their essential "captivation" within the environment they occupy. This conception implies an impossibility to perceive itself as separate from everything else around it—this, according to Heidegger, results in what he terms "poor in world."

16   Gibson, P. (2015) pp. 90–91.

17   Ibid., p. 92.

however not be misread as a provocative flight of fancy or an extravagant proposal relying on the notion of curiosity to trigger interest. The artist's practice is informed by the work of geophilosopher Ben Woodard whose recent work has focused on the speculative realist notion of "ungrounding of the earth."[18] Drawing upon Friedrich Shelling's criticism of the anthropocentric position, which views nature as always external to man, Woodard proposes an ungrounding capable of bridging philosophical knowledge and folk heritage by upturning the ground of thinking—practically and metaphorically focusing on the surface of Earth. Metaphors of digging bring our attention to the surface of soil and plants as interfaces of human/nonhuman interactions of extreme importance in the Anthropocene. Inducing perceptual shifts in the viewer through the critical relocation of plants within the exhibiting space or by staging unconventional encounters with plants, like Cross and Höller have also done, leverages upon the possibility for a productive ungrounding of the human to take place.

It is in the space of the laboratory that a human-plant permeability capable of surpassing the strictures of preinscribed representational tropes, a representational ungrounding can be made to emerge. Slovenian artist Špela Petrič has found in biotechnology a wealth of opportunities to rethink the binary structure of human-plant relations to bypass what she calls "speciest constructs"—the cultural structures that regularly obliterate individuality and difference in human/plant relations. The artist argues that:

> In the deconstruction of plant-human relationships, I searched for modes of human existence that could be perceived as equivalent to plant life. Biotechnology's alienating molecularization of living entities maintained in defined media and sterile plastic containers demonstrate the "human-as-material" and support thinking about

ourselves in terms we afford to plants. Much like algae increasingly employed in the production of biomass and pharmaceuticals, so too are human cells in culture becoming an essential component of our body maintenance program. They can be coaxed into the form and function of a multitude of organs, transplanted into pig embryos, genetically modified to eliminate diseases and selected for particular applications. As cells in culture we are fragmented, decentered, de-essentialised, outsourced, bettered, molded and viscerally spread over large areas.[19]

For the *Strange Encounters* project, Petrič's molecularization of living entities brought her to identify cells of the genus Chlorella, as representative of a plant-lifeform and carcinoma of the bladder as its human counterpart. Chlorella essentially is a type of micro single cell-algae endowed with a high photosynthetic efficiency. The high protein content of Chlorella garnered attention during the 1940s and '50s, when widespread fears of global famine caused by the human population boom prompted research for economic and environmentally viable primary food sources.

Carcinoma of the bladder is caused by cells that grow abnormally, abandoning the preencoded roles they should serve within the organism and ultimately causing its collapse. Petrič's decision to stage a new kind of cellular human/plant encounter *in vitro* is one in which both actants have been deliberately reduced to a minimal level of biological essentialism—the cellular dimension—in an attempt to bypass the stratification of cultural, ethnic, genderial, and social filters that more regularly inform and preencode any types of encounters between humans and nonhumans. Stripping both to the level of basic building blocks, to the essential constituents of bioexistence, obliterates the inherent ability that evolutionary discourses

---

18   Ibid., p. 85.

19   Petrič, S. (2017) Introductory text to 'Strange Encounters', online: [<http://www.spelapetric.org/projects/strange-encounters/strange-encounters-blog/>] accessed on 12 August, 2017.

FIGURE 26.4   Špela Petrič, *Ectogenesis*, photo: Miha Tursic
© ŠPELA PETRIČ.

have to prioritize the human at all costs and to hi-
erarchize life in ways that constantly penalize the
nonhuman on the grounds of comparative inabili-
ties. As Petrič explained, Chlorella and carcinoma
were chosen because of their resilience and tough-
ness and because of the malliablility cells have, as
the smallest and most abundant bio-unit, to form
all organisms. Essentially, Petrič's plant-human
ground zero is a space of equivalence that precedes ontology; a flattened plateau that can only
exist in a Petri-dish; but a field of potentialities
that nonetheless raises questions that appear to be
uncomfortably situated between the pasts and futures of scientific and philosophical intersections.

And this is also where the project performative-
ly engages with seemingly insurmountable issues
related to both: science and philosophy have nurtured an epistemic essentialism designed to dig
deep in search of the essence of things. Isolating
individualized life forms to better grasp biological functioning has been the principal modality of

scientific enquiry since the Enlightenment. Likewise, philosophical abstractism of the kind that
Derrida takes on in "The Animal that Therefore I
Am," his acknowledgement that the word *animal*
harbors a totalizing epistemic force that constantly obliterates biodiversity, has relied on a similar
desire to isolate and individualize. This is the very
epistemic boundary that we need to overcome to
conceive human-nonhuman relations from new
and useful perspectives. The purity that ultimately pervades both methodological approaches is
largely responsible for the current environmental
crisis we face, since it has for a long time prevented us from focusing on ecologies, interconnectedness, and becomings whilst insisting on inherent
notions of identity.

But working and thinking on the cellular level,
Petrič bypasses this form of essentialism in order
to tap into a realm of potentiality that is simultaneously individual and universal, decentred but
essential, and above all *agential*. In another project

titled *Ectogenesis: Plant-Human Monsters*, the artist stages "trans-species intermingling and category mongrelisation; [she] pro-creates plant-human entities, which [she] lovingly calls monsters, via in vitro conception and hormonal alteration."[20] Here human/plant encounters thus turn into becomings in which the very notion of species that has ruled taxonomy gives way to the possibility of something new and biologically uncharted. Care, compassion, and commitment become the relational modalities at play in the laboratory as in glass jar incubators Petrič nurtures the embryonic tissue of thale cress (*Arabidopsis thaliana*), a common plant native to Eurasia. The plant embryos are fed with steroids extracted from the artist's urine. This causes alterations in the embryos epigenetic patterns leading to the productions of morphologies that stray from the recurring plant form in the wild. It is in this sense that these human-plant lives are little monsters: an ontogenesis generating from impossible love, as the artist poetically asserts, and that simultaneously gestures towards shared ancestral biological affinities and the biotechnological promises of a future in which new molecular footprints might provide the answers to many sustainability questions.

Most importantly, in this context, the term "monster" comes to play in a new and nonpejorative sense. Petrič's approach is very far from the genetic provocations of Eduardo Kac and the fear of the kind of monstrousness *GFP Bunny* (2000) evoked. Her human/plant sympoietic organisms are *monsters* in the sense that life on this planet has always been *monstrous*: life on earth is the result of organisms joining others in sometimes unpredictable liaisons and intractive interconnectedness in which purity has no place. As Anna Tsing, Heather Swanson, Elain Gan, and Nils Bubandt argue in the introduction of *Arts of Living on a Damage Planet*, monstrosity was banished by Enlightenment Europe, the light of reason cast monsters into the

obscure corners of the irrational and the archaic;[21] hence their emergence pretty much everywhere in Romantic literature and the visual arts during the nineteenth century. Monsters relentlessly interfere with the taxonomical masterplan; they contradict the rationality of a creation generated by a wise God; and ultimately embody the essence of one's own essential limit in being—the monster is thus cast as that which emerges from the dark edges of humanity, from the anfracts of unreasoning and as such it is very often sterile. It comes from nature, but nature has prevented its reproduction and propagation in a tacit acknowledgement that the monster's place on this planet is ultimately not a legitimate one.

But what potentialities might emerge from the abandonment of the classical conception of monstrosity? What can be at stake in embracing monstrosity as a productivity?

For instance, the untapped potentials of plant/human biological affinity are becoming central to regenerative medicine at the Pelling Laboratory of Biophysical Manipulation (University of Ottawa). In the summer of 2016, researcher Andrew Pelling produced a human ear using a technique he calls *biohacking* in which the cellulose of an apple has been washed of its apple cells and populated with human ones.[22] The process seems paradoxically simple: a McIntosh red apple can be sliced, washed with soap, and sterilized with hot water to provide the cellulose mesh capable of hosting human ones. Once implanted under the skin, cells from the surrounding tissue colonize it, thereafter forming blood vessels. Eight weeks later the implant has been assimilated without rejection from the immune system.

Pelling's apple-ear was produced in response to the highly controversial 1995 Charles Vacanti experiment in which an ear-like scaffolding made of biodegradable polyester fabric was used to induce

20   Petrič, S. (2017) Introductory text to 'Ectogenesis: Plant-Human monsters, online: [<http://www.spelapetric. org/portfolio/ectogenesis/>] accessed on 12 August, 2017.

21   Bubandt, N., Gan, E., Swanson, H., Tsing, A. (Eds.) (2017) *Arts of Living on a Damaged Planet* (Minneapolis: University of Minnesota Press), p. 5.

22   Gamble, J. (2016).

the growth of human-cartilage.[23] The structure was implanted on the back of an OncoMouse deprived of the immune protection necessary to reject human tissue. Bioproximity, as well as disciplinary ontological structures, have brought biomaterial engineers to focus on animal species for the provision of prosthetic structures. Yet, mounting interest in the biocontinuity between humans and plants is reconfiguring this field of research. Pelling argues that the tiny capillaries in asparagus stalks happen to be the right size and shape for spinal cord repairs. Should the use of vegetal biomatter become central to the future of the industry, the now-prohibitive costs of certain procedures might turn out to be within the financial range of many.

---

23   Rader, A.K. (2004) *Making Mice: Standardizing Animals for American Biomedical Research, 1900–1955* (Princeton: Princeton University Press) p. 262.

CHAPTER 27

Of Plants and Robots: Art, Architecture and Technoscience for Mixed Societies

Monika Bakke

The crossroads of technology, science and art is the most common territory for encountering contemporary postnatural vegetal growth such as robot-plant hybrids. Humans' instrumental interests in plants have always demanded that new ways be found to transform plants for our needs; however, the ongoing domestication of plants may also be viewed in terms of coevolution and adaptation. A technoscientific lab has become the contemporary stage for vegetal biopolitics, operating with the use of bioengineering tools and methods allowing direct intervention in plants' bodies on the cellular and molecular level, as well as the creation of plant-robot interfaces, resulting in hybrid plants and other novelty plant entities. It is no longer merely the use of the materiality of plants' bodies that concerns us; it is their sensitivity and their networked, modular, and decentralized mode of operation that is of primary interest. As Stefano Mancuso and Alessandra Viola have noted, "beyond being a source of inspiration for robotics and information science, the plant kingdom may offer numerous innovative solutions to many of our most common technological problems."[1] Yet, with the increased presence of intelligent machines in plants' lives, it is important to remain vigilant and "response-able" towards future visions and contemporary actualizations of plant-machine mixed societies as our own species future becomes inevitably embedded in them.[2]

"Perception, awareness and active assessment," Matthew Hall suggests, "are crucial elements in the behavioral repertoire of plants,"[3] and it is in response to these vegetal abilities that artist Allison Kudla has been interfacing plants with machines. Building a self-monitoring system based on light perception in plants and movement perception in a robot was the goal of her work *Search for Luminosity* (2005–2007). The robotic part of the installation responds to plants' demands for light, and to some degree, allows them to control this system according to their own biological clock.[4] Kudla's installation involves six living *Oxalis Regnelli* plants, well known for their photonastic movements, historically called "sleep movements," which affect the leaves' and flowers' responses to light such as folding and closing. The plants anticipate dawn and adjust the plants' biology to it thanks to their circadian clock, which operates on a twenty-four-hour cycle. The computer controls the activation of the lighting system, where one lamp is dedicated to one plant, and the whole set up operates like a circadian rhythm. When one of the plants starts to open up in anticipation of dawn, the computer turns on the light over it and switches the light off over another plant, inducing its closure and thus influencing the circadian rhythms of the plants.

Sensitivity to light is vital to plants' lives, not only because light is a food source for them, but also because they use light to measure time, which is crucial for determining when to open flowers and when to grow and shed leaves. All of these

---

1 Mancuso, S., and Viola, A. (2015) *Brilliant Green: The Surprising History and Science of Plant Intelligence* (Washington: Island Press) p. 157.

2 The term "mixed society" in the context of robotics was first used in reference to cooperation between machines and animals.

3 Hall, M. (2011) *Plants as Persons* (Albany: SUNY Press) p. 144.

4 Kudla, A. 'The Search for Luminosity', online: [<http://allisonx.com/selected-works/>].

---

calculations work according to seasonal and daily changes. This was first recognized by the French astronomer Jean Jacques d'Ortous de Mairan, who while experimenting with "sensitive" plants (*mimosa pudica*) in 1729, reported that even when the plant is kept in constant darkness, leaf opening and closing continues as if plants were observing night and day.[5] Yet, the most aesthetically rewarding manifestation of this knowledge is *Horologium Florae*: a flower clock designed by Linnaeus and described in his 1751 treatise *Philosophia Botanica*. The clock is actually intended to be a garden comprised of precisely selected flowers which open and close at a specific time. Yet, the difficulty in setting up a functioning flower clock, even today, is apparently due to the fact that although light is a dominant factor, plants follow many other environmental cues, such as temperature and humidity, among others, in determining their flowers' opening and closing. Moreover, recent research suggests that a plant circadian clock is not a simple timekeeper but rather a complex developmental manager with an impact on a plant's fitness and adaptability to the environment, which as Daniel Chamovitz points out "developed early in evolution in single-celled organisms, before the animal and the plant kingdoms split off."[6] Not only does it measure time, it also provides for multilayer communication throughout a complex web involving metabolism, hormones, and stress pathways.[7] Equipped with a circadian clock, plants are able to anticipate predictable changes in their environment and adjust their physiology and developmental traits accordingly. Now that we know the biochemical mechanism responsible for circadian rhythms, the real challenge is "a consideration of

the evolutionary and ecological consequences of variation in clock function" in different life forms,[8] and hence how this behavior fits into a larger system. Kudla's *Search for Luminosity* points out a particular agential reciprocity in plant-robot relations, where in postevolutionary times, intelligent machines are ubiquitous elements of the vital environment.

Growing knowledge about the complexity of plants' perceptive skills and the sensitivity employed in monitoring their environment leads to the conclusion that plants are doing this better than us despite our being equipped with technological tools. For this very reason a team of scientists contributing to the PLEASED (Plants Employed as Sensing Devices) project proposed that instead of using artificial sensing devices commonly employed for monitoring the environment, they use plants themselves as "sensing and decision-making devices."[9] Relying on the ability of plants to generate electrical signals in response to external stimuli, which can then be processed by intelligent machines, the team focused not on individual plants isolated in the labs, but on plants in their natural environments, and on whole communities, such as a forest or meadows. Because they are much more sensitive and responsive and operate as sophisticated networks, in the future, plants could actually replace some of the artificial devices used now to monitor specific environmental parameters, such as humidity, temperature, sunlight, pollution. The real challenge to scientists now, however, is not just measuring the electrical signals emitted by plants in response to environmental changes but actually decoding these signals in order to understand better how and what the forest is communicating.

While the PLEASED team focused on connecting machines to previously established and fully functioning vegetal systems such as forests or meadows, the team involved in *flora robotica* aims

5   Somers, D.E. (1999) 'The Physiology and Molecular Bases of the Circadian Clock', *Plant Physiology*, 121, September, p. 9.

6   Chamovitz, D. (2010) *What a Plant Knows. A Field Guide to the Senses of Your Garden—and Beyond* (Oxford: Oneworld Press) p. 30.

7   Sanchez, E.F., Kay, S.A. (2016) 'The Plant Circadian Clock: From a Simple Timekeeper to a Complex Developmental Manager', in *Cold Spring Harb Perspect Biol*. Dec 1;8(12), pii: a027748. doi: 10.1101/cshperspect.a027748.

8   McClung, C.R. 'Plant Circadian Rhythms', *Plant Cell* 18, 4, April, p. 799.

9   PLEASED (realized from 2012 to 2015) online: [<http://pleased-fp7.eu/>].

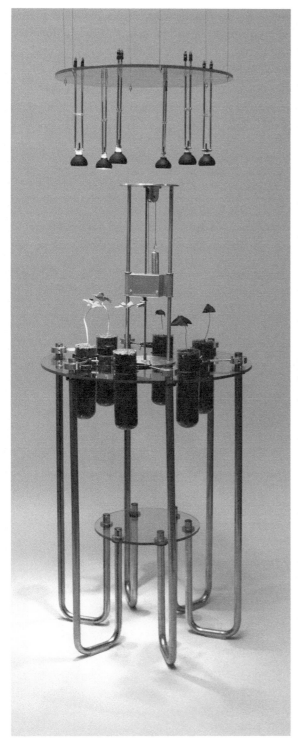

to develop and maintain new plant-machine hybrid systems to explore novel functions in plants and machines.[10] These self-organizing biohybrids will populate future plant-machine mixed societies, forming "an embodied, self-organizing, and distributed cognitive system which is supposed to grow and develop over long periods of time resulting in the creation of meaningful architectural structures,"[11] such as walls, roofs, and benches. In order to grow these architectural artifacts and living spaces, robot components are used for communication and control, enabling the activity of scaffold structures equipped with sensors intertwined with floral components. These self-repairing, self-adapting, and autonomous systems grow slowly alongside their vegetal components and feed themselves on light. The *flora robotica* team has declared their commitment to ensuring the best possible communication and cooperation between organic and nonorganic life forms, resulting in a high level of compatibility between plants and robots, hence "a key idea is to assign equal roles to robots and plants in order to create a highly integrated, symbiotic system."[12]

In the face of the ongoing environmental crisis and in anticipation of a high-tech future of plant-machine-human interconnectivity, it seems crucial to remember that 'these conflicts between human wants and plant needs," as Mathew Hall points out, "should be the primary focus of a wide-scale deliberation on and negotiation of ap-

FIGURE 27.1   Allison Kudla, *Search for Luminosity*, 2005–7.
Courtesy of the artist
© ALLISON KUDLA.

10   *flora robotica* (running from 2015 to 2019), online: [<http://www.florarobotica.eu/>].

11   Hamann, H., Wahby, M., Schmickl, T., Zahadat, P., Hofstadler, D., Stoy, K., Risi, S., Faiña, A., Veenstra, F., Kernbach, S., Kuksin, I., Kernbach, O., Ayres, P., Wojtaszek, P. (2015) *flora robotica*—Mixed Societies of Symbiotic Robot-Plant Bio-Hybrids. IEEE Symposium on Artificial Life (IEEE ALIFE'15), p. 1. online: [<http://www.florarobotica.eu/wp-content/uploads/2016/01/Flora-Robotica-Mixed-Societies_IEEE-ALIFE_2015.pdf>].

12   Ibid.; online: [<http://www.florarobotica.eu/wp-content/uploads/2016/01/Flora-Robotica-Mixed-Societies_IEEE-ALIFE_2015.pdf>].

propriate human-plant relationships."[13] Find-

ing more respectful ways to coexist with plants will require acknowledging our common ancestry and accepting them as active, perceptive, and intelligent beings.

---

13   Hall, M. (2009) 'Plant Autonomy and Human-Plant Ethics' *Environmental Ethics*, 31, 2, Summer 2009, p. 180.

CHAPTER 28

Boundary Plants

Sara Black

Boundary Plants is a series of paintings interrogating the implications of possible anthropogenic effects on ecological systems, in this case concentrations of radiation born of industrial scale energy production. The paintings *Fear Daisy* and *Japanese Persimmon* depict plants, the *Chrysanthemum leucanthem*, commonly know as the "oxeye daisy," and *Dyrospiros kaki*, commonly known as the "Japanese persimmon." Each of these plants has allegedly been subject to radiation contamination in and around Fukushima, Japan, where the 2011 nuclear disaster took place due to a large tsunami destroying the Fukushima Daiichi Nuclear Power Plant. Though images of these plants have made their way to viral status on the Internet, often accompanied by politicized fear speech, the nature of their mutation is contested and controversial. Biologists, citizens, and conspiracy theorists alike claim that the mutations are unquestionably a result of anthropogenic radiation contamination and evidence of endangerment; while others in the scientific community and in residence near the power plant remain skeptical of this allegation, suggesting that the mutations these plants are presenting are "natural," or part of the larger biological systems that have and will continue to exhibit biological mutations on a scale of "normal."[1]

In *Boundary Plants*, species are represented in the tradition of Western botanical illustration, whose earliest surviving forms can be found in a sixth-century illuminated manuscript of *De Materia Medica* by Dioscorides.[2] The form grew in popularity in the sixteenth century when the

FIGURE 28.1   Sara Black, *Boundary Plants* (*Fear Daisy*), Watercolor, 2015.
PRIVATE COLLECTION OF MIKE ANDREWS.

taxonomical system of binomial nomenclature was formalized by Swedish biologist Carl Linnaeus in his epic work *Systemae Natura*.[3] This marks the advent of modern botanical and zoological taxonomy, paved a path for the works of Darwin and the theory of evolution, and might be argued

---

1   Howard, B.C. (2015) 'Are "Mutated" Daisies Really Caused by Fukushima Radiation?' *National Geographic Magazine*, July.

2   'Vienna Dioscurides'. UNESCO Memory of the World Programme. 2009.

3   Manktelow, M. (2010) 'A History of Taxonomy,' Dept. of Systematic Biology, Evolutionary Biology Center. Uppsala University, Sweden.

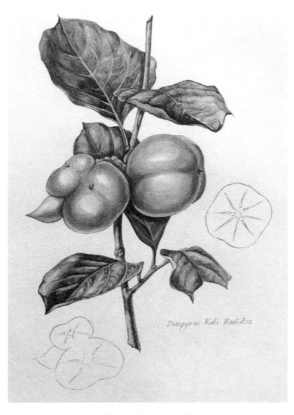

FIGURE 28.1   Sara Black, *Boundary Plants (Japanese Persimmon)*, Watercolor, 2016.
PRIVATE COLLECTION OF TOM AND AMBER GINSBURG.

to have solidified Western conceptions of "nature" and its relation to humanity. The paintings faithfully follow the Linnaean models by presenting a quite "naturalistic" illustration of each plant for clear visual identification, though as opposed to *in situ* observation each illustration is drawn from multiple viral images on the Internet. Rather than presenting these species as they are currently classified and accepted, the paintings represent these plants as novel subspecies that have departed or "branched" from their existing binomial taxonomic classification. They are "new plants." The taxonomical/botanical image assumes a kind of Western scientific authority, but the artistic gesture is rather one of provocation and a means of speculation. That is, through such a reinterpretation,

one may recognize that our human-centered categorical projections, as referenced through the Linnaean classification system are, on a basic level, fictions, born of a particular worldview. Modern botanists name/categorize plant species as a means of ordering and thus distancing "nature," but as we are growing more aware of the physical complexities of earth systems, such a relationship to the nonhuman doesn't accurately reflect the world within which we are actually enmeshed. Mutation is one such complex condition, arguably necessary for the evolution of species, but resistant to the systems of taxonomy and classification so taken for granted. Humans can become very uneasy when seeing rapid mutation taking place, especially if born from anthropogenic intervention or error (e.g., radiation pollution or climate collapse). Across the earth we are now beginning to recognize the various and cumulative effects of the industrial age on species and ecological systems even on a cellular level. It is growing increasingly clear that the clean taxonomical boundaries asserted through the natural sciences are perhaps not so clean after all. What are the implications for our future where these asserted boundaries are clearly more permeable?

A More "Human" Plant

Since the disaster at the Fukushima Daiichi Nuclear Power Plant occurred fairly recently, it remains present in our minds. However, it is by no means a singular example of human industrial endeavoring leading to deep and complex changes within earth systems that are slated to unfold over timescales nearly inconceivable to us now. Similarly, plant malformation allegedly resulting from radiation exposure is by no means the sole effect of the Fukushima meltdown. It was on March 11, 2011, that the Tohoku earthquake led to a large tsunami on the east coast of northern Japan. This tsunami disabled the power supply and cooling of three of the five Fukushima Daiichi reactors, causing all three cores to melt down in the first three days. As a direct result of the earthquake and tsunami, more than fifteen-thousand people died, over five-hundred thousand people were evacuated from the affected regions, and an additional seventy-thousand people were directly exposed to radiation from nearby nonevacuation zones. The disaster leached radioactive material into the North Pacific, constituting the largest radioactive contamination of the oceans recorded, and soil, water, and milk samples have shown high levels of contamination in the region. The extent of the contamination is still being researched.[4] These immediate and concrete outcomes are in many ways traceable and easily described in scientific reports. The long-term outcomes or, "legacy effects" of the industrial and nuclear age on these complex systems, on the other hand, are far less knowable and predictable.

Precedent does exist. Exactly three decades have passed since the infamous nuclear explosion occurred at the Chernobyl nuclear power station located in present-day Pripyat, Ukraine (which was still the Soviet Union in 1986). In April of that year an explosion and fire occurred while a system test was being conducted. Unlike the meltdown in Japan, this disaster was born of human design error and supposed mismanagement. Massive quantities of radioactive contamination were released into the atmosphere and spread over much of western Russia and Europe. Interestingly, the "Chernobyl Exclusion Zone," from which an estimated one-hundred to three-hundred thousand people were evacuated and where human reentry is still largely forbidden, originally constituted only the thirty square kilometers surrounding the plant and now extends to approximately 2600 square kilometers. Again, the human-drawn boundary is in many ways arbitrary.[5] The exclusion zone, for its lack of human presence and subsequent habitation by many nonhuman species, is now being

referred to by some as one of the world's largest wildlife preserves, a concept that seems perverse in many ways, but interesting no less. It is quite true that the tract of now largely forested land is home to thousands and thousands of plant, animal and insect species, some of which are said to be "thriving," some of which have been affected by the high levels of radiation.[6]

One recent expression of concern by members of the scientific community is a growing concern over the lack of human "management" of the forest ecosystem within the "Exclusion Zone." But what of this concept of ecosystem management in the first place? Forest management practices were born of the perceived necessity for humans to suppress fires, manage the "invasion" of nonnative species and, of course, to ensure "optimal" resource extraction for human consumption. For the past thirty years, existing and new growth trees and shrubs at Chernobyl have been actively absorbing radioactive material, drawing it out of the soil and atmosphere. What appears at first glance to be an advantageous circumstance of remediation and sequestering is actually a time bomb of sorts. Fire suppression as a management practice has been nonexistent, and though fires are a necessary element of a forest ecosystem, human occupied or not, they do tend to come less frequently and of a larger scale when human management is not imposed. If the extended growth in the Exclusion Zone does, in fact, catch fire, the radioactive material stored in these trees will be rereleased into the atmosphere. Of course, this cycle would continue until the radioactive materials break down.[7]

The legacy effects of nuclear disaster are yet to be revealed and will continue to reveal themselves over periods of time wholly unrelated to time on a human scale. How then, do we think of a "species" in such a context? The cognitive organization of plant life through human-invented taxonomical systems is one way to project humanness onto the

4   Rosen, A. (2012) 'Effects of the Fukushima Nuclear Meltdowns on Environment and Health' *International Physicians for the Prevention of Nuclear War Conference*, University Clinic Düsseldorf, 9 March.

5   Medvedev, Z. (1992) *The Legacy of Chernobyl* (New York: W.W. Norton & Company).

6   Smith, J.T. (2015) 'Long-term Census Data Reveal Abundant Wildlife Populations at Chernobyl' *Current Biology*, 25, 19, pR824–R826, 5 October.

7   Braxton Little, J. (2013) 'At Chernobyl, Radioactive Danger Lurks in the Trees', *Scientific American*, June.

nonhuman. It is yet another thing when human intervention actually alters a species' genetic material, inscribing change at a cellular level, altering its physical life.

Boundaryless Plants

What are the implications for our future where both taxonomical and physical boundaries are clearly more permeable than we believed? Perhaps we are ushering in an era where categorical distinction is inevitably breaking down. An era where encountering what is commonly called "plant," or more specifically "daisy," is to meet the inadequacy of the idea itself. A time when this inadequacy further deconstructs the environmentalist notion of that Nature is, in fact, a reified thing that we may simply 'relate' to. It is not enough to ask, "what is happening to these plants biologically?" Rather, we are urged to fully reconsider the complex and entangled histories of plant and human. How have human beliefs literally inscribed themselves upon the material existence of the plant and how might this alter our ideas about life itself?

CHAPTER 29

The Illustrated Herbal

Joshi Radin

We—or was it just me?—are at her feet, like puppies. While arranging herself on the bed, sunlight streams in from the east windows, assembled from discounted lumber remnants, arranged symmetrically after the fire. It's a narrow space, just large enough to accommodate the raised platform mattress and bedside tables spilling over with the constant mess attendant to those for whom housecleaning is a lesser virtue. Shelves set into the wall house a spring of books on Buddhism, alternative medicine, and spiritual mystics, as well as a healthy fluffle of dust bunnies, light and airy.

From a wooden jewelry box on the shelf, Maryam or Fatima, depending on how you know her, rustles through a collection of small, cloudy, resealable bags. My anticipation unmasked, I wait, the care in transmission apparent to my adolescent self. It was a teaching moment. Then she finds it. She's animated, excited, at home. Grabbing a magnifying glass, she hands it to me.

"Look closely. Okay, so what you are looking at is a dried flower. It is able to grow like this as long as it is unfertilized. This is a female, *sinsemilla*. See the little curled up guard leaves? They have been trimmed back. See the white, almost transparent crystals? This is what she makes to attract a male. It is her female juice! She wants a mate. She is yearning for sex! And in her yearning, she produces these crystals, her resin, where the THC is concentrated. The cannabinoids. You see the red hairs, too? These are pistils. So yes, when you smoke, the high you experience is the sexual energy of this flower. Take a look, closer...

... So when you're growing, the first thing you do is get rid of all the males. They will fertilize the female plants, and then you'll have seeds. Not what you want. Unless you're pollinating on purpose, but that's different. And seeds are gold—never let a seed get away from you. Yah. Okay, let's try this."

From the bedroom we go up a small set of open stairs to a small square room, from which, like a stage, one can observe the living space. The *Bad Box* is for smoking marijuana, ceremoniously with close friends, or sometimes just us kids. Like a turret, it sits at the top of the house, with windows gazing in three directions into the countryside. Kilim pillows, reminiscent of the time she spent with the former husband she'd met on a train traveling from Munich to Istanbul, line the walls. By the time they made it overland from Istanbul to India, they'd been spontaneously married at the Blue Mosque and had eleven weddings in the interim, because they liked weddings.

Later, she and Omar developed prized strains of sativa plants. One day after moving into a west coast villa recently vacated by musicians, she found a bag of marijuana seeds in a cupboard and cast them into the yard. Thus began her plant cultivation education. And together, they tended a two-story greenhouse. Their crops were well-respected and supported their income. They gave the various strains names like Llama Lightning and Big Al—for Al Capone, whose hitmen once lived in the villa while he did time in Alcatraz.

Next she opens up a velvet satchel and removes a small wooden pipe wrapped in a green silk scarf. From the satchel, wrapped in another scarf, came a deck of tarot cards. Pinching from the bottom of the flower (you must progress up the stem from the bottom), she fills the small wooden pipe with just enough for one of us, about the size of the tip of my pinky fingernail, and raises it above her head, eyes closed, for blessing. Striking a wooden match (never use a lighter, wood burns cleaner, don't breathe gas) she lights the pipe and inhales.

To differentiate the particular effects of each variety, she considered a spectrum of artistic requirements. Dancers, such as herself, looked for lightness in their bodies; to move or dance freely. Thus, sativa varieties would be indicated, to achieve the shimmering, transparent high necessary for their creative practice. *"They need to be lifted, to have lift, to be energized."* A musician however, didn't need to be concerned with such things. They need fluidity in their fingers, as a string player perhaps would, but their bodies could be more melted and relaxed, and an indica variety would give them a more cerebrally creative high to apply to their instrument or tool.

Hashish, on the other hand, is different. Hashish is made from the condensed pollen of male plants. Usually indica. Traditionally, or what I remember as being told was a tradition, it is harvested by walking through the fields of male plants while wearing leather pants. The pollen sticks to the pants, is then scraped off, pressed and weighed out and cut into blocks.

When I first tasted it at thirteen with my father, I hoped to reproduce for myself the significance he'd known while experiencing its effects. But in a distracted haze of alcohol and the adult party taking place, the low lighting and warm laughter, I missed it.

The mark of good grass is that it gets you high with one toke. *"Never smoke anything but 'one toke dope.'"* I took my turn, doing my best to inhale deeply. Next she would give me a reading from the cards. The layouts concerned the past, present and future, guiding principles, overarching archetypes. Maybe we would swim in the pond, she might spend time with my dad or tend her garden, maybe fire up the sauna.

My mother, Isabel, preferred a different route. As her mother-in-law underwent chemotherapy treatments, she developed recipes for palatable treats using a butter substrate for marijuana infusion.

Edith had no interest in expanding her mind, just the desperation to find an antidote to the nausea and wasting from cancer treatment.

The night she taught me to make the infusion was like any other night she labored in the kitchen, a blue floral apron hugging her petite, lightly brown frame, the usual gentleness pouring through her when she held her hands above the bowl. In the same way one might pass down a family cheesecake recipe, I inherited her technique for crafting exceedingly potent edibles. Her confections regularly knocked out the unsuspecting who defied her warnings.

At nineteen, Isabel had learned the process from Willie, an old boyfriend, while living in Mexico City with her father, an agronomist who taught at the UNAM and served in Lopez Portillo's cabinet. They'd met on the west bank of the Mississippi in Minneapolis, a few blocks from the Flash Electric Company. Willie taught her a lot of things—about brown rice, miso, and mescaline. While Mexicans and foreigners were traveling south to Oaxaca to visit with curandera María Sabina to experience her shamanic velada healings with psilocybin mushrooms, Willie, disguised as a priest, sold LSD on the streets, whispering "ácido, ácido, ácido..." to passersby.

A Family Picnic, Good Friday, 1994

We're visiting friends in Hawaii—little sister Teresa, stepfather Ivan, two other local families joined by twin sisters and clothing designers Judy and Joanne—the Strongheart families, Lina, a Lithuanian model, Anna, a Swedish artist and bodyworker, Uncle Joe, who is everyone and no one's uncle. With a large bag of psilocybin mushrooms, we caravan to a black sand beach. Only Zach, Mark and Joanne's ten-year old son, abstains. Perhaps like Walter Pahnke's Good Friday Experiment at Boston University's Marsh Chapel in 1962, our participation was loose but intending toward the sacred. Because there was

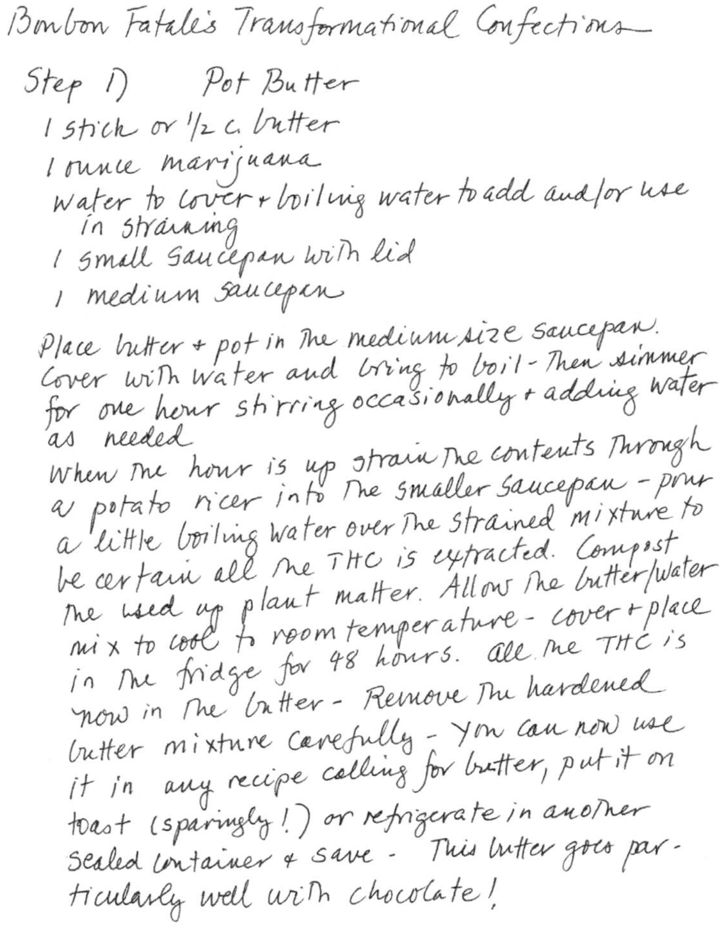

Bonbon Fatale's Transformational Confections—

Step 1)   Pot Butter

1 stick or 1/2 c. butter
1 ounce marijuana
water to cover + boiling water to add and/or use
   in straining
1 small saucepan with lid
1 medium saucepan

Place butter + pot in the medium size saucepan.
Cover with water and bring to boil - Then simmer
for one hour stirring occasionally + adding water
as needed
When the hour is up strain the contents through
a potato ricer into the smaller saucepan - pour
a little boiling water over the strained mixture to
be certain all the THC is extracted. Compost
the used up plant matter. Allow the butter/water
mix to cool to room temperature - cover + place
in the fridge for 48 hours. all the THC is
now in the butter - Remove the hardened
butter mixture carefully - You can now use
it in any recipe calling for butter, put it on
toast (sparingly!) or refrigerate in another
sealed container + save - This butter goes particularly well with chocolate!

FIGURE 29.1   Joshi Radin, *Recipe*, 2017.

something that felt odd to me about seeing the vulnerability of my mother on psilocybin, I escaped to the ocean.

There I could be alone in the waves, muffle the oddities and vulnerabilities of my family and others around me. The water sparkled. The wind held me. The people on shore moved about. Time shifted into sensation and colors, and as light faded I came out of the water. Judy apparently had eaten more mushrooms, and was now lying in her daughter's lap, undone. She was crying, saying, or shrieking over and over, "It is so big!" as Maggie shushed her and assured her she would be okay. As Judy peed herself in Maggie's lap, Ivan, laughing, ate uncooked Tofu Pups out of the plastic packet, his eyes dancing even

behind the sunglasses. Lina, blond hair bouncing in the wind, danced wildly and barefoot on a patch of thorns, telling us they were our friends.

On a few occasions, another home plant brew stepped forward. Due to enduring shyness or lack of interest in boys, my own risk of pregnancy was minimal. Still, the means to manage fertility or abort unwanted pregnancies hovered in the air, in other women near me. Strong teas, either Pennyroyal from the mint family, or ginger root, were known to precipitate a late cycle. It was the hidden resort, if Planned Parenthood or other medical resources were not an option.

When my sister suspected pregnancy after her first year of college, she came home to our mother with a quiet boyfriend. She applied the test, saw the results. The first mode of treatment was Pennyroyal tea, made by the mother, imbibed by the daughter. She remembers it as quite dark, strong. She took it with her back to Pennsylvania in a sealed glass jar packed in a wicker basket. No dice, but also no other side effects. It was only after this failed that she proceeded to the clinic.

Currently, Adam and Maryam live with a Coca plant, a gift from a friend, a real yahoo. Before it was ever refined into cocaine, coca leaves have served as a traditional local anaesthetic and stimulant. Maryam will chew up a leaf if she has a specific need, but it sounds as though for now just successfully growing in the northeast as a tropical native is enough of a service. It is hiding in plain sight, in the company of several dozen other plant residents who have all come indoors for the winter.

To preserve the anonymity of those involved in this account, names of people and places have been altered.

PART 8

Of Other Spaces

∴

CHAPTER 30

(Brief) Encounters

Giovanni Aloi

Individual floor plants in their own containers can be quite stunning, particularly in
smaller lobbies and reception areas. Plants
used this way should be at least 6 to 7 feet
tall to make an impact and not get lost in
the space. People need to be able to move
around the plant, so columnar plants such
as those used in corners are your best choice.
[...] Individual plants are usually used as a
focal point or to offset and draw attention to
an important design element.

KATHY FEDIW, *The Manual of Interior
Plantscaping*[1]

• • •

His waiting room contains five chairs, a table
in one corner and a potted plant on the table.
Above the plant hangs a reproduction of a
sunset by Turner. Rather faded. I usually turn
up at the appointed time on Tuesday but
sometimes Dr. Ellis kindly lets me come later
in the day after dusk has fallen, which suits
me better.

The first time we spoke, I said I hoped
he looked after his patients better than the
plant in the waiting room.

OLAF OLAFFSON, *A Journey Home*[2]

• •
•

In the introduction to his 1967 talk titled "Of Other
Spaces," Foucault stated that "the present epoch
will perhaps be above all the epoch of space." He
assessed that from a phenomenological standpoint space is not homogeneous and empty, as it
might perceptually appear, but that on the contrary, space is a fragmented and simultaneous entity imbued with quantities that "draw us out of
ourselves." "We do not live inside a void that could
be colored with diverse shades of light," Foucault
argued, "we live inside a set of relations that de-
lineates sites which are irreducible to one another
and absolutely not superimposable on one another." In Foucault's conception, space is never an
empty vessel—it has specific agential qualities; it
is a defining entity with inscribed cultural norms
and laws; it is materially as well as relationally specific.[3]

Foucault's focus on the networks of relations
developed in and by space was initially outlined
through his analysis of the panopticon. Jeremy
Bentham's late eighteenth-century design for a
prison-system in which the economy of power is
dispensed through an architectural configuration
imposing visibility for surveillance purposes laid
black on white the reflexivity at play between the
object of study and what can be said about it.[4] The
importance of panopticism in the economies of
power and surveillance gain traction through Foucault's comparative archaeological studies of the
medical gaze at work in the hospital and the spatializations of the prison.[5] But mobilizing the ocu-

1 Fediw, K. (2015) *The Manual of Interior Plantscaping: A
   Guide to Design, Installation, and Maintenance* (Portland:
   Timber Press) p. 68.

2 Olafsson, O. (2007) *A Journey Home: A Novel* (New York:
   Knopf Doubleday Publishing) p. 11.

3 Foucault, M. (1984) 'Of other spaces' *Diacritics*, Spring 1986,
   pp. 22–27.

4 Bentham, J. (1791) *The Works of Jeremy Bentham Vol. IV*
   (Edinburgh: William Tait) 1843.

5 Foucault, M. (1975) *Discipline and Punish: The Birth of the
   Prison*, translation Sheridan, A. 1977 (London: Penguin),

lar metaphor of the panopticon to other spaces, spaces in which humans and plants coexist, for instance, might reveal more nuanced, less polarized, and equally productive biopower relationships.

As it was explained at the beginning, this is the underlying notion connecting the chapters in this book. Every chapter has, in different ways, focused on the networks of relations between humans and plants to effectively capitalize on the irreducibility and nonsuperimposibility of diverse spaces. Within a certain margin of tolerance, each chapter has focused on a more or less delineated space: the forest, the garden, the greenhouse, the gardening center, the supermarket, the house, and the laboratory—all these different spaces have been revealed as specific spatializations that culturally and economically inscribe the blueprints of biopower relationships between humans and plants. The list I have explored in this book is neither comprehensive, nor exhaustive— I have focused on those everyday spaces that have informed the work of contemporary artists and in which human/plant relations are defined by the livingness and undeniable materiality of both parties—this was the most effective way at my disposal to bring plants forward, to equally put our bodies and theirs at risk, and to engage with ontological derailments in which agency is always distributed rather than centralized. But there are many other spaces in which humans and plants come to contact that have remained unexplored. Many of these, in more than one way, fall into the category of what I have called (*brief*) *encounters spaces.* In all honesty, I have developed a difficult relationship with the word "encounter," because it has been substantially abused in human-animal studies arguments—it has generally lost its initial edge, and in time, it has become an abstract cliché stereotyping animal relations under a fictitiously benevolent veneer of reciprocity that can usually only be established with a domesticated animal.

1991 and Foucault, M. (1976) *The History of Sexuality 1—The Will to Knowledge* (London and New York: Penguin Books), 1998.

Therefore, my aim was to keep plants as "feral" as possible despite them being potted and rooted. (Brief) encounters, thus emerge as contingent relational modalities in spaces where plants are not owned by the human that encounters them and where they also are not for sale—to humans, these are public places of transition; to plants, they are spaces of semipermanence. These usually are "loveless spaces" for the simple reason that the temporal dimension in which the human/plant proximity unravels does not last long enough for love to form. Hotel lobbies, office receptions, restaurants, shopping malls, and hospitals for example are spaces in which human-plant interaction most often takes place on the level of the silent glance. It goes without saying that in these spaces, plants are more regularly ontologically aligned to decorative objects than living beings. Tellingly, these are the spaces where the distinction between artificial and living plants can sometimes cease to matter—reproductions of very realistic *Ficus benjamina* are extremely popular with low lighting indoor areas—they fool the eye of most people despite their natural propensity to attract dust like few living plants ever would.

Artificial plants are all surface in every sense— the poorly made ones simply look awful as they grossly approximate the morphology of existing species while involuntarily mocking their formal-integrity to the ground. Their fabric leaves and plastic stems metaphorically encapsulate the essential economies of desire of the plant/human relationship they stage: forever green, in perennial bloom, in full form all year 'round—they aesthetically disavow death while being nothing more than perennially nonliving. They exist on the surface of brief impressions and are deeply rooted in the absence of care. But some artificial specimens have been produced by a pseudoscientific gaze— for a few moments, and from a certain distance, they pass themselves off as their live counterpart so well, thereafter inducing a slight sense of loss in the keen viewer who finally notices the deceit.

Mark Wallinger explored the nature of this superficial relationship in *Double Still Life* (2009) a

FIGURE 30.1   Mark Wallinger, *Double Still Life*, 2009. Silk, plastic urn, lacquered MDF and softwood 272 × 120 × 120 cm
Courtesy the artist and Hauser & Wirth. Photo: Dave Morgan
© MARK WALLINGER.

pair of almost identical, artificial flower compositions. Placed on two stately looking stands, the lush floral assemblages are too colorful to either suggest a funeral or a wedding—their aesthetic evokes a high-end lawyer's waiting room, a luxury hotel lobby, or a prestigious museum entrance—they are ceremonious but not ceremonial. Their ceremoniousness implies institutional authenticity—they are bold, fresh, ordered, and elegant: all positive qualities that implicitly underline the ethical ethos of the hypothetical institution which presents them. From a few feet away, the aesthetic impact equates to that of fresh flowers, but coming closer reveals the bitter truth. Wallinger stages this specific encounter to pose questions related to art and plants alike. Upon noticing the deceit, awe immediately dissipates. But why would we value the composition differently? Why would we desire living flowers when all we do is pass by and merely glance at them, anyway? Wallinger's compositions

gesture towards the fictitious economies of originality and authenticity. Or he might be ironically subverting the *memento mori* paradigm inscribed in still-life flower paintings from the seventeenth century—the impossibility of death which characterizes these flowers echoing the Hegelian notion that nonhuman beings cannot truly die as they do not have a grasp of being alive in the first place. But in the case of plants, death becomes a complex problem on both fronts: the ethical and the biological. While it is fair to say that an animal can be biologically declared dead, matters are more nuanced with plants. Is a cut flower dead or still living? When is a plant truly dead considering that an individual can be splintered apart in multiple cuttings that can thrive as new independent beings? Or that even the fragment of roots, leafs, or tendrils can in some species generate a new plant? Plant life can be fragmented (cuttings and propagation), reconfigured (grafting), networked (rhizomes and bacterial sympoiesis), and can be suspended for extended periods of time. These are all notions that biologically evade the classical construction of individuality, identity, life, and death in ways that apply to mammals and other animals. This is one of the most fascinating and productively charged opportunities plants offer to rethink biosystems and the ways in which we conceive of them. Plant-life is by nature dispersed and self-perpetuating in a constant form of becoming-with its surrounding space—if the conditions of humidity, heat, and light will support it, the plant will strive to develop within it. Move the plant to another space with different humidity, heat, and light variable, and it might perish.

Here lies the ontological shift necessary to conceive plant-life as a compelling nonanthropocentric modality that can enable us to move beyond the binaries of Cartesian thinking. Michael Marder calls this alternative "plant-thinking":

> "Plant-thinking" refers, in the same breath, to (1) the non-cognitive, non-ideational, and non-imagistic mode of thinking proper to plants (hence, what I call "thinking without the head"); (2) our thinking about plants; (3) how human thinking is, to some extent, dehumanized and rendered plantlike, altered by its encounter with the vegetal world; and finally, (4) the ongoing symbiotic relation between this transfigured thinking and the existence of plants.[6]

Marder's theorization of "plant-thinking" essentially constitutes a tool designed to upturn the state of "plant blindness" that has been nurtured by Western philosophy over the past two thousand years. As theorized by botanists James H. Wandersee and Elizabeth E. Schussler, plant blindness is essentially a cultural condition which prevents us from recognizing plant-life complexity beyond

the realm of curiosity or specialistic knowledge.[7] But most importantly, plant blindness is also harbored in what might seem a tangible awareness of them: aesthetic appreciation—only valuing plants for their aesthetic beauty constitutes a totalizing oversimplification which falls straight into the symbolic limitation of knowledge.

It is for this reason that artist Ethan Breckenridge deliberately compromises their aesthetic beauty (without destroying the plant) in order to induce a sense of empathy that is otherwise hard to experience in the transitional spaces in which many superficial human/plant encounters take place everyday. In his installation titled *Too Soon*, staged in Bolivia (2009) and New York (2010), the artist crammed potted plants into carpeted glass cubes. The gray carpet references the corporate desire for homologation and functionality, which aesthetically defines the frugality of office environments around the world. The plants are left in the gardening center plastic-pots they grew in—another sign of capitalist frugality—there is no attempt on behalf of the artist to elevate the plant to a metaphor of nature and culture. Despite the elements in this installation that might point towards that direction, the leaves pressing against the glass, pushing into the corners of the cube, and bending downward in the impossibility of continuing upward are simultaneously heart wrenching and outstandingly defiant—the leaves are green, the plant looks healthy—it makes the most of the given environment filling its every corner, not necessarily pushing to break free, but just engaging with space through economies of sustenance and survival that invite us to think beyond anthropomorphism. And this is one of the biggest challenges at stake with plant-thinking. Can anthropomorphism ever be productive in this context? This is a controversial concept in animal studies already. Do we risk obliterating plant-alterity once again if we empathize with them on the wrong footing?

---

6   Marder, M. (2013) 'What is plant-thinking?' *Klesis—Revue Philosophique*, 25, pp. 124–43.

7   Wandersee, J.H., and Schussler, E.E. (1999) 'Preventing plant blindness' *The American Biology Teacher*, 61, 2 (Feb. 1999), pp. 82+84+86.

Biologically many plants, especially those that have become popular in the transitional spaces of lobbies and waiting rooms favor continuity of light, humidity, and temperature—that's what seems to make them thrive to the best of their domesticated-potential. Breckendrige's glassboxes might recall images of medieval torture devices—yet, what constitutes plant torture? Isn't forcing them to grow in accordance to our own aesthetic liking already a form of torture? Isn't dissecting them for propagation a kind of vivisection? Is hybridizing them a form of eugenics?

Plant-thinking raises these questions not to outline an ethical ground upon which human/plants relations should develop, but to generate awareness of the concealed forms of violence we inflict upon other nonhuman beings—forms of violence that fall outside the remit of the law but that nonetheless exist and that in their existence form the essence of human-nonhuman relations. This should not be intended as an invitation to disregard the suffering of plants—ethical imperatives to treat every living being with respect applies here too. However, plant-blindness is an anthropocentrically induced condition that generates unethicality towards plants—these forms of unethicality can impact plants physically, as just discussed, and also culturally, by relegating them in conveniently objectified conditions.

In this context, the contemporary art gallery is a very peculiar place—although this might seem a paradox, the heightened regime of the gaze which characterizes it imposes upon plants the paradigm of the (brief) encounter, thus flattening into objectification them as long as far as they are contextualized like paintings and sculptures. The first appearance of plants in the gallery space dates back to 1936 when Edward Steichen's *Delphiniums* exhibit was staged at MoMA for one week only.[8] Steichen, who had an extremely successful career as painter, photographer, modern

art promoter, and museum curator, had retired in Connecticut to focus on his horticultural passion. There he presented his engineered and manipulated new breeds of delphiniums; some gigantified to four feet from its more modest natural height. The artist dosed the delphinium seeds in a chemical bath of colchicine, a toxin that induces polyploidy, resulting in the mutated flowers.[9] The exhibition functioned as a metaphorical take on the Aristotelian view that art perfects nature and it furthermore problematized plants with a Duchampian conception of objectification. Steichen's delphiniums posed questions of originality, authorship, value, and temporality. At the time, this proposal pioneered new artistic territories while engaging in important discursivities with contemporary theories and practices. But contemporary art requires a more engaged relationship with the alterity of plant-being—one that attempts to prevent plant objectification at the least or even to do something that might benefit them, as it will be seen towards the end of this chapter.[10]

How can a gallery space then host a different human/plant relational that differs from the objectification of other spaces in which human/plant contact is time-limited and constrained by the encoded cultural norms which define the space itself? To derail plant blindness in the gallery space, it is necessary to unhinge the cultural framework inscribed in its modality of visual consumption to stage the opportunity for new and productive human/plant interactions. Ontologically, the contemporary gallery has its roots in the spaces of optical experimentation, which marked the nineteenth century as a revolutionary time

---

8 Gessert, G. (2012) *Green Light: Toward an Art of Evolution* (Cambridge: MIT Press), p. 48.

9 Stracey F. (2009) 'Bio-art: The ethics behind the aesthetics', in *Perspective*, 10, July, pp. 496–500.

10 Of course, it remains difficult if not impossible to determine whether our intentional well-meaning towards plants effectively equates to something they appreciate—yet, there is something interesting in the possibility to explore aesthetics that might bring these questions to the fore without losing the artistic-edge.

for the history of art and representation more in general. Romantic paintings engaged viewers with a heightened sense of drama, movement, and unbalance. John Martin's sublime paintings were exhibited in theatrical situations that enhanced dramatization through the use of colored lights.[11] Daguerre's diorama exhibits of the 1830s and '40s incorporated even more complex strategies for the purpose of engaging audiences with new visual narratives.[12]

Simultaneously, the reproducibility of the photographic image led to the experimentation with rotating sequences and flickering visions. The Salons of the second half of the nineteenth century that took place in Paris and London were exciting because of the spectacle they proposed and the cultural shocks they sometimes caused.[13] The galleries of the Louvre were a place to study classical art, but not one for experimenting. In this panorama, the essential precursor of the contemporary gallery space is not the Louvre, nor any other public museum of that kind. It's the commercial gallery space, which emerged during the mid-nineteenth century in its already recognizable modern form: the retail space of a dealer who organized temporary exhibitions of specific genres to attract buyers. By 1910, there were hundreds of commercial galleries in London.[14] The Royal Academy of Art and the Louvre were places where the taste and cultural status quo of the establishment were being celebrated and reaffirmed at every step. The commercial gallery was a place where risks, cultural as well as economic, could be taken.

However, it was the Futurist and Dada movements that hijacked the gallery space, turning it into an experimental field. Notably, Dada's disdain for bourgeois values led to controversial artistic gestures which questioned the nature of art itself—their interest for time-based media in opposition to the static of classical art, their new conceptions of space as a three-dimensional theatrical dimension instead of the wall (painting) and the floor (sculpture), their desire to shutter and break instead of constructing or building, their disrespect for skills and privilege for thinking, and their mistrust for the artist's genius as a mystical entity revolutionized the gallery space so that art could actually happen instead of just being exhibited.[15] After the Second World War, as the ideologies of modernism became predominant, the gallery became the sacred space of the white cube.

At this point, the art gallery entered a conceptual dimension charged with new experiential potentialities. As art critic Thomas McEvilley argued: "the white cube was a transitional device that attempted to bleach out the past and at the same time control the future by appealing to supposedly transcendental modes of presence and power."[16] Its very essence is that of being a conduit—a passage between the material world and a Platonic dimension of purified ideas in which modernist objects were removed from historical contexts. The relations the gallery space inscribed, the culturally normative forms of consumption it enabled implicitly excluded livingness—that of the art object and that of the viewer too. It is so that the modernist white cube became a timeless milieu designed to entertain a disembodied eye, thus causing a fragmentation of the self, ultimately alienating the viewer instead of, as Foucault would have it, drawing the viewers out of themselves.

11   Martin Myrone (2013) 'John Martin's *Last Judgement* Triptych: The Apocalyptic Sublime in the Age of Spectacle', in Nigel Llewellyn and Christine Riding (Eds.), *The Art of the Sublime* (London: Tate).

12   Gernsheim, H., and Gernsheim, A. (1968) *L.J.M. Daguerre: The History of the Diorama and the Daguerreotype* (Mineola: Dover Publications).

13   Mainardi, P. (1994) *The End of the Salon* (Cambridge: Cambridge University Press).

14   Fletcher, P. and Helmreich, A. (Eds.) (2011) *The Rise of the Modern Art Market in London, 1850–1939* (Manchester: Manchester UP).

15   O'Doherty, B. (1999) *Inside the White Cube: The Ideology of the Gallery Space* (Berkeley: University of California Press).

16   Ibid., p. 11.

The advent of minimalist art changed this paradigm by introducing what Michael Fried negatively connoted as the theatricality of objecthood in the gallery space: an experience proposing a confrontation involving the beholder. As Fried argued: "once [the beholder] is in the room the work refuses, obstinately, to let him alone—which is to say, it refuses to stop confronting him."[17] Yet a problem remained—minimalist art also incorporated aesthetics of transcendentalism that had little or no concern with the world outside the white cube. As Brian O'Doherty put it, the gallery space became "unshadowed, white, clean, artificial—the space is devoted to the technology of aesthetics."[18] Its specific agential qualities, inscribed cultural norms and laws, and materiality as well as relational specificities rest on an intrinsic Cartesian paradigm, which sanitizes the space and, up until recently, categorically excludes living nonhuman beings.

Because of these reasons, the white cube is not usually a suitable environment for animals and plants—but most importantly, the encounter which it stages in the perimeter of the gallery is more regularly one preencoded by the cultural history and materiality of the space itself. Both animals and plants are vulnerable to an ontological alignment with objects in ways that are as counterproductive than the objectification taking place in zoos and botanical gardens. In the context of the gallery space, plants have been superficially associated with the ready-made objects of Marcel Duchamp—to many, they seem to occupy a pop art/realist dimension in which, they claim, the plant symbolizes that which is outside the boundaries of the gallery space—nature. This interpretation is very limited for it merely situates plant-presence as an institutional critique of the Cartesian dimension defining the gallery space—the plant has become a generalized symbol of nature, it is not its own entity, and individualized body—it has

become a marker of the nature/culture divide and the disinterest the gallery space has nurtured for connecting with not only the world outside, but the living world more precisely. Understanding a plant in the gallery space as an allusion to nature reassesses the lack of seriousness with which living organism are regarded with in art historical discourses. A cultivar in a plastic pot cannot possibly signify nature. With very few exceptions, the majority of artists involving living plants in their work use cultivars produced in gardening centers—these subtexts cannot be ignored in the semantic structure of the work. When encountering a ready-made object in the gallery space, art critics take into careful consideration its materiality, its origin, its (original) function, its age—the man-made-object is an always charged field of agential potentialities. But a plant is quickly "unpacked" by viewers as "nature." This hermeneutical (anthropocentric) limitation constitutes a serious obstacle to a more complex consideration of what plants could do in the gallery space.

Part of the reason why plants are clumsily aligned to ready-made objects, when in the gallery space, is strictly linked to the transitional nature of the white cube itself. Museum displays, as well as the gallery space, have accustomed viewers to a temporally contained consumptive experience inherited from the temporal scales commanded by painting and sculpture. The average person spends fifteen to thirty seconds in front of a painting in any museum in the world.[19] The experience is longer in smaller galleries where the pressure of engaging with an unquantifiable amount art is not incumbent—yet, there is something about the encounter with a plant in the gallery space that just can't be grasped on the time-scale of seconds and minutes—their existence on a different temporal scale from the human one always

---

17   Fried, M. (1967) 'Art and objecthood' in (1998) *Art and Objecthood: Essays and Reviews* (Chicago: University of Chicago Press), pp. 148–72.

18   O'Doherty, B. (1999), p. 15.

19   Rosenbloom, S. (2014) The Art of Slowing Down in a Museum, in *The New York Times*, October 9, online: [<https://www.nytimes.com/2014/10/12/travel/the-art-of-slowing-down-in-a-museum.html>] accessed on February 12, 2016.

pushes them back to the background, as symbolic representations, allegories of human anxieties, and decorative expedients. For this very reason, it is important that the contemporary presence of plants in art should prevent brief encounters from being the main relational modality at play.

Rashid Johnson's installations directly address the anthropocentric axis of modernist power-space frameworks by incorporating potted plants into complex modular structures suspended between the sculptural and the architectural. Johnson's more recent work, like *Antoine's Organ*, exhibited at the Milwaukee Art Museum propose the exemplification of a flat ontology in which everyday objects, plants, light tubes, and structural frames are all of equal importance to the assemblage. The ultimate aim is that of deterritorializing the human, moving the body of the viewer around the structure in order to grasp a sense or meaning. The conclusion, however, is frustrated, since there is no moral or lesson to take away from the piece besides the possibility of resisting the power dynamics that are intrinsic to in the walls of the exhibiting space and with that, therefore resisting the power dynamics of anthropocentrism at play outside the gallery space itself. In Johnson's work, the plants serve two distinct purposes: in one sense, they destabilize the institutional power of the gallery space undermining the museum's necessity to preserve fixity, order, and purity. And in another, according to the artist, the plants are predominantly featured as a call to be present and a call to care. In this way, Johnson subvert the persistent objectification of plants in the tradition of Western art by not giving in to the classical notion of *memento mori* in which plants automatically serve as anthropocentric reminders of death, the passing of time, the demise of (our) beauty, and the importance of making the most of one's time. Johnson's plants occupy the gallery space with a political will to resist past, and very white, cultural tropes, as well as institutional power. They are meant to be cared for and kept alive by an economy of interdependency, which ultimately has the ability of *being present* with them.

Beyond the examples explored in this book, many of which entailed a participatory, experiential dimension, artists have been engaging viewers with plants through performative, video, and sound-based art; scenarios that preclude the brief encounter modality outright. A substantial number of artists, for instance, have staged interactive plant-interactions by capitalizing on the applicability of sonic-art interfaces. Since 1873, it has been known that plants' electrical signals are the most important intracellular signaling system in plant organisms—they are essential to physiological functions like respiration, water uptake, leaf movement, and biotic stress response.[20] Attaching electrodes to plant leaves and channeling the impulses into a system involving a dedicated software interface and amplification, enables us to acoustically encounter plants, thus providing an alternative representational counterpart to their purely aesthetic presence. Mileece Petre produces what she calls "organic electronic music" for the purpose of highlighting plants' sentience as exemplified through the variations in electrical signaling that can be detected in response to different stimuli. In the 1990s, Mileece's father quit a career in the music industry to become a renewable energy entrepreneur. One of the projects father and daughter developed together involved a hydrogen fuel cell system with zero emission that today entirely supports her art installations.

The artist's performances are specifically concerned with bridging the gap we have created between nonhuman beings. As the artist claims:

> We're not really geared, at the moment, to try to take responsibility for things that we feel we don't have any control over, and don't really have a connection with. We're at a loss for how to enable change, especially when dialogue of change is usually baked into the threatening philosophy that we need to

---

20   Volkov, A., G. (2007) *Plant Electrophysiology: Theory and Methods* (Berlin: Springer Science and Business Media).

FIGURE 30.2   Rashid Johnson, *Antoine's Organ*, 2016, at Hauser & Wirth. Courtesy the artist and Hauser & Wirth.
PHOTO: MARTIN PARSEKIAN © RASHID JOHNSON.

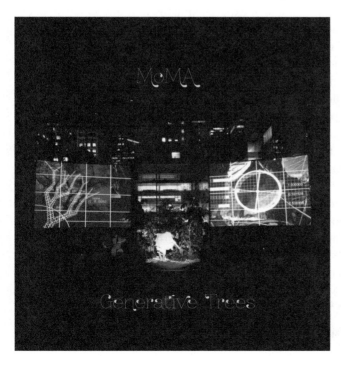

FIGURE 30.3
Mileece, *Speculations: The Future Is ____*, MoMA, 2013
© MILEECE.

move into a kind of austerity in our use of resources, which might effectively reduce or remove our access to technology. Which is very threatening given technology is how we derive our sense of community and communion now.[21]

Mileece's ecocriticist perspective condemns the current ideological attempts being made to mobilize eco-urgency in people. Suggesting that you should care about nature because we are all otherwise going to die is not the way to go, she claims. Her 2013 performance at MoMA's PSA1 series titled 'Speculations: The Future Is ____' kept the audience's attention focused on the plants' bioacoustic live composition for an extended period, enabling those present to appreciate plant's electrical responses to being touched by the artist. This human/plant interaction was slowed down and mediated by technological interfaces capable of translating, transforming, and enhancing human/plant perceptibility.[22]

As engaging audiences on plants and human-plants interaction becomes an imperative, Jonathon Keats has also turned his attention to the limitations which the traditional gallery space imposes on human/plant interaction. His preoccupation was with bridging the contrastingly different human/plant sensorial through the use of video—another time-based medium employed to slow the otherwise brief encounter of the gallery space. Keats has developed an international profile based on a distinct ability to incorporate sound scientific research with poetics and humor in the production of thought-provoking unconventional artworks.

In 2007, the artist staged the first plant porn cinema screening (Chico, California) for a crowd of about a hundred rhododendrons. Straddling a thin, semiserious line of argument, Keats inferred that "pollination was the most titillating experience for plants."[23] He then set out to understand how human and plant sensorial could be poetically aligned to produce footage the plants might actually *enjoy*.

> So I spent a couple of days on the ground, seeing how light and shadow were experienced from their perspective. Once I had a very stark black-and-white image—sun up high, bees flying by. I let it run for a month, and let the plants experience vicarious sex. And let people stand at the periphery and giggle nervously.[24]

Plant's sensitivity to light suggested that cinema would be the perfect medium through which an audience of plants could be effectively drawn into an artistic discourse. Keats came to appreciate the impact of entertainment on nonhuman audiences while choreographing a ballet for honeybees the year before. His projects involving performance and nonhuman beings question the anthropocentric bias according to which only humans are capable of experiencing the nonfunctionalism of art and entertainment. The black and white footage he produced was optimized to be better absorbed by the plants and was projected on their leaves instead of being screened on a wall facing them. Keats made no promise as to the plants' response to the screenings. His intent was to stimulate neither growth nor flowering. In so doing, he deliberately bypassed the notion of cause and effect which governs most of what we do "for plants"—relationships in which we regularly expect something in return.

The success of the first screening led the artist to further explore the potentialities involved in making art for plants titled *Television for Plants*

21   Mileece quoted in Robinsong, E. (2016) 'Mileece: Gardening the future' in *Kadenzeblog*, online: [<https://blog.kadenze.com/2016/10/29/mileece-gardening-the-future/>] accessed on November 10, 2016.

22   MoMA PS1 online: [<http://www.momaps1.org/expo1/image/mileece-lecture/>].

23   Jonathon Keats quoted in Gopnik, A. (2010) 'Plant TV', *The New Yorker*, March 15, online: [<http://www.newyorker.com/magazine/2010/03/15/plant-tv>] accessed on November 17, 2016.

24   Ibid.

FIGURE 30.4
Jonathon Keats, *Cinema Botanica*, Installation, 2009
© JONATHON KEATS.

FIGURE 30.5
Jonathon Keats, *Television for Plants* (2010)
© JONATHON KEATS.

(2010) which once again was designed to give plants something expecting nothing in return. Keats thought that "the subject that would be most interesting to plants is travel. Plants don't get to go anywhere. They're rooted in the ground. But if you're a plant you're not going to get excited about the Eiffel Tower—instead, you're going to be excited about the sky." He thus filmed an Italian sky for over two months to virtually take plants on a trip of a lifetime. He was aware that both NASA and the Soviet-era agronomy schools were interested in plant's perception of light because of their will to grow plants in space or indoors in Siberia. The artist wanted to use the information gathered, like plants sensitivity to color, for the purpose of providing for them a unique experience entirely disentangled from an exploitative economy of sort. He thus invited plant owners to bring their houseplants to the gallery space to share the experience with them. Once again, as for *Cinema Botanica*, Keats's approach is semiserious and yet capable of mobilizing viewers and plants from the static preencoded, objectifying paradigms which most regularly dominate the gallery space. The simple gesture of instilling curiosity about plant-sentience through anthropomorphically-grounded paradoxical situation represents a valuable opportunity for different phito-ontologies to be considered by the general public from a more serious perspective than it might initially seem plausible.

Both, Mileece and Keats, enable the emergence of new agential registers in which plants are somewhat collaborators or participants, and in which their sentient/responsive abilities are emphasized rather than repressed. Both artists slow down the human/plant interaction to a temporality capable of revealing the nuances and complexities of plant-being. They do so through the time-based media of performance, sound, and video art—these are, perhaps surprisingly, some of the most productive media through which the ontological objectification of plants can be subverted in contemporary art. But most importantly, both artists simultaneously pose important questions about the synergy of art and science, challenging the stereotypical view that a solid and close discourse between the two might involve a literalism that precludes poetics and humor from playing essential roles in art designed to make us rethink what we thought we already knew about ourselves and plants.

CHAPTER 31

Places of Maybe: Plants "Making Do" Without the Belly of the Beast

Andrew S. Yang

Of the many aspersions cast about plants, perhaps the most pernicious rumor concerns their immobility. We may come across the occasional Touch-Me-Not, Venus Flytrap, or perhaps enjoy a time-lapse documenting a young, green shoot bursting through the soil. But these apparent exceptions only seem to reinforce our presumptions, as does language: Whether one's feet are firmly "planted on the ground" or a lack of consciousness deems a person as "vegetative," the everyday metaphors of the botanical other make our animal bias all too clear.

In fact most plants can journey far and wide in their most compact of forms, as seeds. This is especially true of flowering plants. By way of animals that eat the fruit in which they are ensconced, seeds travel willingly through the belly of bird or bear alike while at the same time voyaging through the landscape, nomadic by means of the zoological vehicles within which they ride. Upon being passed out the other side, plants then find themselves in a pile of organic fertilizer, ready to take root and grow. The mutualistic logic is evolutionarily superb and adaptively sound; for plants it has made uninterrupted biological sense for many millions of years. That is, until recently. Now in the Anthropocene everything has become a little more complicated.

Belly of the Bird

Birds are by far the most common courier of plants in the form of seeds. Plants move because the birds are moved—compelled—by the aesthetic of the berry or the nut to swallow its seeds. They are carried on the wing often in multispecies mixes across significant distances and at speed.

However the anthropo-scenic visuality of cities disrupts this: annually millions of birds worldwide die when they collide with buildings whose windows offer either false transparency or instead mirror its surroundings, creating a fatal illusion of open space where there is none to be had. At night the situation is no better when birds can find themselves successively attracted to, and disoriented by, the lights of edifices without seeing their impermeable glass surfaces. If birds die with the seeds that they carry, then those seeds become ends without means, orphaned from their living vehicles in a vast ecology of interruption in which millions of possible plants never get a chance to try their luck at sprouting. In my city of Chicago, the birthplace of the skyscraper, the sky is literally scraped of plants.

But from such obstructions seem to grow new forms of opportunity. This is because birds killed in these architectural collisions are collected by teams of volunteers, the Chicago Bird Collision Monitors, who then bring them to the Bird Lab at the Field Museum of Natural History. Once there, the birds are cataloged and their skins and skeletons are accessioned into the museum's collection, but in the process the bellies of these birds—together with their seed stores of trees, flowers, and shrubs that could be—are thrown away. That is, unless you ask them to put the innards aside so that you can forage through them later, which is exactly what I have started to do. Using scissors, tweezers, and sieves, I have been cutting through the stomachs salvaged from these birds in search of the wayward seeds that the birds—sparrows, thrushes, robins, grosbeaks—were carrying within themselves. From this practice emerges a sort of dynamic seed bank from which botanical possibility, these *Flying Gardens of Maybe* (2012–), can be

© KONINKLIJKE BRILL NV, LEIDEN, 2019 | DOI:10.1163/9789004375253_033

FIGURE 31.1   Andrew S. Yang, *Ecologies of Interruption (Flying Gardens of Maybe)* Photo: Andrew S. Yang, 2013
© ANDREW S. YANG.

cashed out. But in what form does such possibility take shape? I have been fashioning stoneware ceramic pots on the wheel to provide a new vessel to replace the one from which I released them in the lab. (Figure 31.1) In these new vessels, each glazed with a pattern evocative of a particular bird species from which the seeds came, the seeds can take the chance to germinate and grow, or not. In this way the gallery in which they grow can become a makeshift greenhouse of (otherwise) lost ecologies. Other seeds are cleaned and put into bird feeders in the possibility that another bird will pick them up, perhaps continuing their passage through the landscape. All told, what comes into view is an ecology interrupted, rerouted, and reconceived—a botanical flux seeking out a new dynamic (Figure 31.2).

A Jawbreaker Syndrome

Meanwhile, on the north side of the city I find thousands of thick, brown, fleshy bean pods littering the sidewalks and streets every spring. Tires of passing cars are the only thing that can even break these sturdy fruits open, scattering their even more impenetrable seeds among cigarette butts and soda cans in the gutter. Dropped by the Kentucky Coffeetree, I have taken to picking up these odd pods and their seeds before they are swept down storm drains or up by street sweepers. But for whom are such strange fruit really intended? They defy the fruitful conceit of attracting animals that might eat pods and swallow the seeds within because they are not only hard as steel, but for most animals ingesting them can lead to anything

FIGURE 31.2   Andrew S. Yang, *Studies for Anachronistic Fruit*. Photo: 2015
                  © ANDREW S. YANG.

from vomiting and muscle paralysis to convulsions and death.[1] This all begs certain existential questions for the Coffeetree, a tree whose silhouette is akin to a rusted, upside down chandelier in winter and whose leaves unfurl so late in spring that it is also known as the Dead Stump Tree. It's a moniker that seems just as apt for its fruits and seeds—apparently purposeless purposes, going nowhere fast, and certainly nowhere that they might grow.

Scientists have made sense of this by proposing that the Coffeetree may be a case of *ecological anachronism*, a situation in which the natural animal partners that once ate its fruit and dispersed its seeds are now, in fact, extinct.[2] This peculiar fruit is thought to have catered to the tastes of mastodons, giant sloths, and other gargantuan mammals that lived in North America until 13,000 years ago, when a changing climate brought warmer weather as well as new humans migrants, whose spears to which the giant animals fell prey. The characteristics of a plant that evolved to encourage the dispersal of its seeds by a specific animal is called the plant's *syndrome*—seed number, fruit flavor, color, size, as well as the hardness of the seeds within the fruit are all crucial traits. The absurdly tough seeds of the Coffeetree suit the hardy mastodon's diet: strong enough to withstand the crushing bite and toxic enough to deter only the most massive of metabolisms. They were the

1   USDA Plant Guide. Online: [<http://plants.usda.gov/plant-guide/pdf/cs_gydi.pdf>].

2   Janzen, D.H., Martin, P.S. (1982) 'Neotropical anachronisms: the fruits the gomphotheres ate', *Science*, 215, 4528, pp. 19–

27. Connie Barlow (2001) 'Anachronistic fruits and the ghosts who haunt them,' *Arnoldia* 61, 2, pp. 14–21.

candy "jawbreakers" for Pleistocene megafauna. Indeed, it suggests what new forms of mutualistic exchange might fill the void of the extinct grazers in the dense urban environs in which the Coffeetree is found today. An updated ecology based on the model of a candy vending machine might just attract the last large mammal left in the Americas, *Homo sapiens*. Filled with evolution's original jawbreakers, it is an adaptation to the contemporary conditions that prioritize visual appeal, monetary exchange, and games of chance—a prosthetic for a plant that is in desperate need to keep up with the times lest it, too, go the way of the mastodon. These are *New Economies for Anachronistic Fruit: A Jawbreaker Syndrome* (2015): A standard gumball dispenser's glassy globe, perched atop a black metal post, is full with the seeds. For a twenty-five-cent coin and a turn of the handle you can get one to three smooth seeds. A free booklet next to the machine gives you cultivation directions (e.g., hacksaws can help abrade the seed coat) and also includes a biography of the Coffeetree, which is essential for evaluating what you—as a newfound mutualist—might gain from planting the seed now in your hand. There are arborists' views on the tree's aesthetic, descriptions of its horticultural virtues, ratings of the quality of the wood, as well as mentions of the various native remedies, potions, and, yes, coffee substitutes, that can be derived from different parts of the tree. A potted Coffeetree seedling also sits by, its purplish stem and soft, green, pinnate leaves a testament to how a newly consummated mutualism between you and this plant could take shape. Some pods are scattered on the floor; there is opportunity.

Making Do: The Tactical Art of Plants

A confession: I am not even that interested in plants, I was trained as a zoologist. Then why dig through the dead bodies of birds or duck traffic to scavenge elusive seeds on the city streets? I am not completely sure. These activities operate under the name of "art," but I want to consider the possibility of whether the artistic agency here lies more with the plants than with me as the presumed artist. Of course, we need to ask what is gained in proposing such an unconceited conceit. Writers like Michael Pollan have invited us to consider the maniacal devotion we have to certain plants in human history as a matter of their adaptive, evolutionary agency taking form as reciprocity and subterfuge alike.[3] Do we cultivate plants or do they cultivate us? This takes on a particular relevance in the case of plants making their way in cities, sites where they are otherwise kept completely marginal to all circumstances outside of the ornamental or photosynthetic. If plants are the epitome of a living "other," then perhaps it is worth extending and hybridizing the evolutionary logic of Charles Darwin with the tactical logic of philosopher Michel de Certeau to understand the role that plants may be taking in such aesthetic gestures. Rather than simply being adaptive, plants may also be *tactical*. As de Certeau describes:

> The place of a tactic belongs to the other. A tactic insinuates itself into the other's place, fragmentarily, without taking it over in its entirety, without being able to keep it at a distance. It has at its disposal no base where it can capitalize on its advantages, prepare its expansions, and secure independence with respect to circumstances... it is always on the watch for opportunities that must be seized "on the wing."[4]

Or—as with the case of the wayward seeds discussed here—seized off the wing and by other means, through "artistic tricks" by which the other must continually "make do" in a world of systematic obstructions. Through that lens we may want to consider how de Certeau's description of indigenous South American, "Indians" making do

---

3   Pollan, M. (2001) *The botany of desire: A plant's-eye view of the world* (London: Random House).

4   de Certeau, M. (1984) *The Practice of Everyday Life* (Berkeley: University of California Press) p. xix.

under the rule of their Spanish colonizers might also apply to the manner in which plants adopt their own tactics to survive in a landscape so thoroughly colonized by the human:

> even when they were subjected, indeed even when they accepted their subjugation, the Indians often used the laws, practices, and representations that were imposed upon them by force or by fascination to ends other than those of their conquerors; they made something else out of them; they subverted them from within—not by rejecting them or transforming them, (though that occurred as well), but by many different ways of using them in the service of rules, customs, or convictions foreign to the colonization which they could not escape.... They remained other within the system which they assimilated and which assimilated them externally. They diverted it without leaving it.[5]

Human ingenuity has both undermined and subjugated the environments that plants enjoyed as their own territories for millions of years prior to our arrival. Is the human artist with an ecological bent the creative agent or, more precisely, simply another node in the network of plants seeking possibility? The city and the humans within it could just as easily be viewed as the mediums through which plants, and other others, "make do" by making use of the institutions (museums and volunteer groups) and devices (vending machines, flower pots, bird feeders) imposed upon them—making use of them as novel means to their own ends.

But what ultimate ends, exactly? Are such artistic gesture performed by either a human medium or cunning plant anything more than pathetic in its potential outcomes? Can the rerouting and "making do" within the larger, technospheric city-system accomplish anything on a scale that is of any ecological relevance? The short answer—in this short now—is "no." However in the long now of the Anthropocene, and every future beyond its horizon, the long answer is a definitive "maybe." After all, if we accept the logic of evolutionary biology, then we also must accept one foundational rule by which it lives, namely the unfathomable improbability of life itself. The whole existence and diversification of all microbes, plants, fungi, animals—and indeed, those creaturely forms that haven't yet even come into existence—is written in the language of the most unlikely of all things actually happening just once. This has been true not only in the very beginnings, but in every subsequent change again, and again, and again that has taken shape so distinctly and persistently over the past 3.8 billion years. Every new species has emerged from the most random, contingent, and statistically improbable of events: a creative mutation inside this tiny cell; the migration of that individual; the survival of one feral seed, on one particular day, in that uncertain place of maybe.

These are the tactics of all life, but especially so the botanical others who insist on flowering—in resistance to as well as to the pleasure of we beasts that still remain.

---

5   Ibid., p. 32.

CHAPTER 32

The Neophyte

Lois Weinberger

Prehistory: In 1988 I began establishing a five-hundred square-meter parcel of land on the outskirts of Vienna as a ruderal area using so-called poor soil.

In so far as the ground was not already populated by plants / I searched for wild plants in the city area / on waysides / vacant lots / rubbish tips / and propagated them in my area in front of the studio building / to then plant them once again / on open land such as abandoned gravel pits and road embankments.

At the same time, I also took plants from these locations and planted them around the city. Plant transfer / field work—a garden as a cell / memory or distributor / plants as living organisms tangent to all the flexible systems of our lives. After some years, the plant cover was complete / I then found the strength / to leave the area in peace / for myself, I experienced this as progress / I had progressed one garden.

From this parcel of field and from the wild seeds / I had brought with me from countries in the south and southeast over many years / grew the plants for the railway tracks in Kassel. In over two-hundred plastic pots / correspondingly filled with the sandy gravelly soil of the tracks / I grew the plants in my area and had them transported to Kassel.

For the (d)OCUMENTA X, in 1997, I planted a one-hundred-meter-long section of decommissioned railway track with neophytes—new immigrants—from South and Southeast Europe as a metaphor for the processes of migration of our time.

Space would be made ready for the development of the unnoticed / for apparently unusable vegetation. An area as a gap in the urban / where boundaries are in a constant state of change.

A place
where the living
manifests
by means of being arranged
how the impossibility
of destruction
in the adventurous future
again and again blossoms
from its opposite
from the conceivable consequences
of the nonsterile. 1994

Now, after twenty years, hardly anything of the original planting could still be seen. The flower stalks had been torn-off from the exotic-looking plants / so that it was no longer possible for them to continue propagating.

Furthermore, bushes such as dewberry and also trees had emerged / making the variety of the lower vegetation no longer viable. The trees and the underbrush overrunning everything / that had proliferated over two decades / had been rooted out / for it to be possible to introduce neophytes once again. On request of the (d)OCUMENTA archive / to preserve the work as a work of art / this regeneration was realized with the help of Kassel's parks department.

Tracking interconnections between nature and society with precise carelessness—passionately and yet from a distance / as well as being part of this without intervening is inherent in my work. The original concept remains as a vague framework / neither inside nor outside my field does anything like security exist / what remains constant / is the eventful up to desertion—like the true essence of blooms are insects / gardens thus lie beneath / in the darkness underneath the grass. One digs them out and climbs down into them. The work with plants has something to do with archaeological processes / facilitating social interconnections. I see the value of a garden / in considering it a substrate for the emergence of meaning / that refers beyond itself and results in noncomparability.

On the already existing growth of plants introduced from South and Southeast Europe in 1996–97:

Ruthenia–Ukraine–White Russia
southern globe thistle
Iberian knapweed

Illyrian–Balkan areas
cotton thistle

Syria
Syrian hogweed

Transylvania–Romania
Transylvanian melic grass

Greece–Peloponnesus–Turkey
Acama thistle
Greek thistle

Pontien–areas around the Black Sea
Pontic mugwort

Iberia–Portugal–Spain–Caucasus
Iberian dragon head

Austria
Hainburger feathered pink
houseleek

Pannonia–Hungary
dwarf iris
Pannonian wormwood

Balearic Islands
Balearic ragwort

FIGURE 32.1 Lois Weinberger, *What is Beyond plants is at One with Them* (*d*)OCUMENTA *X*, Kassel, 1997. Railway track, neophytes from South and Southeastern Europe. Length: 100 m.
PHOTO: DIETER SCHWERDTLE. COURTESY OF THE ARTIST © LOIS WEINBERGER.

Hungary–Turkey
Pannonian immortelle

Sicily–Calabria
purple mullein
Jerusalem sage

CHAPTER 33

Herbarium Perrine: Interview with Mark Dion

Mark Dion and Giovanni Aloi

Dion's work examines the ways in which dominant ideologieos and public institutions shape our understanding of history, knowledge, and the natural world. The job of the artist, he says, is to go against the grain of dominant culture, to challenge perception and convention. Appropriating archaeological, field ecology and other scientific methods of collecting, ordering, and exhibiting objects, Dion creates works that question the distinctions between "objective" ("rational") scientific methods and "subjective" ("irrational") influences. The artist's spectacular and often fantastical curiosity cabinets, modeled on Wunderkammer of the 16th and 17th century, exalt atypical orderings of objects and specimens. Dion also frequently collaborates with museums of natural history, aquariums, zoos, and other institutions mandated to produce public knowledge on the topic of nature. By locating the roots of environmental politics and public policy in the construction of knowledge about nature, Mark Dion questions the objectivity and authoritative role of the scientific voice in contemporary society, tracking how pseudoscience, social agendas and ideology creep into public discourse and knowledge production.

In this interview, Giovanni Aloi and Mark Dion discuss *Herbarium Perrine*, a project dedicated to the work of a doctor, horticulturist, and diplomat, who was one of the first American naturalists to grasp the vast agricultural potential of Florida. As a pioneer in subtropical botany, Dr. Henry Perrine (1797–1840) tirelessly collected previously unknown flora, gathering masses of plants, roots, seeds, shoots, and herbarium specimens. In 1838, the United States Congress awarded Dr. Perrine a vast land grant in southern Florida to establish an experimental botanical station for the research of alien tropical plants introduced to United States

soil. However, before the experimental station was operational, Perrine was murdered in a Seminole raid on Indian Key. During the attack, the house and compound were burned and Perrine's invaluable herbarium and specimens were lost. Dion's distressed portfolio of pressed marine algae specimens is in response to this tragic loss, presenting itself as the few remaining specimens salvaged from the remains of Perrine's herbarium.

Giovanni Aloi: Plants and animals have been a recurring presence in your outstanding career as an environmentally aware artist. What brought you to focus on algae for *Herbarium Perrine*?

Mark Dion: I am drawn to life forms that are uncanny and strange. I have produced works about jellyfish and corals. So, marine algae are kind of like that. While plant-like, seaweeds are not true plants with vascular systems. They have a marvelous diversity and highly varied morphology. The work I produced was part of a meditation on botanical Florida. I was interested in how this amazing semitropical wilderness became the agricultural juggernaut and development nightmare it is today. Horticulturalists like Perrine and early plant hunters and botanists like David Fairchild, with their enthusiasm for economic botany, were a big part of that story. Of course, much scientific material was destroyed when the Indian raid burned Perrine's house. My portfolio mimics a herbarium from the collection and appears to have miraculously escaped the fire.

I am also making reference to the history of the Victorian seaweed preparations. Both scientific and decorative seaweed displays on card and paper were made in the nineteenth century and turned into the most delicate of specimen

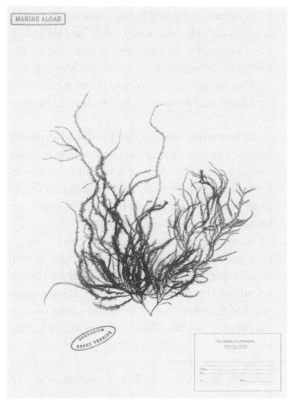

FIGURE 33.1 Mark Dion. *Herbarium Perrine* (*Marine Algae*), 2006. Two portfolios containing pressed seaweed on tea-stained paper, custom vitrine, assorted objects Vitrine: 45 ¾ × 51 1/8 × 26 inches Herbarium closed: 17 × 12 1/8 × 3 ½ inches. Herbarium open: 17 × 24 5/8 × 3 ½ inches.
COURTESY THE ARTIST AND TANYA BONAKDAR GALLERY, NEW YORK
© MARK DION.

books. The chemicals in algae are a perfect glue, adhering the organism to the paper and making them look very like fine drawings.

GA: Fieldwork has been a very important methodological approach to many of your projects. I guess it is fair to say that you understood the importance of localized geographies and ecosystems well before these became an artistic trend a few years ago. What role did fieldwork play in the making of *Herbarium Perrine*?

MD: The *Herbarium Perrine* work is part of a much larger investigation of the issues of plant ecology, conservation, and science in South Florida. The fieldwork aspect involved a variety of extended trips to South Florida and spending time with botanists and historians of science at the Fairchild Botanical Garden and Everglades National Park as well as at the University of South Florida in Tampa. I became interested in drawing a line between the botanical plant collectors of the nineteenth century, which included orchid hunters, and botanists today who are forced to see some of America's rarest habitats go under the bulldozer blade. I built an exhibition around the excitement of discovering new plants and environments and the melancholy of having to watch them disappear.

I heard some botanists at the Fairchild Botanical Garden speak about how they have "rescued" rare plants from a site about to be bulldozed to make room for a housing development. That gave me the idea for the project "The South Florida Wildlife Rescue Unit," a vehicle belonging to a fictional organization which captures and relocates plants and animals from zones threatened by development. These organisms are then released into safe environments. We know that there are few safe zones in the rapidly developing landscape of South Florida.

In order to understand the issues at hand with South Florida ecology and development, I had to spend some time on the ground as well as read a great deal. My partners at the Miami Art Museum, including Peter Boswell and Rene Morales, were marvelous guides and informers regarding the cultural landscape of real-estate development shenanigans. Of course, these aspects of the south Florida landscape do go all the way back to the aspirations of Perrine's vision.

GA: How is this project related to others that have explored the ethics and philosophies of collecting and displaying and thus of constructing nature?

MD: In the original exhibition at Miami Art Museum, there were images of plant hunter's wagons and cars piled high with orchids, bromeliads, and other rare plants. The methods and standards of collection practice of the past were shown in stark contrast to the way we think about threatened landscapes today. Certainly, at the time, when there were still vast wild lands still intact, this type of collecting did not seem extreme. The major menace to wild places in South Florida it turns out was not the wholesale collecting of plant and animal specimens but rather habitat destruction from sprawl and unscrupulous development.

Collecting is an invaluable tool in biology. It is pretty essential to understand individuals, evolutionary history, ecology and biodiversity, but it not practiced without ambience. I am interested in that, of course since where the emotional, subjective and irrational crash into the objective aspirations of science, is the site of my investigation. Most scientists I know truly love their subjects, be they birds, fishes, or plants, and killing them in numbers they find an unsettling necessity. Recently there have been some challenges to collecting practices from ethical perspectives as well as a revolution in taxonomy based on genetic biology. It is an extremely interesting time to follow the developments in collecting ethics.

GA: Henry Perrine was a doctor, horticulturist, and diplomat who was amongst the first to grasp the importance of Florida's agricultural potential. His story is a tragic one—it is marked by loss, not just personal, but also cultural and scientific. Can *Herbarium Perrine* be understood as a reparational work of art in any way?

MD: Yes, in a number of ways. First of all, Dr. Perrine is somewhat of a lost figure in the history of South Florida and America. While numerous streets and features bare his name, few seem to recall that he set a template for agricultural development in the state, with his scientific, economic botany. So, while many, including myself, would be highly critical of the ecological consequences of the field of introducing nonnative crops to unsuitable landscapes, Perrine still is interesting for setting out this model.

Who knows, if he had lived, what kind of landscape South Florida would be today? Would he have advocated the wholesale draining of the Everglades and out of control development that happened there? Would he be a conservation hero and advocate like Marjory Stoneman Douglas?

In terms of valuing the botanical environment of region, his collection, which burned, would have been extremely useful to researchers today. His notebooks and herbariums would have helped to piece together the fragmentary botanical natural history of region.

GA: I have written about herbaria as epistemological sites in which nature was physically as well as metaphorically flattened in order to enter scientific discourses during the Renaissance and the Enlightenment. From an epistemological perspective, what is at stake in making algae visible?

MD: While specimen collections are incredibly valuable for a vast number of reasons, they always pale in use, in contrast to the animal or plant in situ, or in life.

People like you and I are extremely privileged, in that we have access to natural history collections. We are familiar with how nature is stored, sorted, conserved, cataloged, and used in scientific institutions. The violence of collecting, the compromising of the specimens, the limits of what can be saved when making things last, is known to us as it is to any biologist. Many of my works introduce other audiences to these conventions of collection and display for the first time. This is part of the epistemological imperative in the work.

This is why, although I am keen to have the works reference the amateur decorative Victorian arrangements of seaweed, I still insist on the conventions of scientific collections in the herbarium sheets. The labels, intentionally left blank, refer to unfinished labor, and the collection stamps, are essential to herbarium collections.

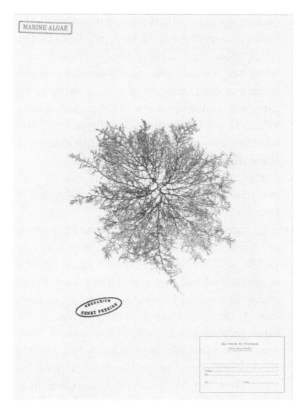

FIGURE 33.2   Mark Dion, *Herbarium Perrine* (*Marine Algae*), 2006. Two portfolios containing pressed seaweed on tea-stained paper, custom vitrine, assorted objects Vitrine: 45 ¾ × 51 1/8 × 26 inches Herbarium closed: 17 × 12 1/8 × 3 ½ inches. Herbarium open: 17 × 24 5/8 × 3 ½ inches.
COURTESY THE ARTIST AND TANYA BONAKDAR GALLERY, NEW YORK
© MARK DION.

GA: You said that algae collected for this project were dried for three weeks in blotter paper and ended up adhering to its surface in ways that resembled the flatness of drawing or ink-painting. I find this of particular interest. It sounds as if the algae, unlike other terrestrial and sturdier plants rendered themselves onto the page as some kind of fossils, through some sort of contact-impression process. Do you read these images as traces? And if so what are they traces of?

MD: The marine algae on the page resemble drawings or the finest watercolor brushwork, more than anything else. I was astonished how the paper seemed to absorb the seaweed into itself, as it drinks the ink of a pen. In the original sheets I produced, the sea organisms seemed both representations as much as the thing itself. This phenomena, and their beauty, seems to me part of the fascination with collecting marine algae in the Victorian period. My extremely capable friends at GraphicStudio did a remarkable job in replicating that effect. The ink of each print was hand applied so as to give the works dimensionality and the sublet variation of living matter.

GA: Your projects are journeys of discovery for the viewer just as much as they are for yourself. What was your relationship to algae prior to embarking on *Herbarium Perrine*? Has this project affected it in any way?

MD: I had collected algae myself and with my wife Dana Sherwood before. Also in the marvelous herbariums and special collections of The British Museum of Natural History and American Museum of Natural History among others, I have often encountered books of pressed seaweeds that they count as some of their greatest and most wonderful treasures. I have collected and attempted to identify algae and produced a work in 1998 titled "The National Botanical Survey (Coastal Collections)." For this I collected specimen with my friend Harrell Fletcher from around the Bay Area. Algae are notoriously difficult to key out and identity. I was mesmerized by the gigantic Pacific forms of algae on the West Coast, and had to make new plant presses a meter long and wide in order to fit the specimens.

GA: Algae appear to be thoroughly enmeshed in the element in which they live. Their structures usually rely on floatation. But besides the obvious morphological difference between terrestrial plants and algae have you become aware of other interesting specificities that define them?

MD: Well marine algae have no vascular system, although the utilize photosynthesis. Algae is a common name that covers a huge diversity of organisms for microscopic algae to the giant kelps. So, this is yet another place where naming causes confusion.

I am close to this group since I grew up on the coast and spent so much time in the tide pools and coastal marshes of Massachusetts. In my exploration, I was interested in how algae created habitat for so many other organisms— crabs, shrimp, worms, fish, echinoderms, etc. Certainly, many seaweeds like the giant kelps that make forests, are keystone species, creating the conditions for a diversity of other life forms.

GA: In the age of virtual reality, do herbaria constitute a completely outdated epistemological space; one that can only reacquire significance within a contemporary art discourse, or do you still see them as relevant in the production of knowledge of the botanical and marine worlds?

MD: Oh, I thoroughly disagree with the notion that herbaria are outdated and supplanted by new technologies. Even given the significant developments of molecular biology there is still so much that can be learned from an encounter with actual specimens. As I said before, a specimen in a basement of a scientific institution cannot speak as well as a living organism in the environment where it evolved, but it can clearly speak more than a mere image. Aspects of a thing like texture, color variation, scale, and a myriad of other aspects of a once living being cannot be sensed by scans of herbarium sheets. Which is not to say that the scans are not useful. They are a wonderful way for institutions to share their holdings around the world.

GA: How important are plants in general to your everyday life? Do you have a special plant in your life?

MD: Of course, plants a critical to the lives of every human on the planet, mostly in ways invisible and underappreciated. Since my life is hectic and full of travel, I can't have house plants in my life. I do have a number of trees that I planted myself in Pennsylvania the same year my son Grey Rabbit was born. They are fifteen years old now as he is and I watch their progress and growth in tandem with his own. There are times when I don't see Rabbit or the trees for some stretch of time and I am always surprised to witness their growth progress.

CHAPTER 34

Burning Flowers: Interview with Mat Collishaw

Mat Collishaw and Giovanni Aloi

An important member of the Young British Artists movement in the 1990s, Mat Collishaw creates work that confronts issues of moral ambiguity with formally stunning and alluring imagery. Coupling references to art history, literature, and the Victorian era with modern imaging technology, the artist renders powerful images and objects that often recontextualize the impact of traditionally disturbing and sinister subject matter. At once poetic and morbid, his sculptures, installations and photo-based works expose elements of beauty within the darkest fantasies, blurring the lines between seduction and repulsion, observation and exploitation, reality and artifice. Much of Collishaw's imagery involves the natural world and plants are particularly recurring in his work. In this interview, Giovanni Aloi and Mat Collishaw discuss the often iconoclastic aesthetic approaches that have characterized the artist's career.

Giovanni Aloi: Opticality and visual perception have been important themes in your body of work. Many of your pieces question the nature of reality and our intrinsic ability to construct nature as external to us. For these reasons, you seldom revisit classical realism, like you did for your iteration of Albrecht Dürer's 1503 masterpiece *Great Piece of Turf*. Besides the striking realism of Dürer's original representation, the fact that "weeds" are central to the image is very meaningful. Considering that the history of baroque painting is filled with beautiful paintings and drawings of sophisticated and expensive cultivars, why did you decide to focus on the humble weed?

Mat Collishaw: I was in hospital, quite ill, and perhaps melodramatically, thought I was dying. I started thinking about this Dürer watercolour and how vividly he had concentrated his attention on a seemingly insignificant clump of weeds. At a time when most painters were preoccupied with religious imagery, it seemed a strange thing to do. But when the likelihood that you might actually be departing from this world becomes tangible, a simple current of wind breathing life into a lowly throng of grass becomes redolent with beauty. The way in which each blade has its own peculiarity and resistance to wind force was a source of mysterious wonder.

GA: Why did you choose to work with video? What does the video dimension bring to the plant materialization in the image?

MC: I decided that, if I ever got out of that hospital bed, I would try to bring that image to life, to recreate my reverence for it—the video dimension allowed that vision to come to fruition.

GA: Beauty and horror have played a substantial role in your work. It is in this context that the notion of sacrifice emerges in your visual representations. You once said that "in the act of producing any work, there has to be some form of sacrifice, even if only the surrendering of reality to the invention of the artwork." This philosophy became central to your series titled *Burning Flowers*. In this case you turned your attention to very colorful and symbolically charged cultivars. How did you come to choose your flowers in this case?

MC: The choice of flowers for these works was entirely practical. Most flowers have a very high water content and just refuse to burn! I tried pretty much every flower I could get my hands on. *Auto Immolation* is a video for this very reason—once again, it is a dimension in which near-impossible things can be made to happen,

FIGURE 34.1   Albrecht Dürer, *The Large Piece of Turf*, 1503. Watercolour.

so the only way I could convincingly make flowers burn was to use digital flames. I wanted a sequence where the flower opened and closed and retained some of its biological strangeness, something that is not apparent when looking at a flower in real time. I spent a substantial amount of time looking at time-lapse videos of flowers opening and closing. The one I eventually chose was an Amaryllis, as the flower had a majestic quality to it. The petals were almost cloak like in the way they opened up, revealing the stamen of the flower, then closed again in a similarly ceremonial fashion. The ritualistic quality of the flowers' movements coupled with the flames echoed ideas of auto immolation, when religious zeal embraces the concept of sacrifice or suicide in order to express its devotion. It's a metaphor about what we do to flowers and the naturalization of our manipulation of them, which becomes their own nature in our eyes.

GA: In *Venal Muse, Envirico* a resin-sculpted orchid sits under a glass case. The work is suspended between symbolic and visceral sets of significations. During the nineteenth century, orchids became precious and delicate objects of desire. They became undisputed symbols of exotic beauty, but the fleshiness of the petals of some species triggered contrasting feelings of attraction and revulsion in viewers. However, closer inspection of this specific orchid reveals new levels of disturbing hyperrealism. How did you come to combine orchids and venereal diseases?

MC: I had a number of sources for these works. First of all was Baudelaire's *Fleur de Mal*, a fascination with the darker side of human nature and an acceptance that beauty can have corruption lurking beneath the surface. Another influence was J.K. Huysmans's *À rebours*, in which the author writes about a collector who has an equally unhealthy obsession with extraordinary looking flowers and works of art. He eventually becomes so removed from the real world that he begins to challenge the boundary between nature and art.

But this very choice, this predilection for the conservatory plants had itself changed under the influence of his mode of thought. Formerly, during his Parisian days, his love for artificiality had led him to abandon real flowers and to use in their place replicas faithfully executed by means of the miracles performed with India rubber and wire, calico and taffeta, paper and silk. He was the possessor of a marvelous collection of tropical plants, the result of the labors of skilful artists who knew how to follow nature and recreate her step by step, taking the flower as a bud, leading it to its full development, even imitating its decline, reaching such a point of perfection as to convey every nuance — the most fugitive expressions of the flower when it opens at dawn and closes at evening, observing the appearance of the petals curled by the wind or rumpled by the rain, applying dew drops of gum on its matutinal corollas; shaping it in full bloom, when the branches bend under the burden of their sap, or showing the dried stem and shrivelled cupules, when calyxes are thrown off and leaves fall to the ground.[1]

This wonderful art had held him entranced for a long while, but now he was dreaming of another experiment. He wished to go one step beyond. Instead of artificial flowers imitating real flowers, natural flowers should mimic the artificial ones.

The obsession mirrored his own pathological descent into a narcissistic madness. Lastly, Jean Genet writes beautifully about his lovers in prison, describing their sores and wounds as magnificent embellishments, almost like military medals that they wear as adornments. All of these influences instigated the series of works *Infectious Flowers* and *The Venal Muse*.

GA: How were the flowers for the *Venal Muse* series made?

MC: I took real flowers and broke them down into several parts, I then made a mold of each part and cast it in resin. Pustules and sores were then added to the cast and it was reassembled, they were then painted in fleshy tones.

GA: In *Gomoria* you have combined a large gothic alter piece with images of flowers into a video-sculpture. Here too what initially seems beautiful reveals itself in a darker light. What is the importance of the Gothic altarpiece and what is the symbolic relevance of the flowers you have chosen in this instance?

MC: The flowers are actually made from real animal flesh decaying on my studio roof and surrounded by flies. The Gothic Altarpiece was added to contextualize this scenario within the tradition of Gothic horror. The Gothic is an architectural form designed to instigate awe and

FIGURE 34.2   Mat Collishaw, *The Venal Muse, Augean*, 2012. Resin, enamel paint, wood and glass vitrine. Overall installed dimensions: 64 × 20 1/2 × 20 1/2 inches; 162.6 × 52.1 × 52.1 cm Courtesy the artist and Tanya Bonakdar Gallery, New York
© MAT COLLISHAW.

wonder and a slightly chilling reverence for powers beyond our control. The video in this work alludes to global meltdown and environmental decay, ideas propagated in scare stories in the media. The work was intended to address issues of emotional manipulation in the media and a sort of spine-tingling pleasure derived from the thrill of divine retribution.

GA: The interest for the ontological distinction between animal and plant has emerged more than

---

1 Huysman, J.K. (1884) *À rebours* (North Charleston: CreateSpace Independent Publishing Platform).

FIGURE 34.3   Mat Collishaw, *Gomoria*, 2012. Wooden
shrine, LED screens, PC. 107 × 88 1/2 × 10 1/4
inches; 271.8 × 224 × 26 cm Edition of 1; 1AP.
Courtesy the artist and Tanya Bonakdar
Gallery, New York
© MAT COLLISHAW.

once in your work. In the mid 1990s you worked
on a series of photographic prints in which the
petals of lilies had been digitally manipulated
to look as if made of leopard or tiger skin. This
series stood as a political statement against the
cosmetically doctored images of flowers produced by popular culture in greeting cards and
calendars. How did this combine of animal and
vegetal surfaces come together?

MC: This series was designed to tease to the surface
the predatory nature of flowers and therefore,
the idea was to liken animals to plants. I wanted

to produce images that reminded people that
flowers are not the pretty objects conceived
by popular culture, but that they are devices
designed for the very purpose of plants' survival—there's a lot more at stake than pretty colors
and fragrance. We are constantly surrounded by
cosmeticized images of flowers that do nothing
but diminish their dignity as integral parts of
plants' biological functioning.

At the same time, I was also quite interested in the way that we adorn ourselves with
animal skins in clothing and interior furnish-
ings—something that also dilutes the meaning of the original function of camouflage in
animals. A leopard-skin miniskirt is devised to
attract attention whereas that very skin, in its
original context, was meant to blend into to the
surrounding terrain. I wanted to combine these
contradictions to make the flowers visible in a
different way.

GA: In 2011, you staged a complex multimedia
installation titled *Sordid Earth* at London's
Roundhouse. This was a collaboration with architect Ron Arad that furthered your exploration of ominous flowers that began with the
series *Infectious Flowers*. Did you envision that
space as a prehistoric reality, or a postapocalyptic scenario?

MC: I designed it to be deliberately ambiguous;
I guess that it could be both: prehistoric or
postapocalyptic. It was important that nature
seemed threatening in a way and that the consequences of interfering with natural processes could be potentially catastrophic. I asked a
group of African drummers to play along with
my projection to communicate a primal feeling, one of ancient spirits being summoned, as
though the Gods were angry and seeking retribution for some unnamed wrong doing. Prehistory was the specter that had come back to
haunt us in a post-apocalyptic onslaught.

GA: How important is scientific accuracy in the
representation of your flowers?

MC: I'm very interested in the science of plants
and flowers and of their evolutionary struggles.

But I use quite a lot of creative license in my depictions of them. I don't let the truth get in the way of a good story because my intentions are probably more poetic than they are empirically based.

GA: Plants and flowers seem to occupy a central role in your personal iconography of catastrophe and decay. Why?

MC: It's been said that nature is the barometer of the world's health, which is one aspect of what I try to represent with the use of plants in my work. But I also frequently use them as metaphors for a certain moral decay and sickness in our relationship to the world more in general. It's almost sacrilegious to deface or abuse flowers so this contingency makes them quite potent images to experiment with.

GA: What is your relationship to plants outside the artistic sphere?

MC: I have a terrace on which I have numerous plants growing; one of the main issues is to keep the dogs from urinating on them. My grandfather grew flowers by the thousands to sell to florists and my father is also a keen gardener and photographer so doubtlessly this all influenced me as I was growing up.

CHAPTER 35

A Program for Plants: In Conversation, Coda

Giovanni Aloi, Brian M. John, Linda Tegg, and Joshi Radin

A Program for Plants was a collaborative research project by SAIC graduate students Joshi Radin, Brian M. John, and Linda Tegg, mentored by Dr. Giovanni Aloi that unfolded during the winter of 2015 and spring 2016. It was both a quest for connection with nonhuman kinds and the overlaying of cultural content, bringing cultural archives and transmissions into unlikely relationships in order to examine empathy and our capacity for empathizing with both plants and art alike.

Through the project's first phase, Radin, John, and Tegg measured the Photosynthetically Active Radiation (light) emitted by the Video Data Bank's 50 most requested videos. They screened the videos to a spectrometer and took measurements (at regular intervals) of the light levels emitted to assess which would be more suited to a plant audience. They then pared the selection down to the top five films with the largest outputs. With the plants in mind, they then produced a film festival, playing the films on a loop directly onto the plants, nourishing them with light.

Top 5 Films for a Plant Audience

5. *Papillon d'amour* / Nicholas Provost
4. *RE:THE_OPERATION* / Paul Chan
3. *Theme Song* / Vito Acconci
2. *Hostage: The Bachar Tapes* (English Version) / Walid Raad and Souheil Bachar
1. *Trio A* / Yvonne Rainer

The PAR measurements identified *Trio A* by Yvonne Rainer as the plants' favourite video. The vegetal beings' verdict prompted the group to consider how *Trio A* might expand our collective capacity to empathize with plants. They, thus, became interested in learning *Trio A* and invited Linda K. Johnson, one of a handful of international dance artists designated by Yvonne Rainer as a custodian/transmitter of her postmodern work to teach a small section of it as part of a three-day workshop.

Initially performed in 1966 by Rainer, David Gordon and Steve Paxton at Judson Church in NYC, *Trio A* is a five-minute sequence of movements that has been considered radical since its very first moment of performance because it proposed an entirely new way to compose, think about, and perform dance. Seminal in its argument that engaging the human body in the straightforward task of simply moving is indeed 'dancing', *Trio A* invites the dancer and the viewer to re-consider the expectations that each bring to the moment of dance. With its evenness of phrasing, specificity of gaze, and use of a seemingly untrained and non-virtuosic movement vocabulary, *Trio A* celebrates the factual elegance of the moving body. Dance historians regard it as a major turning point in the field of dance.[1]

In the text that follows, Radin, John, Tegg, and Aloi summarise the main findings and original contributions of the project.

Joshi Radin: Why don't we start with plants?

Giovanni Aloi: What came first? Did it all begin because Linda was working with plants? Brian isn't your project about empathy in a way? Playing for plants? Do you see that as empathy?

Brian M. John: Absolutely, yes. This started as an idea for something we could do within the show *Mercury*, which Linda and I were collaborating on. We were thinking about the circumstances

---

1 Johnson, L.K. 'Trio A', online: [<http://www.lindakjohnson.net/trio-a/>].

we'd set up, and then thinking what can we do with that, how can we activate it in different ways. We knew the plants were going to be in a gallery exhibition context. We asked, "what can we do for them or with them to activate the exhibition differently," is that fair to say?

Linda Tegg: Yes. We were considering the gallery as a site of cultural production. We had already decided to cultivate plants in the gallery, from within this process we wanted to see where else our thinking might lead, what possibilities would open up. It wasn't a large leap to begin thinking about the Video Data Bank, an archive of video art works that are maintained at the school, as a source of nourishment for the plants. So, I think there is confluence there as well.

BMJ: It was a generous enough gesture towards both, the archive and the plants, that it didn't feel like a subversion, it was more additive than that. I was thinking about how absurd but also how wonderful it would be to take whatever database they had and add this column for every video in their archive, this extra piece of information because of our intervention, that said how good it is for plants. It's this strange metric that no one would bring to their own archive, but again that's additive, it's producing new content, new information. So, it didn't feel like a subversion at first, until we actually started dealing with the thing and got this push back. And they were fine with us doing it, but they weren't willing to come towards us at all.

GA: In a way, what it reveals is how those systems of knowledge work—what is relevant to the Video Data Bank is of course what we think, it's very anthropocentric so, the duration of the film, the data you need to locate material historically and culturally. Who cares about a plant's perception of it? Right? And I guess that's part of the strength of what you've done. Inserting that column is a disturbance of some degree of that anthropocentric stability whereby we categorize these videos this way. But what about using this metric? That's hefty, in a way. I like that

it's productive, and then the subversion is generated as something productive. I wonder if we can think of this idea of productivity more carefully, and in what other senses you think it was productive in an additional, expansive way?

JR: I was interested in issues of empathy and creating meaning in communities that were outside the art institution, and that was the position I came from. I took an interest in nature—Linda's work was very interesting to me, and I was wondering how to evolve those two conversations together. One of the things that's productive in the context of *Mercury* is holding that recentering for an audience that wouldn't normally seek it out; you disrupt normal ways of viewing these elements just by having them in the same space. It's productive in the sense of disrupting perceived ideas. If it were for plants in a garden or greenhouse or space where you'd normally expect to find plants, it wouldn't have the same cultural connection that they're engineering by the site-specificity of that work.

GA: One of the interesting aspects of this project lay in the choice of plants. You did not play with plants with an individualized identity, there were no rose bushes. The plants that were chosen already exist as a pack. Deleuze and Guattari wrote about the pack, as a deterritorializing element, and I'm thinking about the productivity involved as plants are so difficult to relate to as individuals in most cases anyway. They always come off as replaceable multiples. This was particularly visible at the beginning of the project as all seedlings sort of looked like blades of grass for some time.

LT: With Grasslands, in particular, I'm continually challenged with how they're perceived by the human eye. We have to shift our perspective in order to see the complexity in it. In terms of landscape, and of plant communities, it seems as if there is nothing we're more geared to look over and across. Grasslands are historically seen for human use, as either backdrop, or a site of human prospering for agriculture and expansion. I encounter it all the time, the difficulty

FIGURE 35.1   Brian M. John, Linda Tegg, and Joshi Radin, *A Program for Plants*, 2016
© BRIAN M. JOHN, LINDA TEGG, AND JOSHI RADIN.

of shifting human perception to recognize the variance of species in that setting.

GA: Kenneth Shapiro wrote an interesting essay on animals and ontological vulnerability. There he weaves a complex argument about the pack attitude toward certain animals, farm animals especially. A multitude of mass-farmed pigs lose their individuality and therefore that loss enables a base-level of objectification that allows us to, in Shapiro's words, "mow them like blades of grass." The mowing metaphor is important here as it highlights a generalized and indiscriminate approach. But I think the machine-design, and the way it operates, suggests our relationship to the materiality of animals and plants. We're not interested in preserving individual blades of grass, and the machine reflects that. It acts like an equalizer.

BMJ: That was definitely one of the challenges presented by *Mercury*. You can't anthropomorphize a bunch of small shoots in a large field.

BMJ: It seems obvious once you start thinking about plants in this way, but it isn't for an audience that isn't following along this chain of inquiry, so when you present them with a field of plants it's hard to communicate that shift. In *A Program for Plants*, when we were projecting the videos, everybody wanted the plants to be a screen, which was fine because we wanted to give the light to the plants directly. But that was a point of tension—how to present the video work to the plants, and how to maintain the plant audience as the audience.

JR: How not to create a spectacle for a human audience that involves plants.

BMJ: Yes, how to not instrumentalize them.

GA: That is a big question in aesthetics right now. Are you performing for a human audience or are you really trying to create a connection with this nonhuman being that you're claiming you're engaging in the work? There's a lot of controversy about whether you're still performing for an audience of humans rather than doing anything that engages that nonhuman being.

BMJ: I found one empirical study that looked at frequency ranges and how they affected growth of some corn sprouts. It measured the amount the root tendril of the sprout would grow towards the source of the sound through a water medium. It found consistent results for a certain frequency range. There were different results for the sound I curated–not all of the artists were necessarily working with the idea of this frequency range. I made two different pieces that responded directly to that study, but the range is 200–300 hertz, so it's on the low side but well within the range of human hearing. It's not even in that spectrum that you lose as you get older. So, everything we hear, to whatever extent this study applies to other plants, these plants hear. All of my stuff was designed around these frequencies, in both cases modulating music that was originally designed for a human audience–changing it, adapting it to try and create a bridge or a medium between human cultural content and a vision of what cultural content for plants could be.

JR: I feel a lot of the performance work hinged on intention. We spoke a lot about intention with Linda K. Johnson and she brought up the example of experiments on water crystals, which I used to be very dismissive of. I found that when I considered performing for a plant audience as opposed to a human audience, it changed how I felt about it. Linda and I were walking back to the studios, and I was telling her about it, "there I go, anthropomorphizing plants, again, imagining that they're going to somehow be a more generous and receptive audience than humans." When the truth is I just don't know, I have no idea. Perhaps the plants just think I'm full of it, and that I'm a bad dancer. It's the kind of thing where I found myself peeling off layer after layer of constructed meaning that I was imposing. So, getting at the truth of what a phytocentric perspective could be in that context felt very elusive.

BMJ: For me, learning and performing this fragment of *Trio A* was operating on a totally different register than the original video screenings for plants or the music that we made for plants where it was not as much about trying to have a literal material impact on the plants–to actually project culture across this species divide, but that it was more about learning through this work. The process of learning the work was more about opening up our own perceptions. By engaging in this strange process you're opening up all these questions and you're peeling back all these layers of construction. So, for me it was more about that process, revealing these layers of projected meaning that are maybe arbitrary or externally imposed so they're not very meaningful. So, for me it became about boiling down the self and stripping away layers of preconceived notions about these two bodies–the body of the plant and the body of the human. I found it really productive in terms of thinking about ourselves as bodies, and the plants as bodies, and there's a parity in a way. You strip away until you find parity–we're basically living human beings.

GA: Living beings acknowledging each other.

BMJ: Right–I was thinking of it a lot in terms of community, shared community. The video was actually doing this thing to the plants–maybe it's having a material effect on them. But with this I was thinking about how I am a member of a biome with these plants.

JR: It was more about flattening a hierarchical relationship.

JR: It raised questions of absurdity, but it also felt like it raised questions of contemporary occultic practice. In the past there maybe were ritualized dances for the earth or for nonhuman beings, but how do we understand those relationships now, and how do we understand what they were doing or can we reinterpret that relationship? Yvonne's original intention that it would be a folk dance, and a modernist folk dance felt relevant in this way, because here we are trying to forge ahead with these relationships using the tool of this modernist piece and performing it in places where we would look absurd.

GA: It's an interesting point and it makes me think about what Brian said about resisting the scientific engagement and at the same time actually engaging with a folkloric/ritualistic involvement. A lot of contemporary art is concerned with the role of science and what science should and shouldn't be doing and that science could obliterate any sense of the folkloric or tactile sense, or sense-driven contact with a nonhuman being. It's interesting to see how science comes in and out of your work– but then *Trio A* is a derailment of all of that, a constant turning left and right on the specific uses of science. This strikes me as very healthy, and an exciting place to be. I'm not inclined to listen to the 'don't do science mantras' that are going around now that seem to be a bit obscurantist. Okay we understand that too much science can obfuscate any other reading or relationship with the non-human, but no science at all leaves us in the middle ages–with no empirical relational. I think part of the preoccupation with your project as well as other projects out there is how much can this actually translate into everyday life. Is there something we learn from what you have done that can actually be transposed outside the gallery space. I love it that Joshi was performing inside the conservatory, which can operate as a metaphorical setup just as much as real one. It's a place of captivity for plants–you had a captive audience. You perform in a place that's setup for humans to see plants in a certain way, a tropical audience is there for you. And Linda performed in another setup with a captive audience; kept captive by consumerism. They probably were cloned as well. It would be interesting to know. At the same time, they were real spaces. So, you moved from the gallery space to outside, bridging the utopianist setup space of the gallery to the reality out there. You could have just decided to perform *Trio A* to the plants in the gallery—never

mind that they were not there anymore, you could have restaged it.

BMJ: I agree, and I think it's really important, this fluid relationship with science, for myself. I think the boundary between science and other modes of cultural production is unnecessary, for myself. It can be opened up and we can use various pieces of this very closed off methodology. You can pull pieces from it, and I think experimentation is one of those pieces that has been crucial to this project from the beginning in the different modes we approached our content. With *Trio A* there were modes of experimentation. What does it mean to perform this for a plant audience at Home Depot, for the conservatory, at the beach, and then we come back to the studio and what does it mean to perform for plants and humans at the same time. I think it's fundamental to the project–not having preconceptions about what the answers are.

GA: There's a sense of the "lost cause", which goes back to your point about absurdity. It's integral to the project... this idea that all you're doing might be a lost cause. All we're doing might be a lost cause. It seems meaningful because it's set up in certain units of accomplishment that we establish value scales for. Science works within them though, to assess certain data. There might be some discovery or some awareness developing from what might be viewed as a lost cause. Something is a lost cause only because it appears that to be a lost cause in a values system that looks at it as a lost cause. But it can become something else as long as you engage with it and see what happens. I guess part of the danger of western thought and more specifically of capitalism, is that it prevents us from engaging in lost causes. It tells us that we should spend our time productively, and structures are in place to get us to be productive and fast. Therefore, the idea of dancing on the beach in the hope that something might happen between you and the plants is pretty much a lost cause in the best possible productive way.

FIGURE 35.2   Linda K. Johnson performing for a multispecies audience, 2016.

BMJ: Totally. And I think that's one of those things where the space between art and science can change science. If you think that scientific research has to know what it's trying to do, but it can be really open, that can change science and has enormous value, but it's something science is bad at within the constraints of our culture as it stands. It's not good at allowing open-ended research because it wants everything to be productive. We don't fund NASA anymore because it's too open-ended and we don't know what the value of it will be. Even though we can say oh, it's produced enormous cultural value, even so, that's not convincing enough in our short-term focused, productivity-oriented culture. I think that's one of the points that crosses over to everyday life.

JR: There's another aspect relevant to the idea of absurdity which goes back to the plants and nature and current conversation about the end of the world for humans, and end-times, and the significance of acting with that specter in the background. I think it feels different to take on those engagements, questioning human relationships to non-human kinds, in this context and I feel the absurdity and actually quite serious attempts have dual qualities to me.

BMJ: There's an urgency to the ethical questions raised by these projects which wouldn't be there if it weren't for the context and our growing awareness of our species' role in the larger community.

LT: And historically people have thought it absurd that women have rights, that children have rights, or animals. Totally absurd and laughable. I think by extending our empathy toward something we see as inaccessible to us, as plants, opens up so many more possibilities for everything else.

GA: Agency is a hot feature in many discourses right now–I'm thinking of vibrant materialism, for instance. In your project plants were enabled to make choices. They chose *Trio A* for you, for instance...

BMJ: It's a very mediated agency, but I know what you mean.

BMJ: And if you open up your idea of agency and action to include a broader definition that allows plants a kind of agency in determining our decisions with regards to them. Thinking about communication more openly, outside of language, then that issue of captivity becomes really complicated and interesting with regards to plants.

GA: Yep, I think so.

BMJ: I mean it's a huge open-ended question. There are no answers.

JR: It's interesting to me in terms of attributing agency that we frequently think of successful reproduction as an indication of agency, perhaps the primary indication. That all species are looking to reproduce themselves, I wonder about...

GA: It's a Darwinian affectation. The idea that it's always about the strongest species taking over: the survival of the fittest. So we return to your point, Linda, about the seeds in the packet–do they even want to germinate?

JR: Right, but I think that that's something that we can question. What does it mean to be a successful species? Does it mean to reproduce oneself? Or does it mean to have a better quality of life? And how does agency play a role in that? But I think it is harder. I am thinking of humans because they have been so successful at reproducing themselves, they're threatening the life support systems of themselves as well as other species. Is that something that we would define as a success or not?

GA: And then you also have to think about the concept of species itself and whether we need to snap out of that too in order to move the discussion further. I think one of the things that was fascinating about Linda's packets of grains in *One World Rice Pilaf* is the idea that it was a conglomeration, so those packets, the species idea, is obliterated by this almost random gathering of a selection of seeds. Could it be a species in itself? One created by capitalism? If you look at it in the packaging, could that be a species of plants that successfully subjugated us?

Made us dependent, parasitized us by inducing a desire to eat them and therefore to keep growing them. This generates a symbiotic seductive-chain of coevolution. In a sense, you have to start wondering about the differences between plants like the ones in the grain packets and potted plants around us in this apartment. Is there any? These plants have been selected and modified over centuries of cohabitation and coevolution—in a way they have selected us as well and have made us into what we are. We have also diverted or modified what the idea of species was, so in a sense, I am more inclined to think about individual survival rather than species survival in this context. The idea that this individual plant has a drive to flower and propagate seeds more than this species has a desire to overcome another species. I think that is a reading, that is dictated by an anthropomorphic parallelism with human wars, racial conflict ... And I wonder how much of that is valid for all plants. There are plants out there that definitely "think in pack mode" as a network.

LT: That's how I think of it.

BMJ: That's what I was going to say. The whole question then becomes complicated when you're looking at plants and like it makes you realize how focused we have always been in the history of our philosophy on the individual consciousness and on that level of being but you can easily zoom in and zoom out and define entities and define the boundaries between a being and an entity fluidly depending on what level you're looking at. How do you define the difference between a single entity of a plant because it is so...

JR: It's modular.

BMJ: Right. It's so much more fluid, you can take a cutting off a plant and it can grow on its own. Where is the boundary between that and plant communities are so interconnected in a way that is totally different than us, but then even with us, this came up at the symposium, there are all kinds of other living beings that are part of our bodies that boundary becomes much more fluid, the more you look at nonhuman kinds.

LT: One aspect about our collaboration that I found interesting is how we edit documents in real time, seemingly endlessly, together. So, we have this shared headspace which is quite unique, I think within a collaborative group there is that loosening of the boundary and de-stabilization, that challenges me.

GA: I like this idea of a collaboration that has a "shared headspace."

BMJ: Its very cybernetic.

GA: Yeah. But there is something fascinating in this idea of flat ontology if you can allow... what you've done is basically allow the plants to have some agency... and I don't mean "allowed" as a patronizing gesture. I am not saying: "oh let's allow these plants to have agency". But you've sort of taken a step back, deliberately, lots of times, by saying: "let's let the plants decide which is the video we like?" And you've set up this system through which you could enable that choice to emerge and become visible. And I think that's interesting, because if you think about the history of capitalism and humankind in relation to nature, this is never the case. It's never the case of allowing nature to decide, it's always a case of diverting the river. I mean, we live in a city that has actually reversed the flow of the river, which sounds incredible, but it has been done.

The idea of cyborgs that has already come up in this project is something that could be different from a project that could've been similar in the 1960s, right?

JR: I see this a lot. I see the themes recurring, as I've been revisiting this hippie commune, and the plethora of communes that emerged in that time period, after 1968, because of the social crises that were occurring, and that fleeing urban centers to go to the less populated areas as a response to levels of unprecedented violence and social crises. There's a lot of impetus to reorient towards nature now, to reorient towards sustainability and personal responsibility and locality. MIT's Media Lab has a farming group now, which has these ties to that time period, but it's done in this totally... When the Media Lab farms, how do they do it? It's in this cyborgian, techno-heavy way. So, I see these repeating responses but of course they're going to be different now. And they should be.

GA: And thinking about agency once more, and plants... Did you situate agency that you can call agency, and to what degree this agency was detectable, in relation to the presence of the plants in the gallery space? You worked around them, and through them, and with them, right?

JR: They got themselves a gallery show. That's pretty crafty.

Bibliography

Agamben, G. (1995) *Homo Sacer: Sovereign Power and Bare Life* (Stanford: Stanford University Press).

Agamben, G. (2002) *The Open: Man and Animal* (Redwood City: Stanford University Press).

Alam, M., and Subrahmanyam, S. (2012) *Writing the Mughal World: Studies on Culture and Politics* (New York: Columbia University Press).

Alberge, D. (2014) 'The daffodil code: Doubts revived over Leonardo's *Virgin of the Rocks* in London' in *The Guardian*, 9 December, accessed online 08/08/2016: [<https://www.theguardian.com/artanddesign/2014/dec/09/leonardo-da-vinci-virgin-rocks-louvre-national-gallery>].

Alighieri, D. (1320) *The Divine Comedy: Inferno* (New York: Simon and Schuster), 2008.

Allen, R.J. (1887) *Lecture VI: The Medieval Bestiaries—The Rhind Lectures in Archaeology for 1885* (London: Whiting & Co.).

Aloi, G. (2008) 'The Death of the Animal' in *Antennae: The Journal of Nature in Visual Culture*, 5, Spring, pp. 43–53.

Aloi, G. (2011) *Art & Animals* (London: IB Tauris).

Alteveer, I., Brown, M., Wagstaff, S. (2015) *The Roof Garden Commission: Pierre Huyghe* (New York: MoMA).

Angier, N. (2009) 'Sorry Vegans, Brussels Sprouts Like to Live Too' in *The New York Times*, December 22, p. 2.

Appel, H.M., and Cocroft, R.B. (2014) 'Plants Respond to Leaf Vibrations Caused by Insect Herbivore Chewing' in *Oecologia* 175: 4, pp. 1257–66.

Aristotle. Lawson-Tancred, H., trans. (1986) *De Anima (On The Soul)* (New York: Penguin Books).

Aristotle. *The Poetics*. Translated by Allan H. Gilbert in *Literary Criticism: Plato to Dryden* (Detroit: Wayne State UP) 1940.

Ashworth, W.B. (1996) 'Emblematic Natural History in the Renaissance' in Jardine, J., Secord, A., and Spary, E.C. (eds.) *Cultures of Natural History* (Cambridge: Cambridge University Press) pp. 17–37.

Backster, C. (1968) 'Evidence of a primary perception in plant life' in *International Journal of Parapsychology*, X, 4, Winter, pp. 329–48.

Backster, C. (2003) *Primary Perception: Biocommunication with Plants, Living Foods, and Human Cells* (Irwindale: White Rose Millennium Press).

Bailey, O. (n. d.) 'Oscar Bailey: Cirkuits,' *Bailey Panoramas*, online: [<http://baileypanoramas.com/oscar-bailey/>].

Baker, S. (2000) *The Postmodern Animal* (London and New York: Routledge).

Bakke, M. (2012) 'Art for Plants' Sake? Questioning Human Imperialism in the Age of Biotech,' in *Parallax*, 18: 4, pp. 9–25.

Barber, C.L. (2011) *Shakespeare's Festive Comedy: A Study of Dramatic Form and Its Relation to Social Convention* (Princeton: Princeton University).

Barr, M.D., and Trocki, C.A. (eds) (2008) *Paths Not Taken: Political Pluralism in Post-War Singapore* (Singapore: NUS Press).

Barringer, T.J. (1998) *Reading the Pre-Raphaelites* (New Haven: Yale University Press).

Barthes, R. Trans. Lavers, A. (1972) *Mythologies.* (New York: Hill and Wang).

Barto, E., Kathryn, J., Weidenhamer, D., Cipollini, D., and Rillig, M.C. (2012) 'Fungal Superhighways: Do Common Mycorrhizal Networks Enhance below Ground Communication?' in *Trends in Plant Science*, 17: 11, pp. 633–37.

Batchelor, D. (2000) *Chromophobia* (London: Reaktion Books).

Beitiks, M. (2011) 'Everyone who sat with the plant, day two/comment book part one' in *Culture/Nature/Structure*, online: [<http://www.meghanmoebeitiks.com/everyone-who-sat-with-the-plant-day-two-comment-book-part-one/>].

Beitiks, M. (2011) 'The plant is present' in *The Sustainability Review*, online: [<http://www.thesustainabilityreview.org/blog/the-plant-is-present>].

Bennett, J. (2010) *Vibrant Matter: A Political Ecology of Things* (Durham: Duke University Press).

Bentham, J. (1791) *The Works of Jeremy Bentham Vol. IV* (Edinburgh: William Tait) 1843.

Berger, J. (1980) *About Looking* (London: Writers and Readers).

Berger, J. (2009) *Why Look at Animals?* (London: Penguin).

Boetzkes, A. (2010) *The Ethics of Earth Art* (Minneapolis: University of Minnesota Press).

Bonnefoy, Y. (1992) *Roman and European Mythologies* (Chicago: University of Chicago Press).

Bonnet, C. (1779) *Œuvres d'Histoire Naturelle et de Philosophie* (Neuchatel, Switzerland: S. Fauche).

Boursier-Mougenot, C. (2015) *Revolutions* (Arles: Analogues).

Braxton Little, J. (2013) 'At Chernobyl, Radioactive Danger Lurks in the Trees', *Scientific American*, June 24. Online: [<https://www.scientificamerican.com/article/at-chernobyl-radioactive-danger-lurks-in-the-trees/>].

Brettell, R.R. (1995) *Impressionist Paintings, Drawings, and Sculpture* (Dallas: Dallas Museum of Art).

Brockway, L.H. (2002) *Science and Colonial Expansion* (New Haven: Yale University Press).

Broglio, R. (2011) *Surface Encounters: Thinking with Animals and Art* (Minneapolis: Minnesota University Press).

Browne, E.J. (2003) *Charles Darwin: The Power of Place* (London: Jonathan Cape).

Brunfels, O. (1532–36) *Herbarum Vivae Eicones* (Strasburg: Argentorati, Apud Joannem Schottum).

Bryant, L., Srnicek, N., and Harman, G. (2011) *The Speculative Turn: Continental Materialism and Realism* (Melbourne: re.press).

Bubandt, N., Gan, E., Swanson, H., Tsing, A. (eds.) (2017) *Arts of Living on a Damaged Planet* (Minneapolis: University of Minnesota Press).

Buck, L. (2002) 'Champion of the urban weed' in *The Art Newspaper*, December.

Buñuel, L., and Dali S. (1929) *Un Chien Andalou* (France: Les Grands Films Classiques).

Burke, E. (1757) *A Philosophical Enquiry Into The Sublime and Beautiful* (London: Routledge).

Castells-Talens, A., Rodríguez, J.M.R. and Chan Concha, M. (2009) 'Radio, control, and indigenous peoples: the failure of state-invented citizens' media in Mexico' *Development in Practice* 19, 4–5, pp. 525–37.

Caurstemont, S. (2016) 'Trees have an inner life like ours, claims bestseller' in *New Scientist*, October 26.

Celant, G. (1985) *Arte Povera* (Florence: Electa).

Celant, G. (1989) *Giuseppe Penone*, exhibition catalog (Bristol: Arnolfini Gallery).

Chamovitz, D. (2010) *What a Plant Knows. A Field Guide to the Senses of Your Garden—and Beyond* (Oxford: Oneworld Press).

Charlesworth, M. (2011) *Derek Jarman* (London: Reaktion Books).

Colebrook, C. (2016) 'Twilight of the Anthropocene idols' in *After Us* (London: Open Humanities Press).

Colls, R. (2013) *George Orwell: English Rebel* (Oxford: Oxford UP).

Combes, M. (1999). *Gilbert Simondon and the Philosophy of the Transindividual*. Translated by Thomas Lamarre (Cambridge: MIT Press) 2013.

Corrin, L.G., Kwon, M., and Bryson, N. (1997) *Mark Dion* (London: Phaidon).

Crainz, G. (2005) *Storia Del Miracolo Italiano* (Rome: Donzelli Editore).

Cross, D. (2005) *Foxglove: Digitalis purpurea* (DIA: New York) online: [<http://www.diaart.org/program/exhibitions-projects/dorothy-cross-foxglove-digitalis-purpurea-web-project>].

Curley, M.J. (2009) *Physiologus: A Medieval Book of Nature Lore* (Chicago: University of Chicago Press).

DaCosta Kaufmann, T. (2009) *Arcimboldo: Visual Jokes, Natural History, and Still-Life Painting* (Chicago: University of Chicago Press).

Dalton, M.O. (1911) *Byzantine Art and Archaeology* (Mineola: Dover).

Darretta, J.L. (2006) *Before the Sun Has Set: Retribution in the Fiction of Flannery O'Connor* (Bern: Peter Lang).

Darwin Correspondence Project, "Letter no. 4221," accessed on 30 May 2016, online: [<http://www.darwinproject.ac.uk/DCP-LETT-4221>].

Darwin, C. (1898) *The Power of Movement in Plants* (Boston: D. Appleton and Company).

Dash, M. (2010) *Tulipomania: The Story of the World's Most Coveted Flower & the Extraordinary Passions It Aroused* (New York: Crown/Archetype).

Davis, L. (2001) 'In the Company of Trees' in (2011) *Antennae: The Journal of Nature in Visual Culture,* 17, pp. 43–62.

de Certeau, M. (1984) *The Practice of Everyday Life* (Berkeley: University of California Press).

de Certeau, M. (1998) 'Ghosts in the City' in *The Practice of Everyday Life, Volume 2: Living & Cooking* (Minneapolis: University of Minnesota Press) pp. 135–36.

de Saussure, F. 'The Nature of the Linguistic Sign' in (2000) *Routledge Language and Cultural Theory Reader*. Edited by Burke et al., 21–32. (New York: Routledge).

de Saussure, T. (2013) *Chemical Research on Plant Growth* (Berlin: Springer Science & Business Media).

De Vriend, H.J. (ed) (1984) *The Old English Herbarium and Medicina de Quadrupedibus* (London, Oxford, and Toronto: Oxford University Press).

Deacon, T.W. (2012) *Incomplete Nature: How Mind Emerged from Matter* (New York: W.W. Norton).

Deely, J.N. (2015) "Objective reality and the physical world: relation as key to understanding semiosis." In (Eds.) Wheeler, W. and Westling, L. *Green Letters: Studies in Ecocriticism* 19: 3.

Deleuze, G. and Guattari, F. (1980) *A Thousand Plateaus: Capitalism and Schizophrenia* (Minneapolis: University of Minnesota Press) 1988.

Demos, T.J. (2016) *Decolonizing Nature* (Berlin: Sternberg Press).

Derrida, J. (1997) 'The animal that therefore I am (More to follow),' *Critical Inquiry,* 28: 2.

Derrida, J. (2008) *The Animal That Therefore I Am* (New York: Fordham University Press).

Dioscorides, P. (1552) *De Materia Medica* (Lugdunum: Apud Balthazarem Arnolletum).

Drayton, R. (2000) *Nature's Government: Science, Imperial Britain, and the 'Improvement' of the World* (London: Yale University Press).

Duncan, J. (2013) 'Wood Extraction: The Basics' in Balasingamchow, Y. (ed.) *Jalan Jati (Teak Road)* 'The Migrant Ecologies Project the Royal Botanic Garden' (Edinburgh: Migrant Ecologies Project: Singapore) pp. 185–87.

Eckenwalder, J.E. (2009) *Conifers of the World: The Complete Reference* (Portland: Timber Press).

ECNH (2008) *The Dignity of Living Beings with Regard to Plants: Moral Consideration of Plants for Their Own Sake* (ECNH: Berne) online: [<http://www.ekah.admin.ch/fileadmin/ekah-dateien/dokumentation/publikationen/e-Broschure-Wurde-Pflanze-2008.pdf>].

Elhard, K.C. (2005) 'Reopening the book on Arcimboldo's librarian' in *Libraries & Culture,* 40, 2 Spring 2005, pp. 115–27.

Elkins, James. 2010. "How Long Does it Take to Look at a Painting?" *Huffington Post,* online: [<http://www.huffingtonpost.com/james-elkins/how-long-does-it-take-to-_b_779946.html>].

Fairchild, R.D. (2003) *Gardens, Landscape, and Vision* (University Park: Penn State University Press).

Farrell E.J. and Patrick, J. K. (1975) *An Analysis of Indoor Potted Flowering Plants Purchase Behavior* (Voorhees Mall: New Jersey Agricultural Experiment Station).

Fediw, K. (2015) *The Manual of Interior Plantscaping: A Guide to Design, Installation, and Maintenance* (Portland: Timber Press).

Fellini, F. (1973) *Amarcord* (dist. PIC Distribuzione/Warner Brothers).

Findlen, P. (1994) *Possessing Nature: Museums, Collecting, and Scientific Culture in Early Modern Italy* (Berkeley: University of California Press).

Fischer, P. (2015) 'Thinking About Trees' in Fischer, P. and Burgi, B. (Eds.) *About Trees* (Koln: Snoeck).

Fischer, P., and Burgi, B. (Eds.) (2015) *About Trees* (Koln: Snoeck).

Fisher, M. (2009) *Capitalist Realism: Is There No Alternative?* (Portland: Zero Books).

Fletcher, P. and Helmreich, A. (Eds.) (2011) *The Rise of the Modern Art Market in London, 1850–1939* (Manchester: Manchester UP).

Flusser, V. (2013) *Post-History* (Minneapolis: Univocal).

Foucault, M. (1963) *The Birth of the Clinic: An Archaeology of Medical Perception* (London and New York: Routledge) 1973, 2003.

Foucault, M. (1964) *Madness and Civilization: A History of Insanity in the Age of Reason* (New York: Vintage Books), 1967, 1988.

Foucault, M. (1966) *The Order of Things: An Archaeology of The Human Science* (London and New York: Routledge), 1970, 2003.

Foucault, M. (1972) 'The eye of power' in *Power/Knowledge: Selected Interviews and Other Writings, 1972–1977* (Brighton: Harvester Press) pp. 146–165.

Foucault, M. (1972) *Power/Knowledge: Selected Interviews and Other Writings, 1972–1977* (Brighton: The Harvester Press).

Foucault, M. (1972) *The Archaeology of Knowledge* (London: Routledge) 2002.

Foucault, M. (1975–76) *"Society Must Be Defended": Lectures at the Collège de France, 1975–1976* (New York: Picador), 2003.

Foucault, M. (1975) *Discipline and Punish: The Birth of the Prison*, 1977 (London: Penguin), 1991.

Foucault, M. (1976) *The History of Sexuality 1—The Will to Knowledge* (London and New York: Penguin Books), 1998.

Foucault, M. (1976b) 'Questions of Geography', in Gordon, C. (ed.) (1980) *Power/Knowledge: Selected Interviews and Other Writings, 1972–1977* (Brighton: Harvester Press) pp. 63–77.

Foucault, M. (1981) 'The Order of Discourse' in Young, R. (ed.) *Untying the Text: A Post–Structuralist Reader* (London and New York: Routledge) 2006, pp. 70–71.

Foucault, M. (1982) 'The Subject and Power', in Hubert L. Dreyfus and Paul Rabinow, *Michel Foucault: Beyond Structuralism and Hermeneutics* (Chicago: University of Chicago Press) 1983.

Foucault, M. (1984) 'Of other spaces' in *Diacritics*, Spring 1986.

Foucault, M. quoted in Leach, N. (2005) *Rethinking Architecture: A Reader in Cultural Theory* (London: Routledge).

Foumberg, J. (2011) 'Heidi Norton—Ebersmoore' in *Frieze*, Issue 141, September, online: [<https://frieze.com/article/heidi-norton>].

Fountain, H., and Schwartz, J. (2016) 'Spiking Temperatures in the Arctic Startle Scientists' in *The New York Times*, Wednesday, December 21, online: [<http://www.nytimes.com/2016/12/21/science/arctic-global-warming.html>].

Franceschini, A. (2005) *FRUIT Network*, 2005, in *Futurefarmers*, online: [<http://www.futurefarmers.com/#projects/fruit>].

Freedberg, D., and de Vries, J. (1996) *Art in History/History in Art: Studies in Seventeenth-Century Dutch Culture* (Los Angeles: Getty Publications).

Freeman, M. (2011) *Clarence Saunders and the Founding of Piggly Wiggly: The Rise & Fall of a Memphis Maverick* (Mount Pleasant: Arcadia Publishing).

Fried, M. (1967) 'Art and objecthood' in (1998) *Art and Objecthood: Essays and Reviews* (Chicago: University of Chicago Press), pp. 148–72.

Friends of the Earth (2004) 'Every Little Hurts: Why Tesco Needs To Be Tamed,' MPs Briefing, online: [<https://www.foe.co.uk/sites/default/files/downloads/tesco_every_little_hurts.pdf>].

Fuchs, L. (1547) *De Historia Stirpium Commentarii Insignes* (Leipzig: Kurt Wolff Verlag).

Fuchs, L., Meyer, F.G., Heller, J.L., and Emmart Trueblood, E. *The Great Herbal of Leonhart Fuchs: De Historia Stirpium Commentarii Insignes*, 1542, Facsimile (Stanford: Stanford University Press).

Gage, J. (1999) *Color and Culture: Practice and Meaning from Antiquity to Abstraction* (Berkeley: University of California Press).

Gagliano, M. (2012) 'Green Symphonies: A Call for Studies on Acoustic Communication in Plants' in *Behavioral Ecology* 24: 4, pp. 789–96.

Gagliano, M., Grimonprez, M., Depczynski, M., & Renton, M. (2017) 'Tuned in: plant roots use sound to locate water' in *Oecologia* 184, 151–60.

Gagliano, M., Mancuso, S., and Robert, D. (2012) 'Towards understanding plant bioacoustics' *Trends in Plant Science* 17: 6, pp. 323–25.

Gaiman, N. (1990) *Good Omens: The Nice and Accurate Prophecies of Agnes Nutter, Witch* (London: Gollancz).

Gandini, G. (2004) *I Locali Storici di Milano* (Milano: Touring Editore).

Gee, P., Stephenson, D., and Wright, D.E. (1994) 'Temporal Discrimination Learning of Operant Feeding in Goldfish (*Carassius auratus*)' in *Journal of the Experimental Analyses of Behaviour*, 1, pp. 1–13.

Gernsheim, H., and Gernsheim, A. (1968) L.J.M. *Daguerre: The History of the Diorama and the Daguerreotype* (Mineola: Dover Publications).

Gessert, G. (2010) 'The Rainforest of Domestication' in *Green Light: Toward an Art of Evolution* (Cambridge: MIT) pp. 21–31.

Gessert, G. (2012) *Green Light: Toward an Art Of Evolution* (Cambridge: MIT Press).

Gibson, P. (2015) *Janet Laurence: The Pharmacy of Plants* (Sydney: University of New South Wales Press).

Giovannetti, M. et al. (2006) 'At the Root of the Wood Wide Web: Self Recognition and Non-Self Incompatibility in Mycorrhizal Networks' in *Plant Signaling and Behavior*, 1: 1, 1–5.

Glaspell, S. (1921) *The Verge*, in *Plays* (North Charleston: CreateSpace Independent Publishing Platform), 2014.

Gomel, E. (2014) *Narrative Space and Time: Representing Impossible Topologies in Literature* (New York: Routledge).

Gopnik, A. (2010) 'Plant TV', in *The New Yorker*, March 15, online: [<http://www.newyorker.com/magazine/2010/03/15/plant-tv>].

Gordon, A. (2008) *Ghostly Matters: Haunting and the Sociological Imagination* (Minneapolis: Minnesota University Press).

Gordon, R., and Eddison, S. (2002) *Monet the Gardener* (New York: Universe).

Green, C., and Morris, F. (2005) *Henri Rousseau: Jungles in Paris* (London: Tate Publishing).

Hall, M. (2009) 'Plant Autonomy and Human-Plant Ethics' *Environmental Ethics*, 31, 2, Summer 2009.

Hall, M. (2011) *Plants as Persons: A Philosophical Botany* (Albany: SUNY Press).

Hamann, H., Wahby, M., Schmickl, T., Zahadat, P., Hofstadler, D., Stoy, K., Risi, S., Faíña, A., Veenstra, F., Kernbach, S., Kuksin, I., Kernbach, O., Ayres, P., Wojtaszek, P. (2015) *flora robotica*—Mixed Societies of Symbiotic Robot-Plant Bio-Hybrids. IEEE Symposium on Artificial Life (IEEE ALIFE'15) online: [<http://www.florarobotica.eu/wp-content/uploads/2016/01/Flora-Robotica-Mixed-Societies_IEEE-ALIFE_2015.pdf>].

Hamsadeva (1972) *Mriga-Pakshi-Shastra,* English translation (Kalahasti: P.N. Press).

Haraway, D. (1991, 2013) *Simians, Cyborgs, and Women: The Reinvention of Nature* (London: Routledge).

Haraway, D. (2008) *When Species Meet* (Minneapolis: University of Minnesota Press).

Harrison, H.M. and Harrison, N. (2016) *Full Farm*, 1974, *The Harrison Studio*, online: [<http://theharrisonstudio.net/full-farm-1974>].

Harrison, P. (2001) *The Bible, Protestantism, and the Rise of Natural Science* (Cambridge: Cambridge University Press) 1998.

Hobhouse, P. (2002) *The Story of Gardening* (London: Dorling Kindersley).

Hodgson Burnett, F. (1910) *The Secret Garden* (Massachusetts: Trajectory Classics).

Hoffmeyer, J. (2008) *Biosemiotics: An Examination into the Signs of Life and the Life of Signs.* (Eds.) Favareau, D. (Scranton, PA: University of Scranton Press).

Horlock, M., Reitmaier, H., and Schama, S. (2002) *Beat* (London: Tate Gallery Publishing).

Horwood, C. (2011) *Gardening Women* (Windsor: Windsor/Paragon).

Howard, B.C. (2015) 'Are "Mutated" Daisies Really Caused by Fukushima Radiation?' *National Geographic Magazine*, July.

Hustak, C., and Myers, N. (2012) 'Involutionary Momentum: Affective Ecologies and the Sciences of Plant/Insect Encounters.' In *Differences*, 23, no. 3, pp. 74–118.

Huxley, A. (1954) *The Doors of Perception* (US, Harper & Row).

Huysman, J.K. (1884) *À rebours* (North Charleston: CreateSpace Independent Publishing Platform).

Impelluso, L. (2004) S. Sartarelli, trans. *Nature and Its Symbols* (Los Angeles: Getty Publications). Originally published 2003, as *La Natura e i suoi simboli* (Milano: Mondadori Electa).

James, M.R. (1931) 'The Bestiary' in *History: The Quarterly Journal of the Historical Association*, XVI, 61, April, pp. 1–11.

James, M.R. (2011) 'A View from a Hill' in *Collected Ghost Stories* (Oxford and New York: Oxford University Press).

Janzen, D.H., Martin, P.S. (1982) 'Neotropical anachronisms: the fruits the gomphotheres ate', *Science*, 215, 4528, pp. 19–27.

Jarman, D. (1995) *Derek Jarman's Garden* (New York and London: Thames and Hudson).

Kalish, I., Eng, V. (2016) 'Global Powers of Retailing 2016', in *Deloitte*, online: [<https://www2.deloitte.com/global/en/pages/consumer-business/articles/global-powers-of-retailing.html>].

Kanouse, S. (2011) 'Take It to The Air: Radio as Public Art' *Art Journal*, 70, 3, pp. 86–99.

Kant, I. (1790) *Critique of Judgment* (North Chelmsford: Courier Corporation).

Karlson, P. Lüscher, M. (1959) 'Pheromones: a new term for a class of biologically active substances' in *Nature*, 183, 4653, pp. 55–56.

Kleinman, A. (2012) *Published in special DOCUMENTA (13) issue of Mousse Magazine* (Milan: Italy) Summer.

Klingender, F. (1971) *Animals in Art and Thought to the End of the Middle Ages* (Cambridge: MIT Press).

Krishna, N. (2014) *Sacred Animals of India* (New York: Penguin).

Kudla, A. 'The Search for Luminosity', online: [<http://allisonx.com/selected-works/>].

Kusukawa, S. (2010) 'The sources of Gessner's pictures for the Historia animalium' in *Annals of Science*, 76,3, pp. 303–28.

Landolt, J.P. (1997) Sex attractant and aggregation pheromones of male phytophagous insects' in *American Entomologist*, 43:1, pp. 12–22.

Latour, B. (2004) *Politics of Nature* (Cambridge, MA: Harvard University Press).

Latour, B. (2013) "A Secular Gaia," *Facing Gaia: Six Lectures on the political theology of nature, Being the Gifford Lectures on Natural Religion, Edinburgh, 18-28, February 2013*, p. 63. <http://www.bruno-latour.fr/sites/default/files/downloads/GIFFORD-ASSEMBLED.pdf>. Accessed Sept. 3, 2018.

Latour, B. (2015) 'Waiting for Gaia. Composing the common world through art and politics' in Yaneva, A. & Zaera-Polo, A. (Eds.) *What is Cosmopolitical Design?* (Farnham: Ashgate) pp. 21–33.

Lehner, E. and Lehner, J. (2003) *Folklore and Symbolism of Flowers, Plants, and Trees* (Mineola: Dover).

Leick, G. (2002) *A Dictionary of Ancient Near Eastern Mythology* (London: Routledge).

Levinas, E. (1969) *Totality and Infinity: An Essay on Exteriority* (Pittsburgh: Duquesne University Press).

Lowinson, J.H. (2005) *Substance Abuse: A Comprehensive Textbook* (Philadelphia: Lippincott Williams & Wilkins).

Mabey, R. (2010) *Weeds: In Defense of Nature's Most Unwanted Plants* (New York: Ecco).

Mabey, R. (2016) *The Cabaret of Plants* (New York: W.W. Norton & Company).

Mahoney, E. (2008) 'Greenhouse Britain,' in *The Guardian*, March, February 14, online: [<https://www.theguardian.com/artanddesign/2008/mar/14/art1>].

Mainardi, P. (1994) *The End of the Salon* (Cambridge: Cambridge University Press).

Mancuso, S., and Viola, A. (2015) *Brilliant Green: The Surprising History and Science of Plant Intelligence* (Washington, DC: Island Press).

Mansfield, K. (1962) 'Prelude' in *Bliss and Other Stories* (London: Penguin).

Marder, M. (2013) 'Of Plants, and Other Secrets' in *Societies*, 3, 16–23; doi:10.3390/soc3010016.

Marder, M. (2013) 'Plant Intelligence and Attention' in *Plant Signaling & Behavior*, 8, 5 (Landes Bioscience, May 2013), online: [<http://www.ncbi.nlm.nih.gov/pmc/articles/PMC3906434>].

Marder, M. (2013) 'What is plant-thinking?' *Klesis— Revue Philosophique*, 25, pp. 124–43.

Marder, M. (2013) *Plant-Thinking: A Philosophy of Vegetal Life* (New York: Columbia University Press).

Marder, M. (2014) *The Philosopher's Plant* (New York: Columbia University Press).

Marder, M. (2016) *Grafts: Writings on Plants* (Minneapolis: University of Minnesota Press/Univocal).

Marder, M. and Irigaray, L. (2016) *Through Vegetal Being* (New York: Columbia University Press).

Marsh, K. (2002) '"All My Habits of Mind": Performance and Identity in the Novels of Mary McCarthy' *Studies in the Novel*, 34:3.

Marx, K. (1867) *Capital: A Critique of Political Economy*, Vol. 1. (New York: Penguin Books), 2004.

McCarthy, M. (1965) *Birds of America* (New York: Harcourt, Brace, Jovanovich).

McClung, C.R. (2006) 'Plant Circadian Rhythms', *Plant Cell* 18:4, April.

Medvedev, Z. (1992) *The Legacy of Chernobyl* (New York: W.W. Norton & Company).

Mileece quoted in Robinsong, E. (2016) 'Mileece: Gardening the future' in *Kadenzeblog*, online: [<https://blog.kadenze.com/2016/10/29/mileece-gardening-the-future/>].

Montague, J. (2006) *The Stray Shopping Carts of Eastern North America: A Guide to Field Identification* (New York: Abrams).

Moore, J.W. (2014) 'The end of cheap nature. Or how I learned to stop worrying about the environment and love the crisis of capitalism' in *Structures of the World Political Economy and the Future of Global Conflict and Cooperation* (Eds.) C. Suter and C. Chase-Dunn (Berlin: LIT) pp. 285–314.

Moor, J.W. (2015) *Capitalism in the Web of Life: Ecology and the Accumulation of Capital* (New York: Verso Books).

Morton, T. (2007) *Ecology Without Nature* (Cambridge: Harvard University Press).

Morton, T. (2016) *Dark Ecology* (New York: Columbia University Press).

Murakami, H. (2010) *1Q84*. Trans. Jay Rubin and Philip Gabriel (New York: Alfred A. Knopf) 2011.

Museum of Modern Art. (1936) Press Release 18636–17, 'Steichen Delphiniums', June 22.

Myers, N. (2014) 'Sensing Botanical Sensoria: A Kriya for Cultivating Your Inner Plant' in *Centre for Imaginative Ethnography*, 'Imaginings Series: Affect'. online: [<http://imaginativeethnography.org/imaginings/affect/sensing- botanical-sensoria/>].

Myers, N. (2015) 'Conversations on Plant Sensing: Notes from the Field.' *NatureCulture* 3, 'Acting with Non-human Entities' (October) pp. 35–66.

Myers, N. (2016) 'Photosynthesis' in 'Lexicon for an Anthropocene Yet Unseen' (Eds.) Howe, C., and Pandian, A. 'Theorizing the Contemporary', in *Cultural Anthropology*, January, online: [<https://culanth.org/conversations/17-theorizing-the-contemporary>].

Myers, N. (2017a) 'Ungrid-able Ecologies: Decolonizing the Ecological Sensorium in a 10,000-year-old Happening' in *Catalyst: Feminism, Theory, Techno-science*, 3, 2, pp. 1–24.

Myers, N. (2017b) 'Becoming Sensor in Sentient Worlds: A More-than-natural History of a Black Oak Savannah,' in Bakke, G., and Peterson, M. (Eds.) *Between Matter and Method: Encounters in Anthropology and Art* (Durham: Duke University Press) pp. 73–96.

Myrone, M. (2013) 'John Martin's *Last Judgement* Triptych: The Apocalyptic Sublime in the Age of Spectacle', in Nigel Llewellyn and Christine Riding (eds.), *The Art of the Sublime* (London: Tate).

Nagel, T. (1974) 'What is it like to be a bat?' in *The Philosophical Review*, 83: 4, pp. 435–50.

Nellis, D.W. (1997) *Poisonous Plants and Animals of Florida and the Caribbean* (Sarasota: Pineapple Press).

Nemitz, B. (2000) *Trans Plant: Living Vegetation In Contemporary Art* (Berlin: Hatje Cantz).

Nissenbaum, S. (2010) *The Battle of Christmas* (New York: Knopf Doubleday Publishing Group).

O'Connor, F. (1946) 'The Geranium' in *Accent: A Quarterly of New Literature*. Reprinted in (1971) *The Complete Stories* (New York: Farrar, Straus and Giroux).

O'Doherty, B. (1999) *Inside the White Cube: The Ideology of the Gallery Space* (Berkeley: University of California Press).

Olafsson, O. (2007) *A Journey Home: A Novel* (New York: Knopf Doubleday Publishing).

Orwell, G. (1956) *Keep the Aspidistra Flying* (New York: Harcourt).

Payne, M. (2017) 'Before the law: Imagining crimes against trees' in *Fatal Fictions* (Eds.) LaCroix, A.L., McAdams, R.H., and Nussbaum M.C. (Oxford: Oxford University Press).

Pelling, A. quoted in Gamble, J. (2016) 'Are plants the future of regenerative medicine?' in *The Atlantic*, online: [<http://www.theatlantic.com/science/archive/2016/07/growing-organs-on-apples/493265/>].

Pettit, J., Salazar, J.F. and Dagron, A.G. (2009) 'Citizens' media and communication' in *Development in Practice*, 19, 4–5, pp. 443–52.

Petrič, S. (2017) Introductory text to 'Ectogenesis: Plant-Human monsters, online: [<http://www.spelapetric.org/portfolio/ectogenesis/>].

Petrič, S. (2017) Introductory text to 'Strange Encounters', online: [<http://www.spelapetric.org/projects/strange-encounters/strange-encounters-blog/>].

Pollan, M. (2001) *The Botany of Desire: A Plant's-Eye View of the World* (London: Random House).

Pollan, M. (2013) 'The Intelligent Plant', in *The New Yorker*. 23 Dec. pp. 92–14.

Potter, M. (2011). 'Tesco to outpace growth at global rivals—study' in Reuters, 16 February, online: [<http://www.reuters.com/article/tesco-igd-idUSLDE71F1LR20110217>].

Pound, E. (1918) 'Henry James' in *Literary Essays of Ezra Pound* (New York: New Directions Publishing).

Prada, M., Celant, G., Leader, D., Quinn, M. (2000) *Marc Quinn* (Milano: Fondazione Prada).

Press Association. (2003) 'Just how old are the "fresh" fruit & vegetables we eat?' in *The Observer*, 13 July, online: [<https://www.theguardian.com/lifeand-style/2003/jul/13/foodanddrink.features18>].

Press Association. (2016) 'New era of climate change reality as emissions hit symbolic thresholds' in *The Guardian*, October 24, online: [<https://www.theguardian.com/environment/2016/oct/24/new-era-of-climate-change-reality-as-emissions-hit-symbolic-threshold>].

Prest, J.M. (1981) *The Garden of Eden: The Botanic Garden and the Re-Creation of Paradise* (New Haven and London: Yale University Press).

Pseudo-Apuleius (11th century) *Herbarium of Pseudo Apuleius*, Oxford, Bodleian Library, Ashmole, 1431 (7523).

Purves, T., and Selzer, A. (Eds.) (2014) *What We Want Is Free: Critical Exchanges in Recent Art* (Albany: SUNY Press).

Rader, A.K. (2004) *Making Mice: Standardizing Animals for American Biomedical Research, 1900–1955* (Princeton: Princeton University Press).

Ray, C., Burgi, B.M., Druik, D., Fried, M., Neer, R. (2016) *Charles Ray: Sculpture 1997–2014* (New York: Distributed Art Pub Incorporated).

Richards, J. (2000) 'Early Christian Art' in Kemp, M. (ed.) *The Oxford History of Western Art* (Oxford: Oxford University Press).

Rigby, K. (2015) "Art, Nature, and the Poesy of Plants in the Goethezeit: A Biosemiotic Perspective." in *Goethe Yearbook* 22: 23–44. doi: 10.1353/gyr.2015.0000.

Rix, M. (1981) *The Art of Botanical Illustration* (New York: Arch Cape Press).

Roof, J. (2007) 'The Epic Acid' in *The Poetics of DNA* (Minneapolis: University of Minnesota Press) p. 24.

Rosen, A. (2012) 'Effects of the Fukushima Nuclear Meltdowns on Environment and Health' *International Physicians for the Prevention of Nuclear War Conference*, University Clinic Düsseldorf, March 9.

Rosenbloom, S. (2014) 'The Art of Slowing Down in a Museum,' in *The New York Times*, October 9, online: [<https://www.nytimes.com/2014/10/12/travel/the-art-of-slowing-down-in-a-museum.html>].

Rostovtzeff, M.I. (1926) *The Social and Economic History of the Roman Empire* (Cheshire: Biblio and Tunnen).

Sanchez, E.F., Kay, S.A. (2016) 'The Plant Circadian Clock: From a Simple Timekeeper to a Complex Developmental Manager', in *Cold Spring Harb Perspect Biol*. Dec 1;8(12), pii: a027748. doi: 10.1101/cshperspect.a027748.

Savi, G., and Andres, G. (1840) *Istituzioni Botaniche* (Loreto: Tipografia Rossi).

Schiebinger, L. (2014) *Plants and Empire: Colonial Bioprospecting in the Atlantic World* (Boston: Harvard University Press).

Schoenefeldt, H. (2011) 'The Use of Scientific Experimentation in Developing the Glazing for the Palm House at Kew' in *Construction History*, pp. 19–39.

Schryer, S. (2007) 'Mary McCarthy's Field Guide to US Intellectuals: Tradition and Modernization Theory in *Birds of America*' in *Modern Fiction Studies* 53: 4.

Shakespeare, W. (2006) *As You Like It* (Stanford: Cengage Learning Holdings).

Shapiro, J.A. (2011) *Evolution: A View from the 21st Century* (Upper Saddle River, NJ: FT Press Science).

Singer, P. (1993) *Practical Ethics* (Cambridge: Cambridge University Press).

Singer, P. (2000) *Writings on An Ethical Life* (New York: Open Road Media).

Sloane Kennedy, W. (1886) *Art and Life: A Ruskin Anthology* (New York: J.B. Alden).

Smith, J.T. (2015) 'Long-term Census Data Reveal Abundant Wildlife Populations at Chernobyl' *Current Biology*, 25, 19, pR824–R826.

Solnit, R. (2001) *As Eve Said to the Serpent: On Landscape, Gender, and Art* (Athens: University of Georgia Press).

Somers, D.E. (1999) 'The Physiology and Molecular Bases of the Circadian Clock', *Plant Physiology*, 121, September.

Spalding, F. (1998) *Tate: A History* (London: Tate Gallery Publishing).

Stracey F. (2009) 'Bio-art: The ethics behind the aesthetics', in *Perspective*, 10, July, pp. 496–500.

Swan, C. (2005) *Art, Science and Witchcraft* (Cambridge: Cambridge University Press).

Tattfoo. (2006) *SoS Mobile Gardens*, online: [<http://www.tattfoo.com/sos/SOSMobileGarden.html>].

Thoreau, H.D. *Walden* (2006) ed. Jeffrey S. Cramer (New Haven: Yale University Press).

Tju, L.C. (2004) 'Political Prints in Singapore' in *Print Quarterly* 21, 3 (September), pp. 266–81.

Tomasi, T. (2013) 'Gherardo Cibo: un percorso tra arte e scienza' in *Gherardo Cibo: Dilettante di Botanica e Pittore di Paesi* (Ancona: Il Lavoro Editorial).

Tompkins, P., and Bird, C. (1973) *The Secret Life of Plants: A Fascinating Account of the Physical, Emotional, and Spiritual Relations Between Plants and Man* (New York: Harper and Row).

Triciae. (2004–2009) 'Home Depot throwing plants away' in *Houzz*, July 9, online: [<http://forums.gardenweb.com/discussions/1433913/home-depot-throwing-out-plants>].

Tweed Museum of Art (1999) *Botanica: Contemporary Art and the World of Plants* (Duluth: Tweed Museum of Art).

USDA Plant Guide. Online: [<http://plants.usda.gov/plantguide/pdf/cs_gydi.pdf>].

Various Authors. (2011) 'The Silence of the Plants' in *Antennae: The Journal of Nature in Visual Culture*, 18, Autumn, pp. 11–23.

Verheggen, F.J., Haubruge, E., Mescher, M.C. (2010) 'Alarm pheromones-chemical signaling in response to danger' in *Vitam Horm*, 83, pp. 215–39.

Verma, S.P. (2016) *The Illustrated Baburnama* (New York and London: Routledge).

Verne, J. (2015) *Journey to The Centre Of the Earth* (New York: Sheba Blake Publishing).

Vieira, P., Gagliano, M. and Ryan, J. (Eds.) (2015) *The Green Thread: Dialogues with the Vegetal World* (Landham, MD: Rowman & Littlefield).

Viñas, M-J. (2017) 'Massive Iceberg Breaks Off From Antarctica' in *NASA* website, published July 12, online: [<https://www.nasa.gov/feature/goddard/2017/massive-iceberg-breaks-off-from-antarctica>].

Volkov, A.G. (2007) *Plant Electrophysiology: Theory and Methods* (Berlin: Springer Science and Business Media).

von Goethe, J.W. (2009) *The Metamorphosis of Plants* (Cambridge: The MIT Press).

von Goethe, J.W. (1872) *Elective Affinities* (Boston: D.W. Niles).

von Uexküll, J. (1982) "Introduction to the first edition of The Theory of Meaning." *Semiotica* 42: 1 25–82.

von Uexküll, J., Uexküll, M. and O'Neil, J.D. (2010) *A Foray Into the Worlds of Animals and Humans: With a Theory of Meaning* (Minneapolis: Minnesota University Press).

Wandersee, J.H., and Schussler, E.E. (1999) 'Preventing plant blindness' *The American Biology Teacher*, 61, 2 (Feb. 1999), pp. 82+84+86.

Waterson, R. (1990) *The Living House: An Anthropology of Architecture in South-East Asia* (Singapore: Oxford University Press).

Weil, K. (2012) *Thinking Animals: Why Animal Studies Now?* (New York: Columbia University Press).

Weintraub, L. (2012) *To Life!: Eco Art in Pursuit of a Sustainable Planet* (Berkeley: University of California Press).

Wheeler, W. (2016) *Expecting the Earth: Life|Culture|Biosemiotics* (London: Lawrence & Wishart).

Whippo, C.W. (2006) 'Phototropism: Bending towards Enlightenment' *The Plant Cell*, May 18, 5, pp. 1110–19.

Whistler, A. (2000) *Tropical Ornamentals: A Guide* (Portland: Timber Press).

Williams, D. (2012) *The Afterlife of Ophelia* (New York: Springer).

Wohlleben, P. (2016) *The Hidden Life of Trees: What They Feel, How They Communicate—Discoveries from a Secret World* (New York: Penguin).

Wolfe, C. (2010) *What Is Posthumanism?* (Minneapolis: Minnesota University Press).

Wolfe, C. (2013) *Before the Law: Humans and Other Animals in a Biopolitical Frame* (Chicago: University of Chicago Press).

Woods, M., and Warren, A.S. (1988) *Glass Houses: A History of Greenhouses, Orangeries, and Conservatories* (Milan: Rizzoli).

Woolf, V. (1973) *Orlando; a Biography*. 1928. Reprint. (New York: Harcourt Brace Jovanovich).

Woolf, V. (1974) 'Craftsmanship.' *The Death of the Moth and Other Essays* (New York: Harcourt Brace Jovanovich).

Worland, J. (2015) 'The Weird Effect Climate Change Will Have On Plant Growth' in *Time*, Thursday, June 11, online: [<http://time.com/3916200/climate-change-plant-growth/>].

Worrall, S. (2016) 'There Is Such a Thing as Plant Intelligence' in *National Geographic*, February 21, online: [<http://news.nationalgeographic.com/2016/ 02/160221-plant-science-botany-evolution-mabey- ngbooktalk/>].

Worringer, W. (1953) *Abstraction and Empathy: A Con- tribution to the Psychology of Style* (Chicago: Ivan R. Dee), 1997.

Ziegler, C. (2007) *Favored Flowers: Culture and Economy*

in a Global Culture (Durham: Duke University Press).

Žižek, S. (2013) 'Slavoj Žižek: Ecology is the new opiate of the masses' in *Dustysojourner.Wordpress*, online: [<https://dustysojourner.wordpress.com/2013/01/15/ slavoj-zizek-ecology-is-the-new-opiate-of-the-mass es/>].

Index

Printed in the United States
By Bookmasters